Sources of World Civilization

Sources of World Civilization

Volume I
A Diversity of Traditions

THIRD EDITION

Edited by

OLIVER A. JOHNSON
University of California Riverside

JAMES L. HALVERSON
Judson College

PEARSON
Prentice Hall

Upper Saddle River, New Jersey 07458

Library of Congress Cataloging-in-Publication Data

Sources of world civilization / Oliver A. Johnson, James L. Halverson. -- 3rd ed.
    p. cm.
    Contents: v. l. Before 1500 -- v. 2. Since 1500.
    ISBN 0-13-182483-X (v. 1) -- ISBN 0-13-183505-X (v. 2)
    1. Civilization -- History -- Sources. I. Johnson, Oliver A. II. Halverson,
    James L.

CB69.S68 2004
909--dc21

                                                            2003048687

Acquisitions Editor: Charles Cavaliere
Editor-in-Chief: Charlyce Jones Owen
Associate Editor: Emsal Hasan
Editorial Assistant: Adrienne Paul
Marketing Manager: Heather Shelstad
Marketing Assistant: Jennifer Bryant
Production Editor: Laura A. Lawrie
Manufacturing Buyer: Tricia Kenny
Cover Design: Kiwi Design

Cover Illustration: Two relief panels
from the stupa of Bharhut, middle of
the second century B.C. Courtesy of the
Library of Congress.
Composition: This book was set
in 10/12 Palatino by Integra

Credits and acknowledgments borrowed from other sources and reproduced, with
permission, in this textbook appear on appropriate page within text.

The Scripture quotations contained herein are from the New Revised Standard
Version Bible, Copyright © 1989 by the Division of Christian Education of the
National Council of the Churches of Christ in the U.S.A., and are used by
permission. All rights reserved.

Copyright © 2004, 2000, 1994, by Pearson Education, Inc.,
Upper Saddle River, New Jersey, 07458.
Pearson Prentice Hall. All rights reserved. Printed in the United States of America.
This publication is protected by Copyright and permission should be obtained from
the publisher prior to any prohibited reproduction, storage in a retrieval system, or
transmission in any form or by any means, electronic, mechanical, photocopying,
recording, or likewise. For information regarding permission(s), write to: Rights
and Permissions Department.

Pearson Prentice Hall™ is a trademark of Pearson Education, Inc.
Pearson® is a registered trademark of Pearson plc
Prentice Hall® is a registered trademark of Pearson Education, Inc.

Pearson Education LTD.
Pearson Education Singapore, Pte. Ltd.
Pearson Education Canada, Ltd.
Pearson Education—Japan

Pearson Education Australia PTY, Limited
Pearson Education North Asia, Ltd.
Pearson Educación de Mexico, S.A. de C.V.
Pearson Education Malaysia, Pte. Ltd.

10 9 8 7 6 5 4 3
ISBN 0-13-182483-X

CONTENTS

CLASSICAL CIVILIZATIONS 70

PREFACE

Those familiar with previous editions of this book will immediately notice some significant changes. First, the number of selections has been greatly reduced. Second, sources from Western civilization are less predominant. Finally, study questions have been added before each selection and at the end of each major section of the book. These changes reflect my desire to update the book and at the same time remain true to the vision of previous editions. For this edition, the total length of the book needed to be reduced, while the geographic scope needed to be widened. This could have been done by either shortening the selections or by eliminating entire selections. I chose to keep the selections relatively long. There are other world history readers on the market that include a great number of brief excerpts. I have found this to be bewildering to my own students. Thus, this edition continues to affirm that any document significant enough to be included in an anthology such as this deserves to be excerpted in such a way that it retains some of its integrity and meaning. To make room for a broader scope of sources, I eliminated many of the documents pertaining to Western civilization. Even so, there is still a bias toward Western sources in this volume. As in previous editions, the assumption is that North American college students not only should be introduced to a variety of world cultures but also should dig more deeply into the origins of the culture in which they find themselves.

Acknowledgments

There are, as always, many people to thank at the end of a project like this. I would not have been involved in this project if the editors at Prentice Hall had not asked me. Nor could this project have gone forward had Dr. Johnson's estate not trusted me with making changes to the previous edition. Reviewers of the second edition, Nupur Chaudhuri (Texas Southern University), John Lyons (Joliet Junior College), Kurt J. Peterson (North Park University), and Robert Walker (Jackson State University), provided valuable insights into how this book might be improved. This project would have gone on much longer and been much less pleasant without the help of my assistant, Kelley Burke. Judson College greatly facilitated my work by awarding me a Surbeck Research Grant and relieving me of some of my faculty duties. My children, C.J., Tommy, and Anna, were constant sources of rejuvenation. But all this would have been for naught without the encouragement, patience, and support of my wife, Terri.

GENERAL INTRODUCTION

The purpose of this book is to introduce students to the history of world civilization through the documents that have formed and shaped that civilization. One word in the title of the book needs explanation. Our use of the singular "civilization," rather than "civilizations," is not meant to be question-begging. We are not implying by its use that world history is the story of a single civilization or even that the myriad societies that have occupied various parts of the world during the past five thousand years have much more in common than the shared humanity of their people. Our intent, rather, is the much more modest one of simply indicating that the book is concerned with the history of people who have lived together in organized and stable societies.

An attempt might be made to give the term "civilization" in the history of the world some substantive, positive content by selecting a central theme to serve as an overarching principle capable of uniting the various historical societies into a single world civilization. Such a theme could be used as an organizing device for these documents, giving this book a coherence and unity that it may seem to lack. But any such principle, whether chosen from politics, religion, economics, philosophy, or another field, would distort history by reducing the variety and complexity of historical societies into artificial and unreal unity. Although there are continuities in history and similarities among cultures that need to be recognized, there also are discontinuities and diversities as well. However convenient it might be for us to try, we cannot fit world history into a straitjacket. Although we have not found a central thread from which to hang the selections in this book, we have not chosen them arbitrarily. Instead, we have adopted three general criteria to guide the selection of documents: (1) that the document be of major significance, shaping the history of an important society or succession of societies through time; (2) that the document give us substantial insights into the nature of the society from which it sprang, either at a given period in its history or over a long period of time; and (3) that the document be intrinsically interesting. Almost all of the selections in this book satisfy one of the first two criteria; those that satisfy the third may appear (at least to students) to be fewer in number.

Even with the help of our criteria, the process of selecting the documents to include in this book has been difficult. It would be unrealistic to assume that all (or even much) of the significant literature of the societies of the world throughout history can be encapsulated within less than a hundred documents. Of necessity, innumerable items, some arguably as worthy of inclusion as those selected, have not been chosen. Readers of this book will, on occasion, undoubtedly question some of the decisions we have made, preferring other selections to those contained here. It is our hope, however, that readers will recognize that none of these decisions was made arbitrarily but all with consideration and with careful weighing of the alternative possibilities.

One way in which we might have eased the task of selection would have been through the inclusion of a much larger number of selections in the book. But, because of constraints on the length of the book, any increase in the number of selections would have necessitated a decrease in their average length. In deciding against this procedure, we have been guided by educational principles. We are convinced that to gain the fullest possible understanding of history through reading of original source materials, students must have these materials presented to them at length and in detail. Short extracts excerpted from the original sources too often fail to provide a reader with anything more than a superficial and fragmented acquaintance with the society under study. If a document chosen for inclusion satisfies our criteria for selection, it should yield an understanding of the society from which it sprang that justifies its being reproduced in its entirety or, where that is not possible, at sufficient length so that contribution to the history of that society is rendered clear.

Although its various introductions contain a considerable amount of historical information, this book is not designed to be a history of world civilization. The function of the introductory materials is, rather, to provide a background framework in which to exhibit the source documents themselves. Or, to reverse the metaphor, the book can be viewed as a gallery filled with documents that illuminate the societies of which they are a product. To anyone who wishes a full understanding of the course of world civilization, we recommend the study of the documents included in this book be supplemented by a reading of a standard work on the history of civilization.

Sources of World Civilization

EARLY CIVILIZATIONS

When did civilization begin? We have strong evidence that human—or closely similar—beings have lived on the earth for millions of years, but no one suggests that any civilization approaches that extreme age. To cope with our initial question, we need to address a prior one: What constitutes civilization? Although no simple answer can be given to this question, sufficient consensus exists among archaeologists and historians that we can identify the earliest of the ancient civilizations and the approximate times of their beginnings. Civilization requires a society, or a group of people living together over a period of time in the same place. Accepting these conditions of civilized life, we can conclude that a precondition of the existence of a civilization is the development of agriculture, for people who must hunt for their food cannot lead a settled, communal life. Agriculture, in its turn, leads to the domestication of animals, the tillage of fields, the acquisition of property, trade, and commerce, and, eventually, to the growth of towns and cities. With all of these we have a fully developed civilization. For our purpose, which is to present a history of civilization, one other requirement needs mention—the written word. Although not essential (for some civilizations have existed for long periods with their past preserved in oral traditions), written records furnish the solid foundations on which the story of humankind rests.

Even if we accept these constituents of civilization, we cannot place a definite date on the first civilizations, for archaeologists continue to unearth early remains in widely scattered locations. At the present time, they can point to towns they have excavated in the Near East that flourished as early as the eighth millennium B.C. Although we cannot review the entire list of ancient civilizations here, we shall concentrate on those that, because of their importance or their continuity, have made significant contributions to later history.

We begin with the great river civilizations, of which three are outstanding. That complex and stable societies should have grown up first in river valleys is understandable; here the land was level and the soil rich and deep and water was available, ideal conditions for the development of agriculture. Archaeologists generally agree that the earliest of these civilizations began in the Tigris and Euphrates valleys of Mesopotamia, in what is now Iraq. Apparently the first permanent settlers in the valleys were called Subarians, but they were conquered by the Sumerians, who had a well-established and flourishing society before the end of the fourth millennium B.C. They founded a number of cities, such as Lagash, Ur, and

Uruk, the walled city of Gilgamesh. Their system of agriculture, with its intricate irrigation systems, as well as their cities, in which trade flourished, required political organization and the development of legal systems. The latter are summarized in the famous Code of Hammurabi, which dates from about 1700 B.C. but is a codification of laws of earlier origin. We know much about the early history of Mesopotamia because the inhabitants of the valleys developed a form of writing on clay tablets, called cuneiform. Since the nineteenth century, thousands of these tablets have been discovered and translated.

Much of the early history of Mesopotamia is a record of turmoil as city-states strove with each other to dominate the rich land. But, with the passage of time, powerful leaders arose who created empires. During the course of about two thousand years, four major empires came to power and passed away. First was the Akkadian empire under Sargon I, with its capital city at Assur on the upper Tigris. This was followed by the Babylonian empire, founded by Hammurabi the lawgiver, its capital city being Babylon on the Euphrates. After a considerable lapse of time, a third empire, the Assyrian, arose with its capital at Ninevah, also on the upper Tigris. The final empire—one of the greatest in the history of the world—was the Persian, founded by Cyrus the Great around 550 B.C. This empire, which was centered to the east of Mesopotamia in what is now Iran, rapidly expanded until it covered most of the Near East, extending as far east as India. Under Darius I and later under Xerxes I the Persians moved westward, crossing the Hellespont and invading the Greek city-states. There the stage was set for one of the crucial military confrontations in history, whose outcome shaped the future course of civilization in the Western world.

The second ancient river civilization arose along the banks of the Nile, which has its source deep in Africa, to flow northward into the southeast corner of the Mediterranean Sea. This is Egypt, whose civilization rivals that of Mesopotamia in antiquity. Farms, and farming communities, developed on the banks of the long river in the fourth millennium B.C. and toward its end two kingdoms, Upper and Lower Egypt, had come into existence. According to tradition, about 3100 B.C. Menes, a strong leader, united the two kingdoms and inaugurated the dynastic age, whose pharaohs were to rule Egypt for millennia. The history of ancient Egypt, unlike that of Mesopotamia, was quite tranquil. The Nile overflowed its banks each year, enriching the soil, and the farmers reaped their crops, just as they still do. Although the land suffered a few invasions, and the Egyptians as a result came under foreign domination, for the most part they remained free from conquest. The explanation of this is largely geographical. Egypt is separated from the Near East by the Red Sea, and the Nile valley is protected on both sides by forbidding deserts, more than sufficient to give a potential invader pause.

We know much about both the history and the daily life of Egyptians from extensive records that survive, written in hieroglyphics, picture-writing dating from the fourth millennium. Another major source of knowledge results from the Egyptian faith in immortality. Believing in a life after death much like that on earth, the Egyptians filled the tombs of their dead with everything necessary for a prosperous, happy afterlife. Preserved intact through the ages in the dry desert air, ancient tombs like that of the pharaoh Tutankhamen, who reigned in the fourteenth century B.C., have yielded sufficient works of art and dazzling treasures to modern archaeologists.

The third great river civilization arose in the Far East, first in the floodplain of the lower Yellow River and later in that of the Yangtze River of China. In the rich soils of these river valleys a form of intensive farming developed, highly dependant on human labor, which continues to this day. Although the origins of the Chinese river civilization are shrouded in mythology, archaeologists believe that it developed at a somewhat later date than the previous two, probably around the middle of the third millennium B.C. The earliest royal dynasty, known as the Hsia, is said to have reigned over China (actually all the area between the Yellow and Yangtze rivers) throughout the second millennium; however, we have no firm records to verify accounts of these rulers. The first dynasty of which we can speak with assurance was the Shang, which governed China from 1523 to 1028 B.C. The last capital of this dynasty, Anyang (located just north of the Yellow River) was discovered and excavated early in the twentieth century; it has yielded much information about early Chinese civilization. The art of writing had been perfected, in the form of pictographs, by the time of the Shang. We have evidence, too, that the practice of ancestor worship dates at least from their time. Coupled with it is a concentration on the family (extended to include ancestors) as the focal point of the individual person's life.

The Shang dynasty was followed by the Chou, which ruled China for nearly a thousand years (until 256 B.C.). During the Chou Dynasty, the borders of imperial China were greatly expanded; however, imperial rule over all but the heartland became increasingly dependent on the goodwill of often unruly local chieftains. By the end of the dynasty China had literally disintegrated into a large number of independent principalities. Traditional Chinese historians refer to the last two centuries of the Chou as the "period warring states."

The ancient world contained another major river civilization, which was completely destroyed around 1500 B.C. and disappeared from historical memory until its remains were discovered and excavated early in the twentieth century. This civilization, which is thought to have developed around the middle of the third millennium B.C., occupied the valleys of the Indus River and its tributaries in the northwest corner of the Indian subcontinent in what is present-day Pakistan. Although we have scant evidence on which to base our speculations (the written language has not been deciphered), archaeological remains indicate that this was an advanced civilization comparable to Mesopotamia and Egypt. Two large cities have been excavated. They contain the remains of substantial buildings, built of brick and laid out on a grid system of streets. They even had a municipal sewer system. Numerous high-quality art objects have been found and evidence indicates that trade was carried on with the Sumerians in Mesopotamia. What happened to the Indus valley civilization? The best hypothesis is that it was overrun and obliterated by groups of warrior-tribesmen who moved into the valleys from the north-west, or what is now Afghanistan. These invaders, who are known as the Aryans, had been gradually moving east from Iran and central Asia. They later continued their migrations beyond the Indus valley pushing into the Ganges basin of northern India. There they subdued the local inhabitants, who still lived in a state of precivilization, turning these natives into their slaves. From these beginnings the caste system, which was to become a per-manent feature of Indian society, was later to emerge.

Undoubtedly advanced civilizations developed elsewhere in the world at an early time but we lack information about them. Mention should be made, however, of civilizations in the Western Hemisphere, because archaeological and other evidence indicates that they were com-parable to those we have already described. Two centers were particularly important: Central America and Mexico, where the Mayan civilization flourished, and the Andean region of South America, where several pre-Inca centers of civilization developed. Our knowledge of these civilizations is limited, but, from the evidence that remains, it is clear that both achieved a high level of culture.

The Epic of Gilgamesh

The epic of Gilgamesh is one of the oldest stories of which we have a written record. Presumably recited orally for generations before it was inscribed on clay tablets in cuneiform script, it tells of the life and exploits of a young nobleman and king, who ruled the city of Uruk in ancient Sumer, probably between 2700 and 2600 B.C. Sumer, generally recognized to be the earliest human civilization, was centered in the lower valley between the Tigris and Euphrates rivers in what is contemporary Iraq; Uruk was not far from the present capital city of Baghdad.

It is almost fortuitous that we have the epic in written form today. In the seventh century B.C. (two thousand years after the time of Gilgamesh) the Assyrian king Assurbanipal, who ruled over the territory including what had been the ancient Sumerian civilization, built a great library in his capital city of Ninevah. Included among its holdings was a copy of the epic. But in 612 B.C. an invading army of Medes and Babylonians overran Ninevah, destroying the city and burying it (with its library) beneath the desert sands. There all remained lost and virtually forgotten for over two millennia until, in 1839, a young English archaeologist stumbled on this magnificent treasure. Over several decades the tablets containing the epic (as well as many other ancient writings) were unearthed and deciphered. Later other copies were discovered elsewhere. The epic, as we now have it, is a collation pieced together from these various cuneiform tablets. Although the epic is sufficiently complete to tell its story, some portions are missing and have been reconstructed by the translator.

---

1. What are Gilgamesh's virtues? What are his faults? What does this tell us about the values and assumptions of the community that produced and preserved this story?

2. What does this story teach about human nature and the human condition? What does it teach about the nature of the gods and their relationship with humans?

Gilgamesh

All things he saw, even to the ends of the earth,
He underwent all, learned to know all,
He peered through all secrets,
Through wisdom's mantle that veileth all.
What was hidden he saw,
What was covered he undid;
Of times before the stormflood he brought report.
He went on a long far way,
Giving himself toil and distress;
Wrote then on a stone-tablet the whole of his labour.
He built the walls of ramparted Uruk,
He laid the foundations, steadfast as bronze,
Of holy Eanna, the pure temple . . .

Two thirds of him is god,
One third of him is man,
There's none can match the form of his body . . .

[*The inhabitants of Uruk call upon the gods for help:*]

"Gilgamesh keeps the son from the father,
Building the walls through the day, through the night.
He is herdsman of ramparted Uruk,
He is herdsman and lord of his folk,
Strong and splendid, knowing wisdom.
Gilgamesh keeps the lover from the maiden,
The daughter of a hero,
The chosen of a noble!"
The great gods heard their outcries.
The gods of heaven called the lord Anu:
"Was he not of thy making, this almighty wild bull,
This hero Gilgamesh?
He hath not his like in the whole land . . .
Gilgamesh keeps the son from the father,
Building the walls through the day, through the night.
He is herdsman of ramparted Uruk,
He is herdsman and lord of his folk,
Strong and splendid,
Knowing wisdom.

From *Gilgamesh* by William Ellery Leonard, translated by William Ellery Leonard. Translation copyright 1934 by William Ellery Leonard, renewed © 1962 by Barbara A. Hayward. Used by permission of Viking Penguin, a division of Penguin Books USA Inc.

Gilgamesh keeps the lover from the maiden,
The daughter of a hero,
The chosen of a noble!"
The great god Anu lent ear to their cries.
Aruru was summoned, she the great goddess:
"Thou, Aruru, madest Gilgamesh;
Now make another like unto him.
So long as he pleases
Let him come at Gilgamesh.
Let them contend together,
That Uruk may have peace."

As Aruru this heard,
She shaped in her heart a warrior of Anu.
Aruru washed her hands,
She pinched up some clay and spat on it.
She moulded Engidu,
Fashioned a hero, a glorious scion,
A fighter of Ninurta's.
His whole body was shaggy with hair,
Hair he bore on his head like a woman,
The plenty of his hair sprouted like grain.
He knew naught of land and people,
He was clothed like the god of the herds.
With the gazelles he eats the plants,
With the wild beasts he drinks at the watering-place,
With the throng at the water he makes glad his heart.

He walked to the watering-place
Toward a hunter, a stalker of wild beasts;
On one day, on a second, and a third,
Toward the hunter he walked to the watering-place.
The hunter saw him, the hunter's face grew troubled.
Without his quarry he turned back to his house.
He was down-cast, troubled; he shrieked.
His heart was afraid and his face was dark.
Grief made way into his heart,
And he looked like a wanderer of far ways.

• • •

[The hunter] started on the way, he entered into Uruk.
He goes to Gilgamesh, and to him he says:
"A man that came from the hills

Hath become strong indeed in the land.
Mighty in power like a fighter of Anu's.
Ever he goeth along on the hills,
He is ever beside the wild beasts,
Ever are his feet at the watering-place.
I am afraid, I cannot go near to him.
He hath filled my pits which I dug;
My traps which I laid
He hath destroyed.
So from my hands he let my quarry get away,
The throngs of the fields;
No catch he allows me."

Gilgamesh says to him, to the hunter:
"Go, my hunter, and get thee a priestess.
When the wild beasts come to the watering-place,
Then let her cast her garment off,
That he may take his fill of her.
When he sees her, he will draw near;
Then will he become a stranger to his wild beasts,
Who on his own steppes grew up with him."

The hunter went yonder and got him a priestess.
They made themselves ready, went forth straight on.
On the third day they came to their goal:
The hunter and the priestess sat themselves down.
One day, a second day, they sat by the watering-place.
The wild beasts come along and drink at the watering-place.
Glad is the throng of the flood.
So too comes he, Engidu . . .
With the gazelles he eats the plants,
With the beasts he drinks at the watering-place,
His heart is happy with the throng of the flood.
Then the priestess saw him, the great strong one,
The wild fellow, the man of the steppes:
"There he is, woman!
Loosen thy buckle,
Unveil thy delight,
That he may take his fill of thee!
Hang not back, take up his lust!
When he sees thee, he will draw near.
Open thy robe that he rest upon thee!
Arouse in him rapture, the work of woman.
Then will he become a stranger to his wild beasts,

Who on his own steppes grew up with him.
His bosom will press against thee."
Then the priestess loosened her buckle,
Unveiled her delight,
For him to take his fill of her.
She hung not back, she took up his lust,
She opened her robe that he rest upon her.
She aroused in him rapture, the work of woman.
His bosom pressed against her.
Engidu forgot where he was born.
For six days and seven nights
Was Engidu given over to love with the priestess.
When he had sated himself with the fill of her,
He raised up his face to his wild ones:
At sight of Engidu, the gazelles flee away,
The wild of the fields shrink back before him.
Then Engidu marvelled,
His body stood as in a spell,
His knees quivered, because his wild ran off . . .
The speed of his onset is not what it was.
He hearkens and opens his ear:
He turns about and sits down at the feet of the priestess.
He looks the priestess in the face,
And to what the priestess now speaks
His ears give heed.

The priestess says to him, to Engidu:
"Engidu, how beautiful thou, how like a god!
Why must thou rush with animals over the steppes?
Come, I will lead thee into ramparted Uruk,
To a pure house, the dwelling of Anu and Ishtar,
Where Gilgamesh lives, matchless in might,
And like a wild bull lords it over the folk . . ."
She talks to him, till he likes her words.
Knowing his own heart, he seeketh a friend.
Engidu says to her, to the priestess:
"Woman, go to! Lead me to the pure, the holy house,
The dwelling of Anu and Ishtar,
Where Gilgamesh lives, matchless in might,
And like a wild bull lords it over the folk.
I will challenge him to a fight.
I will call the strong one.
I will call out in Uruk:
'I too am a strong one!'

I alone can alter fate,
I, born on the steppes, matchless in might.
O Gilgamesh, may I behold thy face!
Well I know what the outcome will be."

• • •

Engidu goes along the market-street
Of ramparted Uruk.
Marvelling he looks at the mighty work;
He bars the way of the warriors of Uruk;
Then the folk of Uruk crowd against him,
The land is assembled . . .
But in fear the folk turn away.
They fall down . . . like a weak child . . .
The couch had been spread for goddess Ishtar. . .
At the gates of her house
Engidu barred the going-to,
Allowed not Gilgamesh that he enter in.
They grappled each other at the gates of her house.
They fought in the street . . .
That the doorposts quaked and the wall swayed . . .
Gilgamesh crumpled his leg to the ground,
His anger softened, he checked his onset.
When he had checked his onset,
Says Engidu to him, to Gilgamesh:
"Thee, as one matchless, thy mother bore,
The wild cow of the fold, the goddess Ninsun.
Over all men is thy head lifted up,
Ellil to thee hath allotted
The kingdom over mankind!"

• • •

[After their wrestling match Gilgamesh and Engidu become good friends. Together they trek into a far-distant cedar forest where they slay the monster, Khumbaba. But Gilgamesh later spurns the goddess, Ishtar, who then persuades her father, Anu, to send the bull of heaven to kill Gilgamesh.—Ed.]

Anu lent ear to [Ishtar's] words,
Let a bull-of-heaven descend
And come unto Uruk . . .
At his first snort he kills
Three hundred warriors.

And Engidu grasped the bull-of-heaven
By his horns.
At his second snort
Two hundred warriors he knocks over.
At his third snort
Engidu stalks up to him,
Leaps on his back,
And grasps him by the thick of the tail . . .
Then Engidu opened his mouth and speaks,
Says to Gilgamesh:
"My friend,
We have made our name glorious. . ."
And Gilgamesh, like a huntsman,
Thrusts his sword between nape and horns.
When they had laid low the bull-of-heaven,
Their heart had peace . . .
And in front of Shamash they sat down to their rest,
Both of the brothers.

Then Ishtar mounted the walls of ramparted Uruk,
Sprang on the battlements and shrieked down:
"Woe unto Gilgamesh who affronted me,
Who killed the bull-of-heaven."
As Engidu heard these words of Ishtar,
He tore loose a thigh-bone from the bull-of-heaven,
And flung it into her face:
"Could I but get hold of thee,
I would do unto thee as unto him!
Round thy neck would I hang his entrails!"
Then Ishtar assembled the damsels of the temple,
The harlots and the priestesses;
Over the thigh-bone of the bull-of-heaven
They wailed a chant . . .
Gilgamesh called the masters, the handworkers all.
The masters praise the thickness of the horns;
Thirty pounds of lapis lazuli was the weight of each.
Two fingers thick was their shell.
Six measures of oil (as much as both horns held)
Did he pour, as oil of anointing,
To his god, Lugalmaradda;
Brought the horns to his god's temple,
And fastened them on his throne.
Then they washed their hands in the Euphrates,
Start off and wander along

On the market-street of Uruk.
The people of Uruk stand assembled
And gaze upon them.

Gilgamesh speaks thus
To the maid-servants of his palace:
"Who is the most beautiful among the heroes?
Who is the mightiest among men?"

"Gilgamesh is the most beautiful among the heroes!
Gilgamesh is the mightiest among men!" . . .
Then Gilgamesh makes in his palace
A feast of rejoicing.

The warriors rest in their beds of night.
Also Engidu rests, beholding dreams.
Then Engidu rose up,
Tells the dreams, and speaks to his friend:
"Gilgamesh, my friend,
I beheld dreams this last night:
The heavens called, the earth answered.
In the dark night am I standing there alone,
I see a man with forbidding face . . .
He is hideous to look on,
His nails are eagle-talons . . .
He made my arms into wings like a bird's:
'Descend, descend, I say, into the house of darkness,
To the dwelling of Irkalla,
To the house
Which none leave again who have betrodden it,
To a way whose road turneth not,
To the house whose inhabitants do without light,
Where dust is their nourishment and clay their food.
They are as birds clothed with wings,
They see not the light,
They dwell in the darkness.'
In the house of dust which I entered . . .
Are kings' crowns bowed down.
There do dwell the mighty ones
Who from the days of old ruled the land . . .
In the house of dust which I entered
Dwell priest-prince and wailing-priests,
Dwell the conjurers and the rapt seers,
Dwell the high-priests of the great gods . . .

Dwells the queen of the earth, Eresh-Kigal.
Belit-Seri, she the scribe of the earth,
Standeth bowed before her . . .
And readeth to her aloud.
Then she raised her head and saw me,
She stretched out her hand and took me to herself" . . .

[*Then Gilgamesh moaned and said:*]

"My friend,
Who with me hast ranged through all hardships . . .
My friend, the dream comes true! . . ."
On the day when he saw the dream
His fate was fulfilled.
Engidu lies stricken,
For one day,
For a second day,
Engidu suffers pain in his bed.
For a third day, and a fourth,
Engidu lies stricken.
For a fifth, a sixth, and a seventh,
For an eighth, a ninth, and a tenth day.
Engidu's pain grows great.
For an eleventh and a twelfth day,
Engidu lies in his bed . . .
He calls Gilgamesh and speaks:
"A god hath cursed me, my friend.
Not like one wounded in battle
Is it mine to die.
I once feared the fight . . .
But, my friend,
He who falls in the fight is happy.
As to me, I must die in my bed . . ."

• • •

[*And Gilgamesh returns to Engidu's bed and speaks:*]

"Engidu, my young friend,
Thou panther of the steppes,
Who couldst do all things,
So that we climbed the mountain,
Overthrew Khumbaba,
Who housed in the cedar-forest,
So that we seized and slew the bull-of-heaven,
What kind of sleep is this

That hath now seized upon thee?
Dark is thy look,
And thine ears take not my voice!"
But he lifts up his eyes no more.
Gilgamesh touched him on the heart,
But the heart beats no more.
Then he covered up his friend like a bride.

Like as a lion, Gilgamesh raised his voice,
Like as a lioness, he roared out.
He turns round to his friend,
He tears his hair and strews it forth . . .
Soon as beamed the first shimmer of morning,
Gilgamesh raised a new cry:
"I made thee to rest on a bed well-prepared,
I made thee to dwell in a quiet dwelling-place . . .
I made princes of the earth kiss thy feet.
Now will I make the people of ramparted Uruk
Beweep thee and sorrow for thee;
Much people will I make to serve thee,
And I will myself put on mourning for thee,
Will clothe myself in a lion's skin,
And haste away over the steppes . . ."

Gilgamesh weeps bitterly
For his friend Engidu,
And hastes away over the steppes:

• • •

[After many wanderings over steppes and mountains Gilgamesh reaches the sea.—*Ed.*]

Siduri, she the divine cup-bearer,
Sits there by the rim of the sea.
Sits there and looks afar off . . .
She is wrapped in a shawl . . .
Gilgamesh ran thither and drew nigh unto her.
He is clad in skins,
His shape is awesome,
His body godlike,
Woe is in his heart.
He is like a wanderer of far ways.
The face of her, the cup-bearer, looks afar off,
She talks to herself and says the word,

Takes counsel in her heart:
"Is he yonder one who deviseth ill?
Whither is he going in the wrath of his heart?"
As Siduri saw him, she locked her gate,
Locked her portal, locked her chamber . . .

Gilgamesh says to her, to the cup-bearer:
"Cup-bearer, what ails thee,
That thou lockest thy gate,
Lockest thy portal,
Lockest thy chamber?
I will crash the door, I will break the lock . . ."
The cup-bearer says to him, to Gilgamesh:
"Why are thy cheeks so wasted,
Thy visage so sunken,
Thy heart so sad,
Thy shape so undone?
Why is woe in thy heart?
Why art thou like a wanderer of far ways?
Why is thy countenance
So destroyed with grief and pain?
Why hast thou from wide-away
Made haste over the steppes?"
Gilgamesh says to her, to the cup-bearer:
"Why should my cheeks not be so wasted,
My visage so sunken,
My heart so sad,
My shape so undone?
How should woe not be in my heart?
Why should I not be like
A wanderer of far ways?
Why should not my countenance
Be destroyed with grief and pain?
Why should I not to the far-away
Make haste over the steppes?
My belovèd friend, the panther of the steppes,
Engidu, my belovèd friend,
The panther of the steppes who could do all things,
So that we climbed the mountain,
Overthrew Khumbaba,
Who housed in the cedar-forest,
So that we seized and slew the bull-of-heaven,
So that we laid lions low
In the ravines of the mountain,

My friend,
Who with me ranged through all hardships,
Engidu, my friend, who killed lions with me,
Who with me ranged through all hardships,
Him hath the fate of mankind overtaken.
Six days and six nights have I wept over him,
Until the seventh day
Would I not have him buried.
Then I began to be afraid . . .
Fear of death seized upon me.
Therefore I make away over the steppes.
The fate of my friend weighs me down.
Therefore I make haste
On a far way over the steppes.
The fate of Engidu, my friend,
Weigheth me down.
Therefore I make haste on a long road over the steppes.
Why should I be silent thereon?
Why should I not cry it forth?
My friend, whom I love,
Hath turned into earth.
Must not I too, as he,
Lay me down
And rise not up again
For ever and for ever?—
Ever since he is gone, I cannot find Life,
And rove, like a hunter, round over the fields.
Cup-bearer, now I behold thy face;
But Death, whom I fear, I would not behold."

The cup-bearer, she says to him, to Gilgamesh:
"Gilgamesh, whither runnest thou?
Life, which thou seekest, thou wilt not find.
When the gods created mankind,
They allotted to mankind Death,
But Life they withheld in their hands.
So, Gilgamesh, fill thy body,
Make merry by day and night,
Keep each day a feast of rejoicing!
Day and night leap and have thy delight!
Put on clean raiment,
Wash thy head and bathe thee in water,
Look cheerily at the child who holdeth thy hand,
And may thy wife have joy in thy arms!"

Gilgamesh says again to her, to the cup-bearer:
"Go to, cup-bearer!
Where is the way to Utnapishtim?
What is his sign? Give it to me!
If it can be done,
I will pass over the sea;
If it cannot be done,
I will make away over the steppes."
The cup-bearer she says to him, to Gilgamesh:
"Never, Gilgamesh, was there a place of crossing,
And no one who came since the days of old
Could pass over that sea.
Only Shamash, the hero,
Hath passed over that sea.
But who except Shamash can pass over it?
There is no getting to the place of crossing,
Toilsome the way thereunto,
The waters of death are deep
That lie there to thwart thee.
Where wilt thou, Gilgamesh, pass over that sea?
When thou comest to the waters of death,
What, then, wilt thou do?
Gilgamesh, Ur-Shanabi is there,
The shipman of Utnapishtim,
Who hath with him coffers of stone.
He picks plants in the forest.
Him do thou seek out.
If it can be done, fare across with him;
If it cannot be done, turn again back."

● ●

[*Gilgamesh seeks for Ur-Shanabi, but finds at first only his stone coffers, which he breaks to pieces in his anger. Then suddenly he beholds Ur-Shanabi.*]

Ur-Shanabi says to him, to Gilgamesh:
"What is thy name? Say forth!
I am Ur-Shanabi,
Man-servant of Utnapishtim, the far one."

Gilgamesh speaks to him, to Ur-Shanabi:
"My name is Gilgamesh,
I have come from long away . . .
At last, Ur-Shanabi, I behold thy face.
Let me look on Utnapishtim, the far one."

And Gilgamesh says again to him,
To Ur-Shanabi, the shipman:
"Come, Ur-Shanabi, where is the way to Utnapishtim?
What is his sign? Give it to me!
Give me, give me his sign!
If it can be done,
I will pass over the sea;
If it cannot be done,
I will make away over the steppes."

Ur-Shanabi says to him, to Gilgamesh:
"Thy hands, O Gilgamesh,
Have hindered a landing.
Thou brakest to pieces the coffers of stone,
The coffers of stone are to-broken;
And so I cannot ferry thee over.
Gilgamesh, take the axe in thy arm,
Go down to the forest,
Cut poles of length sixty ells,
Smear them with pitch and bear them to me."

As Gilgamesh this heard,
He took the axe in his arm,
Drew the sword from his girdle,
Went down to the forest,
And cut poles of length sixty ells,
Smeared them with pitch . . .
And brought them to Ur-Shanabi.

Gilgamesh and Ur-Shanabi boarded the ship,
They headed the ship into the flood,
And sailed forth,
A way of one month and fifteen days.
As he took his bearings on the third day,
Ur-Shanabi had reached the waters of death.
Ur-Shanabi says to him, to Gilgamesh:
"Quick, Gilgamesh, take a pole!
For thy hands must not touch
The waters of death.
A second, a third, a fourth pole,
Take, Gilgamesh!
An fifth, a sixth, a seventh pole,
Take, Gilgamesh!
An eighth, a ninth, a tenth pole,

Take, Gilgamesh!
An eleventh, a twelfth pole,
Take, Gilgamesh!"

At a hundred and twenty
Gilgamesh had used up the poles.
Now he made his hips free . . .
Gilgamesh stripped off his garment,
And with his hands made high the mast.
Utnapishtim descrieth his face afar;
Talks to himself and saith the word,
Takes counsel in his heart:
"Why are the stone-coffers
Of the ship all to-broken?
And one who belongs not to me
Sails in the ship!
He who comes yonder, he cannot be man! . . .
I gaze thither, but I understand it not.
I gaze thither, but I grasp it not." . . .

Utnapishtim says to him, to Gilgamesh:
"What is thy name? Say forth!
I am Utnapishtim who hath found Life."

• • •

Gilgamesh says to him, to Utnapishtim:
"Methought, I will go and see
Utnapishtim, of whom men tell.
So I betook me through all lands to and fro,
So I betook me over the mountains
That are hard to cross over,
So I fared over all seas.
With good have I not been glutted . . .
I filled my body with pain;
Ere ever I got to Siduri, the cup-bearer,
Was my clothing gone . . .
I had to hunt all the wild of the fields,
Lions and panthers,
Hyenas, and deer, and ibex.
Their flesh do I eat,
With their skins do I clothe me."

• • •

"I look upon thee, Utnapishtim:
Thy form is not unlike;

Even as I, so too art thou;
Yes, thou art not unlike;
Even as I, so too art thou.
Yet I was born unto this:
To fight and to do battle.
But thou art idle and liest on thy back.
How camest thou, then, into the assembly
Of the gods and foundest Life?"

Utnapishtim says to him, to Gilgamesh:
"I will lay open before thee, Gilgamesh,
Knowledge deep-hidden,
And a secret of the gods will I tell thee:
Shurippak is a city (thou thyself knowest her),
Which lieth on Euphrates' banks.
She is an ancient city,
And the gods are kind to her.
Once the great gods conceived a plan
To make a stormflood.
There foregathered Anu, their father,
Their overlord, the hero Ellil,
Their herald Ninurta, their prince Ennugi.
The bright-eyed Ea had sat with them at counsel.
He told their discussion to a reed-hut:[1]
'Reed-hut, reed-hut! Hut-wall, hut-wall!
Reed-hut, listen! Wall, take it in!
Thou man from Shurippak, son of Ubara-Tutu,[2]
Tear down thy house, build a ship!
Let riches go, seek Life,
Despise possessions, save thy life!
Bring living things of all kinds into the ship!
The ship that thou art to build,
Be its measurements strictly laid out,
For its length and its breadth to match—
On the holy lake set it at anchor!
I understood, and I say to Ea, my lord:
'I perceive, my lord, what thou sayest;
I hold it dear, and will carry it out.'

• • •

[1]In which Utnapishtim lives.
[2]That is, Utnapishtim himself, who is revealing the "knowledge deep-hidden" to Gilgamesh.

Before sunset the ship was finished . . .
All that I had I laded upon it,
All that I had of silver I laded upon it,
I laded upon it all that I had of gold,
I laded upon it all that I had
Of living things of all kinds.
I made my whole family and kin
To go aboard the ship;
Cattle of the field, animals of the field,
All handworkers I made go aboard.
Shamash had given me the appointed time:
'Of an evening will the Sender of darkness
Let a cloudburst stream from on high.
Then enter the ship and close thy door.'
This appointed time came on.
The Sender of darkness
Of an evening let a cloudburst come down.
I observed the look of the tempest,
I was afraid to gaze on the tempest,
I went within the ship and shut my gate.

●●●

Six days and six nights swirls the stormflood,
And the southstorm is a weight on the land.
As the seventh day came on,
The southstorm gave up the fight,
Which it had fought like an army.
The sea grew quiet, and gathered up its waters.
The stormflood ceased.
I looked for the tempest, all had become still.
The whole race of man was turned to earth.
Like a flat roof were the plains.
Then I opened a hatch,
And light streamed into my face.
I sat me down weeping,
And my tears ran over my face.
I gazed about for solid earth
In the dominions of the sea.
After twelve hours an island emerged.
The ship drove for Mount Nissir.
Mount Nissir holds the ship fast
And keeps it from rocking.
One day, a second day, Mount Nissir
Holds the ship fast and keeps it from rocking.

A third and fourth day Mount Nissir
Holds the ship fast and keeps it from rocking.
A fifth, a sixth day Mount Nissir
Holds the ship fast and keeps it from rocking.

"As the seventh day came on,
I held a dove outside and set it free;
The dove flew forth and came back.
She found no resting-place, so she turned home.
I held a swallow outside and set it free;
The swallow flew forth and came back.
She found no resting-place, so she turned home.
I held a raven outside and set it free;
The raven flew forth, saw the water run dry,
He feeds, scrapes, croaks, and turned not home.

"Then I let all out unto the four winds,
And offered a sacrifice,
Set up a burnt-offering
On the top of the mountain.

• • •

Gilgamesh and Ur-Shanabi boarded the ship,
They headed the ship into the flood,
And sailed away.
Then said his wife to him,
To Utnapishtim, the far one:
"Gilgamesh hath set forth;
He hath worn himself out, and suffered torments.
What wilt thou give him,
That with it he may reach his homeland?"

And Gilgamesh has already lifted the pole,
And brings the ship again near the shore:
Utnapishtim says to him, to Gilgamesh:
"Gilgamesh, thou hast set forth;
Thou hast worn thyself out, and suffered torments.
What shall I give thee
That with it thou reachest thy homeland?
I will lay open before thee
Knowledge deep-hidden;
About a plant of life will I tell thee.
The plant looks like the prick-thorn . . .
Its thorn like the thorn of the rose

Can prick the hand hard.
When thou gettest this plant in thy hands,
Eat thereof and thou wilt live."

When Gilgamesh learned of this . . .
He bound heavy stones on his feet;
These drew him down deep in the sea.
He himself took the plant,
And it pricked his hand hard.
He cut off the heavy stones . . .
And laid the plant beside him.
Gilgamesh says to him,
To Ur-Shanabi, the shipman:
"Ur-Shanabi, this plant
Is a plant-of-promise,
Whereby a man obtains his desire.
I will bring it to ramparted Uruk;
I will make the warriors eat thereof . . .
Its name is: 'The-old-man-becomes-young-again.'
I myself will eat thereof,
And return back to my youth."
After twenty miles they took a little food,
After thirty miles they rested for the night.
Then Gilgamesh saw a pit with cool water;
He stepped into it and bathed in the water.
Then a serpent savoured the smell of the plant;
She crept along and took the plant . . .
When he returned, he shrieked out a curse.
Gilgamesh sat himself down and weeps,
His tears run over his face.
He speaks and says to Ur-Shanabi, the shipman:
"For whom, Ur-Shanabi,
Have my arms worn themselves out?
For whom hath been spent the blood of my heart?
I worked good not for myself—
For the worm of the earth have I wrought good. . . ."

Daily Life in Egypt

Because of the dry climate of Egypt, historians have a wealth of written and physical remains with which to study the civilization that arose along the Nile valley. Although reading and writing were skills known only to the elite, we can learn something of ancient Egyptian life in general from the following texts. One can easily picture congregations of Egyptian worshippers singing their praises to the Nile. The Nile was essential to Egyptian life. Its annual flooding inundated the valley, thus enriching the soil and producing a much greater yield than would otherwise have occurred. As the ancient Greek historian Herodotus so aptly put it, "Egypt is the gift of the Nile." In their worship of the Nile, ancient Egyptians were exemplifying a form of religious belief common among early civilizations—animism, or the deification of objects of nature. It is clear that the Nile is being worshipped as one among many gods, so the religion is not only animistic but also polytheistic. The date of the Hymn to the Nile is not known, but scholars believe that it was sung during an annual festival held at Thebes (in upper Egypt), celebrating the inundation of the land by the Nile. It has, unfortunately, not survived intact, but is still sufficiently complete so that its content is clear.

The second document is a letter of advice from a high-level government official to his son, exhorting him to learn the skills of a scribe. This document gives us insight into the demanding and perilous existence of the majority of the ancient Egyptian population, as well as the attitude of Egyptian elites toward various types of work.

---

1. What was the Egyptian attitude toward the Nile River?

2. Egyptian religious texts tend to paint an optimistic picture of prosperity and stability. While the advice of the government official to his son is certainly exaggerated, what does it tell us about the reality of life in ancient Egypt?

3. What sorts of class distinctions are described in the second document?

Hymn to the Nile

Praise to thee, O Nile, that issueth from the earth, and cometh to nourish Egypt. Of hidden nature, a darkness in the day-time. . . .

Trans. A. M. Blackman.

That watereth the meadows, he that Rē [1] hath created to nourish all cattle. That giveth drink to the desert places, which are far from water; it is his dew that falleth from heaven.

Beloved of Kēb,[2] director of the corn-god; that maketh to flourish every workshop of Ptah.[3]

Lord of fish, that maketh the water-fowl to go upstream. . . .

That maketh barley and createth wheat, so that he may cause the temples to keep festivals.

If he be sluggish,[4] the nostrils are stopped up,[5] and all men are improverished; the victuals of the gods are diminished, and millions of men perish.

If he be niggardly the whole land is in terror and great and small lament. . . . Khnum[6] hath fashioned him. When he riseth, the land is in exultation and every body is in joy. All jaws begin to laugh and every tooth is revealed.

He that bringeth victuals and is rich in food, that createth all that is good. The revered, sweet-smelling. . . . That createth herbage for the cattle, and giveth sacrifice to every god, be he in the underworld, in heaven, or upon earth. . . . That filleth the storehouses, and maketh wide the granaries, that giveth things to the poor.

He that maketh trees to grow according to every wish, and men have no lack thereof; the ship is built by his power, for there is no joinery with stones. . . .

. . . thy young folk and thy children shout for joy over thee, and men hail thee as king. Unchanging of laws, when he cometh forth in the presence of Upper and Lower Egypt. Men drink the water. . . .

He that was in sorrow is become glad, and every heart is joyful. Sobk,[7] the child of Neith, laugheth, and the divine Ennead, that is in thee, is glorious.

Thou that vomitest forth, giving the fields to drink and making strong the people. He that maketh the one rich and loveth the other. He maketh no distinctions, and boundaries are not made for him.

Thou light, that cometh from the darkness! Thou fat for his cattle. He is a strong one, that createth. . . .

---

[1] The sun-god.
[2] The earth-god.
[3] Ptah, the craftsman, who fashions everything, could effect nothing without the Nile.
[4] On the occasion of a deficient inundation.
[5] Men no longer breathe and live.
[6] The ram-headed god, who fashions all that is.
[7] Sobk has the form of a crocodile and will originally have been a water-god, who rejoices in the inundation.

. . . one beholdeth the wealthy as him that is full of care, one beholdeth each one with his implements. . . . None that (otherwise) goeth clad, is clad,[8] and the children of notables are unadorned. . . .

He that establisheth right, whom men love. . . . It would be but lies to compare thee with the sea, that bringeth no corn. . . . no bird descendeth in the desert. . . .

Men begin to play to thee on the harp, and men sing to thee with the hand.[9] Thy young folk and thy children shout for joy over thee, and deputations to thee are appointed.

He that cometh with splendid things and adorneth the earth! That causeth the ship to prosper before men; that quickeneth the hearts in them that are with child; that would fain have there be a multitude of all kinds of cattle.

When thou art risen in the city of the sovereign, then men are satisfied with a goodly list.[10] "I would like lotus flowers," saith the little one, "and all manner of things," saith the . . . commander, "and all manner of herbs," say the children. Eating bringeth forgetfulness of him.[11] Good things are scattered over the dwelling. . . .

When the Nile floodeth, offering is made to thee, cattle are slaughtered for thee, a great oblation is made for thee. Birds are fattened for thee, antelopes are hunted for thee in the desert. Good is recompensed unto thee.

Offering is also made to every other god, even as is done for the Nile, with incense, oxen, cattle, and birds (upon) the flame. The Nile hath made him his cave in Thebes, and his name shall be known no more in the underworld. . . .

All ye men, extol the Nine Gods, and stand in awe of the might which his son, the Lord of All, hath displayed, even he that maketh green the Two River-banks. Thou art verdant, O Nile, thou art verdant. He that maketh man to live on his cattle, and his cattle on the meadow! Thou art verdant, thou art verdant: O Nile, thou art verdant.

Papyrus Lansing

Title

[Beginning of the instruction in letter-writing made by the royal scribe and chief overseer of the cattle of Amen-Re, King of Gods, Nebmare-nakht] for his apprentice, the scribe Wenemdiamun.

---

[8]For hard work, clothes are taken off.
[9]It is an old custom to beat time with the hand while singing.
[10]*i.e.*, a multitude of good things.
[11]The Nile.
Mirian Lichtheim, *Ancient Egyptian Literature: A Book of Readings. Vol. II: The New Kingdom* (Berkeley: University of California Press, 1976), pp. 168–172.

Praise of the Scribe's Profession

[The royal scribe] and chief overseer of the cattle of Amen-[Re, King of Gods. Nebmare-nakht speaks to the scribe Wenemdiamun]. [Apply yourself to this] noble profession. . . . You will find it useful. . . . You will be advanced by your superiors. You will be sent on a mission. . . . Love writing, shun dancing; then you become a worthy official. Do not long for the marsh thicket. Turn your back on throw stick and chase. By day write with your fingers; recite by night. Befriend the scroll, the palette. It pleases more than wine. Writing for him who knows it is better than all other professions. It pleases more than bread and beer, more than clothing and ointment. It is worth more than an inheritance in Egypt, than a tomb in the west.

Advice to the Unwilling Pupil

Young fellow, how conceited you are! You do not listen when I speak. Your heart is denser than a great obelisk, a hundred cubits high, ten cubits thick. When it is finished and ready for loading, many work gangs draw it. It hears the words of men; it is loaded on a barge. Departing from Yebu it is conveyed, until it comes to rest on its place in Thebes.

So also a cow is bought this year, and it plows the following year. It learns to listen to the herdsman; it only lacks words. Horses brought from the field, they forget their mothers. Yoked they go up and down on all his majesty's errands. They become like those that bore them, that stand in the stable. They do their utmost for fear of a beating.

But though I beat you with every kind of stick, you do not listen. If I knew another way of doing it, I would do it for you, that you might listen. You are a person fit for writing, though you have not yet known a woman. Your heart discerns, your fingers are skilled, your mouth is apt for reciting.

Writing is more enjoyable than enjoying a basket of . . . and beans; more enjoyable than a mother's giving birth, when her heart knows no distaste. She is constant in nursing her son; her breast is in his mouth every day. Happy is the heart [of] him who writes; he is young each day.

All Occupations Are Bad Except That of the Scribe

See for yourself with your own eye. The occupations lie before you.

The washerman's day is going up, going down. All his limbs are weak, [from] whitening his neighbors' clothes every day, from washing their linen.

The maker of pots is smeared with soil, like one whose relations have died. His hands, his feet are full of clay, he is like one who lives in the bog.

The cobbler mingles with vats. His odor is penetrating. His hands are red with madder, like one who is smeared with blood. He looks behind him for the kite, like one whose flesh is exposed.

The watchman prepares garlands and polishes vase-stands. He spends a night of toil just as one on whom the sun shines.

The merchants travel downstream and upstream. They are as busy as can be, carrying goods from one town to another. They supply him who has wants. But the tax collectors carry off the gold, that most precious of metals.

The ships' crews from every house (of commerce), they receive their loads. They depart from Egypt for Syria, and each man's god is with him. (But) not one of them says: "We shall see Egypt again!"

The carpenter who is in the shipyard carries the timber and stacks it. If he gives today the output of yesterday, woe to his limbs! The shipwright stands behind him to tell him evil things.

His outworker who is in the fields, his is the toughest of all the jobs. He spends the day loaded with his tools, tied to his tool-box. When he returns home at night, he is loaded with the tool-box and the timbers, his drinking mug, and his whet-stones.

The scribe, he alone, records the output of all of them. Take note of it!

The Misfortunes of the Peasant

Let me also expound to you the situation of the peasant, that other tough occupation. [Comes] the inundation and soaks him . . . , he attends to his equipment. By day he cuts his farming tools; by night he twists rope. Even his midday hour he spends on farm labor. He equips himself to go to the field as if he were a warrior. The dried field lies before him; he goes out to get his team. When he has been after the herdsman for many days, he gets his team and comes back with it. He makes for it a place in the field. Comes dawn, he goes to make a start and does not find it in its place. He spends three days searching for it; he finds it in the bog. He finds no hides on them; the jackals have chewed them. He comes out, his garment in his hand, to beg for himself a team.

When he reaches his field he finds [it] broken up. He spends time cultivating, and the snake is after him. It finishes off the seed as it is cast to the ground. He does not see a green blade. He does three plowings with borrowed grain. His wife has gone down to the merchants and found nothing for barter. Now the scribe lands on the shore. He surveys the harvest. Attendants are behind him with staffs, Nubians with clubs. One says (to him): "Give grain." "There is none." He is beaten savagely. He is bound, thrown in the well, submerged head down. His wife is bound in his presence. His children are in fetters. His neighbors abandon them and flee. When it's over, there's no grain.

If you have any sense, be a scribe. If you have learned about the peasant, you will not be able to be one. Take note of it! . . .

The Scribe Does Not Suffer Like the Soldier

Furthermore. Look, I instruct you to make you sound; to make you hold the palette freely. To make you become one whom the king trusts; to make you gain entrance to treasury and granary. To make you receive the ship-load at the gate of the granary. To make you issue the offerings on feast days. You are dressed in fine clothes; you own horses. Your boat is on the river; you are supplied with attendants. You stride about inspecting. A mansion is built in your town. You have a powerful office, given you by the king. Male and female slaves are about you. Those who are in the fields grasp your hand, on plots that you have made. Look, I make you into a staff of life! Put the writings in your heart, and you will be protected from all kinds of toil. You will become a worthy official.

Do you not recall the (fate of) the unskilled man? His name is not known. He is ever burdened [like an ass carrying] in front of the scribe who knows what he is about.

Come, [let me tell] you the woes of the soldier, and how many are his superiors: the general, the troop-commander, the officer who leads, the standard-bearer, the lieutenant, the scribe, the commander of fifty, and the garrison-captain. They go in and out in the halls of the palace, saying: "Get laborers!" He is awakened at any hour. One is after him as (after) a donkey. He toils until the Aten (*sun*) sets in his darkness of night. He is hungry, his belly hurts; he is dead while yet alive. When he receives the grain-ration, having been released from duty, it is not good for grinding.

He is called up for Syria. He may not rest. There are no clothes, no sandals. The weapons of war are assembled at the fortress of Sile. His march is uphill through mountains. He drinks water every third day: it is smelly and tastes of salt. His body is ravaged by illness. The enemy comes, surrounds him with missiles, and life recedes from him. He is told: "Quick, forward, valiant soldier! Win for yourself a good name!" He does not know what he is about. His body is weak, his legs fail him. When victory is won, the captives are handed over to his majesty, to be taken to Egypt. The foreign woman faints on the march; she hangs herself [on] the soldier's neck. His knapsack drops, another grabs it while he is burdened with the woman. His wife and children are in their village; he dies and does not reach it. If he comes out alive, he is worn out from marching. Be he at large, be he detained, the soldier suffers. If he leaps and joins the deserters, all his people are imprisoned. He dies on the edge of the desert, and there is none to perpetuate his name. He suffers in death as in life. A big sack is brought for him; he does not know his resting place.

Be a scribe, and be spared from soldiering! You call and one says: "Here I am." You are safe from torments. Every man seeks to raise himself up. Take note of it!

The Code of Hammurabi

At the beginning of the twentieth century, a French archaeological expedition unearthed one of the most magnificent finds of our times—a stele, or tablet, on which was inscribed the entire Code of Hammurabi. Found at Susa in western Persia, where it had been taken by an Elamite king as war booty in the twelfth century B.C., the stele is of stone, about eight feet tall, and contains approximately thirty-six hundred lines of writing. Although the stone has been damaged slightly, most of the writing, in cuneiform script, is legible. At the top of the stele is a well-executed carving showing Hammurabi receiving the laws from Marduk, the sun god of Babylonia. After its discovery the stele was taken to Paris and placed in the Louvre, where it can still be seen.

Hammurabi (whose tribe, the Amorites, had occupied the middle Euphrates valley), established himself in power and founded the city of Babylon along the lower river, then reigned as king of Babylonia from 1728 to 1686 B.C. Although he was responsible for formulating and publishing the Code, he did not originate the laws it contains. Rather, the Code is a compilation and revision of older laws of the Sumerians and Akkadians (tribes occupying the same general region). These deal with almost every facet of life in the ancient Near East, including marriage and the family, relationships among social classes, regulations concerning land and business, labor relations, military service, religion, and crime. They are important not only for the light they shed on the quite complex society of that time but also for the influence they had on later Near Eastern law codes.

The selection that follows includes the most important legal provisions of the Code; regulations of lesser significance have been omitted.

---

1. What does the law code tell us about Babylonian society concerning gender, class, and family?

2. Based on the selections below, what issues most concerned the Babylonian government? What seem to be the most basic problems of early urban life?

The Code of Hammurabi

1.   If a man has accused another of laying a death spell upon him, but has not proved it, he shall be put to death.

2.   If a man has accused another of laying a spell upon him, but has not proved it, the accused shall go to the sacred river, he shall plunge into the sacred river, and if the sacred river shall conquer him, he that accused him shall take possession of his house. If the sacred river shall show his innocence and he is saved, his accuser shall be put to death. He that plunged into the sacred river shall appropriate the house of him that accused him.

3.   If a man has borne false witness in a trial, or has not established the statement that he has made, if that case be a capital trial, that man shall be put to death.

4.   If he has borne false witness in a civil law case, he shall pay the damages in that suit.

5.   If a judge has given a verdict, rendered a decision, granted a written judgment, and afterward has altered his judgment, that judge shall be prosecuted for altering the judgment he gave and shall pay twelvefold the penalty laid down in that judgment. Further, he shall be publicly expelled from his judgment-seat and shall not return nor take his seat with the judges at a trial.

6.   If a man has stolen goods from a temple, or house, he shall be put to death; and he that has received the stolen property from him shall be put to death.

• • •

14.   If a man has stolen a child, he shall be put to death.

15.   If a man has induced either a male or female slave from the house of a patrician, or plebeian, to leave the city, he shall be put to death.

16.   If a man has harbored in his house a male or female slave from a patrician's or plebeian's house, and has not caused the fugitive to leave on the demand of the officer over the slaves condemned to public forced labor, that householder shall be put to death.

• • •

22.   If a man has committed highway robbery and has been caught, that man shall be put to death.

23.   If the highwayman has not been caught, the man that has been robbed shall state on oath what he has lost and the city or district governor

"The Code of Hammurabi", trans. T. J. Meek, in *The Ancient Near East*, ed. J. B. Pritchard (Princeton University Press, 1958). Used by permission of Princeton University Press.

in whose territory or district the robbery took place shall restore to him what he has lost.

• • •

25.   If a fire has broken out in a man's house and one who has come to put it out has coveted the property of the householder and appropriated any of it, that man shall be cast into the self-same fire.

26.   If a levy-master, or warrant-officer, who has been detailed on the king's service, has not gone, or has hired a substitute in his place, that levy-master, or warrant-officer, shall be put to death and the hired substitute shall take his office.

27.   If a levy-master, or warrant-officer, has been assigned to garrison duty, and in his absence his field and garden have been given to another who has carried on his duty, when the absentee has returned and regained his city, his field and garden shall be given back to him and he shall resume his duty.

28.   If a levy-master, or warrant-officer, has been assigned to garrison duty, and has a son able to carry on his official duty, the field and garden shall be given to him and he shall carry on his father's duty.

29.   If the son be a child and is not able to carry on his father's duty, one-third of the field and garden shall be given to his mother to educate him.

• • •

34.   If either a governor, or a prefect, has appropriated the property of a levy-master, has hired him out, has robbed him by high-handedness at a trial, has taken the salary which the king gave to him, that governor, or prefect, shall be put to death.

35.   If a man has bought from a levy-master the sheep, or oxen, which the king gave him, he shall lose his money.

36.   The field, garden, or house, of a levy-master, warrant-officer, or tributary shall not be sold.

• • •

42.   If a man has hired a field to cultivate and has caused no corn to grow on the field, he shall be held responsible for not doing the work on the field and shall pay an average rent.

45.   If a man has let his field to a farmer and has received his rent for the field but afterward the field has been flooded by rain, or a storm has carried off the crop, the loss shall be the farmer's.

46.   If he has not received the rent of his field, whether he let it for a half, or for a third, of the crop, the farmer and the owner of the field shall share the corn that is left in the field, according to their agreement.

• • •

53, 54.   If a man has neglected to strengthen his dike and has not kept his dike strong, and a breach has broken out in his dike, and the waters have flooded the meadow, the man in whose dike the breach has broken out shall restore the corn he has caused to be lost. [54]. If he be not able to restore the corn, he and his goods shall be sold, and the owners of the meadow whose corn the water has carried away shall share the money.

• • •

100.   [If an agent has received money of a merchant, he shall write down the amount] and [what is to be] the interest of the money, and when his time is up, he shall settle with his merchant.

101.   If he has not had success on his travels, he shall return double what he received to the merchant.

102, 103.   If the merchant has given money, as a speculation, to the agent, who during his travels has met with misfortune, he shall return the full sum to the merchant. [103]. If, on his travels, an enemy has forced him to give up some of the goods he was carrying, the agent shall specify the amount on oath and shall be acquitted.

• • •

106.   If an agent has taken money of a merchant, and his principal suspects him, that principal shall prosecute his agent, put him on oath before the elders, as to the money taken; the agent shall pay to the merchant threefold what he misappropriated.

107.   If the principal has overcharged the agent and the agent has [really] returned to his principal whatever his principal gave him, and if the principal has disputed what the agent has given him, that agent shall put his principal on oath before the elders, and the merchant, because he has defrauded the agent, shall pay to the agent sixfold what he misappropriated.

108.   If the mistress of a beer-shop has not received corn as the price of beer or has demanded silver on an excessive scale, and has made the measure of beer less than the measure of corn, that beer-seller shall be prosecuted and drowned.

109.   If the mistress of a beer-shop has assembled seditious slanderers in her house and those seditious persons have not been captured and have not been haled to the palace, that beer-seller shall be put to death.

110.   If a votary, who is not living in the convent, open a beer-shop, or enter a beer-shop for drink, that woman shall be put to death.

• • •

120.   If a man has deposited his corn for safe keeping in another's house and it has suffered damage in the granary, or if the owner of the house has opened the store and taken the corn, or has disputed the amount of the corn that was stored in his house, the owner of the corn shall declare

on oath the amount of his corn, and the owner of the house shall return him double.

• • •

122.   If a man has given another gold, silver, or any goods whatever, on deposit, all that he gives shall he show to witnesses, and take a bond and so give on deposit.

123.   If he has given on deposit without witnesses and bonds, and has been defrauded where he made his deposit, he has no claim to prosecute.

124.   If a man has given on deposit to another, before witnesses, gold, silver, or any goods whatever, and his claim has been contested, he shall prosecute that man, and [the man] shall return double what he disputed.

125.   If a man has given anything whatever on deposit, and, where he has made his deposit, something of his has been lost together with something belonging to the owner of the house, either by house-breaking or a rebellion, the owner of the house who is in default shall make good all that has been given him on deposit, which he has lost, and shall return it to the owner of the goods. The owner of the house shall look after what he has lost and recover it from the thief.

126.   If a man has said that something of his is lost, which is not lost, or has alleged a depreciation, though nothing of his is lost, he shall estimate the depreciation on oath, and he shall pay double whatever he has claimed.

• • •

128.   If a man has taken a wife and has not executed a marriage-contract, that woman is not a wife.

129.   If a man's wife be caught lying with another, they shall be strangled and cast into the water. If the wife's husband would save his wife, the king can save his servant.

130.   If a man has ravished another's betrothed wife, who is a virgin, while still living in her father's house, and has been caught in the act, that man shall be put to death; the woman shall go free.

131. If a man's wife has been accused by her husband, and has not been caught lying with another, she shall swear her innocence, and return to her house.

132.   If a man's wife has the finger pointed at her on account of another, but has not been caught lying with him, for her husband's sake she shall plunge into the sacred river.

• • •

138.   If a man has divorced his wife, who has not borne him children, he shall pay over to her as much money as was given for her bride-price and the marriage-portion which she brought from her father's house, and so shall divorce her.

139.   If there was no bride-price, he shall give her one mina of silver, as a price of divorce.

140.   If he be a plebeian, he shall give her one-third of a mina of silver.

141.   If a man's wife, living in her husband's house, has persisted in going out, has acted the fool, has wasted her house, has belittled her husband, he shall prosecute her. If her husband has said, "I divorce her," she shall go her way; he shall give her nothing as her price of divorce. If her husband has said. "I will not divorce her," he may take another woman to wife; the wife shall live as a slave in her husband's house.

142.   If a woman has hated her husband and has said, "You shall not possess me," her past shall be inquired into, as to what she lacks. If she has been discreet, and has no vice, and her husband has gone out, and has greatly belittled her, that woman has no blame, she shall take her marriage-portion and go off to her father's house.

143.   If she has not been discreet, has gone out, ruined her house, belittled her husband, she shall be drowned.

• • •

150.   If a man has presented field, garden, house, or goods to his wife, has granted her a deed of gift, her children, after her husband's death, shall not dispute her right; the mother shall leave it after her death to that one of her children whom she loves best. She shall not leave it to her kindred.

151.   If a woman, who is living in a man's house, has persuaded her husband to bind himself, and grant her a deed to the effect that she shall not be held for debt by a creditor of her husband's; if that man had a debt upon him before he married that woman, his creditor shall not take his wife for it. Also, if that woman had a debt upon her before she entered that man's house, her creditor shall not take her husband for it.

152.   From the time that that woman entered into the man's house they together shall be liable for all debts subsequently incurred.

153.   If a man's wife, for the sake of another, has caused her husband to be killed, that woman shall be impaled.

154.   If a man has committed incest with his daughter, that man shall be banished from the city.

155.   If a man has betrothed a maiden to his son and his son has known her, and afterward the man has lain in her bosom, and been caught, that man shall be strangled and she shall be cast into the water.

156.   If a man has betrothed a maiden to his son, and his son has not known her, and that man has lain in her bosom, he shall pay her half a mina of silver, and shall pay over to her whatever she brought from her father's house, and the husband of her choice shall marry her.

157.   If a man, after his father's death, has lain in the bosom of his mother, they shall both of them be burnt together.

• • •

159.   If a man, who has presented a gift to the house of his prospective father-in-law and has given the brideprice, has afterward looked upon another woman and has said to his father-in-law, "I will not marry your daughter"; the father of the girl shall keep whatever he has brought as a present.

160.   If a man has presented a gift to the house of his prospective father-in-law, and has given the brideprice, but the father of the girl has said, "I will not give you my daughter," the father shall return double all that was presented him.

• • •

162.   If a man has married a wife, and she has borne him children, and that woman has gone to her fate, her father shall lay no claim to her marriage-portion. Her marriage-portion is her children's only.

163.   If a man has married a wife, and she has not borne him children, and that woman has gone to her fate; if his father-in-law has returned to him the bride-price, which that man brought into the house of his father-in-law, her husband shall have no claim on the marriage-portion of that woman. Her marriage-portion indeed belongs to her father's house.

• • •

168.   If a man has determined to disinherit his son and has declared before the judge, "I cut off my son," the judge shall inquire into the son's past, and, if the son has not committed a grave misdemeanor such as should cut him off from sonship, the father shall not disinherit his son.

169.   If he has committed a grave crime against his father, which cuts off from sonship, for the first offence he shall pardon him. If he has committed a grave crime a second time, the father shall cut off his son from sonship.

170.   If a man has had children borne to him by his wife, and also by a maid, if the father in his lifetime has said, "My sons," to the children whom his maid bore him, and has reckoned them with the sons of his wife; then after the father has gone to his fate, the children of the wife and of the maid shall share equally. The children of the wife shall apportion the shares and make their own selections.

171.   And if the father, in his lifetime, has not said, "My sons," to the children whom the maid bore him, after the father has gone to his fate, the children of the maid shall not share with the children of the wife in the goods of their father's house. The maid and her children, however, shall obtain their freedom. The children of the wife have no claim for service on the children of the maid.

The wife shall take her marriage-portion, and any gift that her husband has given her and for which he has written a deed of gift and she shall dwell in her husband's house; as long as she lives, she shall enjoy it, she shall not sell it. After her death it is indeed her children's.

• • •

175. If either a slave of a patrician, or of a plebeian, has married the daughter of a free man, and she has borne children, the owner of the slave shall have no claim for service on the children of a free woman. And if a slave, either of a patrician or of a plebeian, has married a free woman and when he married her she entered the slave's house with a marriage-portion from her father's estate, be he slave of a patrician or of a plebeian, and from the time that they started to keep house, they have acquired property; after the slave, whether of a patrician or of a plebeian, has gone to his fate, the free woman shall take her marriage-portion, and whatever her husband and she acquired, since they started house-keeping. She shall divide it into two portions. The master of the slave shall take one half, the other half the free woman shall take for her children.

176. If the free woman had no marriage-portion, whatever her husband and she acquired since they started house-keeping he shall divide into two portions. The owner of the slave shall take one half, the other half the free woman shall take for her children.

177. If a widow, whose children are young, has determined to marry again, she shall not marry without consent of the judge. When she is allowed to remarry, the judge shall inquire as to what remains of the property of her former husband, and shall intrust the property of her former husband to that woman and her second husband. He shall give them an inventory. They shall watch over the property, and bring up the children. Not a utensil shall they sell. A buyer of any utensil belonging to the widow's children shall lose his money and shall return the article to its owners.

• • •

181. If a father has vowed his daughter to a god, as a temple maid, or a virgin, and has given her no portion; after the father has gone to his fate, she shall share in the property of her father's estate, taking one-third of a child's share. She shall enjoy her share, as long as she lives. After her, it belongs to her brothers.

• • •

185. If a man has taken a young child, a natural son of his, to be his son, and has brought him up, no one shall make a claim against that foster child.

186. If a man has taken a young child to be his son, and after he has taken him, the child discover his own parents, he shall return to his father's house.

• • •

188, 189. If a craftsman has taken a child to bring up and has taught him his handicraft, he shall not be reclaimed. If he has not taught him his handicraft that foster child shall return to his father's house.

• • •

195.   If a son has struck his father, his hands shall be cut off.

196.   If a man has knocked out the eye of a patrician, his eye shall be knocked out.

197.   If he has broken the limb of a patrician, his limb shall be broken.

198.   If he has knocked out the eye of a plebeian or has broken the limb of a plebeian, he shall pay one mina of silver.

199.   If he has knocked out the eye of a patrician's servant, or broken the limb of a patrician's servant, he shall pay half his value.

200.   If a patrician has knocked out the tooth of a man that is his equal, his tooth shall be knocked out.

201.   If he has knocked out the tooth of a plebeian, he shall pay one-third of a mina of silver.

202.   If a man has smitten the privates of a man, higher in rank than he, he shall be scourged with sixty blows of an ox-hide scourge, in the assembly.

• • •

209.   If a man has struck a free woman with child, and has caused her to miscarry, he shall pay ten shekels for her miscarriage.

210.   If that woman die, his daughter shall be killed.

• • •

215.   If a surgeon has operated with the bronze lancet on a patrician for a serious injury, and has cured him, or has removed with a bronze lancet a cataract for a patrician, and has cured his eye, he shall take ten shekels of silver.

• • •

218.   If a surgeon has operated with the bronze lancet on a patrician for a serious injury, and has caused his death, or has removed a cataract for a patrician, with the bronze lancet, and has made him lose his eye, his hands shall be cut off.

• • •

224.   If a veterinary surgeon has treated an ox, or an ass, for a severe injury, and cured it, the owner of the ox, or the ass, shall pay the surgeon one-sixth of a shekel of silver, as his fee.

225.   If he has treated an ox, or an ass, for a severe injury, and caused it to die, he shall pay one-quarter of its value to the owner of the ox, or the ass.

226.   If a brander has cut out a mark on a slave, without the consent of his owner, that brander shall have his hands cut off.

• • •

229.   If a builder has built a house for a man, and has not made his work sound, and the house he built has fallen, and caused the death of its owner, that builder shall be put to death.

230.   If it is the owner's son that is killed, the builder's son shall be put to death.

231.   If it is the slave of the owner that is killed, the builder shall give slave for slave to the owner of the house.

• • •

236.   If a man has let his boat to a boatman, and the boatman has been careless and the boat has been sunk or lost, the boatman shall restore a boat to the owner.

237.   If a man has hired a boat and boatman, and loaded it with corn, wool, oil or dates, or whatever it be, and the boatman has been careless, and sunk the boat, or lost what is in it, the boatman shall restore the boat which he sank, and whatever he lost that was in it.

• • •

244.   If a man has hired an ox, or an ass, and a lion has killed it in the open field, the loss falls on its owner.

245.   If a man has hired an ox and has caused its death, by carelessness, or blows, he shall restore ox for ox, to the owner of the ox.

• • •

249.   If a man has hired an ox, and God has struck it, and it has died, the man that hired the ox shall make affidavit and go free.

250.   If a bull has gone wild and gored a man, and caused his death, there can be no suit against the owner.

251.   If a man's ox be a gorer, and has revealed its evil propensity as a gorer, and he has not blunted its horn, or shut up the ox, and then that ox has gored a free man, and caused his death, the owner shall pay half a mina of silver.

• • •

265.   If a herdsman, to whom oxen or sheep have been given, has defaulted, has altered the price, or sold them, he shall be prosecuted, and shall restore oxen, or sheep, tenfold, to their owner.

266.   If lighting has struck a fold, or a lion has made a slaughter, the herdsman shall purge himself by oath, and the owner of the fold shall bear the loss of the fold.

267.   If the herdsman has been careless, and a loss has occurred in the fold, the herdsman shall make good the loss in the fold; he shall repay the oxen, or sheep, to their owner.

• • •

278.   If a man has bought a male or female slave and the slave has not fulfilled his month, but the *bennu* disease has fallen upon him, he shall return the slave to the seller and the buyer shall take back the money he paid.

279.   If a man has bought a male or female slave and a claim has been raised, the seller shall answer the claim.

280.   If a man, in a foreign land, has bought a male, or female, slave of another, and if when he has come home the owner of the male or female slave has recognized his slave, and if the slave be a native of the land, he shall grant him his liberty without money.

281.   If the slave was a native of another country, the buyer shall declare on oath the amount of money he paid, and the owner of the slave shall repay the merchant what he paid and keep his slave.

282.   If a slave has said to his master, "You are not my master," he shall be brought to account as his slave, and his master shall cut off his ear.

Hebrew Scriptures

The Hebrew Scriptures (commonly called the Old Testament) are, arguably, the most influential texts in the Western tradition. Modern Jews, Christians, and Muslims, some three billion people or 40 to 50 percent of the world's population, claim to follow the God depicted in the Hebrew Scriptures. While most of the literature produced in the ancient Near East has either been lost, is indecipherable, or is accessible only to scholars, the Hebrew Scriptures are available in inexpensive, accessible translations all over the world.

The Hebrew Scriptures contain law codes, poetry, prophetic visions, proverbs, and histories. Whatever the genre, the texts of the Hebrew Scriptures focus on the relationship between God and his chosen people, Israel. While the book of Genesis begins with an account of creation and the distant past, this is prologue to the central story of God making a covenant with Abraham. The covenant includes a promise by God to bless and protect Abraham and his descendents contingent upon Abraham and his descendents honoring and worshipping only God. The Hebrew Scriptures then describe how Abraham's descendents are enslaved in Egypt; freed and led to a new land by God; try and fail to live as a nation that honors the covenant; and their eventual defeat and dispersal by successive invasions by Assyria and Babylon.

The first selections come from the book of Genesis and deal with the creation of the world, including humans, and the eventual calling of Abraham. The last two selections are from the prophetic writings. In the first, Isaiah reminds Israel who their God is and what the covenant entails. Finally, Jeremiah describes and explains the destruction of Jerusalem by Babylonian armies.

1. What does God expect from the Israelites? What can they expect from God?

2. How is the religion of the Israelites different from their Ancient Near Eastern neighbors?

3. What behaviors and attitudes are considered virtuous in the Hebrew Scriptures? What sorts of behaviors and attitudes are condemned?

GENESIS 6.11–8.22

11 Now the earth was corrupt in God's sight, and the earth was filled with violence. [12] And God saw that the earth was corrupt; for all flesh had corrupted its ways upon the earth. [13]And God said to Noah, "I have determined to make an end of all flesh, for the earth is filled with violence because of them; now I am going to destroy them along with the earth. [14]Make yourself an ark of cypress[a] wood; make rooms in the ark, and cover it inside and out with pitch. [15]This is how you are to make it: the length of the ark three hundred cubits, its width fifty cubits, and its height thirty cubits. [16]Make a roof [b] for the ark, and finish it to a cubit above; and put the door of the ark in its side; make it with lower, second, and third decks. [17]For my part, I am going to bring a flood of waters on the earth, to destroy from under heaven all flesh in which is the breath of life; everything that is on the earth shall die. [18]But I will establish my covenant with you; and you shall come into the ark, you, your sons, your wife, and your sons' wives with you. [19]And of every living thing, of all flesh, you shall bring two of every kind into the ark, to keep them alive with you; they shall be male and female. [20]Of the birds according to their kinds, and of the animals according to their kinds, of every creeping thing of the ground according to its kind, two of every kind shall come in to you, to keep them alive. [21]Also take with you every kind of food that is eaten, and store it up; and it shall serve as food for you and for them." [22]Noah did this; he did all that God commanded him.

7 Then the LORD said to Noah, "Go into the ark, you and all your household, for I have seen that you alone are righteous before me in this generation. [2]Take with you seven pairs of all clean animals, the male and its mate; and a pair of the animals that are not clean, the male and its mate; [3]and seven pairs of the birds of the air also, male and female, to keep their kind alive on the face of all the earth. [4]For in seven days I will send rain on the earth for forty days and forty nights; and every living thing that I have made I will blot out from the face of the ground." [5]And Noah did all that the LORD had commanded him.

6 Noah was six hundred years old when the flood of waters came on the earth. [7]And Noah with his sons and his wife and his sons' wives went into the ark to escape the waters of the flood. [8]Of clean animals, and of animals that are not clean, and of birds, and of everything that creeps on the ground, [9]two and two, male and female, went into the ark with Noah, as God had commanded Noah. [10]And after seven days the waters of the flood came on the earth.

11 In the six hundredth year of Noah's life, in the second month, on the seventeenth day of the month, on that day all the fountains of the great deep burst forth, and the windows of the heavens were opened. [12]The rain fell on

[a]Meaning of Heb uncertain
[b]Or *window*

the earth forty days and forty nights. [13]On the very same day Noah with his sons, Shem and Ham and Japheth, and Noah's wife and the three wives of his sons entered the ark, [14]they and every wild animal of every kind, and all domestic animals of every kind, and every creeping thing that creeps on the earth, and every bird of every kind—every bird, every winged creature. [15]They went into the ark with Noah, two and two of all flesh in which there was the breath of life. [16]And those that entered, male and female of all flesh, went in as God had commanded him; and the LORD shut him in.

17 The flood continued forty days on the earth; and the waters increased, and bore up the ark, and it rose high above the earth. [18]The waters swelled and increased greatly on the earth; and the ark floated on the face of the waters. [19]The waters swelled so mightily on the earth that all the high mountains under the whole heaven were covered; [20]the waters swelled above the mountains, covering them fifteen cubits deep. [21]And all flesh died that moved on the earth, birds, domestic animals, wild animals, all swarming creatures that swarm on the earth, and all human beings; [22]everything on dry land in whose nostrils was the breath of life died. [23]He blotted out every living thing that was on the face of the ground, human beings and animals and creeping things and birds of the air; they were blotted out from the earth. Only Noah was left, and those that were with him in the ark. [24]And the waters swelled on the earth for one hundred fifty days.

8 But God remembered Noah and all the wild animals and all the domestic animals that were with him in the ark. And God made a wind blow over the earth, and the waters subsided; [2]the fountains of the deep and the windows of the heavens were closed, the rain from the heavens was restrained, [3]and the waters gradually receded from the earth. At the end of one hundred fifty days the waters had abated; [4]and in the seventh month, on the seventeenth day of the month, the ark came to rest on the mountains of Ararat. [5]The waters continued to abate until the tenth month; in the tenth month, on the first day of the month, the tops of the mountains appeared.

6 At the end of forty days Noah opened the window of the ark that he had made [7]and sent out the raven; and it went to and fro until the waters were dried up from the earth. [8]Then he sent out the dove from him, to see if the waters had subsided from the face of the ground; [9]but the dove found no place to set its foot, and it returned to him to the ark, for the waters were still on the face of the whole earth. So he put out his hand and took it and brought it into the ark with him. [10]He waited another seven days, and again he sent out the dove from the ark; [11]and the dove came back to him in the evening, and there in its beak was a freshly plucked olive leaf; so Noah knew that the waters had subsided from the earth. [12]Then he waited another seven days, and sent out the dove; and it did not return to him any more.

13 In the six hundred first year, in the first month, on the first day of the month, the waters were dried up from the earth; and Noah removed the covering of the ark, and looked, and saw that the face of the ground was drying.

¹⁴In the second month, on the twenty-seventh day of the month, the earth was dry. ¹⁵Then God said to Noah, ¹⁶"Go out of the ark, you and your wife, and your sons and your sons' wives with you. ¹⁷Bring out with you every living thing that is with you of all flesh—birds and animals and every creeping thing that creeps on the earth—so that they may abound on the earth, and be fruitful and multiply on the earth." ¹⁸So Noah went out with his sons and his wife and his sons' wives. ¹⁹And every animal, every creeping thing, and every bird, everything that moves on the earth, went out of the ark by families.

20 Then Noah built an altar to the LORD, and took of every clean animal and of every clean bird, and offered burnt offerings on the altar. ²¹And when the LORD smelled the pleasing odor, the LORD said in his heart, "I will never again curse the ground because of humankind, for the inclination of the human heart is evil from youth; nor will I ever again destroy every living creature as I have done.

22 As long as the earth endures, seedtime and harvest, cold and heat, summer and winter, day and night, shall not cease."

12 Now the LORD said to Abram, "Go from your country and your kindred and your father's house to the land that I will show you. ²I will make of you a great nation, and I will bless you, and make your name great, so that you will be a blessing. ³I will bless those who bless you, and the one who curses you I will curse; and in you all the families of the earth shall be blessed."

15 After these things the word of the LORD came to Abram in a vision, "Do not be afraid, Abram, I am your shield; your reward shall be very great." ²But Abram said, "O Lord GOD, what will you give me, for I continue childless, and the heir of my house is Eliezer of Damascus?" ³And Abram said, "You have given me no offspring, and so a slave born in my house is to be my heir." ⁴But the word of the LORD came to him, "This man shall not be your heir; no one but your very own issue shall be your heir." ⁵He brought him outside and said, "Look toward heaven and count the stars, if you are able to count them." Then he said to him, "So shall your descendants be." ⁶And he believed the LORD; and the LORD reckoned it to him as righteousness.

7 Then he said to him, "I am the LORD who brought you from Ur of the Chaldeans, to give you this land to possess." ⁸But he said, "O Lord GOD, how am I to know that I shall possess it?" ⁹He said to him, "Bring me a heifer three years old, a female goat three years old, a ram three years old, a turtledove, and a young pigeon." ¹⁰He brought him all these and cut them in two, laying each half over against the other; but he did not cut the birds in two. ¹¹And when birds of prey came down on the carcasses, Abram drove them away.

12 As the sun was going down, a deep sleep fell upon Abram, and a deep and terrifying darkness descended upon him. ¹³Then the LORD said to Abram, "Know this for certain, that your offspring shall be aliens in a land

that is not theirs, and shall be slaves there, and they shall be oppressed for four hundred years; [14]but I will bring judgment on the nation that they serve, and afterward they shall come out with great possessions. [15]As for yourself, you shall go to your ancestors in peace; you shall be buried in a good old age. [16]And they shall come back here in the fourth generation; for the iniquity of the Amorites is not yet complete."

17 When the sun had gone down and it was dark, a smoking fire pot and a flaming torch passed between these pieces. [18]On that day the LORD made a covenant with Abram, saying, "To your descendants I give this land, from the river of Egypt to the great river, the river Euphrates, [19]the land of the Kenites, the Kenizzites, the Kadmonites, [20]the Hittites, the Perizzites, the Rephaim, [21]the Amorites, the Canaanites, the Girgashites, and the Jebusites."

ISAIAH 44.1–44.19

44 But now hear, O Jacob my servant,
  Israel whom I have chosen!
[2]Thus says the LORD who made you,
  who formed you in the womb and will help you:
Do not fear, O Jacob my servant,
  Jeshurun whom I have chosen.
[3]For I will pour water on the thirsty land,
  and streams on the dry ground;
I will pour my spirit upon your descendants,
  and my blessing on your offspring.
[4]They shall spring up like a green tamarisk,
  like willows by flowing streams.
[5]This one will say, "I am the LORD's,"
  another will be called by the name of Jacob,
yet another will write on the hand,
  "The LORD's,"
  and adopt the name of Israel.
[6]Thus says the LORD, the King of Israel,
  and his Redeemer, the LORD of hosts:
I am the first and I am the last;
  besides me there is no god.
[7]Who is like me? Let them proclaim it,
  let them declare and set it forth before me.
Who has announced from of old the things to come?
  Let them tell us what is yet to be.
[8]Do not fear, or be afraid;
  have I not told you from of old and declared it?
  You are my witnesses!
Is there any god besides me?
  There is no other rock; I know not one.

9 All who make idols are nothing, and the things they delight in do not profit; their witnesses neither see nor know. And so they will be put to shame. [10]Who would fashion a god or cast an image that can do no good? [11]Look, all its devotees shall be put to shame; the artisans too are merely human. Let them all assemble, let them stand up; they shall be terrified, they shall all be put to shame.

12 The ironsmith fashions it[a] and works it over the coals, shaping it with hammers, and forging it with his strong arm; he becomes hungry and his strength fails, he drinks no water and is faint. [13]The carpenter stretches a line, marks it out with a stylus, fashions it with planes, and marks it with a compass; he makes it in human form, with human beauty, to be set up in a shrine. [14]He cuts down cedars or chooses a holm tree or an oak and lets it grow strong among the trees of the forest. He plants a cedar and the rain nourishes it. [15]Then it can be used as fuel. Part of it he takes and warms himself; he kindles a fire and bakes bread. Then he makes a god and worships it, makes it a carved image and bows down before it. [16]Half of it he burns in the fire; over this half he roasts meat, eats it and is satisfied. He also warms himself and says, "Ah, I am warm, I can feel the fire!" [17]The rest of it he makes into a god, his idol, bows down to it and worships it; he prays to it and says, "Save me, for you are my god!"

18 They do not know, nor do they comprehend; for their eyes are shut, so that they cannot see, and their minds as well, so that they cannot understand. [19]No one considers, nor is there knowledge or discernment to say, "Half of it I burned in the fire; I also baked bread on its coals, I roasted meat and have eaten. Now shall I make the rest of it an abomination? Shall I fall down before a block of wood?"

ISAIAH 45.5–45.25

[5]I am the LORD, and there is no other;
   besides me there is no god.
   I arm you, though you do not know me,
[6]so that they may know, from the rising of the sun
   and from the west, that there is no one besides me;
   I am the LORD, and there is no other.
[7]I form light and create darkness,
   I make weal and create woe;
   I the LORD do all these things.
[8]Shower, O heavens, from above,
   and let the skies rain down righteousness;
   let the earth open, that salvation may spring up,

a. an axe

and let it cause righteousness to sprout up also;
    I the LORD have created it.
[9]Woe to you who strive with your Maker,
    earthen vessels with the potter!
Does the clay say to the one who fashions it, "What are you making"?
    or "Your work has no handles"?
[10]Woe to anyone who says to a father,
    "What are you begetting?"
    or to a woman, "With what are you in labor?"
[11]Thus says the LORD,
    the Holy One of Israel, and its Maker:
Will you question me about my children,
    or command me concerning the work of my hands?
[12]I made the earth,
    and created humankind upon it;
it was my hands that stretched out the heavens,
    and I commanded all their host.
[13]I have aroused Cyrus in righteousness,
    and I will make all his paths straight;
he shall build my city and set my exiles free,
not for price or reward,
    says the LORD of hosts.
[14]Thus says the LORD:
The wealth of Egypt and the merchandise of Ethiopia,
    and the Sabeans, tall of stature,
shall come over to you and be yours, they shall follow you;
    they shall come over in chains and bow down to you.
They will make supplication to you, saying,
    "God is with you alone, and there is no other;
    there is no god besides him."
[15]Truly, you are a God who hides himself,
    O God of Israel, the Savior.
[16]All of them are put to shame and confounded,
    the makers of idols go in confusion together.
[17]But Israel is saved by the LORD with everlasting salvation;
you shall not be put to shame or confounded to all eternity.
[18]For thus says the LORD,
who created the heavens (he is God!),
who formed the earth and made it (he established it;
he did not create it a chaos,
    he formed it to be inhabited!):
I am the LORD, and there is no other.
[19]I did not speak in secret,
    in a land of darkness;

I did not say to the offspring of Jacob,
   "Seek me in chaos."
I the LORD speak the truth,
   I declare what is right.
20Assemble yourselves and come together,
   draw near, you survivors of the nations!
They have no knowledge—those who carry about their wooden idols,
and keep on praying to a god that cannot save.
21Declare and present your case;
   let them take counsel together!
Who told this long ago?
   Who declared it of old?
Was it not I, the LORD?
   There is no other god besides me,
a righteous God and a Savior;
   there is no one besides me.
22Turn to me and be saved,
   all the ends of the earth!
   For I am God, and there is no other.
23By myself I have sworn,
   from my mouth has gone forth in righteousness
   a word that shall not return:
"To me every knee shall bow,
   every tongue shall swear."
24Only in the LORD, it shall be said of me,
   are righteousness and strength;
all who were incensed against him shall come to him and be
   ashamed.
25In the LORD all the offspring of Israel shall triumph in glory.

LAMENTATIONS

1 How lonely sits the city that once was full of people!
How like a widow she has become,
   she that was great among the nations!
She that was a princess among the provinces
   has become a vassal.

2She weeps bitterly in the night,
   with tears on her cheeks;
among all her lovers she has no one to comfort her;
all her friends have dealt treacherously with her,
they have become her enemies.

³Judah has gone into exile with suffering
  and hard servitude;
she lives now among the nations,
  and finds no resting place;
her pursuers have all overtaken her in the midst of her distress.

⁴The roads to Zion mourn,
  for no one comes to the festivals;
all her gates are desolate,
  her priests groan;
her young girls grieve,
  and her lot is bitter.

⁵Her foes have become the masters,
  her enemies prosper,
because the Lord has made her suffer
  for the multitude of her transgressions;
her children have gone away,
  captives before the foe.

⁶From daughter Zion has departed all her majesty.
Her princes have become like stags that find no pasture;
they fled without strength before the pursuer.

⁷Jerusalem remembers,
in the days of her affliction and wandering,
all the precious things that were hers in days of old.
When her people fell into the hand of the foe,
  and there was no one to help her,
the foe looked on mocking over her downfall.

⁸Jerusalem sinned grievously,
  so she has become a mockery;
all who honored her despise her,
  for they have seen her nakedness;
she herself groans,
  and turns her face away.

⁹Her uncleanness was in her skirts;
  she took no thought of her future;
her downfall was appalling,
  with none to comfort her.
"O Lord, look at my affliction,
  for the enemy has triumphed!"

[10]Enemies have stretched out their hands
   over all her precious things;
she has even seen the nations invade her sanctuary,
those whom you forbade to enter your congregation.

[11]All her people groan as they search for bread;
they trade their treasures for food to revive their strength.
Look, O Lord, and see how worthless I have become.

[12]Is it nothing to you, all you who pass by?
   Look and see
if there is any sorrow like my sorrow,
   which was brought upon me,
which the Lord inflicted on the day of his fierce anger.

[13]From on high he sent fire;
   it went deep into my bones;
he spread a net for my feet;
   he turned me back;
he has left me stunned,
   faint all day long.

[14]My transgressions were bound into a yoke;
   by his hand they were fastened together;
they weigh on my neck,
   sapping my strength;
the Lord handed me over to those whom I cannot withstand.

[15]The Lord has rejected
   all my warriors in the midst of me;
he proclaimed a time against me to crush my young men;
the Lord has trodden as in a wine press the virgin daughter Judah.

[16]For these things I weep;
   my eyes flow with tears;
for a comforter is far from me,
   one to revive my courage;
my children are desolate,
   for the enemy has prevailed.

[17]Zion stretches out her hands,
   but there is no one to comfort her;
the Lord has commanded against Jacob
   that his neighbors should become his foes;
Jerusalem has become a filthy thing among them.

[18]The L ORD is in the right,
   for I have rebelled against his word;
but hear, all you peoples,
   and behold my suffering;
my young women and young men have gone into captivity.

[19]I called to my lovers
   but they deceived me;
my priests and elders
   perished in the city
while seeking food
   to revive their strength.

[20]See, O L ORD, how distressed I am;
   my stomach churns,
my heart is wrung within me,
   because I have been very rebellious.
In the street the sword bereaves;
   in the house it is like death.

[21]They heard how I was groaning,
   with no one to comfort me.
All my enemies heard of my trouble;
   they are glad that you have done it.
Bring on the day you have announced,
   and let them be as I am.

[22]Let all their evil doing come before you;
   and deal with them
as you have dealt with me
   because of all my transgressions;
for my groans are many and my heart is faint.

Rig Veda

Most religions, whether they have their origin in the Far East, the Middle East, or in the Western Hemisphere, contain creation "myths." The term, "myth," however, can be misleading. It should not be taken to imply that these accounts are simply "fairy stories," lacking any kind of rational foundation. On the contrary, they represent the attempts made by their originators to give answers to some of the most profound questions that we can ask, such as, How did the universe come into being? and How and when were human beings created? Such questions are still pertinent today; even though science has made great strides in providing explanations of them, the answers to the most fundamental of them still remain shrouded in mystery.

This book contains a number of creation myths, taken from various cultures throughout the world. Most of them are quite detailed and elaborate. An exception is the short poem that follows. It is taken from the *Rig Veda*, a large collection of religious poems sacred to the early period of Indian Hinduism. Because the poem was handed down by oral tradition long before being written, the time of its original composition is not known. However, it is believed to date from around 1000 to 900 B.C. The poem has been included in this book for a special reason. Although it offers what is a variation on a standard theme of creation myths, even in its short length it contains lines that set it apart from all of the others, giving it a level of intellectual sophistication that is impressive by any standards.

1. How is the creation of the world explained in this text?

2. What role do gods or a God play in creation?

Song of Creation

Then there was neither being nor not-being.
The atmosphere was not, nor sky above it.
What covered all? and where? by what protected?
Was there the fathomless abyss of waters?

Trans. A. Kaegi and R. Arrowsmith. Hymm X:129. The title has been added.

Then neither death nor deathlessness existed;
Of day and night there was yet no distinction.
Alone that One breathed calmly, self-supported,
Other than It was none, nor aught above It.

Darkness there was at first in darkness hidden;
This universe was undistinguished water.
That which in void and emptiness lay hidden
Alone by power of fervor was developed.

Then for the first time there arose desire,
Which was the primal germ of mind, within it.
And sages, searching in their heart, discovered
In Nothing the connecting bond of Being.

And straight across their cord was then extended:
What then was there above? or what beneath it?
Life giving principles and powers existed;
Below the origin,—the striving upward.

Who is it knows? Who here can tell us surely
From what and how this universe has risen?
And whether not till after it the gods lived?
Who then can know from what it has arisen?

The source from which this universe has risen
And whether it was made, or uncreated,
He only knows, who from the highest heaven
Rules, the all-seeing lord.—or does not He know?

The Hindu Caste System

The beginnings of the caste system are shrouded in the remote past, but it seems to have developed following the Aryan invasion of India in the second millennium B.C. Although references to it can be found in much early literature, its formal elaboration appears in *The Laws of Manu*, a large compendium of Hindu regulations from which the following selection is taken. These laws were, according to Hindu doctrine, established by the demigod Manu, himself a manifestation of Brahma, so represent divine commands. They divide society into four castes—the priests and scholars (Brahmanas), the nobles and warriors (Kshatriyas), the merchants and farmers (Vaisyas), and the common laborers and servants (Sudras). Although the Brahmanas (who wrote the laws that separated society into castes) were preeminent in prestige and honor, all of the first three castes shared the attribute of being "twice-born." Besides their original human first birth, they experienced a "second birth" consisting of their initiation into the mysteries of the Hindu religion. The Sudras were excluded from the "second birth" so could aspire to no higher rank than that of servants to the privileged castes. It should be added that the castes as here described offer an idealized oversimplification of the system, as it has actually existed in India. In fact, there are literally thousands of subcastes, based on such things as different occupations, area of the country, and so on.

Hindus found a religio-moral justification for the caste system. According to the divine law of Karma, an individual in each of his reincarnations is born into a rank and level of society that results from the quality of the life he had lived in his previous incarnation. Thus, a member of the Sudra caste has earned that status; his position as a servant is just what he deserves. Furthermore, any attempt to change one's status or to modify the caste system itself would be immoral, as well as a breach of divine law.

Two further points should be added. Closely associated with the caste system is a set of regulations governing marriage, the status of women, and family relationships in general. Also, it should be mentioned that a substantial portion of the population of India does not fit into any of the four castes. These are the outcasts or "untouchables" who rank far below the Sudras—indeed, are often treated with less respect than animals. These are people literally "beyond the pale."

In the selection that follows from *The Laws of Manu* an attempt has been made to offer some insight into the extraordinary complexities of the caste system. To do this, illustrative "laws" have been chosen and reorganized from the original to enhance their coherence; also section headings have been added.

1. What distinguishes each caste? What distinguishes those within the caste system from outcasts? What do these distinctions tell us about ancient Indian society?

2. Describe the gender roles assumed and reinforced in this text. How do gender roles fit into the caste system?

The Laws of Manu

Manu the Lawgiver

The great sages approached Manu,* who was seated with a collected mind, and, having duly worshipped him, spoke as follows:

"Deign, divine one, to declare to us precisely and in due order the sacred laws of each of the four chief castes and of the intermediate ones.

"For thou, O Lord, alone knowest the purport, the rites, and the knowledge of the soul, taught in this whole ordinance of the Self-existent, which is unknowable and unfathomable."

He, whose power is measureless, being thus asked by the high-minded great sages, duly honored them, and answered, "Listen!"

The Four Castes

For the sake of the prosperity of the worlds, he caused the Brahmana, the Kshatriya, the Vaisya, and the Sudra to proceed from his mouth, his arms, his thighs, and his feet.

The Brahmana, the Kshatriya, and the Vaisya castes are the twice-born ones, but the fourth, the Sudra, has one birth only; there is no fifth caste.

To Brahmanas he assigned teaching and studying the Veda, sacrificing for their own benefit and for others, giving and accepting of alms. The Kshatriya he commanded to protect the people, to bestow gifts, to offer sacrifices, to study the Veda, and to abstain from attaching himself to sensual pleasures; the Vaisya to tend cattle, to bestow gifts, to offer sacrifices, to

---

Trans. G. Bühler. Some minor modifications have been made in the text.
*Manu in Hindu mythology is a being who is both divine and human.

study the Veda, to trade, to lend money, and to cultivate land. One occupation only the lord prescribed to the Sudra, to serve meekly even these other three castes.

The seniority of Brahmanas is from sacred knowledge, that of Kshatriyas from valor, that of Vaisyas from wealth in grain and other goods, but that of Sudras from age alone.

A twice-born man who knowingly eats mushrooms, a village pig, garlic, a village cock, onions or leeks, will become an outcast.

Some wealthy Brahmana shall compassionately support both a Kshatriya and a Vaisya if they are distressed for a livelihood, employing them on work which is suitable for their castes. But a Brahmana who, because he is powerful, out of greed makes initiated men of the twice-born castes against their will do the work of slaves shall be fined by the king. But a Sudra, whether bought or unbought, he may compel to do servile work; for he was created by the Self-existent to be the slave of a Brahmana. A Sudra, though emancipated by his master, is not released from servitude; since that is innate in him, who can set him free from it?

With whatever limb a man of a low caste does hurt to a man of the three highest castes, even that limb shall be cut off; that is the teaching of Manu. He who raises his hand or a stick shall have his hand cut off; he who in anger kicks with his foot shall have his foot cut off.

A low-caste man who tries to place himself on the same seat with a man of a high caste shall be branded on his hip and be banished, or the king shall cause his buttock to be gashed. If out of arrogance he spits on a superior the king shall cause both his lips to be cut off; if he urines on him, the penis; if he breaks wind against him, the anus.

A man of low caste who through covetousness lives by the occupations of a higher one the king shall deprive of his property and banish.

Abstention from injuring creatures, veracity, abstention from unlawfully appropriating the goods of others, purity, and control of the organs, Manu has declared to be the summary of the law for the four castes.

The Brahmana

Of created beings the most excellent are said to be those which are animated; of the animated, those which subsist by intelligence; of the intelligent, mankind; and of men, the Brahmanas. Of Brahmanas, those learned in the Veda; of the learned, those who recognize the necessity and the manner of performing the prescribed duties; of those who possess this knowledge, those who perform them; of the performers, those who know the Brahman.

The very birth of a Brahmana is an eternal incarnation of the sacred law; for he is born to fulfil the sacred law, and becomes one with Brahman.

A Brahmana, coming into existence, is born as the highest on earth, the lord of all created beings, for the protection of the treasury of the law.

Whatever exists in the world is the property of the Brahmana; on account of the excellence of his origin the Brahmana is, indeed, entitled to it all. The Brahmana eats but his own food, wears but his own apparel, bestows but his own in alms; other mortals subsist through the benevolence of the Brahmana.

In order to clearly settle his duties and those of the other castes according to their order wise Manu, sprung from the Self-existent, composed these Institutes of the sacred law. A learned Brahmana must carefully study them and he must duly instruct his pupils in them, but nobody else shall do it. A Brahmana who studies these Institutes and faithfully fulfils the duties prescribed therein is never tainted by sins, arising from thoughts, words, or deeds. He sanctifies any company which he may enter, seven ancestors and seven descendents, and he alone deserves to possess this whole earth.

To study this work is the best means of securing welfare; it increases understanding, it procures fame and long life, it leads to supreme bliss. In this work the sacred law has been fully stated as well as the good and bad qualities of human actions and the immemorial rule of conduct to be followed by all the four castes. The rule of conduct is transcendent law, whether it be taught in the revealed texts or in the sacred tradition; hence a twice-born man who possesses regard for himself should be always careful to follow it. A Brahmana who departs from the rule of conduct does not reap the fruit of the Veda, but he who duly follows it will obtain the full reward.

Man is stated to be purer above the navel than below; hence the Self-existent has declared the purest part of him to be his mouth. As the Brahmana sprang from Brahman's mouth, as he was the first-born, and as he possesses the Veda, he is by right the Lord of this whole creation.

A Brahmana must seek a means of subsistence which either causes no, or at least little pain to others and live by that except in times of distress. For the purpose of gaining bare subsistence let him accumulate property by following those irreproachable occupations which are prescribed for his caste, without unduly fatiguing his body. He may either possess enough to fill a granary, or a store filling a grain-jar; or he may collect what suffices for three days, or make no provision for the morrow. Let him never, for the sake of subsistence, follow the ways of the world; let him live the pure, straightforward, honest life of a Brahmana.

A Brahmana who knows the law need not bring any offence to the notice of the king; by his own power alone he can punish those men who injure him. His own power is greater than the power of the king; the Brahmana, therefore, may punish his foes by his own power alone.

A Brahmana shall never beg from a Sudra property for a sacrifice; for a sacrificer having begged it from such a man, after death is born again as a Kandala ["the lowest of men"].

Let him not entertain at a Sraddha [sacrificial meal] one who wears his hair in braids (a student), one who has not studied the Veda, one afflicted with a skin disease, a gambler, nor those who sacrifice for a multitude of others.

Physicians, temple-priests, sellers of meat, and those who subsist by shop-keeping must be avoided at sacrifices offered to the gods and to the manes [spirits]; a paid servant of a village or of a king, a man with deformed nails or black teeth, one who opposes his teacher, one who has forsaken the sacred fire, and a usurer; one suffering from consumption, one who subsists by tending cattle, a younger brother who marries or kindles the sacred fire before the elder, one who neglects the five great sacrifices, an enemy of the Brahmana race, an elder brother who marries or kindles the sacred fire after the younger, and one who belongs to a company or corporation; an actor or singer, one who has broken the vows of studentship, one whose only or first wife is a Sudra female, the son of a remarried woman, a one-eyed man, and he in whose house a paramour of his wife resides; he who teaches for a stipulated fee and he who is taught on that condition, he who instructs Sudra pupils and he whose teacher is a Sudra, he who speaks rudely, the son of an adulteress, and the son of a widow; he who forsakes his mother, his father, or a teacher without a sufficient reason, he who has contracted an alliance with outcasts either through the Veda or through a marriage; an incendiary, a prisoner, he who eats the food given by the son of an adulteress, a seller of Soma, he who undertakes voyages by sea, a bard, an oil-man, a suborner to perjury; he who wrangles or goes to law with his father, the keeper of a gambling-house, a drunkard, he who is afflicted with a disease in punishment of former crimes, he who is accused of a mortal sin, a hypocrite, a seller of substances used for flavoring food; a maker of bows and of arrows, he who lasciviously dallies with a brother's window, the betrayer of a friend, one who subsists by gambling, he who learns the Veda from his son; an epileptic man, one who suffers from scrofulous swellings of the glands, one afflicted with white leprosy, an informer, a madman, a blind man, and he who cavils at the Veda must all be avoided.

A trainer of elephants, oxen, horses, or camels, he who subsists by astrology, a bird-fancier, and he who teaches the use of arms; he who diverts water-courses, and he who delights in obstructing them, an architect, a messenger, and he who plants trees for money; a breeder of sporting-dogs, a falconer, one who defiles maidens, he who delights in injuring living creatures, he who gains his subsistence from Sudras, and he who offers sacrifices to the Ganas; he who does not follow the rule of conduct, a man destitute of energy like a eunuch, one who constantly asks for favors, he who lives by agriculture, a club-footed man, and he who is censured by virtuous men; a shepherd, a keeper of buffaloes, the husband of a remarried woman, and a carrier of dead bodies, all these must be carefully avoided.

A Brahmana who knows the sacred law should shun at sacrifices both to the gods and to the manes these lowest of twice-born men, whose conduct is reprehensible, and who are unworthy to sit in the company at a repast.

Let the king, after rising early in the morning, worship Brahmanas who are well versed in the threefold sacred science and learned in polity, and follow their advice. Let him daily worship aged Brahmanas who know the Veda and are pure. Let him honor those Brahmanas who have returned from their teacher's house after studying the Veda; for that money which is given to Brahmanas is declared to be an imperishable treasure for kings. Not to turn back in battle, to protect the people, to honor the Brahmanas, is the best means for a king to secure happiness.

The slayer of a Brahmana enters the womb of a dog, a pig, an ass, a camel, a cow, a goat, a sheep, a deer, a bird, a Kandala, and a Pukkasa.

The Kshatriya

Kings and Kshatriyas, the domestic priests of kings, and those who delight in the warfare of disputations constitute the middling rank of the states caused by Activity.

As the Earth supports all created beings equally, thus a king who supports all his subjects takes upon himself the office of the Earth. Employing these and other means, the king shall, ever untired, restrain thieves both in his own dominions and in those of others.

Let him not, though fallen into the deepest distress, provoke Brahmanas to anger for they, when angered, could instantly destroy him together with his army and his vehicles. Who could escape destruction, when he provokes to anger those men by whom the fire was made to consume all things, by whom the water of the ocean was made undrinkable, and by whom the moon was made to wane and to increase again? Who could prosper, while he injures those men who, provoked to anger, could create other worlds and other guardians of the world, and deprive the gods of their divine station? What man, desirous of life, would injure them to whose support the three worlds and the gods ever owe their existence, and whose wealth is the Veda?

A Brahmana, be he ignorant or learned, is a great divinity, just as the fire, whether carried forth for the performance of a burnt-oblation or not carried forth, is a great divinity. The brilliant fire is not contaminated even in burial-places, and when presented with oblations of butter at sacrifices, it again increases mightily. Thus, though Brahmanas employ themselves in all sorts of mean occupations, they must be honored in every way for each of them is a very great deity.

When the Kshatriyas become in any way overbearing towards the Brahmanas, the Brahmanas themselves shall duly restrain them, for the Kshatriyas sprang from the Brahmanas. Fire sprang from water, Kshatriyas from Brahmanas, iron from stone; the all-penetrating force of those three has no effect on that whence they were produced. Kshatriyas prosper not without Brahmanas, Brahmanas prosper not without Kshatriyas. Brahmanas and Kshatriyas, being closely united, prosper in this world and in the next. But a king who feels his end drawing nigh shall bestow all his wealth accumulated from fines on Brahmanas, make over his kingdom to his son, and then seek death in battle.

Know that a Brahmana of ten years and a Kshatriya of a hundred years stand to each other in the relation of father and son; but between those two the Brahmana is the father.

The Vaisya

Know that the following rules apply in due order to the duties of Vaisyas:

After a Vaisya has received the sacraments and has taken a wife, he shall be always attentive to the business whereby he may subsist and to that of tending cattle. For when the Lord of creatures created cattle he made them over to the Vaisya; to the Brahmana and to the king he entrusted all created beings. A Vaisya must never conceive this wish, "I will not keep cattle," and if a Vaisya is willing to keep them they must never be kept by men of other castes.

A Vaisya must know the respective value of gems, of pearls, of coral, of metals, of cloth made of thread, of perfumes, and of condiments. He must be acquainted with the manner of sowing of seeds and of the good and bad qualities of fields and he must perfectly know all measures and weights; moreover, the excellence and defects of commodities, the advantages and disadvantages of different countries, the probable profit and loss on merchandise, and the means of properly rearing cattle.

He must be acquainted with the proper wages of servants, with the various languages of men, with the manner of keeping goods, and the rules of purchase and sale. Let him exert himself to the utmost in order to increase his property in a righteous manner, and let him zealously give food to all created beings.

The king should order a Vaisya to trade, to lend money, to cultivate the land, or to tend cattle.

There are seven lawful modes of acquiring property: Inheritance, finding or friendly donation, purchase, conquest, lending at interest, the performance of work, and the acceptance of gifts from virtuous men.

Learning, mechanical arts, work for wages, service, rearing cattle, traffic, agriculture, contentment with little, alms, and receiving interest on money are the ten modes of subsistence permitted to all men in times of distress. Neither a Brahmana nor a Kshatriya must lend money at interest but at his pleasure either of them may, in times of distress when he requires money for sacred purposes, lend to a very sinful man at a small interest.

A king (Kshatriya) who, in times of distress, takes even the fourth part of the crops is free from guilt, if he protects his subjects to the best of his ability. His peculiar duty is conquest and he must not turn back in danger; having protected the Vaisyas by his weapons, he may cause the legal tax to be collected—from the Vaisyas one-eighth as the tax on grain, one-twentieth on the profits on gold and cattle.

The Sudra

That kingdom where Sudras are very numerous, which is infested by atheists and destitute of twice-born inhabitants, soon entirely perishes, afflicted by famine and disease.

A Brahmana may confidently seize the goods of his Sudra for, as that slave can have no property, his master may take his possessions.

A Brahmana who takes a Sudra wife to his bed will after death sink into hell; if he begets a child of her he will lose the rank of a Brahmana. The son whom a Brahmana begets through lust on a Sudra female is, though alive, a corpse and hence called a living corpse.

A Sudra who has intercourse with a woman of a twice-born caste, guarded or unguarded, shall be punished in the following manner: If she was unguarded he loses the offending part and all his property; if she was guarded, everything, even his life.

The foolish man who, after having eaten a dinner, gives the leavings to a Sudra falls headlong into hell.

A Sudra who is pure, the servant of his betters, gentle in his speech, and free from pride, and always seeks refuge with Brahmanas attains in his next life a higher caste.

The Dasyus

All those tribes in this world which are excluded from the community of those born from the mouth, the arms, the thighs, and the feet of Brahman are called Dasyus, whether they speak the language of the barbarians or that of the Aryans.

The dwellings of Kandalas and Svapakas [low-order Dasyus] shall be outside the village and their wealth shall be dogs and donkeys. Their dress shall be the garments of the dead, they shall eat their food from broken dishes, black iron shall be their ornaments, and they must always wander from place to place.

A man who fulfils a religious duty shall not seek intercourse with them; their transactions shall be among themselves and their marriages with their equals.

Their food shall be given to them by others than an Aryan giver in a broken dish; at night they shall not walk about in villages and in towns. By day they may go about for the purpose of their work, distinguished by marks at the king's command, and they shall carry out the corpses of persons who have no relatives; that is a settled rule.

By the king's order they shall always execute the criminals, in accordance with the law, and they shall take for themselves the clothes, the beds, and the ornaments of such criminals.

A Kandala, a village pig, a cock, a dog, a menstruating woman, and a eunuch must not look at the Brahmanas while they eat.

Let a Brahmana gently place on the ground some food for dogs, outcasts, Kandalas, those afflicted with diseases that are punishments of former sins, crows, and insects.

Marriage and Family

A twice-born man shall marry a wife of equal caste who is endowed with auspicious bodily marks. A damsel who is neither a Sapinda on the mother's side, nor belongs to the same family on the father's side, is recommended to twice-born men for wedlock and conjugal union. In connecting himself with a wife, let him carefully avoid the ten following families, be they ever so great or rich in kine, horses, sheep, grain, or other property: One which neglects the sacred rites, one in which no male children are born, one in which the Veda is not studied, one the members of which have thick hair on the body, those which are subject to hemorrhoids, phthisis, weakness of digestion, epilepsy, or white and black leprosy.

Let him not marry a maiden with reddish hair, nor one who has a redundant member, nor one who is sickly, nor one either with no hair on the body or too much, nor one who is garrulous or has red eyes, nor one named after a constellation, a tree, or a river, nor one bearing the name of a low caste, or of a mountain, nor one named after a bird, a snake, or a slave, nor one whose name inspires terror. Let him wed a female free from bodily defects, who has an agreeable name, the graceful gait of a Hamsa or of an elephant, a moderate quantity of hair on the body and on the head, small teeth, and soft limbs.

A man aged thirty years shall marry a maiden of twelve who pleases him or a man of twenty-four a girl eight years of age; if the performance of his duties would otherwise be impeded he must marry sooner.

The husband receives his wife from the gods, he does not wed her according to his own will; doing what is agreeable to the gods he must always support her while she is faithful.

He only is a perfect man who consists of three persons united—his wife, himself, and his offspring; thus says the Veda and learned Brahmanas propound this maxim likewise, "The husband is declared to be one with the wife."

Women must be honored and adorned by their fathers, brothers, husbands, and brothers-in-law, who desire their own welfare. Where women are honored there the gods are pleased but where they are not honored no sacred rite yields rewards. Where the female relations live in grief the family soon wholly perishes but that family where they are not unhappy ever prospers. The houses on which female relations, not being duly honored, pronounce a curse perish completely, as if destroyed by magic. Hence men who seek their own welfare should always honor women on holidays and festivals with gifts of ornaments, clothes, and dainty food.

"Let mutual fidelity continue until death"—this may be considered as the summary of the highest law for husband and wife.

A virtuous wife who after the death of her husband constantly remains chaste reaches heaven, though she have no son, just like those chaste men. But a woman who from a desire to have offspring violates her duty towards her deceased husband brings on herself disgrace in this world and loses her place with her husband in heaven.

Offspring begotten by another man is here not considered lawful nor does offspring begotten on another man's wife belong to the begetter nor is a second husband anywhere prescribed for virtuous women.

She who cohabits with a man of higher caste, forsaking her own husband who belongs to a lower one, will become contemptible in this world, and is called a remarried woman. By violating her duty towards her husband a wife is disgraced in this world; after death she enters the womb of a jackal and is tormented by diseases, the punishment of her sin.

She who, controlling her thoughts, words, and deeds, never slights her Lord resides after death with her husband in heaven and is called a virtuous wife. In reward of such conduct a female who controls her thoughts, speech, and actions gains in this life highest renown and in the next world a place near her husband.

Between wives who are destined to bear children, who are worthy of worship and irradiate their dwellings, and between the goddesses of fortune who reside in the houses of men there is no difference whatsoever.

The production of children, the nurture of those born, and the daily life of men, of these matters woman is visibly the cause. Offspring, the due performance of religious rites, faithful service, highest conjugal happiness and heavenly bliss for the ancestors and oneself depend on one's wife alone.

Though destitute of virtue, or seeking pleasure elsewhere, or devoid of good qualities, yet a husband must be constantly worshipped as a god by a faithful wife. No sacrifice, no vow, no fast must be performed by women apart from their husbands; if a wife obeys her husband she will for that reason alone be exalted in heaven.

A faithful wife who desires to dwell after death with her husband must never do anything that might displease him who took her hand, whether he be alive or dead. At her pleasure let her emaciate her body by living on pure flowers, roots, and fruit but she must never even mention the name of another man after her husband has died.

When the purpose of the appointment to cohabit with the widow has been attained in accordance with the law those two shall behave towards each other like a father and a daughter-in-law. If those two being thus appointed deviate from the rule and act from carnal desire they will both become outcasts, as men who defile the bed of a daughter-in-law or of a Guru.

By twice-born men a widow must not be appointed to cohabit with any other than her husband for they who appoint her to another man will violate the eternal law. In the sacred texts which refer to marriage the appointment of widows is nowhere mentioned, nor is the re-marriage of widows prescribed in the rules concerning marriage. This practice is reprehended by the learned of the twice-born castes as fit for cattle.

A wife, a son, and a slave, these three are declared to have no property; the wealth which they earn is acquired for him to whom they belong.

A wife, a son, a slave, a pupil, and a younger brother of the full blood who have committed faults may be beaten with a rope or a split bamboo. But on the back part of the body only, never on a noble part.

To a distinguished, handsome suitor of equal caste should a father give his daughter in accordance with the prescribed rule, though she have not attained the proper age. But the maiden, though marriageable, should rather stop in the father's house until death than that he should ever give her to a man destitute of good qualities.

For the first marriage of twice-born men wives of equal caste are recommended but for those who through desire proceed to marry again, the following females, chosen according to the direct order of the castes, are most approved: It is declared that a Sudra woman alone can be the wife of a Sudra; she and one of his own caste the wives of a Vaisya; those two and one of his own caste the wives of a Kshatriya; those three and one of his own caste the wives of a Brahmana. A Sudra woman is not mentioned even in any ancient story as the first wife of a Brahmana or of a Kshatriya, though they lived in the greatest distress. Twice-born men who, in their folly, wed wives of the low Sudra caste soon degrade their families and their children to the state of Sudras.

In all castes those children only which are begotten in the direct order on wedded wives, equal in caste and married as virgins, are to be considered as belonging to the same caste as their father. Sons, begotten by twice-born men on wives of the next lower castes, they declare to be similar to their fathers but blamed on account of the fault inherent in their mothers. Such is the eternal law concerning children born of wives one degree lower than their husbands.

Women

Women do not care for beauty, nor is their attention fixed on age; thinking, "It is enough that he is a man," they give themselves to the handsome and to the ugly. Through their passion for men, through their mutable temper, through their natural heartlessness, they become disloyal towards their husbands, however carefully they may be guarded in this world.

Knowing their disposition, which the Lord of creatures laid in them at the creation, to be such, every man should most strenuously exert himself to guard them. When creating them Manu allotted to women a love of their bed, of their seat and of ornament, impure desires, wrath, dishonesty, malice, and bad conduct.

It is the nature of women to seduce men in this world; for that reason the wise are never unguarded in the company of females. For women are able to lead astray in this world not only a fool but even a learned man and to make him a slave of desire and anger.

Day and night women must be kept in dependence by the males of their families and, if they attach themselves to sensual enjoyments, they must be kept under one's control. Her father protects her in childhood, her husband protects her in youth, and her sons protect her in old age; a woman is never fit for independence.

Reprehensible is the father who gives not his daughter in marriage at the proper time, reprehensible is the husband who approaches not his wife in due season, and reprehensible is the son who does not protect his mother after her husband has died.

A female must not seek to separate herself from her father, husband, or sons; by leaving them she would make both her own and her husband's families contemptible. She must always be cheerful, clever in the management of her household affairs, careful in cleaning her utensils, and economical in expenditure. Him to whom her father may give her, or her brother with the father's permission, she shall obey as long as he lives and when he is dead she must not insult his memory.

Drinking spirituous liquor, associating with wicked people, separation from the husband, rambling abroad, sleeping at unseasonable hours, and dwelling in other men's houses are the six causes of the ruin of women.

The Mandate of Heaven

Traditional Chinese history begins with a series of legendary rulers who are credited with many of the accomplishments and discoveries of an early civilization: writing, agricultural techniques, controlling water supplies, and so on. After these legendary rulers, the histories tell of three dynasties, the Hsia (2205–1766 B.C.), Shang (1766–1050 B.C.), and the Chou (1050–256 B.C.). Since the earliest Chinese historical documents can be dated only to the eleventh century B.C., historians used to believe that the Hsia and Shang dynasties also were legendary. Early in this century, however, archeological discoveries have confirmed the existence of the Shang Dynasty and have supported the traditional description of it. While the existence of the Hsia still lacks empirical verification, scholars now view traditional Chinese history as fairly reliable.

Even though early Chinese historians strove to be accurate and reliable, that does not mean that they practiced history in the contemporary sense. In two very important ways, the early Chinese historians are very different from a modern historian. First, traditional Chinese history focuses almost exclusively on the ruling family. These histories give us glimpses of Chinese culture only as it has to do with imperial policy and only from the point of view of the very elite. Second, these histories were not meant to be dispassionate descriptions of events, but commentaries on the virtues and vices of the various rulers. In many cases, these histories were written to justify the current regime and discredit the previous one. While traditional Chinese historians may have been accurate in terms of recounting the facts, they were highly biased in their interpretation of those facts.

The following document is the earliest example of this way of writing history. In the eleventh century, the Chou family led an aristocratic revolt against the last Shang emperor, who was morally corrupt and politically irresponsible. After defeating the Shang, the Chou faced the task of convincing their subjects that they were the legitimate rulers of the empire. They claimed that a dynasty was legitimate because it had the Mandate of Heaven (divine sanction or approval). The Mandate of Heaven could be removed if the dynasty failed to fulfill its responsibilities as rulers. The Chou claimed that their military victory was evidence that the Mandate of Heaven had been withdrawn from the Shang and given to them. This proved to be a very successful idea for the Chou—so successful, that all subsequent Chinese imperial dynasties would appeal to it.

1. How is the Mandate of Heaven gained and lost? How should the new emperors remember the emperors of the Hsia and Shang (Yin) dynasties?

2. What seem to be the primary roles of the emperor? What are the most important virtues of an emperor?

In the second month, third quarter, sixth day *i-wei*, the king in the morning proceeded from Chou and arrived in Feng. The Grand Guardian, the Duke of Shao, preceded the Duke of Chou to inspect the site. In the third month, the day *mou-shen*, the third day after the first appearance of the new moon on *ping-wu*, the Grand Guardian arrived in the morning at Lo and consulted the tortoise oracle about the site. When he had obtained the oracle he planned and laid out the city. On the third day *keng-hsü*, the Grand Guardian with all the Yin people started work on the emplacements at the bend of the Lo River, and on the fifth day *chia-yin* the emplacements were determined. The next day *i-mao*, the Duke of Chou arrived in the morning at Lo and thoroughly inspected the plans for the new city. On the third day *ting-ssu*, he sacrificed two oxen as victims on the suburban altar, and on the next day *mou-wu* he sacrificed to the God of the Soil in the new city one ox, one sheep, and one pig. On the seventh day *chia-tzu* the Duke of Chou by written documents gave charges to all the rulers of the states of the Hou, Tien. and Nan zones in the Yin realm. When orders had been given to the Yin multitude they arose with vigor to do their work. The Grand Guardian then together with all the ruling princes of the states went out and took gifts and entered again and gave them to the Duke of Chou. The Duke of Chou said: "I salute and bow down my head and I extol the king and your Grace. I make an announcement to all Yin and managers of affairs. Oh, august Heaven, the Lord-on-High, has changed his principal son [i.e., the ruler] and this great state Yin's mandate. Now that the king has received the mandate, unbounded is the grace, but also unbounded is the solicitude. Oh, how can he be but careful! Heaven has removed and made an end to the great state Yin's mandate. There are many former wise kings of Yin in Heaven, and the later kings and people here managed their mandate. But in the end [under the last king] wise and good men lived in misery so that, leading their wives and carrying their children, wailing and calling to Heaven, they went to where no one could come and seize them. Oh, Heaven had pity on the people of the four quarters, and looking with affection and giving its mandate, it employed the zealous ones [i.e., the leaders of the Chou]. May the king now urgently pay careful attention to his virtue. Look at the ancient predecessors, the lords of Hsia; Heaven indulged them and cherished and protected them. They strove to comprehend the obedience to Heaven; but in these times they have lost their mandate. Now a young son is the successor; may he not neglect the aged elders. Then he will comprehend our ancient men's virtue, nay still more it will occur that he is able to comprehend and endeavor to follow Heaven. . . . May the king come and take over the work of the Lord-on-High, and himself manage the government in the center of the land. I, Tan, say: having made the great city, he shall from here be a counterpart to august Heaven. He shall carefully sacrifice to the upper and lower spirits, and from here centrally govern. . . . We should not fail to mirror ourselves in the lords of Hsia; we likewise should not fail to mirror ourselves in the lords of Yin. We do not presume to know and say that the lords of Hsia undertook Heaven's mandate so as to have it for so-and-so many years; we do not presume to know and say that it could not have been prolonged. It was that they did not reverently attend to their virtue, and so they prematurely renounced their mandate. We do not presume to know and say that the lords of Yin received Heaven's mandate for so-and-so many years: we do not know and say that it could not have been prolonged. It was that they did not reverently attend to their virtue and so they prematurely threw away their mandate. Now the king has succeded to and received their mandate. We should then also remember the mandates of these two states and in succeeding to them equal their merits. . . . Being king, his position will be that of a leader in virtue; the small people will then imitate him in all the world. . . . May those above and below [i.e., the king and his servants] labor and be anxiously careful; may they say: we have received Heaven's mandate, may it grandly equal the span of years of the lords of Hsia and not miss the span of years of the lords of Yin.".

King Wen

1

King Wen is on high;
Oh, he shines in Heaven!
Chou is an old people,
But its charge is new.
The leaders of Chou became illustrious;
Was not God's charge timely given?
King Wen ascends and descends
On the left and right of God.

• • •

4

August was King Wen,
Continuously bright and reverent.
Great, indeed, was the appointment of Heaven.

There were Shang's grandsons and sons,
Shang's grandsons and sons;
Was their number not a hundred thousand?
But the Lord-on-High gave his command
And they bowed down to Chou.

• • •

7

The charge is not easy to keep;
May it not end in your persons.
Display and make bright your good fame.
And consider what Yin had received from Heaven.
The doings of high Heaven
Have no sound, no smell.
Make King Wen your pattern
And all the states will trust in you.

THINKING ACROSS CULTURES

1. River valley civilizations depend on the regular flooding of rivers. It is no surprise that the floods play a major role in ancient Near Eastern texts. Compare and contrast how rivers and floods are depicted in the Epic of Gilgamesh, the Hebrew Scriptures, and the Hymn to the Nile.

2. In general, what seems to be the status of women in ancient civilizations? Are there differences in gender roles and expectations among the various cultures?

3. How is the caste system of India different from the class distinctions in other ancient societies?

4. What seem to be some common issues and problems faced by early river valley civilizations?

CLASSICAL CIVILIZATIONS

The early river valley civilizations dealt in various ways with the very basic problems of urban, civilized life. In some cases, these civilizations left enduring cultural legacies such as the Hebrew Scriptures or the caste system in India. For the most part, however, the early civilizations were overshadowed by three later civilizations that flourished around the Mediterranean, the northern part of the Indian subcontinent, and northern China in the period between 500 B.C. and 500 A.D. These civilizations are commonly called the "classical" civilizations, because they are often seen by subsequent civilizations in those regions as "golden ages," whence their basic values and cultural assumptions are derived. While these civilizations did not cover the world, they had broad influence over time and space. Classical Mediterranean civilization was a model, in varying degrees, for both European civilization, and thus an on any culture in the world of European descent, and the Islamic civilization in North Africa and the Middle East. Classical Chinese civilization became a model not only in China but also in Korea, Japan, and Vietnamese territories. Classical Indian culture spread to influence all of what are now India, Sri Lanka, and most of Southeastern Asia.

Classical Mediterranean civilization flourished first around Greek speaking city-states on the coasts of the Aegean Sea and was later adopted and spread by the Roman Empire. The defeat of the Persian Empire by the Greeks at the battles of Marathon and Salamis in the early fifth century B.C. is the symbolic beginning of this period. Following these victories, Greece, especially Athens, entered a golden age that, although little longer than a century, left an indelible mark on the future. For instance, the Greeks were the founders of theoretical science. Although many significant scientific discoveries had been made prior to their time, by civilizations as disparate as the Egyptian and Mayan, these were for the most part practical—scientific knowledge gained to control the environment to secure specific results. With the Greeks we find a different approach to science—the search for generality. They wanted to understand how the universe works; not just to put it to work for them but, rather, simply to understand. The Greeks did not confine their theoretical approach to the study of nature but generalized even beyond the scientific world. Plato, in his great work *The Republic*, reached the metaphysical conclusion that ultimate Reality consists of the Form of the Good. This idea, so important to all later Western thought, is the fundamental expression of classical Greek rationalism and optimism.

But in more prosaic areas as well, the Greeks sought to generalize. Thucydides, in the preface to his *History*, made it clear that he was interested not only in describing the events of the Peloponnesian War but of war in general. And the most famous statement in Aristole's *Politics*—"Man is a political animal"—is a generalization about human nature. But Aristotle meant more than this by his statement. The sentence as he wrote it actually reads, "Man is by nature an animal intended to live in a polis." Thus Aristotle implied that the form of political organization developed in classical Greece—the polis (whence our word "politics")—was ideally suited for human life. Greece was divided into scores of these poleis, or small city-states, each independent and many with quite different forms of government. Athens, the most important, was, during the golden age of the fifth century, a democracy. But, whatever its form, the polis was the center of each individual's life and the object of his pride and devotion. Pericles, in his Funeral Oration eulogizing the dead after the first year of the Peloponnesian War, said of them "they were worthy of Athens"; no greater praise could he have accorded them.

But the Greek poleis represented an anomaly. Whereas they generalized in their theories, the Greeks failed to do so in their practical politics. The separate poleis were often at odds with each other, culminating in the disastrous Peloponnesian War in the late fifth century B.C., which so weakened them, defeated Athens in particular, that they fell easy prey to the organized Macedonian hosts who moved on them from the north.

As these events were occurring in the eastern Mediterranean, another city-state halfway across the sea to the west was pursuing its destiny—Rome. According to tradition, Rome was founded in 753 B.C. Ruled at first by kings, it became a republic, much as described by Polybius in his *Histories*, in 509 B.C. Not long afterward it began a process of expansion that, before it ended, had transformed this tiny city-state into one of the most powerful empires the world has ever known. Unlike the Greeks, with their theories and generalizations, the Romans were an intensely practical people. Where the former pursued mathematics for its rational elegance, for example, the latter put it to use in engineering, to build highways and aqueducts.

To conquer the Western world required the Romans to develop their military might. This they did through recruiting citizen-soldiers who were highly trained, disciplined, and dedicated to their legion. To maintain their empire, however, involved them in much more complex functions. They had to develop a code of laws that could be applied to a wide variety of places and political traditions, administrators capable of governing the far-flung outposts of empire, and systems of communication and transportation to link them all together. This the Romans accomplished with remarkable efficiency and success. The history of Rome is divided almost equally in half. In the early period, until the first century B.C., the government was republican, with a tripartite division of political power among Consuls, the Senate, and the people. Then, after several decades of turmoil, Rome emerged an empire—meaning by this term that power rested in the hands of a supreme ruler. Imperial rule continued until the disintegration of Roman power in the fifth century A.D. under the onslaught of invasions by tribal warriors from the north and east. One event, almost unnoticed at the time, occurred early in the in period, during the reign of Caesar Augustus. This was the birth, in a remote province of the empire, of the child Jesus. It is not necessary to comment on the influence his life and teachings has had on the subsequent civilization.

At about the same time that Rome was expanding and consolidating its empire the Chinese empire was in the process of disintegration, as the centralized government of the Chou dynasty more and more lost control over the provinces. To conclude from this that Chinese civilization was in decline, however, would be a mistake. Quite the opposite, for the later centuries of the Chou are often referred to as China's Golden Age. The preeminent figure of the age was Confucius, who flourished early in the fifth century B.C. The teachings of Confucius were essentially conservative. He believed in the importance of tradition and the following of traditional ways, urging his students and also those who held political power to devote their efforts to the preservation of an orderly and stable society. This attitude, with its respect for the past, was to become a controlling influence on Chinese civilization through much of its history.

At the same time that Confucius was teaching, a quite different movement was stirring in China, which was to rival Confucianism at the time and throughout succeeding millennia. This was Taoism, a mystical form of religion said to have been founded by a man named Lao-Tzu. The Taoists, unlike the Confucians—who instilled in their followers a sense of duty to society and the state—were individualists. Instead of conforming to society, they believed one should conform to nature. For them the best life was one in which a person separated himself from the social scene to commune in isolation with nature. The political disintegration of the later Chou was brought to an end by the Ch'in dynasty, which, although it held power for only a few years (221–206 B.C.), succeeded in uniting China under its iron rule. Its head, Shi Huang, took the title Emperor of Ch'in (China), a title that was held by monarchs until the revolution of 1912. Another accomplishment of the Ch'in dynasty was the construction of the Great Wall, to protect the country from invaders from the north. It came finally to stretch along China's border for fifteen hundred miles and remains today a sight for tourists' eyes.

The Ch'in dynasty, which did not long outlive its founder, was followed by the Han, which ruled China for more than four hundred years (until A.D. 220), a period of general peace and prosperity. Once again, however, disintegration finally set in and China experienced a period of fluctuating political fortunes. Two developments of the Han period are worthy of note. With Chinese leadership the "silk road" was constructed, linking China by a long and arduous route to the Mediterranean Sea, thus promoting both trade and greater contact between these two classical civilizations.

Also, Buddhism was introduced into China from India, the first major step leading to its spread throughout the Far East.

The other great civilization of the classical world was India. Here the Aryan invaders moved east from their original foothold in the Indus valley, gradually expanding their power and subjugating the local population. By around 600 B.C. they controlled most of the Ganges plain. Unlike China, which developed a largely secular society, Indian life from early times was dominated by religion. Hinduism, the predominant religion of India, developed out of an amalgamation of aboriginal cults with those of the invading Aryans. The priests, or Brahmins, who developed the religion and compiled its scriptures, gave themselves a preeminent status in the social structure, organizing the society into four occupational groups that later hardened into the unique caste system of India, described in the *Laws of Manu*. At the beginning of the fifth century B.C., two new religions were born in India. The first was Jainism, which taught an extreme form of asceticism. Although it still has a following in India, it never spread beyond that country. The second was Buddhism. Founded by a young Indian prince, Siddhartha Gautama (who was an almost exact contemporary of Confucius), Buddhism later spread throughout Asia.

Political consolidation of India dates from the Mauryan dynasty whose first king, Chandragupta, conquered most of northern India at the end of the fourth century B.C. More important, however, was his grandson, Asoka (273–232 B.C.), the most famous of Indian kings, who conquered all but the southern tip of the peninsula. A convert to Buddhism, Asoka sent out missionaries to spread the religion to other parts of the world. Shortly after the death of Asoka the Maurya empire disintegrated. After a period of Greek influence, India experienced a long interim of divided rule. But, in the fourth century A.D., a new dynasty, the Guptas, again began to consolidate much of the land. The Gupta Empire was brought to an end after two hundred years, by invading Huns from the north, in the sixth century A.D.

Homer

Homer's *Iliad*, the great epic of the Trojan wars, is based on the legend of the seduction and abduction of Helen, wife of King Minolaus of Sparta (in southern Greece), by the young prince Paris of Troy, or Ilium, a city in Asia Minor, not far from present-day Istanbul. Helen, who is considered to have been one of the great beauties of history, fell in love with Paris and gladly accompanied him to Troy. Her husband, understandably, was not pleased, so he sent a Spartan army to Troy to bring her back home. Once there, however, the Greeks found themselves unable to penetrate the walls of the city. Always ingenious, the Greeks built a wooden horse, the famous "Trojan Horse," and filled it with soldiers. The curious Trojans pulled it inside the city, and the Greek soldiers leaped out, took the city, and recaptured Helen. Prominent in all these activities was the formidable Greek warrior, Achilles.

The story of the return of the Greek chief Odysseus to Ithaca and his long-suffering wife, Penelope, is recounted in the *Odyssey* the second of Homer's great epics. It traces his two decades of wandering throughout the Mediterranean—even venturing past Gibraltar into the Atlantic Ocean—to Odysseus' homecoming to Ithaca, in Southern Greece.

Little is known of the life of Homer. He lived in the eighth century B.C. and is thought to have been blind. It is probable that he did not actually compose the *Iliad* and *Odyssey* in writing but recited them to his disciples who presumably then transcribed them.

---

1. Achilles and Odysseus served as legendary role models, or heroes, for Greek men. What character traits do these figures model? Based on these two characters, what is a hero?

2. Does the character of Penelope give us any insight into attitudes toward women in classical Greece?

The Iliad

Book XXII

To such I call the gods! one constant state
Of lasting rancour and eternal hate:
No thought but rage, and never-ceasing strife,
Till death extinguish rage, and thought, and life.
Rouse then thy forces this important hour,
Collect thy soul, and call forth all thy power.
No further subterfuge, no further chance;
'Tis Pallas, Pallas gives thee to my lance.
Each Grecian ghost, by thee deprived of breath,
Now hovers round, and calls thee to thy death.
    He spoke, and launch'd his javelin at the foe;
But Hector shunn'd the mediated blow:
He stoop'd, while o'er his head the flying spear
Sang innocent, and spent its force in air.
Minerva watch'd it falling on the land,
Then drew, and gave to great Achilles' hand,
Unseen of Hector, who, elate with joy,
Now shakes his lance, and braves the dread of Troy.
'The life you boasted to that javelin given,
Prince! you have miss'd. My fate depends on Heaven.
To thee, presumptuous as thou art, unknown,
Or what must prove my fortune, or thy own.
Boasting is but an art, our fears to blind,
And with false terrors sink another's mind.
But know, whatever fate I am to try,
By no dishonest wound shall Hector die.
I shall not fall a fugitive at least,
My soul shall bravely issue from my breast.
But first, try thou my arm; and may this dart
End all my country's woes, deep buried in thy heart.'
    The weapon flew, its course unerring held,
Unerring, but the heavenly shield repell'd
The mortal dart; resulting with a bound
From off the ringing orb, it struck the ground.
Hector beheld his javelin fall in vain,
Nor other lance, nor other hope remain;
He calls Deïphobus, demands a spear—

Trans. Alexander Pope

In vain, for no Deïphobus was there.
All comfortless he stands: then, with a sigh:
'Tis so—Heaven wills it, and my hour is nigh!
I deem'd Deïphobus had heard my call,
But he secure lies guarded in the wall.
A god deceived me; Pallas, 'twas thy deed,
Death and black fate approach! 'tis I must bleed.
No refuge now, no succour from above,
Great Jove deserts me, and the son of Jove,
Propitious once, and kind! Then, welcome fate!
'Tis true I perish, yet I perish great:
Yet in a mighty deed I shall expire,
Let future ages hear it, and admire!'
   Fierce, at the word, his weighty sword he drew,
And, all collected, on Achilles flew.
So Jove's bold bird, high balanced in the air,
Stoops from the clouds to truss the quivering hare.
Nor less Achilles his fierce soul prepares:
Before his breast the flaming shield he bears,
Refulgent orb! above his fourfold cone
The gilded horse-hair sparkled in the sun,
Nodding at every step: (Vulcanian frame!)
And as he moved, his figure seem'd on flame.
As radiant Hesper shines with keener light,
Far-beaming o'er the silver host of night,
When all the starry train emblaze the sphere:
So shone the point of great Achilles' spear.
In his right hand he waves the weapon round,
Eyes the whole man, and meditates the wound;
But the rich mail Patroclus lately wore
Securely cased the warrior's body o'er.
One space at length he spies, to let in fate,
Where 'twixt the neck and throat the jointed plate
Gave entrance: through that penetrable part
Furious he drove the well-directed dart:
Nor pierced the windpipe yet, nor took the power
Of speech, unhappy! from thy dying hour.
Prone on the field the bleeding warrior lies,
While, thus triumphing, stern Achilles cries:

'At last is Hector stretch'd upon the plain,
Who fear'd no vengeance for Patroclus slain:
Then, prince! you should have fear'd, what now you feel;
Achilles absent was Achilles still: . . .

The Odyssey

Odysseus and Penelope

Chuckling as she went, the old woman bustled upstairs to tell her mistress that her beloved husband was in the house. Her legs could hardly carry her fast enough, and her feet twinkled in their haste. As she reached the head of the bedstead, she cried: 'Wake up, Penelope, dear child, and see a sight you've longed for all these many days. Odysseus has come home, and high time too! And he's killed the rogues who turned his whole house inside out, ate up his wealth, and bullied his son.'

Penelope was not caught off her guard. 'My dear nurse,' she said, 'the gods have made you daft. It's as easy for them to rob the wisest of their wits as to make stupid people wise. And now they've addled *your* brains, which used to be so sound. How dare you make sport of my distress by waking me when I had closed my eyes for a comfortable nap, only to tell me this nonsense? Never have I slept so soundly since Odysseus sailed away to that accursed place I cannot bring myself to mention. Off with you now downstairs and back into your quarters! If any of the other maids had come and awakened me to listen to such stuff, I'd soon have packed her off to her own place with a box on the ears. You can thank your age for saving you from that.'

But this did not silence the old nurse. 'I am not making fun of you, dear child,' she said. 'Odysseus really has come home, just as I told you. He's the stranger whom they all scoffed at in the hall. Telemachus has known for some time that he was back, but had the sense to keep his father's plans a secret till he'd made those upstarts pay for their villainy.'

Penelope's heart leapt up. She sprang from the bed and clung to the old woman, with the tears streaming from her eyes and the eager words from her lips. 'Dear nurse,' she cried, 'I beg you for the truth! If he is really home, as you say, how on earth did he manage single-handed against that rascally crew who always hang about the house in a pack?'

'I never saw a thing,' said Eurycleia, 'I knew nothing about it. All I heard was the groans of dying men. We sat petrified in a corner of our quarters, with the doors shut tightly on us, till your son Telemachus shouted to me to come out. His father had sent him to fetch me. And then I found Odysseus standing among the bodies of the dead. They lay round him in heaps all over the hard floor. It would have done you good to see him, spattered with blood and filth like a lion. By now all the corpses have been gathered together at the courtyard gate, while he has had a big fire made and is fumigating the palace. He sent me to call you to him. So come with me now, so that you two may enter into your happiness together after all the sorrows

Trans. E. V. Rieu (Harmonds Worth, 1946), pp. 341–350.

you have had. The hope you cherished so long is fulfilled for you today. Odysseus has come back to his own hearth alive, he has found both you and his son in the home, and he has had his revenge in his own palace on every one of the Suitors who were doing him such wrong.'

'Don't laugh too soon, dear nurse, don't boast about them yet,' said Penelope in her prudence. 'You know how everyone at home would welcome the sight of him, and nobody more than myself and the son we brought into the world. But this tale of yours does not ring true. It must be one of the immortal gods that has killed the young lords, provoked, no doubt, by their galling insolence and wicked ways. For they respected nobody they met—good men and bad were all the same to them. And now their iniquities have brought them to this pass. Meanwhile Odysseus in some distant land has lost his chance of ever getting home, and with it lost his life.'

'My child,' her old nurse exclaimed, 'how can you say such things! Here is your husband at his own fireside, and you declare he never will get home. What little faith you have always had! But let me tell you something else—a fact that proves the truth. You know the scar he had where he was wounded long ago by the white tusk of a boar? I saw that very scar when I was washing him, and would have told you of it, if Odysseus, for his own crafty purposes, hadn't seized me by the throat and prevented me. Come with me now. I'll stake my life upon it. If I've played you false, then kill me in the cruellest way you can.'

'Dear nurse,' Penelope replied, 'you are a very wise old woman, but even you cannot probe into the minds of the everlasting gods. However, let us go to my son, so that I can see my suitors dead, together with the man who killed them.'

As she spoke she left her room and made her way downstairs, a prey to indecision. Should she remain aloof as she questioned her husband, or go straight up to him and kiss his head and hands? What she actually did, when she had crossed the stone threshold into the hall, was to take a chair in the firelight by the wall, on the opposite side to Odysseus, who was sitting by one of the great columns with his eyes on the ground, waiting to see whether his good wife would say anything to him when she saw him. For a long while Penelope, overwhelmed by wonder, sat there without a word. But her eyes were busy, at one moment resting full on his face, and at the next falling on the ragged clothes that made him seem a stranger once again. It was Telemachus who broke the silence, but only to rebuke her.

'Mother,' he said, 'you strange, hard-hearted mother of mine, why do you keep so far from my father? Why aren't you sitting at his side, talking and asking questions all the while? No other woman would have had the perversity to hold out like this against a husband she had just got back after nineteen years of misadventure. But then your heart was always harder than flint.'

'My child, the shock has numbed it,' she admitted. 'I cannot find a word to say to him; I cannot ask him anything at all; I cannot even look him in the face. But if it really is Odysseus home again, we two shall surely recognize each other, and in an even better way; for there are tokens between us which only we two know and no one else has heard of.'

Patient Odysseus smiled, then turning briskly to his son he said: 'Telemachus, leave your mother to put me to the proof here in our home. She will soon come to a better mind. At the moment, because I'm dirty and in rags, she gives me the cold shoulder and won't admit that I'm Odysseus. But you and I must consider what is best to be done. When a man has killed a fellow-citizen, just one, with hardly any friends to carry on the feud, he is outlawed, he leaves his kith and kin and flies the country. But we have killed the pick of the Ithacan nobility, the mainstay of our state. There is a problem for you.'

'One you must grapple with yourself, dear father,' Telemachus shrewdly rejoined. 'For at getting out of a difficulty you are held to be the best man in the world, with no one else to touch you. We will follow your lead with alacrity, and I may say with no lack of courage either, so far as in us lies.'

Odysseus was not at a loss. 'As I see it, then,' he said, 'our best plan will be this. Wash yourselves first, put on your tunics, and tell the maids in the house to get dressed. Then let our excellent minstrel strike up a merry dance-tune for us, loud as his lyre can play, so that if the music is heard outside by anyone passing in the road or by one of our neighbours, they may imagine there is a wedding-feast. That will prevent the news of the Suitors' death from spreading through the town before we can beat a retreat to our farm among the orchards. Once there, we shall see. Providence may play into our hands.'

They promptly put his idea into practice. The men washed and donned their tunics, while the women decked themselves out. The admirable bard took up his hollow lyre and had them soon intent on nothing but the melodies of song and the niceties of the dance. They made the great hall echo round them to the feet of dancing men and women richly clad. 'Ah!' said the passers-by as the sounds reached their ears. 'Somebody has married our much-courted queen. The heartless creature! Too fickle to keep patient watch over the great house till her lawful husband should come back!' Which shows how little they knew what had really happened.

Meanwhile the great Odysseus, in his own home again, had himself bathed and rubbed with oil by the housekeeper Eurynome, and was fitted out by her in a beautiful cloak and tunic. Athene also played her part by enhancing his comeliness from head to foot. She made him look taller and sturdier than ever; she caused the bushy locks to hang from his head thick as the petals of the hyacinth in bloom; and just as a craftsman trained by Hephaestus and herself in the secrets of his art takes pains to put a graceful finish to his work by overlaying silver-ware with gold, she finished now by endowing his head and shoulders with an added beauty. He came out from the bath looking like one of the everlasting gods, then went and sat down once more in the chair opposite his wife.

'What a strange creature!' he exclaimed. 'Heaven made you as you are, but for sheer obstinacy you put all the rest of your sex in the shade. No other wife could have steeled herself to keep so long out of the arms of a husband she had just got back after nineteen years of misadventure. Well, nurse, make a bed for me to sleep alone in. For my wife's heart is just about as hard as iron.'

'You too are strange,' said the cautious Penelope. 'I am not being haughty or indifferent. I am not even unduly surprised. But I have too clear a picture of you in my mind as you were when you sailed from Ithaca in your long-oared ship. Come, Eurycleia, make him a comfortable bed outside the bedroom that he built so well himself. Place the big bed out there, and make it up with rugs and blankets, and with laundered sheets.'

This was her way of putting her husband to the test. But Odysseus flared up at once and rounded on his loyal wife. 'Penelope,' he cried, 'you exasperate me! Who, if you please, has moved my bed elsewhere? Short of a miracle, it would be hard even for a skilled workman to shift it somewhere else, and the strongest young fellow alive would have a job to budge it. For a great secret went into the making of that complicated bed; and it was my work and mine alone. Inside the court there was a long-leaved olive-tree, which had grown to full height with a stem as thick as a pillar. Round this I built my room of close-set stone-work, and when that was finished, I roofed it over throughly, and put in a solid, neatly fitted, double door. Next I lopped all the twigs off the olive, trimmed the stem from the root up, rounded it smoothly and carefully with my adze and trued it to the line, to make my bedpost. This I drilled through where necessary, and used as a basis for the bed itself, which I worked away at till that too was done, when I finished it off with an inlay of gold, silver, and ivory, and fixed a set of purple straps across the frame.

'There is our secret, and I have shown you that I know it. What I don't know, madam, is whether my bedstead stands where it did, or whether someone has cut the tree-trunk through and shifted it elsewhere.'

Her knees began to tremble as she realized the complete fidelity of his description. All at once her heart melted. Bursting into tears she ran up to Odysseus, threw her arms round his neck and kissed his head. 'Odysseus,' she cried, 'do not be cross with me, you who were always the most reasonable of men. All our unhappiness is due to the gods, who couldn't bear to see us share the joys of youth and reach the threshold of old age together. But don't be angry with me now, or hurt because the moment when I saw you first I did not kiss you as I kiss you now. For I had always had the cold fear in my heart that somebody might come here and bewitch me with his talk. There are plenty of rogues who would seize such a chance; and though Argive Helen would never have slept in her foreign lover's arms had she known that her countrymen would go to war to fetch her back to Argos, even she, the daughter of Zeus, was tempted by the goddess and fell, though the idea of such madness had never entered her head till that moment, which was so fateful for the world and proved the starting-point of all our sorrows too. But now all's well. You have faithfully described our token, the secret of our bed, which no one ever saw but you and I and one maid, Actoris, who was my father's gift when first I came to you, and sat as sentry at our bedroom door. You have convinced your unbelieving wife.'

Penelope's surrender melted Odysseus' heart, and he wept as he held his dear wife in his arms, so loyal and so true. Sweet moment too for her, sweet as the sight of land to sailors struggling in the sea, when the Sea-god by dint of wind and wave has wrecked their gallant ship. What happiness for the few swimmers that have fought their way through the white surf to the shore, when, caked with brine but safe and sound, they tread on solid earth! If that is bliss, what bliss it was for her to see her husband once again! She kept her white arms round his neck and never quite let go. Dawn with her roses would have caught them at their tears, had not Athene of the flashing eyes bestirred herself on their behalf. She held the long night lingering in the West, and in the East at Ocean's Stream she kept Dawn waiting by her golden throne, and would not let her yoke the nimble steeds who bring us light, Lampus and Phaethon, the colts that draw the chariot of Day.

But there was one thing which Odysseus had the wisdom soon to tell his wife. 'My dear,' he said, 'we have not yet come to the end of our trials. There lies before me still a great and hazardous adventure, which I must see through to the very end however far that end may be. That was what Teiresias' soul predicted for me when I went down to the House of Hades to find a way home for my followers and myself. So come to bed now, my dear wife, and let us comfort ourselves while we can with a sweet sleep in each other's arms.'

Prudent Penelope answered: 'Your bed shall be ready the moment you wish to use it, now that the gods have brought you back to your own country and your lovely home. But since it did occur to you to speak of this new ordeal, please tell me all about it; for I shall certainly find out later, and it could be no worse to hear at once.'

'Why drag it out of me?' he asked reproachfully. 'Well, you shall hear the whole tale. I'll make no secret of it. Not that you'll find it to your liking! I am not pleased myself. For he told me to take a well-cut oar and wander on from city to city, till I came to a people who know nothing of the sea, and never use salt with their food, so that our crimson-painted ships and the long oars that serve those ships as wings are quite beyond their ken. Of this, he said that I should find conclusive proof, as you shall hear, when I met some other traveller who spoke of the "winnowingfan" I was carrying on my shoulder. Then, he said, the time would have come for me to plant my oar in the earth and offer the Lord Poseidon the rich sacrifice of a ram, a bull, and a breeding boar. After that I was to go back home and make ceremonial sacrifices to the everlasting gods who live in the far-flung heavens, to all of them, this time, in due precedence. As for my end, he said that Death would come to me in his gentlest form out of the sea, and that when he took me I should be worn out after an easy old age and surrounded by a prosperous folk. He swore that I should find all this come true.'

'Well then,' Penelope sagely replied, 'if Providence plans to make you happier in old age, you can always be confident of escaping from your troubles.'

While they were talking, Eurynome and the nurse, by the light of torches, were putting soft bedclothes for them on their bed. When the work was done and the bed lay comfortably spread, the old woman went back into her own quarters for the night, and the housekeeper Eurynome, with a torch in her hands, lit them on their way to bed, taking her leave when she had brought them to their room. And glad indeed they were to lie once more together in the bed that had known them long ago. Meanwhile Telemachus, the cowman, and the swineherd brought their dancing feet to rest, made the women finish too, and lay down for the night in the darkened hall.

But Odysseus and Penelope, after their love had taken its sweet course, turned to the fresh delights of talk, and interchanged their news. He heard this noble wife tell of all she had put up with in his home, watching that gang of wreckers at their work, of all the cattle and fat sheep that they had slaughtered for her sake, of all the vessels they had emptied of their wine. And in his turn, royal Odysseus told her of all the discomfiture he had inflicted on his foes and all the miseries which he himself had undergone. She listened spell-bound, and her eyelids never closed in sleep till the whole tale was finished.

He began with his first victory over the Cicones and his visit to the fertile land where the Lotus-eaters live. He spoke of what the Cyclops did, and the price he had made him pay for the gallant men he ruthlessly devoured. He told her of his stay with Aeolus, so friendly when he came and helpful when he left; and how the gale, since Providence would not let him reach his home so soon, had caught him up once more and driven him in misery down the highways of the fish. Next came his call at Telepylus on the Laestrygonian coast, where the savages destroyed his fleet and all his fighting men, the black ship that carried him being the only one to get away. He spoke of Circe and her magic arts; of how he sailed across the seas to the mouldering Halls of Hades to consult the soul of Theban Teiresias, and saw all his former comrades and the mother who had borne him and nursed him as a child. He told her how he had listened to the rich music of the Sirens' song; how he had sailed by the Wandering Rocks, by dread Charybdis, and by Scylla, whom no sailors pass unscathed; how his men had killed the cattle of the Sun; how Zeus the Thunderer had struck his good ship with a flaming bolt, and all his loyal band had been killed at one fell swoop, though he escaped their dreadful fate himself. He described his arrival at the Isle of

Ogygia and his reception by the Nymph Calypso, who had so much desired to marry him that she kept him in her cavern home, a pampered guest, tempted by promises of immortality and ageless youth, but inwardly rebellious to the end. Finally he came to his disastrous voyage to Scherie, where the kind-hearted Phaeacians had treated him like a god and sent him home by ship with generous gifts of bronze ware and of gold, and woven stuffs. He had just finished this last tale, when sleep came suddenly upon him, relaxing all his limbs as it resolved his cares.

Once more Athene of the flashing eyes took thought on his behalf. Not till she was satisfied that he had had his fill of love and sleep in his wife's arms, did she arouse the lazy Dawn to leave her golden throne by Ocean Stream and to bring daylight to the world. At last Odysseus rose from that soft bed of his and told Penelope his plans. 'Dear wife,' he said, 'the pair of us have had our share of trials, you here in tears because misfortune dogged each step I took to reach you, and I yearning to get back to Ithaca but kept in cheerless exile by Zeus and all the gods there are. Nevertheless we have had what we desired, a night spent in each other's arms. So now I leave the house and my belongings in your care. As for the ravages that gang of profligates have made among my flocks, I shall repair the greater part by raiding on my own, and the people must contribute too, till they have filled up all my folds again. But at the moment I am going to our orchard farm, to see my good father, who has been so miserable on my account. And this, my dear, is what I wish you to do, though you are too wise to need my instructions. Since it will be common knowledge, as soon as the sun is up, that I have killed the Suitors in the palace, go with your ladies-in-waiting to your room upstairs and stay quietly there, see nobody, and ask no questions.'

Odysseus donned his splendid body-armour, woke up Telemachus, the cowman, and the swineherd, and told them all to arm themselves with weapons. They carried out his orders and were soon equipped in bronze. Then they opened the doors and sallied out with Odysseus at their head. It was broad daylight already, but Athene hid them in darkness and soon had them clear of the town.

Plato

The son of a wealthy and noble family—on his mother's side he was descended from the great lawgiver, Solon—Plato (427–347 B.C.) was preparing for a career in politics when the trial and execution of Socrates changed the course of his life. He abandoned his political career and turned to philosophy, opening a school on the outskirts of Athens dedicated to the Socratic search for wisdom. Plato's school, known as the Academy, was the first university in the history of the West. It continued operating for over nine hundred years, from 387 B.C. until it was closed by an edict of the Roman emperor Justinian in A.D. 529.

Plato's writings are in the form of dialogues, with Socrates as the principal speaker. In the selection that follows, the Allegory of the Cave (perhaps the most famous passage in all his works), Plato describes symbolically the predicament in which human beings find themselves and proposes a way of salvation. In addition, the allegory presents, in brief form, most of Plato's main philosophical theories: his belief that the world revealed by our senses is not the real world but only a poor copy of it, and that the real world can be apprehended only intellectually; his idea that knowledge cannot be transferred from teacher to student but, rather, that education consists in directing students' minds toward what is real and important and allowing them to apprehend it for themselves; his faith that the universe ultimately is good; his conviction that enlightened individuals have an obligation to the rest of society, and that a good society must be one in which the truly wise are the rulers. Woven into these themes is a defense of the life of Socrates and a condemnation of Athenian society for having executed him.

The allegory is from Book VII of Plato's best-known work, *The Republic*, which represents a conversation between Socrates and some friends on the nature of justice, and which include Plato's plan for an ideal state ruled by philosophers.

---

1. According to Plato, who should govern the perfect state?

2. How does one acquire wisdom?

The Republic

The Allegory of the Cave

Next, said I [Socrates], here is a parable to illustrate the degrees in which our nature may be enlightened or unenlightened. Imagine the condition of men living in a sort of cavernous chamber underground, with an entrance open to the light and a long passage all down the cave. Here they have been from childhood, chained by the leg and also by the neck, so that they cannot move and can see only what is in front of them, because the chains will not let them turn their heads. At some distance higher up is the light of a fire burning behind them; and between the prisoners and the fire is a track with a parapet built along it, like the screen at a puppet-show, which hides the performers while they show their puppets over the top.

I see, said he [Glaucon].[1]

Now behind this parapet imagine persons carrying along various artificial objects, including figures of men and animals in wood or stone or other materials, which project above the parapet. Naturally, some of these persons will be talking, others silent.[2]

It is a strange picture, he said, and a strange sort of prisoners.

Like ourselves, I replied; for in the first place prisoners so confined would have seen nothing of themselves or of one another, except the shadows thrown by the fire-light on the wall of the Cave facing them, would they?

Not if all their lives they had been prevented from moving their heads.

And they would have seen as little of the objects carried past.

Of course.

Now, if they could talk to one another, would they not suppose that their words referred only to those passing shadows which they saw?

Necessarily.

And suppose their prison had an echo from the wall facing them? When one of the people crossing behind them spoke, they could only suppose that the sound came from the shadow passing before their eyes.

No doubt.

In every way, then, such prisoners would recognize as reality nothing but the shadows of those artificial objects.

[1][A brother of Plato.—*Ed.*]

[2][A modern Plato would compare his Cave to an underground cinema, where the audience watch the play of shadows thrown by the film passing before a light at their backs. The film itself is only an image of "real" things and events in the world outside the cinema. For the film Plato has to substitute the clumsier apparatus of a procession of artificial objects carried on their heads by persons who are merely part of the machinery, providing for the movement of the objects and the sounds whose echo the prisoners hear. The parapet prevents these persons' shadows from being cast on the wall of the Cave.—*Trans.*]

The Republic of Plato, trans. F. M. Cornford (Oxford: The Clarendon Press, 1941). Reprinted by permission of Oxford University Press.

Inevitably.

Now consider what would happen if their release from the chains and the healing of their unwisdom should come about in this way. Suppose one of them set free and forced suddenly to stand up, turn his head, and walk with eyes lifted to the light; all these movements would be painful, and he would be too dazzled to make out the objects whose shadows he had been used to see. What do you think he would say, if someone told him that what he had formerly seen was meaningless illusion, but now, being somewhat nearer to reality and turned towards more real objects, he was getting a truer view? Suppose further that he were shown the various objects being carried by and were made to say, in reply to questions, what each of them was. Would he not be perplexed and believe the objects now shown him to be not so real as what he formerly saw?

Yes, not nearly so real.

And if he were forced to look at the fire-light itself, would not his eyes ache, so that he would try to escape and turn back to the things which he could see distinctly, convinced that they really were clearer than these other objects now being shown to him?

Yes.

And suppose someone were to drag him away forcibly up the steep and rugged ascent and not let him go until he had hauled him out into the sunlight, would he not suffer pain and vexation at such treatment, and, when he had come out into the light, find his eyes so full of its radiance that he could not see a single one of the things that he was now told were real?

Certainly he would not see them all at once.

He would need, then, to grow accustomed before he could see things in that upper world. At first it would be easiest to make out shadows, and then the images of men and things reflected in water, and later on the things themselves. After that, it would be easier to watch the heavenly bodies and the sky itself by night, looking at the light of the moon and stars rather than the Sun and the Sun's light in the day-time.

Yes, surely.

Last of all, he would be able to look at the Sun and contemplate its nature, not as it appears when reflected in water or any alien medium, but as it is in itself in its own domain.

No doubt.

And now he would begin to draw the conclusion that it is the Sun that produces the seasons and the course of the year and controls everything in the visible world, and moreover is in a way the cause of all that he and his companions used to see.

Clearly he would come at last to that conclusion.

Then if he called to mind his fellow prisoners and what passed for wisdom in his former dwelling-place, he would surely think himself happy in

the change and be sorry for them. They may have had a practice of honour-
ing and commending one another, with prizes for the man who had the
keenest eye for the passing shadows and the best memory for the order in
which they followed or accompanied one another, so that he could make a
good guess as to which was going to come next. Would our released prisoner
be likely to covet those prizes or to envy the men exalted to honour and
power in the Cave? Would he not feel like Homer's Achilles, that he would
far sooner "be on earth as a hired servant in the house of a landless man"
or endure anything rather than go back to his old beliefs and live in the
old way?"

Yes, he would prefer any fate to such a life.

Now imagine what would happen if he went down again to take his
former seat in the Cave. Coming suddenly out of the sunlight, his eyes
would be filled with darkness. He might be required once more to deliver his
opinion on those shadows, in competition with the prisoners who had never
been released, while his eyesight was still dim and unsteady; and it might
take some time to become used to the darkness. They would laugh at him
and say that he had gone up only to come back with his sight ruined; it was
worth no one's while even to attempt the ascent. If they could lay hands on
the man who was trying to set them free and lead them up, they would
kill him.[3]

Yes, they would.

Every feature in this parable, my dear Glaucon, is meant to fit our earlier analysis. The prison dwelling corresponds to the region revealed to us
through the sense of sight, and the fire-light within it to the power of the
Sun. The ascent to see the things in the upper world you may take as standing for the upward journey of the soul into the region of the intelligible; then
you will be in possession of what I surmise, since that is what you wish to
be told. Heaven knows whether it is true; but this, at any rate, is how it
appears to me. In the world of knowledge, the last thing to be perceived and
only with great difficulty is the essential Form of Goodness. Once it is perceived, the conclusion must follow that, for all things, this is the cause of
whatever is right and good; in the visible world it gives birth to light and to
the lord of light, while it is itself sovereign in the intelligible world and the
parent of intelligence and truth. Without having had a vision of this Form no
one can act with wisdom, either in his own life or in matters of state.

So far as I can understand, I share your belief.

Then you may also agree that it is no wonder if those who have reached
this height are reluctant to manage the affairs of men. Their souls long to
spend all their time in that upper world—naturally enough, if here once more
our parable holds true. Nor, again, is it at all strange that one who comes from
the contemplation of divine things to the miseries of human life should

[3][An allusion to the fate of Socrates.— *Trans.*]

appear awkward and ridiculous when, with eyes still dazed and not yet accustomed to the darkness, he is compelled, in a law-court or elsewhere, to dispute about the shadows of justice or the images that cast those shadows, and to wrangle over the notions of what is right in the minds of men who have never beheld Justice itself.

It is not at all strange.

No; a sensible man will remember that the eyes may be confused in two ways—by a change from light to darkness or from darkness to light; and he will recognize that the same thing happens to the soul. When he sees it troubled and unable to discern anything clearly, instead of laughing thoughtlessly, he will ask whether, coming from a brighter existence, its unaccustomed vision is obscured by the darkness, in which case he will think its condition enviable and its life a happy one; or whether, emerging from the depths of ignorance, it is dazzled by excess of light. If so, he will rather feel sorry for it; or, if he were inclined to laugh, that would be less ridiculous than to laugh at the soul which has come down from the light.

That is a fair statement.

If this is true, then, we must conclude that education is not what it is said to be by some, who profess to put knowledge into a soul which does not possess it, as if they could put sight into blind eyes. On the contrary, our own account signifies that the soul of every man does possess the power of learning the truth and the organ to see with; and that, just as one might have to turn the whole body round in order that the eye should see light instead of darkness, so that entire soul must be turned away from this changing world, until its eye can bear to contemplate reality and that supreme splendour which we have called the Good. Hence there may well be an art whose aim would be to effect this very thing, the conversion of the soul, in the readiest way; not to put the power of sight into the soul's eye, which already has it, but to ensure that, instead of looking in the wrong direction, it is turned the way it ought to be.

Yes, it may well be so.

It looks, then, as though wisdom were different from those ordinary virtues, as they are called, which are not far removed from bodily qualities, in that they can be produced by habituation and exercise in a soul which has not possessed them from the first. Wisdom, it seems, is certainly the virtue of some diviner faculty, which never loses its power, though its use for good or harm depends on the direction towards which it is turned. You must have noticed in dishonest men with a reputation for sagacity the shrewd glance of a narrow intelligence piercing the objects to which it is directed. There is nothing wrong with their power of vision, but it has been forced into the service of evil, so that the keener its sight, the more harm it works.

Quite true.

And yet if the growth of a nature like this had been pruned from earliest childhood, cleared of those clinging overgrowths which come of gluttony and all luxurious pleasure and, like leaden weights charged with affinity to this mortal world, hang upon the soul, bending its vision downwards; if, freed from these, the soul were turned round towards true reality, then this same power in these very men would see the truth as keenly as the objects it is turned to now.

Yes, very likely.

Is it not also likely, or indeed certain after what has been said, that a state can never be properly governed either by the uneducated who know nothing of truth or by men who are allowed to spend all their days in the pursuit of culture? The ignorant have no single mark before their eyes at which they must aim in all the conduct of their own lives and of affairs of state; and the others will not engage in action if they can help it, dreaming that, while still alive, they have been translated to the Islands of the Blest.

Quite true.

It is for us, then, as founders of a commonwealth, to bring compulsion to bear on the noblest natures. They must be made to climb the ascent to the vision of Goodness, which we called the highest object of knowledge; and, when they have looked upon it long enough, they must not be allowed, as they now are, to remain on the heights, refusing to come down again to the prisoners or to take any part in their labours and rewards, however much or little these may be worth.

Shall we not be doing them an injustice, if we force on them a worse life than they might have?

You have forgotten again, my friend, that the law is not concerned to make any one class specially happy, but to ensure the welfare of the commonwealth as a whole. By persuasion or constraint it will unite the citizens in harmony, making them share whatever benefits each class can contribute to the common good; and its purpose in forming men of the spirit was not that each should be left to go his own way, but that they should be instrumental in binding the community into one.

True, I had forgotten.

You will see, then, Glaucon, that there will be no real injustice in compelling our philosophers to watch over and care for the other citizens. We can fairly tell them that their compeers in other states may quite reasonably refuse to collaborate: there they have sprung up, like a selfsown plant, in despite of their country's institutions; no one has fostered their growth, and they cannot be expected to show gratitude for a care they have never received. "But," we shall say, "it is not so with you. We have brought you into existence for your country's sake as well as for your own, to be like leaders and king-bees in a hive; you have been better and more thoroughly educated than those others and hence you are more capable of playing your part both as men of thought and as men of action. You must go down, then, each in his turn, to live with the rest and let your eyes grow accustomed to the darkness. You will then see a thousand times better than those who live there always; you will recognize every image for what it is and know what it represents, because you have seen justice, beauty, and goodness in their reality; and so you and we shall find life in our commonwealth no mere dream, as it is in most existing states, where men live fighting one another about shadows and quarrelling for power, as if that were a great prize; whereas in truth government can be at its best and free from dissension only where the destined rulers are least desirous of holding office."

Quite true.

Then will our pupils refuse to listen and to take their turns at sharing in the work of the community, though they may live together for most of their time in a purer air?

No; it is a fair demand, and they are fair-minded men. No doubt, unlike any ruler of the present day, they will think of holding power as an unavoidable necessity.

Yes, my friend; for the truth is that you can have a well-governed society only if you can discover for your future rulers a better way of life than being in office; then only will power be in the hands of men who are rich, not in gold, but in wealth that brings happiness, a good and wise life. All goes wrong when, starved for lack of anything good in their own lives, men turn to public affairs hoping to snatch from thence the happiness they hunger for. They set about fighting for power, and this internecine conflict ruins them and their country. The life of true philosophy is the only one that looks down upon offices of state; and access to power must be confined to men who are not in love with it; otherwise rivals will start fighting. So whom else can you compel to undertake the guardianship of the commonwealth, if not those who, besides understanding best the principles of government, enjoy a nobler life than the politician's and look for rewards of a different kind?

There is indeed no other choice.

Aristotle

Aristotle (384–322 B.C.) was a native of Macedonia. At the age of eighteen he journeyed to Athens and enrolled as a student in the Academy, where he remained for twenty years until the death of Plato. He then moved to Asia Minor to become political adviser to the ruler of a small kingdom. There he married the king's niece. It is said that he spent his honeymoon gathering seashells for use in scientific studies. From Asia Minor he was called back to his native Macedonia to serve as tutor to Alexander (later "the Great"), who was then a boy of twelve. When Alexander set out to conquer the world, Aristotle returned to Athens and established a school of his own, the Lyceum, as a rival to the Academy. For the next eleven years he divided his time among teaching, public lecturing, and writing. His philosophical system is known as the *peripatetic* (or "walking") philosophy, a title derived from his habit of pacing back and forth as he lectured. At the death of Alexander in 323 B.C., Aristotle, because of his former association with the conqueror, found himself unpopular in Athens. Fearing the anger of the mob and remembering the fate of Socrates, he fled the city, not wishing, as he put it, "to give the Athenians a second chance of sinning against philosophy." He died in exile the following year.

Aristotle was a remarkably productive and versatile thinker. His extant works include major treatises on physics, astronomy, zoology, biology, botany, psychology, logic, ethics, metaphysics, political theory, constitutional history, rhetoric, and the theory of art. His influence on intellectual history has been comparable to that of Plato. Wherever his works have been studied, there has been intellectual ferment, activity, and development. Partly as a result of Aristotle's influence, the Muslims of the Near East enjoyed an intellectual golden age while Europe was still deep in the Dark Ages. The rediscovery of Aristotle by Europeans, through their contacts with the Muslims, contributed directly to the cultural awakening in Europe that culminated in the High Middle Ages of the thirteenth century. Although the philosophy of Aristotle has come under increasingly sharp attack since the rise of modern science, many of his main concepts and theories still remain alive and vigorous.

The following selection is from one of Aristotle's major works, *The Politics*. His views in *The Politics* on the social nature of humanity, the purpose of government, and the most desirable kind of society have formed the basis, along with Plato's *Republic*, for almost all subsequent political theory in the West.

1. In your own words, describe the relationship among the individual, the state, and the family according to Aristotle.

2. What kinds of states are there? What are the pros and cons of each?

The Politics

Book I

Every state is a community of some kind, and every community is established with a view to some good; for mankind always act in order to obtain that which they think good. But, if all communities aim at some good, the state or political community, which is the highest of all, and which embraces all the rest, aims, and in a greater degree than any other, at the highest good.

Now there is an erroneous opinion that a statesman, king, householder, and master are the same, and that they differ, not in kind, but only in the number of their subjects. For example, the ruler over a few is called a master; over more, the manager of a household; over a still larger number, a statesman or king, as if there were no difference between a great household and a small state. The distinction which is made between the king and the statesman is as follows: When the government is personal, the ruler is a king; when, according to the principles of the political science, the citizens rule and are ruled in turn, then he is called a statesman.

But all this is a mistake; for governments differ in kind, as will be evident to any one who considers the matter according to the method which has hitherto guided us. As in other departments of science, so in politics, the compound should always be resolved into the simple elements or least parts of the whole. We must therefore look at the elements of which the state is composed, in order that we may see in what they differ from one another, and whether any scientific distinction can be drawn between the different kinds of rule.

He who thus considers things in their first growth and origin, whether a state or anything else, will obtain the clearest view of them. In the first place (1) there must be a union of those who cannot exist without each other; for example, of male and female, that the race may continue; and this is a union which is formed, not of deliberate purpose, but because, in common with other animals and with plants, mankind have a natural desire to leave behind them an image of themselves. And (2) there must be a union of natural ruler and subject, that both may be preserved. For he who can foresee with his mind is by nature intended to be lord and master, and he who can

Trans. B. Jowett.

work with his body is a subject, and by nature a slave; hence master and slave have the same interest. Nature, however, has distinguished between the female and the slave. For she is not niggardly, like the smith who fashions the Delphian knife for many uses; she makes each thing for a single use, and every instrument is best made when intended for one and not for many uses. But among barbarians no distinction is made between women and slaves, because there is no natural ruler among them: they are a community of slaves, male and female. Wherefore the poets say—

"It is meet that Hellenes should rule over barbarians;"

as if they thought that the barbarian and the slave were by nature one.

Out of these two relationships between man and woman, master and slave, the family first arises, and Hesiod is right when he says—

"First house and wife and an ox for the plough,"

for the ox is the poor man's slave. The family is the association established by nature for the supply of men's every day wants, and the members of it are called by Charondas "companions of the cupboard," and by Epimenides the Cretan, "companions of the manger." But when several families are united, and the association aims at something more than the supply of daily needs, then comes into existence the village. And the most natural form of the village appears to be that of a colony from the family, composed of the children and grandchildren, who are said to be "suckled with the same milk." And this is the reason why Hellenic states were originally governed by kings; because the Hellenes were under royal rule before they came together, as the barbarians still are. Every family is ruled by the eldest, and therefore in the colonies of the family the kingly form of government prevailed because they were of the same blood. As Homer says [of the Cyclopes]:—

"Each one gives law to his children and to his wives."

For they lived dispersedly, as was the manner in ancient times. Wherefore men say that the Gods have a king, because they themselves either are or were in ancient times under the rule of a king. For they imagine, not only the forms of the Gods, but their ways of life to be like their own.

When several villages are united in a single community, perfect and large enough to be nearly or quite self-sufficing, the state comes into existence, originating in the bare needs of life, and continuing in existence for the sake of a good life. And therefore, if the earlier forms of society are natural, so is the state, for it is the end of them, and the completed nature is the end. For what each thing is when fully developed, we call its nature, whether we are speaking of a man, a horse, or a family. Besides, the final cause and end of a thing is the best, and to be self-sufficing is the end and the best.

Hence it is evident that the state is a creation of nature, and that man is by nature a political animal. And he who by nature and not by mere accident is without a state, is either above humanity, or below it; he is the

"Tribeless, lawless, heartless one,"

whom Homer denounces—the outcast who is a lover of war; he may be compared to a bird which flies alone.

Now the reason why man is more of a political animal than bees or any other gregarious animals is evident. Nature, as we often say, makes nothing in vain, and man is the only animal whom she has endowed with the gift of speech. And whereas mere sound is but an indication of pleasure or pain, and is therefore found in other animals (for their nature attains to the perception of pleasure and pain and the intimation of them to one another, and no further), the power of speech is intended to set forth the expedient and inexpedient, and likewise the just and the unjust. And it is a characteristic of man that he alone has any sense of good and evil, of just and unjust, and the association of living beings who have this sense makes a family and a state.

Thus the state is by nature clearly prior to the family and to the individual, since the whole is of necessity prior to the part; for example, if the whole body be destroyed, there will be no foot or hand, except in an equivocal sense, as we might speak of a stone hand; for when destroyed the hand will be no better. But things are defined by their working and power; and we ought not to say that they are the same when they are no longer the same, but only that they have the same name. The proof that the state is a creation of nature and prior to the individual is that the individual, when isolated, is not self-sufficing; and therefore he is like a part in relation to the whole. But he who is unable to live in society, or who has no need because he is sufficient for himself, must be either a beast or a god: he is no part of a state. A social instinct is implanted in all men by nature, and yet he who first founded the state was the greatest of benefactors. For man, when perfected, is the best of animals, but, when separated from law and justice, he is the worst of all; since armed injustice is the more dangerous, and he is equipped at birth with the arms of intelligence and with moral qualities which he may use for the worst ends. Wherefore, if he have not virtue, he is the most unholy and the most savage of animals, and the most full of lust and gluttony. But justice is the bond of men in states, and the administration of justice, which is the determination of what is just, is the principle of order in political society.

• • •

Book III

Having determined these questions, we have next to consider whether there is only one form of government or many, and if many, what they are, and how many, and what are the differences between them.

A constitution is the arrangement of magistracies in a State, especially of the highest of all. The government is everywhere sovereign in the State, and the constitution is in fact the government. For example, in democracies the people are supreme, but in oligarchies, the few; and, therefore, we say that these two forms of government are different: and so in other cases.

First, let us consider what is the purpose of a State, and how many forms of government there are by which human society is regulated. We have already said, in the former part of this treatise, when drawing a distinction between household management and the rule of a master, that man is by nature a political animal. And therefore, men, even when they do not require one another's help, desire to live together all the same, and are in fact brought together by their common interests in proportion as they severally attain to any measure of well-being. This is certainly the chief end, both of individuals and of States. And also for the sake of mere life (in which there is possibly some noble element) mankind meet together and maintain the political community, so long as the evils of existence do not greatly overbalance the good. And we all see that men cling to life even in the midst of misfortune, seeming to find in it a natural sweetness and happiness.

There is no difficulty in distinguishing the various kinds of authority; they have been often defined already in popular works. The rule of a master, although the slave by nature and the master by nature have in reality the same interests, is nevertheless exercised primarily with a view to the interest of the master, but accidentally considers the slave, since, if the slave perish, the rule of the master perishes with him. On the other hand, the government of a wife and children and of a household, which we have called household management, is exercised in the first instance for the good of the governed or for the common good of both parties, but essentially for the good of the governed, as we see to be the case in medicine, gymnastic, and the arts in general, which are only accidentally concerned with the good of the artists themselves. (For there is no reason why the trainer may not sometimes practise gymnastics, and the pilot is always one of the crew.) The trainer or the pilot considers the good of those committed to his care. But, when he is one of the persons taken care of, he accidentally participates in the advantage, for the pilot is also a sailor, and the trainer becomes one of those in training. And so in politics: when the State is framed upon the principle of equality and likeness, the citizens think that they ought to hold office by turns. In the order of nature everyone would take his turn of service; and then again, somebody else would look after his interest, just as he, while in office, had looked after theirs. But nowadays, for the sake of the advantage which is to be gained from the public revenues and from office, men want to be always in office. One might imagine that the rulers, being sickly, were only kept in health while they continued in office; in that case we may be sure that they would be hunting after places. The conclusion is evident: that governments, which have a regard to the common interest, are constituted in accordance with strict principles of justice, and are therefore true forms; but those which regard only the interest of the rulers are all defective and perverted forms, for they are despotic, whereas a State is a community of freemen.

Having determined these points, we have next to consider how many forms of government there are, and what they are; and in the first place what are the true forms, for when they are determined the perversions of them will at once be apparent. The words "constitution" and "government" have the same meaning, and the government, which is the supreme authority in States, must be in the hands of one, or of a few, or of many. The true forms of government, therefore, are those in which the one, or the few, or the many, govern with a view to the common interest; but governments which rule with a view to the private interest, whether of the one, or of the few, or of the many, are perversions. For citizens, if they are truly citizens, ought to participate in the advantages of a State. Of forms of government in which one rules, we call that which regards the common interests, kingship or royalty; that in which more than one, but not many, rule, aristocracy [the rule of the best]; and it is so called, either because the rulers are the best men, or because they have at heart the best interests of the State and of the citizens. But when the citizens at large administer the State for the common interest, the government is called by the generic name—a constitution. And there is a reason for this use of language. One man or a few may excel in virtue; but of virtue there are many kinds: and as the number increases it becomes more difficult for them to attain perfection in every kind, though they may in military virtue, for this is found in the masses. Hence, in a constitutional government the fighting-men have the supreme power, and those who possess arms are the citizens.

Of the above mentioned forms, the perversions are as follows:—of royalty, tyranny; of aristocracy, oligarchy; of constitutional government, democracy. For tyranny is a kind of monarchy which has in view the interest of the monarch only; oligarchy has in view the interest of the wealthy democracy, of the needy: none of them the common good of all.

Tyranny, as I was saying, is monarchy exercising the rule of a master over political society; oligarchy is when men of property have the government in their hands; democracy, the opposite, when the indigent, and not the men of property, are the rulers.

● ● ●

But a State exists for the sake of a good life, and not for the sake of life only: if life only were the object, slaves and brute animals might form a State, but they cannot, for they have no share in happiness or in a life of free choice. Nor does a State exist for the sake of alliance and security from injustice, nor yet for the sake of exchange and mutual intercourse; for then the Tyrrhenians and the Carthaginians, and all who have commercial treaties with one another, would be the citizens of one State. True, they have agreements about imports, and engagements that they will do no wrong to one another, and written articles of alliance. But there are no magistracies common to the contracting parties who will enforce their engagements; different States have each their own magistracies. Nor does one State take care that the citizens of the other are such as they ought to be, nor see that those who come under the terms of the treaty do no wrong or wickedness at all, but only that they do no injustice to one another. Whereas, those who care for good government take into consideration [the larger question of] virtue and vice in States. Whence it may be further inferred that virtue must be the serious care of a State which truly deserves the name: for [without this ethical end] the community becomes a mere alliance which differs only in place from alliances of which the members live apart; and law is only a convention, "a surety to one another of justice," as the sophist Lycophron says, and has no real power to make the citizens good and just.

This is obvious; for suppose distinct places, such as Corinth and Megara, to be united by a wall, still they would not be one city, not even if the citizens had the right to intermarry, which is one of the rights peculiarly characteristic of States. Again, if men dwelt at a distance from one another, but not so far off as to have no intercourse, and there were laws among them that they should not wrong each other in their exchanges, neither would this be a State. Let us suppose that one man is a carpenter, another a husbandman, another a shoemaker, and so on, and that their number is ten thousand: nevertheless, if they have nothing in common but exchange, alliance, and the like, that would not constitute a State. Why is this? Surely not because they are at a distance from one another: for even supposing that such a community were to meet in one place, and that each man had a house of his own, which was in a manner his State, and that they made alliance with one another, but only against evil-doers; still an accurate thinker would not deem this to be a State, if their intercourse with one another was of the same character after as before their union. It is clear then that a State is not a mere society, having a common place, established for the prevention of crime and for the sake of exchange. These are conditions without which a State cannot exist; but all of them together do not constitute a State, which is a community of well-being in families and aggregations of families, for the sake of a perfect and self-sufficing life. Such a community can only be established among those who live in the same place and intermarry. Hence arise in cities family connections, brotherhoods, common sacrifices, amusements which draw men together. They are created by friendship, for friendship is the motive of society. The end is the good life, and these are the means towards

it. And the State is the union of families and villages having for an end a perfect and self-sufficing life, by which we mean a happy and honorable life.

Our conclusion, then, is that political society exists for the sake of noble
actions, and not of mere companionship. And they who contribute most to
such a society have a greater share in it than those who have the same or a
greater freedom or nobility of birth but are inferior to them in political
virtue; or than those who exceed them in wealth but are surpassed by them
in virtue.

From what has been said it will be clearly seen that all the partisans of
different forms of government speak of a part of justice only.

There is also a doubt as to what is to be the supreme power in the
State:—Is it the multitude? Or the wealthy? Or the good? Or the one best
man? Or a tyrant? Any of these alternatives seems to involve disagreeable
consequences. If the poor, for example, because they are more in number,
divide among themselves the property of the rich—is not this unjust? No, by
heaven (will be the reply), for the lawful authority [i.e. the people] willed it.
But if this is not injustice, pray what is? Again, when [in the first division] all
has been taken, and the majority divide anew the property of the minority,
is it not evident, if this goes on, that they will ruin the State? Yet surely, virtue
is not the ruin of those who possess her, nor is justice destructive of a State;
and therefore this law of confiscation clearly cannot be just. If it were, all
the acts of a tyrant must of necessity be just; for he only coerces other men
by superior power, just as the multitude coerce the rich. But is it just then
that the few and the wealthy should be the rulers? And what if they, in like
manner, rob and plunder the people—is this just? If so, the other case [i.e.,
the case of the majority plundering the minority] will likewise be just. But
there can be no doubt that all these things are wrong and unjust.

Then ought the good to rule and have supreme power? But in that case
everybody else, being excluded from power, will be dishonored. For the
offices of a State are posts of honor; and if one set of men always hold them,
the rest must be deprived of them. Then will it be well that the one best man
should rule? Nay, that is still more oligarchical, for the number of those who
are dishonored is thereby increased. Some one may say that it is bad for a
man, subject as he is to all the accidents of human passion, to have the
supreme power, rather than the law. But what if the law itself be democrati-
cal or oligarchical, how will that help us out of our difficulties? Not at all; the
same consequences will follow.

Most of these questions may be reserved for another occasion. The
principle that the multitude ought to be supreme rather than the few best is
capable of a satisfactory explanation, and, though not free from difficulty, yet
seems to contain an element of truth. For the many, of whom each individual is but an ordinary person, when they meet together may very likely be
better than the few good, if regarded not individually but collectively, just as
a feast to which many contribute is better than a dinner provided out of

a single purse. For each individual among the many has a share of virtue and prudence, and when they meet together they become in a manner one man, who has many feet, and hands, and senses; that is a figure of their mind and disposition. Hence the many are better judges than a single man of music and poetry; for some understand one part, and some another, and among them, they understand the whole. There is a similar combination of qualities in good men, who differ from any individual of the many, as the beautiful are said to differ from those who are not beautiful, and works of art from realities, because in them the scattered elements are combined, although, if taken separately, the eye of one person or some other feature in another person would be fairer than in the picture.

•••

In all sciences and arts the end is a good, and especially and above all in the highest of all—this is the political science of which the good is justice, in other words, the common interest. All men think justice to be a sort of equality; and to a certain extent they agree in the philosophical distinctions which have been laid down by us about ethics. For they admit that justice is a thing having relation to persons, and that equals ought to have equality. But there still remains a question; equality or inequality of what? here is a difficulty which the political philosopher has to resolve. For very likely some persons will say that offices of State ought to be unequally distributed according to superior excellence, in whatever respect, of the citizen, although there is no other difference between him and the rest of the community; for that those who differ in any one respect have different rights and claims. But, surely, if this is true, the complexion or height of a man, or any other advantage, will be a reason for his obtaining a greater share of political rights. The error here lies upon the surface, and may be illustrated from the other arts and sciences. When a number of flute-players are equal in their art, there is no reason why those of them who are better born should have better flutes given to them; for they will not play any better on the flute, and the superior instrument should be reserved for him who is the superior artist. If what I am saying is still obscure, it will be made clearer as we proceed. For if there were a superior flute-player who was far inferior in birth and beauty, although either of these may be a greater good than the art of flute-playing, and persons gifted with these qualities may excel the flute-player in a greater ratio than he excels them in his art, still he ought to have the best flutes given to him, unless the advantages of wealth and birth contribute to excellence in flute-playing, which they do not. Moreover upon this principle any good may be compared with any other. For if a given height, then height in general may be measured either against height or against freedom. Thus if A excels in height more than B in virtue, and height in general is more excellent than virtue, all things will be commensurable [which is absurd]; for if a certain magnitude is greater than some other, it is clear that some other will be equal. But since no such comparison can be made, it is evident that there is good reason why in politics men do not ground their claim to office on every sort of inequality any more than in the arts. For if some be slow, and others swift, that is no reason why the one should have little and the others much; it is in gymnastic contests that such excellence is rewarded. Whereas the rival claims of candidates for office can only be based on the possession of elements which enter into the composition of a State [such as wealth, virtue, etc.]. And therefore the noble, or free-born, or rich, may with good reason claim office; for holders of offices must be freemen and taxpayers: a State can be no more composed entirely of poor men than entirely of slaves. But if wealth and freedom are necessary elements, justice and valor are equally so; for without the former a State cannot exist at all, without the latter not well.

If the existence of the State is alone to be considered, then it would seem that all, or some at least, of these claims are just; but, if we take into account a good life, as I have already said, education and virtue have superior claims. As, however, those who are equal in one thing ought not to be equal in all, nor those who are unequal in one thing to be unequal in all, it is certain that all forms of government which rest on either of these principles are perversions. All men have a claim in a certain sense, as I have already admitted, but they have not an absolute claim. The rich claim because they have a greater share in the land, and land is the common element of the State; also they are generally more trustworthy in contracts. The free claim under the same title as the noble; for they are nearly akin. And the noble are citizens in a truer sense than the ignoble, since good birth is always valued in a man's own home and country. Another reason is, that those who are sprung from better ancestors are likely to be better men, for nobility is excellence of race. Virtue, too, may be truly said to have a claim, for justice has been acknowledged by us to be a social virtue, and it implies all others. Again, the many urge their claim against the few; for, when taken collectively, and compared with the few, they are stronger and richer and better. But, what if the good, the rich, the noble, and the other classes who make up a State, are all living together in the same city, will there, or will there not, be any doubt who shall rule?—No doubt at all in determining who ought to rule in each of the above-mentioned forms of government. For States are characterized by differences in their governing bodies—one of them has a government of the rich, another of the virtuous, and so on. But a difficulty arises when all these elements coexist. How are we to decide? Suppose the virtuous to be very few in number; may we consider their numbers in relation to their duties, and ask whether they are enough to administer a State, or must they be so many as will make up a State? Objections may be urged against all the aspirants to political power. For those who found their claims on wealth or family have no basis of justice; on this principle, if any one person were richer than all the rest, it is clear that he ought to be the ruler of them. In like manner he who is very distinguished by his birth ought to have the superiority over all those who claim on the ground that they are free-born. In an aristocracy, or government of the best, a like difficulty occurs about virtue; for if one citizen be better than the other members of the government, however good they may be, he too, upon the same principle of justice, should rule over them. And if the people are to be supreme because they are stronger than the few, then if one man, or more than one, but not a majority, is stronger than the many, they ought to rule, and not the many.

Book IV

We have now to inquire what is the best constitution for most States, and the best life for most men, neither assuming a standard of virtue which is above ordinary persons, nor an education which is exceptionally favored by nature and circumstances, nor yet an ideal State which is an aspiration only, but having regard to the life in which the majority are able to share, and to the form of government which States in general can attain. As to those aristocracies, as they are called, of which we were just now speaking, they either lie beyond the possibilities of the greater number of States, or they approximate to the so-called constitutional government, and therefore need no separate discussion. And in fact the conclusion at which we arrive respecting all these forms rests upon the same grounds. For if it has been truly said in the "Ethics" that the happy life is the life according to unimpeded virtue, and that virtue is a mean, then the life which is in a mean, and in a mean attainable by everyone, must be the best.* And the same principles of virtue and vice are characteristic of cities and of constitutions; for the constitution is in a figure the life of a city.

Now in all States there are three elements; one class is very rich, another very poor, and a third in a mean. It is admitted that moderation and the mean are best, and therefore it will clearly be best to possess the gifts of fortune in moderation; for in that condition of life men are most ready to listen to reason. But he who greatly excels in beauty, strength, birth or wealth, or on the other hand who is very poor, or very weak, or very much disgraced, finds it difficult to follow reason. Of these two the one sort grow into violent and great criminals, the others into rogues and petty rascals. And two sorts of offences correspond to them, the one committed from violence, the other from roguery. The petty rogues are disinclined to hold office, whether military or civil, and their aversion to these two duties is as great an injury to the State as their tendency to crime. Again, those who have too much of the goods of fortune, strength, wealth, friends, and the like, are

---

*[Following a middle path between excess and deficiency.—*Ed.*]

neither willing nor able to submit to authority. The evil begins at home: for when they are boys, by reason of the luxury in which they are brought up, they never learn, even at school, the habit of obedience. On the other hand, the very poor, who are in the opposite extreme, are too degraded. So that the one class cannot obey, and can only rule despotically; the other knows not how to command and must be ruled like slaves. Thus arises a city, not of freemen, but of masters and slaves, the one despising, the other envying; and nothing can be more fatal to friendship and good-fellowship in States than this: for good-fellowship tends to friendship; when men are at enmity with one another, they would rather not even share the same path. But a city ought to be composed, as far as possible, of equals and similars; and these are generally the middle classes. Wherefore the city which is composed of middle-class citizens is necessarily best governed; they are, as we say, the natural elements of a State. And this is the class of citizens which is most secure in a State, for they do not, like the poor, covet their neighbors' goods; nor do others covet theirs, as the poor covet the goods of the rich; and as they neither plot against others, nor are themselves plotted against, they pass through life safely. Wisely then did Phocylides pray, "Many things are best in the mean; I desire to be of a middle condition in my city."

Polybius

It is easy to misunderstand what Polybius meant when he wrote that he was going to interrupt his history of Rome to enter on a disquisition "on the Roman constitution." We may think that he will then go on to describe some document comparable to our own Constitution, but this is far from his intent. What Polybius meant by "constitution" is the organization of the Roman people themselves, and particularly of their political powers and relationships. His ultimate aim was to explain the success of the Roman social and political system, and, especially, to account for Rome's quick and phenomenal rise to domination of "nearly the whole world." To do this he chose as his crucial date the very time of one of Rome's greatest military defeats, at the hands of the Carthaginians in 216 B.C.

The social and political structure that Polybius is describing in the following selection is, of course, that of the Roman republic, as it existed more than a century before the revolutions and power struggles that eventuated in a quite different system—that of imperial Rome. Behind the details that he discusses there emerges the picture of an arrangement that bears a curious resemblance to our own; namely, the balance of powers. That the balance, between the Consuls, the Senate, and the people, was a success is amply verified by the longevity and stability of republican Rome. But its very success was a major contributor to its ultimate downfall. Rome became powerful, rich, and increasingly corrupt—so eventually fell prey to adventurers and despots.

Although his exact dates are not known, Polybius was probably born around 200 B.C. He was a Greek from the Peloponnesus. How such a person should come to write the history of Rome is of special interest. As a young man Polybius became a political leader of the Achaean League in southern Greece. Their Roman masters, convinced that the Greeks were plotting to throw off Roman rule, in 168 B.C. arrested one thousand members of the League, including Polybius, and transported them to Italy as hostages. There Polybius remained in exile for the next sixteen years. With his career destroyed and far from his homeland Polybius devoted his time to study. Fortunately, he was sent to Rome where he had ready access to records and documents, so he took that government as the subject of his scholarship. The result was the *Histories*. Polybius was finally set free in 151 B.C. and returned to Greece, where he again became active in political and diplomatic affairs.

1. Using Aristotle's taxonomy of states, what kind of state is Rome as Polybius describes it?

2. Why does Polybius think it is important to study the Roman state?

Histories

Book VI

1. I am aware that some will be at a loss to account for my interrupting the course of my narrative for the sake of entering upon the following disquisition on the Roman constitution. But I think that I have already in many passages made it fully evident that this particular branch of my work was one of the necessities imposed on me by the nature of my original design; and I pointed this out with special clearness in the preface which explained the scope of my history. I there stated that the feature of my work which was at once the best in itself, and the most instructive to the students of it, was that it would enable them to know and fully realise in what manner, and under what kind of constitution, it came about that nearly the whole world fell under the power of Rome in somewhat less than fifty-three years—an event certainly without precedent. This being my settled purpose, I could see no more fitting period than the present for making a pause, and examining the truth of the remarks about to be made on this constitution. In private life if you wish to satisfy yourself as to the badness or goodness of particular persons, you would not, if you wish to get a genuine test, examine their conduct at a time of uneventful repose, but in the hour of brilliant success or conspicuous reverse. For the true test of a perfect man is the power of bearing with spirit and dignity violent changes of fortune. An examination of a constitution should be conducted in the same way: and therefore being unable to find in our day a more rapid or more signal change than that which has happened to Rome, I reserve my disquisition on its constitution for this place. . . .

    What is really educational and beneficial to students of history is the clear view of the causes of events, and the consequent power of choosing the better policy in a particular case. Now in every practical undertaking by a state we must regard as the most powerful agent for success or failure the form of its constitution; for from this as from a fountainhead all conceptions and plans of action not only proceed, but attain their consummation.

• • •

Trans. Evelyn S. Shuckburgh.

11.   . . . I will now endeavour to describe [the constitution] of Rome at the period of their disastrous defeat at Cannae [in 216 B.C.]. . . .

As for the Roman constitution, it had three elements, each of them possessing sovereign powers: and their respective share of power in the whole state had been regulated with such a scrupulous regard to equality and equilibrium, that no one could say for certain, not even a native, whether the constitution as a whole were an aristocracy or democracy or despotism. And no wonder: for if we confine our observation to the power of the Consuls we should be inclined to regard it as despotic; if on that of the Senate, as aristocractic; and if finally one looks at the power possessed by the people it would seem a clear case of democracy. What the exact powers of these several parts were, and still, with slight modifications, are, I will now state.

12.   The Consuls, before leading out the legions, remain in Rome and are supreme masters of the administration. All other magistrates, except the Tribunes, are under them and take their orders. They introduce foreign ambassadors to the Senate; bring matters requiring deliberation before it; and see to the execution of its decrees. If, again, there are any matters of state which require the authorisation of the people, it is their business to see to them, to summon the popular meetings, to bring the proposals before them, and to carry out the decrees of the majority. In the preparations for war, also, and in a word in the entire administration of a campaign, they have all but absolute power. It is competent to them to impose on the allies such levies as they think good, to appoint the Military Tribunes, to make up the roll for soldiers and select those that are suitable. Besides they have absolute power of inflicting punishment on all who are under their command while on active service: and they have authority to expend as much of the public money as they choose, being accompanied by a quaestor who is entirely at their orders. A survey of these powers would in fact justify our describing the constitution as despotic,—a clear case of royal government. Nor will it affect the truth of my description, if any of the institutions I have described are changed in our time, or in that of our posterity: and the same remarks apply to what follows.

13.   The Senate has first of all the control of the treasury, and regulates the receipts and disbursements alike. For the quaestors cannot issue any public money for the various departments of the state without a decree of the Senate, except for the service of the Consuls. The Senate controls also what is by far the largest and most important expenditure, that, namely, which is made by the censors every lustrum for the repair or construction of public buildings; this money cannot be obtained by the censors except by the grant of the Senate. Similarly all crimes committed in Italy requiring a public investigation, such as treason, conspiracy, poisoning, or wilful murder, are in the hands of the Senate. Besides, if any individual or state among the Italian allies requires a controversy to be settled, a penalty to be assessed, help or protection to be afforded,—all this is the province of the Senate.

Or again, outside Italy, if it is necessary to send an embassy to reconcile warring communities, or to remind them of their duty, or sometimes to impose requisitions upon them, or to receive their submission, or finally to proclaim war against them,—this too is the business of the Senate. In like manner the reception to be given foreign ambassadors in Rome, and the answers to be returned to them, are decided by the Senate. With such business the people have nothing to do. Consequently, if one were staying at Rome when the Consuls were not in town, one would imagine the constitution to be a complete aristocracy: and this has been the idea entertained by many Greeks, and by many kings as well, from the fact that nearly all the business they had to do with Rome was settled by the Senate.

14.   After this one would naturally be inclined to ask what part is left for the people in the constitution, when the Senate has these various functions, especially the control of the receipts and expenditure of the exchequer; and when the Consuls, again, have absolute power over the details of military preparation, and an absolute authority in the field? There is, however, a part left the people, and it is a most important one. For the people is the sole fountain of honour and of punishment; and it is by these two things and these alone that dynasties and constitutions and, in a word, human society are held together: for where the distinction between them is not sharply drawn both in theory and practice, there no undertaking can be properly administered,—as indeed we might expect when good and bad are held in exactly the same honour. The people then is the only court to decide matters of life and death; and even in cases where the penalty is money, if the sum to be assessed is sufficiently serious, and especially when the accused have held the higher magistracies. And in regard to this arrangement there is one point deserving especial commendation and record. Men who are on trial for their lives at Rome, while sentence is in process of being voted,—if even only one of the tribes whose votes are needed to ratify the sentence has not voted,—have the privilege at Rome of openly departing and condemning themselves to a voluntary exile. Such men are safe at Naples or Praeneste or at Tibur, and at other towns with which this arrangement has been duly ratified on oath.

Again, it is the people who bestow offices on the deserving, which are the most honourable rewards of virtue. It has also the absolute power of passing or repealing laws; and, most important of all, it is the people who deliberate on the question of peace and war. And when provisional terms are made for alliance, suspension of hostilities, or treaties, it is the people who ratify them or the reverse.

These considerations again would lead one to say that the chief power in the state was the people's, and that the constitution was a democracy.

15.   Such, then, is the distribution of power between the several parts of the state. I must now show how each of these several parts can, when they choose, oppose or support each other.

The Consul, then, when he has started on an expedition with the powers I have described, is to all appearance absolute in the administration of the business in hand; still he has need of the support both of people and Senate, and, without them, is quite unable to bring the matter to a successful conclusion. For it is plain that he must have supplies sent to his legions from time to time; but without a decree of the Senate they can be supplied neither with corn, nor clothes, nor pay, so that all the plans of a commander must be futile, if the Senate is resolved either to shrink from danger or hamper his plans. And again, whether a Consul shall bring any undertaking to a conclusion or no depends entirely on the Senate: for it has absolute authority at the end of a year to send another Consul to supersede him, or to continue the existing one in his command. Again, even to the successes of the generals, the Senate has the power to add distinction and glory, and on the other hand to obscure their merits and lower their credit. For these high achievements are brought in tangible form before the eyes of the citizens by what are called "triumphs." But in these triumphs the commanders cannot celebrate with proper pomp, or in some cases celebrate at all, unless the Senate concurs and grants the necessary money. As for the people, the Consuls are pre-eminently obliged to court their favour, however distant from home may be the field of their operations; for it is the people, as I have said before, that ratifies, or refuses to ratify, terms of peace and treaties; but most of all because when laying down their office they have to give account of their administration before it. Therefore in no case is it safe for the Consuls to neglect either the Senate or the goodwill of the people.

16. As for the Senate, which possesses the immense power I have described, in the first place it is obliged in public affairs to take the multitude into account, and respect the wishes of the people; and it cannot put into execution the penalty for offences against the republic, which are punishable with death, unless the people first ratifies its decrees. Similarly even in matters which directly affect the senators,—for instance, in the case of a law depriving senators of certain dignities and offices, or even actually cutting down their property,—even in such cases the people has the sole power of passing or rejecting the law. But most important of all is the fact that, if the Tribunes interpose their veto, the Senate not only is unable to pass a decree, but cannot even hold a meeting at all, whether formal or informal. Now, the Tribunes are always bound to carry out the decree of the people, and above all things to have regard for their wishes: therefore, for all these reasons the Senate stands in awe of the multitude, and cannot neglect the feelings of the people.

17. In like manner the people on its part is far from being independent of the Senate, and is bound to take its wishes into account both collectively and individually. For contracts, too numerous to count, are given out by the censors in all parts of Italy, for the repairs or construction of public

buildings; there is also the collection of revenue, from many rivers, harbours, gardens, mines, and land—every thing, in a word, that comes under
the control of the Roman government: and in all these the people at large
are engaged; so that there is scarcely a man, so to speak, who is not interested either as a contractor or as being employed in the works. For some
purchase the contracts from the censors for themselves; and others go
partners with them; while others again go security for these contractors, or
actually pledge their property to the treasury for them. Now over all these
transactions the Senate has absolute control. It can grant an extension of
time; and in case of unforeseen accident can relieve the contractors from a
portion of their obligation, or release them from it altogether, if they are
absolutely unable to fill it. And there are many details in which the Senate
can inflict great hardships, or, on the other hand, grant great indulgences to
the contractors: for in every case the appeal is to it. But the most important
point of all is that the judges are taken from its members in the majority of
trials, whether public or private, in which the charges are heavy.
Consequently, all citizens are much at its mercy; and being alarmed at the
uncertainty as to when they may need its aid, are cautious about resisting
or actively opposing its will. And for a similar reason men do not rashly
resist the wishes of the Consuls, because one and all may become subject to
their absolute authority on a campaign.

18.   The result of this power of the several estates for mutual help or
harm is a union sufficiently firm for all emergencies, and a constitution than
which it is impossible to find a better. For whenever any danger from without compels them to unite and work together, the strength which is developed by the State is so extraordinary, that everything required is unfailingly
carried out by the eager rivalry shown by all classes to devote their whole
minds to the needs of the hour, and to secure that any determination come
to should not fail for want of promptitude; while each individual works, privately and publicly alike, for the accomplishment of the business in hand.
Accordingly, the peculiar constitution of the State makes it irresistible, and
certain of obtaining whatever it determines to attempt. Nay, even when
these external alarms are past, and the people are enjoying their good fortune and the fruits of their victories, and, as usually happens, growing corrupted by flattery and idleness, show a tendency to violence and
arrogance,—it is in these circumstances, more than ever, that the constitution
is seen to possess within itself the power of correcting abuses. For when any
one of the three classes becomes puffed up, and manifests an inclination to
be contentious and unduly encroaching, the mutual interdependency of all
the three, and the possibility of the pretentions of any one being checked and
thwarted by the others, must plainly check this tendency: and so the proper
equilibrium is maintained by the impulsiveness of the one part being
checked by its fear of the other.

THE ROMAN REPUBLIC COMPARED WITH OTHERS

51.   Now the Carthaginian constitution seems to me originally to have been well contrived in these most distinctively important particulars. For they had kings, and the Gerusia had the powers of an aristocracy, and the multitude were supreme in such things as affected them; and on the whole the adjustment of its several parts was very like that of Rome and Sparta. But about the period of its entering on the Hannibalian war the political state of Carthage was on the decline, that of Rome improving. For whereas there is in every body, or polity, or business a natural stage of growth, zenith, and decay; and whereas everything in them is best at the zenith; we may thereby judge of the difference between these two constitutions as they existed at that period. For exactly so far as the strength and prosperity of Carthage preceded that of Rome in point of time, by so much was Carthage then past its prime, while Rome was exactly at its zenith, as far as its political constitution was concerned. In Carthage therefore the influence of the people in the policy of the state had already risen to be supreme, while at Rome the Senate was at the height of its power: and so, as in the one measures were deliberated upon by the many, in the other by the best men, the policy of the Romans in all public undertakings proved the stronger; on which account, though they met with capital disasters, by force of prudent counsels they finally conquered the Carthaginians in the war.

52.   If we look however at separate details, for instance at the provisions for carrying on a war, we shall find that whereas for a naval expedition the Carthaginians are the better trained and prepared,—as it is only natural with a people with whom it has been hereditary for many generations to practise this craft, and to follow the seaman's trade above all nations in the world,—yet, in regard to military service on land, the Romans train themselves to a much higher pitch than the Carthaginians. The former bestow their whole attention upon this department: whereas the Carthaginians wholly neglect their infantry, though they do take some slight interest in the cavalry. The reason of this is that they employ foreign mercenaries, the Romans native and citizen levies. It is in this point that the latter policy is preferable to the former. They have their hopes of freedom ever resting on the courage of mercenary troops: the Romans on the valour of their own citizens and the aid of their allies. The result is that even if the Romans have suffered a defeat at first, they renew the war with undiminished forces, which the Carthaginians cannot do. For, as the Romans are fighting for country and children, it is impossible for them to relax the fury of their struggle; but they persist with obstinate resolution until they have overcome their enemies. What has happened in regard to their navy is an instance in point. In skill the Romans are much behind the Carthaginians, as I have already said; yet the upshot of the whole naval war has been a decided triumph for the Romans, owing to the valour of their men. For although nautical science

contributes largely to success in sea-fights, still it is the courage of the marines that turns the scale most decisively in favour of victory. The fact is that Italians as a nation are by nature superior to Phoenicians and Libyans both in physical strength and courage; but still their habits also do much to inspire the youth with enthusiasm for such exploits. One example will be sufficient of the pains taken by the Roman state to turn out men ready to endure anything to win a reputation in their country for valour.

53. Whenever one of their illustrious men dies, in the course of his funeral, the body with all its paraphernalia is carried into the forum to the Rostra, as a raised platform there is called, and sometimes is propped upright upon it so as to be conspicuous, or, more rarely, is laid upon it. Then with all the people standing round, his son, if he has left one of full age and he is there, or, failing him, one of his relations, mounts the Rostra and delivers a speech concerning the virtues of the deceased, and the successful exploits performed by him in his lifetime. By these means the people are reminded of what has been done, and made to see it with their own eyes,— not only such as were engaged in the actual transactions but those also who were not;—and their sympathies are so deeply moved, that the loss appears not to be confined to the actual mourners, but to be a public one affecting the whole people. After the burial and all the usual ceremonies have been performed, they place the likeness of the deceased in the most conspicuous spot in his house, surmounted by a wooden canopy or shrine. This likeness consists of a mask made to represent the deceased with extraordinary fidelity both in shape and colour. These likenesses they display at public sacrifices adorned with much care. And when any illustrious member of the family dies, they carry these masks to the funeral, putting them on men whom they thought as like the originals as possible in height and other personal peculiarities. And these substitutes assume clothes according to the rank of the person represented; if he was a consul or praetor, a toga with purple stripes; if a censor, whole purple; if he had also celebrated a triumph or performed any exploit of that kind, a toga embroidered with gold. These representatives also ride themselves in chariots, while the fasces and axes, and all the other customary insignia of the particular offices, lead the way, according to the dignity of the rank in the state enjoyed by the deceased in his lifetime; and on arriving at the Rostra they all take their seats on ivory chairs in their order. There could not easily be a more inspiring spectacle than this for a young man of noble ambitions and virtuous aspirations. For can we conceive any one to be unmoved at the sight of all the likenesses collected together of the men who have earned glory, all as if they were living and breathing? Or what could be a more glorious spectacle?

54. Besides, the speaker over the body about to be buried, after having finished the panegyric of this particular person, starts upon the others whose representatives are present, beginning with the most ancient, and recounts the successes and achievements of each. By this means the glorious

memory of brave men is continually renewed; the fame of those who have performed any noble deed is never allowed to die; and the renown of those who have done good service to their country becomes a matter of common knowledge to the multitude, and part of the heritage of posterity. But the chief benefit of the ceremony is that it inspires young men to shrink from no exertion for the general welfare, in the hope of obtaining the glory which awaits the brave. And what I say is confirmed by this fact. Many Romans have volunteered to decide a whole battle by single combat; not a few have deliberately accepted certain death, some in time of war to secure the safety of the rest, some in time of peace to preserve the safety of the common-wealth. There have also been instances of men in office putting their own sons to death, in defiance of every custom and law, because they rated the interests of their country higher than those of natural ties even with their nearest and dearest. There are many stories of this kind, related of many men in Roman history; but one will be enough for our present purpose; and I will give the name as an instance to prove the truth of my words.

55.   The story goes that Horatius Cocles, while fighting with two ene-mies at the head of the bridge over the Tiber, which is the entrance to the city on the north, seeing a large body of men advancing to support his enemies, and fearing that they would force their way into the city, turned round, and shouted to those behind him to hasten back to the other side and break down the bridge. They obeyed him: and whilst they were breaking the bridge, he remained at his post receiving numerous wounds, and checked the progress of the enemy: his opponents being panic stricken, not so much by his strength as by the audacity with which he held his ground. When the bridge had been broken down, the attack of the enemy was stopped; and Cocles then threw himself into the river with his armour on and deliberately sacri-ficed his life, because the valued the safety of his country and his own future reputation more highly than his present life, and the years of existence that remained to him. Such is the enthusiasm and emulation for noble deeds that are engendered among the Romans by their customs.

56.   Again the Roman customs and principles regarding money trans-actions are better than those of the Carthaginians. In the view of the latter nothing is disgraceful that makes for gain; with the former nothing is more disgraceful than to receive bribes and to make profit by improper means. For they regard wealth obtained form unlawful transactions to be as much a subject of reproach, as a fair profit from the most unquestioned source is of commendation. A proof of the fact is this. The Carthaginians obtain office by open bribery, but among the Romans the penalty for it is death. With such a radical difference, therefore, between the rewards offered to virtue among the two people, it is natural that the ways adopted for obtaining them should be different also.

But the most important difference for the better which the Roman commonwealth appears to me to display is in their religious beliefs. For

I conceive that what in other nations is looked upon as a reproach, I mean a scrupulous fear of the gods, is the very thing which keeps the Roman Commonwealth together. To such an extraordinary height is this carried among them, both in private and public business, that nothing could exceed it. Many people might think this unaccountable; but in my opinion their object is to use it as a check upon the common people. If it were possible to form a state wholly of philosophers, such a custom would perhaps be unnecessary. But seeing that every multitude is fickle, and full of lawless desires, unreasoning anger, and violent passion, the only resource is to keep them in check by mysterious terrors and scenic effects of this sort. Wherefore, to my mind, the ancients were not acting without purpose or at random, when they brought in among the vulgar those opinions about the gods, and the belief in the punishments in Hades: much rather do I think that men nowadays are acting rashly and foolishly in rejecting them. This is the reason why, apart from anything else, Greek statesmen, if entrusted with a single talent, though protected by ten checking-clerks, as many seals, and twice as many witnesses, yet cannot be induced to keep faith: whereas among the Romans, in their magistracies and embassies, men have the handling of a great amount of money, and yet from pure respect to their oath keep their faith intact. And, again, in other nations it is a rare thing to find a man who keeps his hands out of the public purse, and is entirely pure in such matters: but among the Romans it is a rare thing to detect a man in the act of committing such a crime.

Suetonius

Julius Caesar was one of the most successful military men of all times. More than that, he was an extraordinarily popular political leader. As a conqueror he dramatically expanded the Roman Empire and in doing so brought the benefits of Roman civilization to large areas, particularly of Western Europe, that were then culturally primitive. As a statesman he enacted a series of laws that substantially benefited the soldiers and ordinary citizens but he did so often at the expense of the liberties that the people had enjoyed under the republic. In any event, Caesar held power for only two years after his return to Rome after his military adventures in Western Europe and the Near East, before being assassinated by his political enemies.

We know a good deal about the life and character of Caesar, thanks mainly to the writings of two gifted biographers—Plutarch and Suetonius—both of whom lived about a hundred years after the death of their subject. Little is known about Suetonius, from whom the following selection is taken, except that he was at one time secretary to the emperor Hadrian. The biography, which is part of a larger work, *Lives of the Caesars*, is by no means adulatory; indeed, the author often seems intent on destroying the reputation of Caesar. On the other hand he is generous in his estimate of Caesar's strengths. Above all the entire piece gives a vivid picture of the political intrigues, turbulence, and violence of the years of the decline and collapse of republican Rome.

---

1. How have the checks and balances in the Roman state as described by Polybius broken down?

2. Is Rome still a republic after Caesar wins the civil wars? Why or why not?

The Lives of the Caesars

Book I

The Deified Julius

•••

Backed by his father-in-law and son-in-law, out of all the numerous provinces [Caesar] made the Gauls his choice, as the most likely to enrich him and furnish suitable material for triumphs. At first, it is true, by the bill of Vatinius he received only Cisalpine Gaul* with the addition of Illyricum; but presently he was assigned Gallia Comata as well by the senate, since the members feared that even if they should refuse it, the people would give him this also. Transported with joy at this success, he could not keep from boasting a few days later before a crowded house, that having gained his heart's desire to the grief and lamentation of his opponents, he would therefore from that time mount on their heads; and when someone insultingly remarked that that would be no easy matter for any woman, he replied in the same vein that Semiramis too had been queen in Syria and the Amazons in days of old had held sway over a great part of Asia.

When at the close of his consulship the praetors Gaius Memmius and Lucius Domitius moved an inquiry into his conduct the previous year, Caesar laid the matter before the senate; and when they failed to take it up, and three days had been wasted in fruitless wrangling, went off to his province. Whereupon his quaestor was at once arraigned on several counts, as a preliminary to his own impeachment. Presently he himself too was prosecuted by Lucius Antistius, tribune of the commons, and it was only by appealing to the whole college that he contrived not to be brought to trial, on the ground that he was absent on public service. Then to secure himself for the future, he took great pains always to put the magistrates for the year under personal obligation, and not to aid any candidates or suffer any to be elected, save as guaranteed to defend him in his absence. And he did not hesitate in some cases to exact an oath to keep this pledge or even a written contract.

When however Lucius Domitius, candidate for the consulship, openly threatened to effect as consul what he had been unable to do as praetor, and to take his armies from him, Caesar compelled Pompeius and Crassus to come to Luca, a city in his province, where he prevailed on them to stand for a second consulship, to defeat Domitius; and he also succeeded through their influence in having his term as governor of Gaul made five years longer. Encouraged by this, he added to the legions which he had received from the state others at his own cost, one actually composed of men of Transalpine Gaul and bearing a Gallic name too (for it was called Alauda), which he trained in the Roman tactics and equipped with Roman arms; and later on he gave every man of it citizenship. After that he did not let slip any pretext for war, however unjust and dangerous it might be, picking quarrels as well with allied as with hostile and barbarous nations; so that once the senate decreed that a commission be sent to inquire into the condition of the Gallic provinces, and some even recommended that Caesar be handed over to the enemy. But as his enterprises prospered, thanksgivings were appointed in his honour oftener and for longer periods than for anyone before his time.

*[Roughly Northern Italy.—Ed.]
Trans. J. C. Rolfe.

During the nine years of his command this is in substance what he did. All that part of Gaul which is bounded by the Pyrenees, the Alps and the Cevennes, and by the Rhine and Rhone rivers, a circuit of some thirty-two hundred miles, with the exception of some allied states which had rendered him good service, he reduced to the form of a province; and imposed upon it a yearly tribute of forty million sesterces. He was the first Roman to build a bridge and attack the Germans beyond the Rhine, and he inflicted heavy losses upon them. He invaded the Britons too, a people unknown before, vanquished them, and exacted moneys and hostages. Amid all these successes he met with adverse fortune but three times in all: in Britain, where his fleet narrowly escaped destruction in a violent storm; in Gaul, when one of his legions was routed at Gergovia; and on the borders of Germany, when his lieutenants Titurius and Aurunculeius were ambushed and slain.

Within this same space of time he lost first his mother, then his daughter, and soon afterwards his grandchild. Meanwhile, as the community was aghast at the murder of Publius Clodius, the senate had voted that only one consul should be chosen, and expressly named Gnaeus Pompeius. When the tribunes planned to make him Pompey's colleague, Caesar urged them rather to propose to the people that he be permitted to stand for a second consulship without coming to Rome, when the term of his governorship drew near its end, to prevent his being forced for the sake of the office to leave his province prematurely and without finishing the war. On the granting of this, aiming still higher and flushed with hope, he neglected nothing in the way of lavish expenditure or of favours to anyone, either in his public capacity or privately. He began a forum with the proceeds of his spoils, the ground for which cost more than a hundred million sesterces. He announced a combat of gladiators and a feast for the people in memory of his daughter, a thing quite without precedent. To raise the expectation of these events to the highest possible pitch, he had the material for the banquet prepared in part by his own household, although he had let contracts to the markets as well. He gave orders too that whenever famous gladiators fought without winning the favour of the people, they should be rescued by force and kept for him. He had the novices trained, not in a gladiatorial school by professionals, but in private houses by Roman knights and even by senators who were skilled in arms, earnestly beseeching them, as is shown by his own letters, to give the recruits individual attention and personally direct their exercises. He doubled the pay of the legions for all time. Whenever grain was plentiful, he distributed it to them without stint or measure, and now and then gave each man a slave from among the captives.

Moreover, to retain his relationship and friendship with Pompey, Caesar offered him his sister's granddaughter Octavia in marriage, although she was already the wife of Gaius Marcellus, and asked for the hand of

Pompey's daughter, who was promised to Faustus Sulla. When he had put all Pompey's friends under obligation, as well as the great part of the senate, through loans made without interest or at a low rate, he lavished gifts on men of all other classes, both those whom he invited to accept his bounty and those who applied to him unasked, including even freedmen and slaves who were special favourites of their masters or patrons. In short, he was the sole and ever ready help of all who were in legal difficulties or in debt and of young spendthrifts, excepting only those whose burden of guilt or of poverty was so heavy, or who were so given up to riotous living, that even he could not save them; and to these he declared in the plainest terms that what they needed was a civil war.

He took no less pains to win the devotion of princes and provinces all over the world, offering prisoners to some by the thousand as a gift, and sending auxiliary troops to the aid of others whenever they wished, and as often as they wished, without the sanction of the senate or people, besides adorning the principal cities of Asia and Greece with magnificent public works, as well as those of Italy and the provinces of Gaul and Spain. At last, when all were thunderstruck at his actions and wondered what their purpose could be, the consul Marcus Claudius Marcellus, after first making proclamation that he purposed to bring before the senate a matter of the highest public moment, proposed that a successor to Caesar be appointed before the end of his term, on the ground that the war was ended, peace was established, and the victorious army ought to be disbanded; also that no account be taken of Caesar at the elections, unless he were present, since Pompey's subsequent action had not annulled the decree of the people. And it was true that when Pompey proposed a bill touching the privileges of officials, in the clause where he debarred absentees from candidacy for office he forgot to make a special exception in Caesar's case, and did not correct the oversight until the law had been inscribed on a tablet of bronze and deposited in the treasury. Not content with depriving Caesar of his provinces and his privilege, Marcellus also moved that the colonists whom Caesar had settled in Novum Comum by the bill of Vatinius should lose their citizenship, on the ground that it had been given from political motives and was not authorized by the law.

Greatly troubled by these measures, and thinking, as they say he was often heard to remark, that now that he was the leading man of the state, it was harder to push him down from the first place to the second than it would be from the second to the lowest, Caesar stoutly resisted Marcellus, partly through vetoes of the tribunes and partly through the other consul, Servius Sulpicius. When next year Gaius Marcellus, who had succeeded his cousin Marcus as consul, tried the same thing, Caesar by a heavy bribe secured the support of the other consul, Aemilius Paulus, and of Gaius Curio, the most reckless of the tribunes. But seeing that everything was being pushed most persistently, and that even the consuls-elect were among the opposition, he sent a written appeal to the senate, not to take from him the privilege which the people had granted, or else to compel the others in command of armies to resign also; feeling sure, it was thought, that he could more readily muster his veterans as soon as he wished, than Pompey his newly levied troops. He further proposed a compromise to his opponents, that after giving up eight legions and Transalpine Gaul, he be allowed to keep two legions and Cisalpine Gaul, or at least one legion and Illyricum, until he was elected consul.

But when the senate declined to interfere, and his opponents declared that they would accept no compromise in a matter affecting the public welfare, he crossed to Hither Gaul, and after holding all the assizes, halted at Ravenna, intending to resort to war if the senate took any drastic action against the tribunes of the commons who interposed vetoes in his behalf. Now this was his excuse for the civil war, but it is believed that he had other motives. Gnaeus Pompeius used to declare that since Caesar's own means were not sufficient to complete the works which he had planned, nor to do all that he had led the people to expect on his return, he desired a state of general unrest and turmoil. Others say that he dreaded the necessity of rendering an account for what he had done in his first consulship contrary to the auspices and the laws, and regardless of vetoes; for Marcus Cato often declared, and took oath too, that he would impeach Caesar the moment he had disbanded his army. It was openly said too that if he was out of office on his return, he would be obliged, like Milo, to make his defence in a court hedged about by armed men. The latter opinion is the more credible one in view of the assertion of Asinius Pollio, that when Caesar at the battle of Pharsalus saw his enemies slain or in flight, he said, word for word: "They would have it so. Even I, Gaius Caesar, after so many great deeds, should have been found guilty, if I had not turned to my army for help." Some think that habit had given him a love of power, and that weighing the strength of his adversaries against his own, he grasped the opportunity of usurping the depotism which had been his heart's desire from early youth. Cicero too was seemingly of this opinion, when he wrote in the third book of his *De Officiis* that Caesar ever had upon his lips these lines of Euripides, of which Cicero himself adds a version:—

If wrong may e'er be right, for a throne's sake
Were wrong most right:—be God in all else feared.

Accordingly, when word came that the veto of the tribunes had been set aside and they themselves had left the city, he at once sent on a few cohorts with all secrecy, and then, to disarm suspicion, concealed his purpose by appearing at a public show, inspecting the plans of a gladiatorial school which he intended building, and joining as usual in a banquet with a large company. It was not until after sunset that he set out very privily with a small company, taking the mules from a bakeshop hard by and harnessing them to a carriage; and when his lights went out and he lost his way, he was astray for some time, but at last found a guide at dawn and got back to the road on foot by narrow by-paths. Then, overtaking his cohorts at the river Rubicon, which was the boundary of his province, he paused for a while, and realising what a step he was taking, he turned to those about him and said: "Even yet we may draw back; but once cross yon little bridge, and the whole issue is with the sword."

As he stood in doubt, this sign was given him. On a sudden there appeared hard by a being of wondrous stature and beauty, who sat and played upon a reed; and when not only the shepherds flocked to hear him, but many of the soldiers left their posts, and among them some of the trumpeters, the apparition snatched a trumpet from one of them, rushed to the river, and sounding the war-note with mightly blast, strode to the opposite bank. Then Caesar cried: "Take we the course which the signs of the gods and the false dealing of our foes point out. The die is cast," said he.

Accordingly, crossing with his army, and welcoming the tribunes of the commons, who had come to him after being driven from Rome, he harangued the soldiers with tears, and rending his robe from his breast besought their faithful service. It is even thought that he promised every man a knight's estate, but that came of a misunderstanding; for since he often pointed to the finger of his left hand as he addressed them and urged them on, declaring that to satisfy all those who helped him to defend his honor he would gladly tear his very ring from his hand, those on the edge of the assembly, who could see him better than they could hear his words, assumed that he said what his gesture seemed to mean; and so the report went about that he had promised them the right of the ring and four hundred thousand sesterces as well.

The sum total of his movements after that is, in their order, as follows: He overran Umbria, Picenum, and Etruria, took prisoner Lucius Domitius, who had been irregularly named his successor, and was holding Corfinium with a garrison, let him go free, and then proceeded along the Adriatic to Brundisium, where Pompey and the consuls had taken refuge, intending to cross the sea as soon as might be. After vainly trying by every kind of hindrance to prevent their sailing, he marched off to Rome, and after calling the senate together to discuss public business, went to attack Pompey's strongest forces, which were in Spain under command of three of his lieutenants—Marcus Petreius, Lucius Afranius, and Marcus Varro—saying to his friends before he left, "I go to meet an army without a leader, and I shall return to meet a leader without an army." And in fact, though his advance was delayed by the siege of Massilia, which had shut its gates against him, and by extreme scarcity of supplies, he nevertheless quickly gained a complete victory.

Returning thence to Rome, he crossed into Macedonia, and after blockading Pompey for almost four months behind mighty ramparts, finally routed him in the battle at Pharsalus, followed him in his flight to Alexandria, and when he learned that his rival had been slain, made war on King Ptolemy, whom he perceived to be plotting against his own safety as well; a war in truth of great difficulty, conveninent neither in time nor place, but carried on during the winter season, within the walls of a well-provisioned and crafty foeman, while Caesar himself was without supplies of any kind and ill-prepared. Victor in spite of all, he turned over the rule of Egypt to Cleopatra and her young brother, fearing that if he made a province of it, it might one day under a headstrong governor be a source of revolution. From Alexandria he crossed to Syria, and from there went to Pontus, spurred on by the news that Pharnaces, son of Mithridates the Great, had taken advantage of the situation to make war, and was already flushed with numerous successes; but Caesar vanquished him in a single battle within five days after his arrival and four hours after getting sight of him, often remarking on Pompey's good luck in gaining his principal fame as a general by victories over such feeble foemen. Then he overcame Scipio and Juba, who were patching up the remnants of their party in Africa, and the sons of Pompey in Spain.

In all the civil wars he suffered not a single disaster except through his lieutenants, of whom Gaius Curio perished in Africa, Gaius Antonius fell into the hands of the enemy in Illyricum, Publius Dolabella lost a fleet also off Illyricum, and Gnaeus Domitius Calvinus an army in Pontus. Personally he always fought with the utmost success, and the issue was never even in doubt save twice: once at Dyrrachium, where he was put to flight, and said of Pompey, who failed to follow up his success, that he did not know how to use a victory; again in Spain, in the final struggle, when, believing the battle lost, he actually thought of suicide.

Having ended the wars, he celebrated five triumphs, four in a single month, but at intervals of a few days, after vanquishing Scipio; and another on defeating Pompey's sons. The first and most splendid was the Gallic triumph, the next the Alexandrian, then the Pontic, after that the African, and finally the Spanish, each differing from the rest in its equipment and display of spoils. As he rode through the Velabrum on the day of his Gallic triumph, the axle of his chariot broke, and he was all but thrown out; and he mounted the Capitol by torchlight, with forty elephants bearing lamps on his right and his left. In his Pontic triumph he displayed among the show-pieces of the procession an inscription of but three words, "I came, I saw, I conquered," not indicating the events of the war, as the others did, but the speed with which it was finished.

To each and every foot-soldier of his veteran legions he gave twenty-four thousand sesterces by way of booty, over and above the two thousand apiece which he had paid them at the beginning of the civil strife. He also assigned them lands, but not side by side, to avoid dispossessing any of the former owners. To every man of the people, besides ten pecks of grain and the same number of pounds of oil, he distributed the three hundred sesterces which he had promised at first, and one hundred apiece to boot because of the delay. He also remitted a year's rent in Rome to tenants who paid two thousand sesterces or less, and in Italy up to five hundred sesterces. He added a banquet and a dole of meat, and after his Spanish victory two dinners; for deeming that the former of these had not been served with a liberality creditable to his generosity, he gave another five days later on a most lavish scale.

He gave entertainments of divers kinds: a combat of gladiators and also stage-plays in every ward all over the city, peformed too by actors of all languages, as well as races in the circus, athletic contests, and a sham sea-fight. In the gladiatorial contest in the Forum, Furius Leptinus, a man of praetorian stock, and Quintus Calpenus, a former senator and pleader at the bar, fought to a finish. A Pyrrhic dance was performed by the sons of the princes of Asia and Bithynia. During the plays Decimus Laberius, a Roman Knight, acted a farce of his own composition, and having been presented with five hundred thousand sesterces and a gold ring, passed from the stage through the orchestra and took his place in the fourteen rows. For the races the circus was lengthened at either end and a broad canal was dug all about it; then young men of the highest rank drove four-horse and two-horse chariots and rode pairs of horses, vaulting from one to the other. The game called Troy was performed by two troops, of younger and of older boys. Combats with wild beasts were presented on five successive days, and last of all there was a battle between two opposing armies, in which five hundred foot-soldiers, twenty elephants and thirty horsemen engaged on each side. To make room for this, the goals were taken down and in their place two camps were pitched over against each other. The athletic competitions lasted for three days in a temporary stadium built for the purpose in the region of the Campus Martius. For the naval battle a pool was dug in the lesser Codeta and there was a contest of ships of two, three, and four banks of oars, belonging to the Tyrian and Egyptian fleets, manned by a large force of fighting men. Such a throng flocked to all these shows from every quarter, that many strangers had to lodge in tents pitched in the streets or along the roads, and the press was often such that many were crushed to death, including two senators.

Then turning his attention to the reorganisation of the state, he reformed the calendar, which the negligence of the pontiffs had long since so disordered, through their privilege of adding months or days at pleasure, that the harvest festivals did not come in summer nor those of the vintage in the autumn; and he adjusted the year to the sun's course by making it consist of three hundred and sixty-five days, abolishing the intercalary month, and adding one day every fourth year. Furthermore, that the correct reckoning of seasons might begin with the next Kalends of January, he inserted two other months between those of November and December; hence the year in which these arrangements were made was one of fifteen months, including the intercalary month, which belonged to that year according to the former custom.

He filled the vacancies in the senate, enrolled additional particians, and increased the number of praetors, aediles, and quaestors, as well as of the minor officials; he reinstated those who had been degraded by official action of the censors or found guilty of bribery by verdict of the jurors. He shared the elections with the people on this basis: that except in the case of the consulship, half of the magistrates should be appointed by the people's choice, while the rest should be those whom he had personally nominated. And these he announced in brief notes like the following, circulated in each tribe: "Caesar the Dictator to this or that tribe. I commend to you so and so, to hold their positions by your votes." He admitted to office even the sons of those who had been proscribed. He limited the right of serving as jurors to two classes, the equestrain and senatorial orders, disqualifying the third class, the tribunes of the treasury.

He made the enumeration of the people neither in the usual manner nor place, but from street to street aided by the owners of blocks of houses, and reduced the number of those who received grain at public expense from three hundred and twenty thousand to one hundred and fifty thousand. And to prevent the calling of additional meetings at any future time for purposes of enrollment, he provided that the places of such as died should be filled each year by the praetors from those who were not on the list.

Moreover, to keep up the population of the city, depleted as it was by the assignment of eighty thousand citizens to colonies across the sea, he made a law that no citizen older than twenty or younger than forty, who was not detained by service in the army, should be absent from Italy for more than three successive years; that no senator's son should go abroad except as the companion of a magistrate or on his staff; and that those who made a business of grazing should have among their herdsmen at least one-third who were men of free birth. He conferred citizenship on all who practised medicine at Rome, and on all teachers of the liberal arts, to make them more desirous of living in the city and to induce others to resort to it.

As to debts, he disappointed those who looked for their cancellation, which was often agitated, but finally decreed that the debtors should satisfy their creditors according to a valuation of their possessions at the price which they had paid for them before the civil war, deducting from the principal whatever interest had been paid in cash or pledged through bankers; an arrangement which wiped out about a fourth part of their indebtedness. He dissolved all guilds, except those of ancient foundation. He increased the penalties for crimes; and inasmuch as the rich involved themselves in guilt with less hesitation because they merely suffered exile, without any loss of property, he punished murderers of freemen by the confiscation of all their goods, as Cicero writes, and others by the loss of one-half.

He administered justice with the utmost conscientiousness and strictness. Those convicted of extortion he even dismissed from the senatorial order. He annulled the marriage of an ex-praetor, who had married a woman the very day after her divorce, although there was no suspicion of adultery. He imposed duties on foreign wares. He denied the use of litters and the wearing of scarlet robes or pearls to all except to those of a designated position and age, and on set days. In particular he enforced the law against extravagance, setting watchmen in various parts of the market, to seize and bring to him dainties which were exposed for sale in violation of the law; and sometimes he sent his lictors and soldiers to take from a dining-room any articles which had escaped the vigilance of his watchmen, even after they had been served.

In particular, for the adornment and convenience of the city, also for the protection and extension of the Empire, he formed more projects and more extensive ones every day: first of all, to rear a temple to Mars, greater than any in existence, filling up and levelling the pool in which he had exhibited the sea-fight, and to build a theatre of vast size, sloping down from the Tarpeian rock; to reduce the civil code to fixed limits, and of the vast and prolix mass of statutes to include only the best and most essential in a limited number of volumes; to open to the public the greatest possible libraries of Greek and Latin books, assigning to Marcus Varro the charge of procuring and classifying them; to drain the Pomptine marshes; to let out the water from Lake Fucinus; to make a highway from the Adriatic across the summit of the Apennines as far as the Tiber; to cut a canal through the Isthmus; to check the Dacians, who had poured into Pontus and Thrace; then to make war on the Parthians by way of Lesser Armenia, but not to risk a battle with them until he had first tested their mettle.

All these enterprises and plans were cut short by his death. But before I speak of that, it will not be amiss to describe briefly his personal appearance, his dress, his mode of life, and his character, as well as his conduct in civil and military life.

He is said to have been tall of stature, with a fair complexion, shapely limbs, a somewhat full face, and keen black eyes; sound of health, except that towards the end he was subject to sudden fainting fits and to nightmare as well. He was twice attacked by the falling sickness during his campaigns. He was somewhat over-nice in the care of his person, being not only carefully trimmed and shaved, but even having superfluous hair plucked out, as some have charged; while his baldness was a disfigurement which troubled him greatly, since he found that it was often the subject of the gibes of his detractors. Because of it he used to comb forward his scanty locks from the crown of his head, and of all the honours voted him by the senate people there was none which he received or made use of more gladly than the privilege of wearing a laurel wreath at all times. They say, too, that he was remarkable in his dress; that he wore a senator's tunic with fringed sleeves reaching to the wrist, and always had a girdle over it, though rather a loose one; and this, they say, was the occasion of Sulla's *mot*, when he often warned the nobles to keep an eye on the ill-girt boy.

He lived at first in the Subura in a modest house, but after he became pontifex maximus, in the official residence of the Sacred Way. Many have written that he was very fond of elegance and luxury; that having laid the foundations of a country-house on his estate at Nemi and finished it at great cost, he tore it all down because it did not suit him in every particular, although at the time he was still poor and heavily in debt; and that he carried tessellated and mosaic floors about with him on his campaigns.

They say that he was led to invade Britain by the hope of getting pearls, and that in comparing their size he sometimes weighted them with his own hand; that he was always a most enthusiastic collector of gems, carvings, statues, and pictures by early artists; also of slaves of exceptional figure and training at enormous prices, of which he himself was so ashamed that he forbade their entry in his accounts.

It is futher reported that in the provinces he gave banquets constantly in two dining-halls, in one of which his officers of Greek companions, in the other Roman civilians and the more distinguished of the provincials reclined at table. He was so punctilious and strict in the management of his household, in small matters as well as in those of greater importance, that he put his baker in irons for serving him with one kind of bread and his guests with another; and he inflicted capital punishment on a favorite freedman for adultery with the wife of a Roman knight, although no complaint was made against him.

There was no stain on his reputation for chastity except his intimacy with King Nicomedes, but that was a deep and lasting reproach, which laid him open to insults from every quarter. I say nothing of the notorious lines of Licinius Calvus:

Whate'er Bithynia had, and Caesar's paramour.

I pass over, too, the invectives of Dolabella and the elder Curio, in which Dolabella calls him "the queen's rival, the inner partner of the royal couch," and Curio, "the brothel of Nicomedes and the stew of Bithynia." I take no account of the edicts of Bibulus, in which he posted his colleague as "the queen of Bithynia," saying that "of yore he was enamoured of a king, but now of a king's estate." At this same time, so Marcus Brutus declares, one Octavius, a man whose disordered mind made him somewhat free with his tongue, after saluting Pompey as "king" in a crowded assembly, greeted Caesar as "queen." But Gaius Memmius makes the direct charge that he acted as cupbearer to Nicomedes with the rest of his wantons at a large dinner party, and that among the guests were some merchants from Rome, whose names Memmius gives. Cicero, indeed, is not content with having written in sundry letters that Caesar was led by the king's attendants to the royal apartments, that he lay on a golden couch arrayed in purple, and that the virginity of this son of Venus was lost in Bithynia; but when Caesar was once addressing the senate in defence of Nysa, daughter of Nicomedes, and was enumerating his obligations to the king, Cicero cried: "No more of that, pray, for it is well known what he gave you, and what you gave him in turn." Finally, in his Gallic triumph his soldiers, among the bantering songs which are usually sung by those who follow the chariot, shouted these lines, which became a by-word:—

> All the Gauls did Caesar vanquish,
>   Nicomedes vanquished him:
> Lo! now Caesar rides in triumph,
>   victor over all the Gauls,
> Nicomedes does not triumph, who
>   subdued the conqueror.

That he was unbridled and extravagant in his intrigues is the general opinion, and that he seduced many illustrious women, among them Postumia, wife of Servius Sulpicius, Lollia, wife of Aulus Gabinius, Tertulla, wife of Marcus Crassus, and even Gnaeus Pompey's wife Mucia. At all events there is no doubt that Pompey was taken to task by the elder and the younger Curio, as well as by many others, because through a desire for power he had afterwards married the daughter of a man on whose account he divorced a wife who had borne him three children, and whom he had often referred to with a groan as an Aegisthus. But beyond all others Caesar loved Servilla, the mother of Marcus Brutus, for whom in his first consulship he bought a pearl costing six million sesterces. During the civil war, too, besides other presents, he knocked down some fine estates to her in a public auction at a nominal price, and when some expressed their surprise at the low figure, Cicero wittily remarked: "It's a better bargain than you think, for there is a third off." And in fact it was thought that Servilla was prostituting her own daughter Tertia to Caesar.

That he did not refrain from intrigues in the provinces is shown in particular by this couplet, which was also shouted by the soldiers in his Gallic triumph:—

> Men of Rome, keep close your
>   consorts, here's a bald adulterer.
> Gold in Gaul you spent in dalliance,
>   which you borrowed here in Rome.

He had love affairs with queens too, including Eunoe that Moor, wife of Bogudes, on whom, as well as on her husband, he bestowed many splendid presents, as Naso writes; but above all with Cleopatra, with whom he often feasted until daybreak, and he would have gone through Egypt with her in her statebarge almost to Aethiopia, had not his soldiers refused to follow him. Finally he called her to Rome and did not let her leave until he had ladened her with high honours and rich gifts, and he allowed her to give his name to the child which she bore. In fact, according to certain Greek writers, this child was very like Caesar in looks and carriage. Mark Anthony declared to the senate that Caesar had really acknowledged the boy, and that Gaius Matius, Gaius Oppius, and other friends of Caesar knew this. Of these Gaius Oppius, as if admitting that the situation required apology and defence, published a book, to prove that the child whom Cleopatra fathered on Caesar was not his. Helvius Cinna, tribune of the commons, admitted to several that he had a bill drawn up in due form, which Caesar had ordered him to propose to the people in his absence, making it lawful for Caesar to marry what wives he wished, "for the purpose of begetting children." But to remove all doubt that he had an evil reputation for shameless vice and for adultery, I have only to add that the elder Curio in one of his speeches calls him "every woman's man and every man's woman."

That he drank very little wine not even his enemies denied. There is a saying of Marcus Cato that Caesar was the only man who undertook to overthrow the state when sober. Even in the matter of food Gaius Oppius tells us that he was so indifferent, that once when his host served stale oil instead of fresh, and the other guests would have none of it, Caesar partook even more plentifully than usual, not to seem to charge his host with carelessness or lack of manners.

Neither when in command of armies nor as a magistrate at Rome did he show a scrupulous integrity; for as certain men have declared in their memoirs, when he was proconsul in Spain, he not only begged money from the allies, to help pay his debts, but also attacked and sacked some towns of the Lusitanians although they did not refuse his terms and opened their gates to him on his arrival. In Gaul he pillaged shrines and temples of the gods filled with offerings, and oftener sacked towns for the sake of plunder than for any fault. In consequence he had more gold than he knew what to do with, and offered it for sale throughout Italy and the provinces at the rate of three thousand sesterces the pound. In his first consulship he stole three thousand pounds of gold from the Capitol, replacing it with the same weight of gilded bronze. He made alliances and thrones a matter of barter, for he extorted from Ptolemy alone in his own name and that of Pompey nearly six thousand talents, while later on he met the heavy expenses of the civil wars and of his triumphs and entertainments by the most barefaced pillage and sacrilege.

In eloquence and in the art of war he either equalled or surpassed the fame of their most eminent representatives. After his accusation of Dolabella, he was without question numbered with the leading advocates. At all events when Cicero reviews the orators in his *Brutus*, he says that he does not see to whom Caesar ought to yield the palm, declaring that his style is elegant as well as transparent, even grand and in a sense noble. Again in a letter to Cornelius Nepos he writes thus of Caesar: "Come now, what orator would you rank above him of those who have devoted themselves to nothing else? Who has cleverer or more frequent epigrams? Who is either more picturesque or more choice in diction?" He appears, at least in his youth, to have imitated the manner of Caesar Strabo, from whose speech entitled "For the Sardinians" he actually transferred some passages word for word to a trial address of his own. He is said to have delivered himself in a high-pitched voice with impassioned action and gestures, which were not without grace. He left several speeches, including some which are attributed to him on insufficient evidence. Augustus had good reason to think that the speech "For Quintus Metellus" was rather taken down by shorthand writers who could not keep pace with his delivery, than published by Caesar himself; for in some copies I find that even the title is not "For Metellus," but, "Which He Wrote for Metellus," although the discourse purports to be from Caesar's lips, defending Metellus and himself against the charges of their common detractors. Augustus also questions the authenticity of the address "To His Soldiers in Spain," although there are two sections of it, one purporting to have been spoken at the first battle, the other at the second, when Asinius Pollio writes that because of the sudden onslaught of the enemy he actually did not have time to make an harangue.

He left memoirs too of his deeds in the Gallic war and in the civil strife with Pompey; for the author of the Alexandrian, African, and Spanish Wars is unknown; some think it was Oppius, others Hirtius, who also supplied the final book of the Gallic War, which Caesar left unwritten. With regard to Caesar's memoirs Cicero, also in the *Brutus* speaks in the following terms: "He wrote memoirs which deserve the highest praise; they are naked in their simplicity, straightforward yet graceful, stripped of all rhetorical adornment, as of a garment; but while his purpose was to supply material to others, on which those who wished to write history might draw, he haply gratified silly folk, who will try to use the curling-irons on his narrative, but he has kept men of any sense from touching the subject." Of these same memoirs Hirtius uses this emphatic language: "They are so highly rated in the judgment of all men, that he seems to have deprived writers of an opportunity, rather than given them one; yet our admiration for this feat is greater than that of others; for they know how well and faultlessly he wrote, while we know besides how easily and rapidly he finished his task." Asinius Pollio thinks that they were put together somewhat carelessly and without strict regard for truth; since in many cases Caesar was too ready to believe the accounts which others gave of their actions, and gave a perverted account of his own, either designedly or perhaps from forgetfulness; and he thinks that he intended to rewrite and revise them. He left besides a work in two volumes "On Analogy," the same number of "Speeches Criticising Cato," in addition to a poem, entitled "The Journey." He wrote the first of these works while crossing the Alps and returning to his army from Hither Gaul, where he had held the assizes; the second about the time of the battle of Munda, and the third in the course of a twenty-four days' journey from Rome to Farther Spain. Some letters of his to the senate are also preserved, and he seems to have been the first to reduce such documents to pages and the form of a notebook, whereas previously consuls and generals sent their reports written right across the sheet. There are also letters of his to Cicero, as well as to his intimates on private affairs, and in the latter, if he had anything confidential to say, he wrote it in cipher, that is, by so changing the order of the letters of the alphabet, that not a word could be made out. If anyone wishes to decipher these, and get at their meaning, he must substitute the fourth letter of the alphabet, namely D, for A, and so with the others. We also have mention of certain writings of his boyhood and early youth, such as the "Praises of Hercules," a tragedy "Oedipus," and a "Collection of Apophthegms"; but Augustus forbade the publication of all these minor works in a very brief and frank letter sent to Pompeius Macer, whom he had selected to set his libraries in order.

He was highly skilled in arms and horsemanship, and of incredible powers of endurance. On the march he headed his army, sometimes on horseback, but oftener on foot, bareheaded both in the heat of the sun and in the rain. He covered great distances with incredible speed, making a hundred miles a day in a hired carriage and with little baggage, swimming the rivers which barred his path or crossing them on inflated skins, and very often arriving before the messengers sent to announce his coming.

In the conduct of his campaigns it is a question whether he was more cautious or more daring, for he never led his army where ambuscades were possible without carefully reconnoitering the country, and he did not cross to Britain without making personal inquiries about the harbours, the course, and the approach to the island. But on the other hand, when news came that his camp in Germany was beleaguered, he made his way to his men through the enemies' pickets, disguised as a Gaul. He crossed from Brundisium to Dyrrachium in winter time, running the blockade of the enemy's fleets; and when the troops which he had ordered to follow him delayed to do so, and he had sent to fetch them many times in vain, at last in secret and alone he boarded a small boat at night with his head muffled up; and he did not reveal who he was, or suffer the helmsman to give way to the gale blowing in their teeth, until he was all but overwhelmed by the waves.

No regard for religion ever turned him from any undertaking, or even delayed him. Though the victim escaped as he was offering sacrifice, he did not put off his expedition against Scipio and Juba. Even when he had a fall as he disembarked, he gave the omen a favourable turn by crying: "I hold thee fast, Africa." Furthermore, to make the prophecies ridiculous which declared that the stock of the Scipios was fated to be fortunate and invincible in that province, he kept with him in camp a contemptible fellow belonging to the Cornelian family, to whom the nickname Salvito had been given as a reproach for his manner of life.

He joined battle, not only after planning his movements in advance but on a sudden opportunity, often immediately at the end of a march, and sometimes in the foulest weather, when one would least expect him to make a move. It was not until his later years that he became slower to engage, through a conviction that the oftener he had been victor, the less he ought to tempt, fate, and that he could not possibly gain as much by success as he might lose by a defeat. He never put his enemy to flight without also driving him from his camp, thus giving him no respite in his panic. When the issue was doubtful, he used to send away the horses, and his own among the first, to impose upon his troops the greater necessity of standing their ground by taking away that aid to flight.

He rode a remarkable horse, too, with feet that were almost human; for its hoofs were cloven in such a way as to look like toes. This horse was foaled on his own place, and since the soothsayer had declared that it foretold the rule of the world for its master, he reared it with the greatest care, and was the first to mount it, for it would endure no other rider. Afterwards, too, he dedicated a statute of it before the temple of Venus Genetrix.

Juvenal

The typical present-day picture of ancient Rome is one of awesome grandeur. Although the monuments—like the Colosseum, the Forum, and the triumphal arches—have been damaged by the ravages of time, they still convey a sense of the Imperial City. But Rome, as it really existed, was much more than these monuments; it was the great urban metropolis of the Western world. It is about Rome, the metropolis, that Juvenal writes in his "Third Satire." From his description of life in urban Rome during the early empire it is abundantly clear that Juvenal envied his friend, Umbricius, who decided to abandon the city to settle in a quiet village in the country.

Was Rome actually as dirty and debauched as Juvenal describes it? Certainly his was not the only negative voice; other contemporary writers (like Tacitus) have given us similar critical appraisals. But two points can help us to keep a proper perspective. First, Juvenal was a satirist. Not only is it apparent from "The Third Satire" that he detested Rome but also that he found joy in depicting its shortcomings in picturesque and lurid detail. So we must use some judgment in evaluating the accuracy of his description. Second, Rome was a big city and anyone who has lived in a modern big city can recognize that many of the things Juvenal talks about could, if translated into contemporary terms, be said about any of our great metropolitan centers. But that does not mean that they lack all redeeming qualities. So, too, of ancient Rome.

Little is known of the life of Juvenal. He was born Decimus Junius Juvenalis, probably around A.D. 55. He obviously knew the city of Rome very well and presumably lived in or near it most of his life. There is a story, which cannot be verified, that he was exiled, perhaps by the emperor Domitian, and spent a number of years in Egypt. He may also have served in the Roman army. He probably died sometime around the year 140 but the exact date is unknown.

Altogether we have sixteen satires that Juvenal wrote, on a wide range of topics, including a long one titled "Against Women." Although the translation of "The Third Satire," as given in the following selection, is somewhat free, it conveys very well the flavor of Juvenal's verse.

---

1. Taking into account the exaggerations in the text, what are some of the problems with living in an ancient city like Rome?

2. Based on the things that Juvenal criticizes, what does he value?

The Third Satire

Against the City of Rome

Troubled because my old friend is going, I still must commend him
For his decision to settle down in the ghost town of Cumae,
Giving the Sibyl one citizen more. That's the gateway to Baiae
There, a pleasant shore, a delightful retreat. I'd prefer
Even a barren rock in that bay to the brawl of Subura.
Where have we ever seen a place so dismal and lonely
We'd not be better off there, than afraid, as we are here, of fires,
Roofs caving in, and the thousand risks of this terrible city
Where the poets recite all through the dog days of August?

While they are loading his goods on one little four-wheeled wagon,
Here he waits, by the old archways which the aqueducts moisten.
This is where Numa, by night, came to visit his goddess.
That once holy grove, its sacred spring, and its temple,
Now are let out to the Jews, if they have some straw and a basket.
Every tree, these days, has to pay rent to the people.
Kick the Muses out; the forest is swarming with beggars.
So we go down to Egeria's vale, with its modern improvements.
How much more close the presence would be, were there lawns
    by the water.
Turf to the curve of the pool, not this unnatural marble!
Umbricius has much on his mind. "Since there's no place in the city,"
He says, "For an honest man, and no reward for his labors,
Since I have less today than yesterday, since by tomorrow
That will have dwindled still more, I have made my decision.
    I'm going
To the place where, I've heard, Daedalus put off his wings,
While my white hair is still new, my old age in the prime of
    its straightness,
While my fate spinner still has yarn on her spool, while I'm able
Still to support myself on two good legs, without crutches.
Rome, good-bye! Let the rest stay in the town if they want to,
Fellows like A, B, and C, who make black white at their pleasure,
Finding it easy to grab contracts for rivers and harbors,
Putting up temples, or cleaning out sewers, or hauling off corpses,
Or, if it comes to that, auctioning slaves in the market.

The Satires of Juvenal, trans. Rolfe Humphries (Bloomington: Indiana University Press, 1958).
Courtesy of Indiana University Press.

Once they used to be hornblowers, working the carneys;
Every wide place in the road knew their puffed-out cheeks and
    their squealing.
Now they give shows of their own. Thumbs up! Thumbs down!
    And the killers
Spare or slay, and then go back to concessions for private privies.
Nothing they won't take on. Why not?— since the kindness of
    Fortune (Fortune is out for laughs) has exalted them out of
    the gutter.

"What should I do in Rome? I am no good at lying.
If a book's bad, I can't praise it, or go around ordering copies.
I don't know the stars; I can't hire out as assassin
When some young man wants his father knocked off for a price;
    I have never
Studied the guts of frogs, and plenty of others know better
How to convey to a bride the gifts of the first man she cheats with.
I am no lookout for thieves, so I cannot expect a commission
On some governor's staff. I'm a useless corpse, or a cripple.
Who has a pull these days, except your yes men and stooges
With blackmail in their hearts, yet smart enough to keep silent?
No honest man feels in debt to those he admits to his secrets,
But your Verres must love the man who can tattle on Verres
Any old time that he wants. Never let the gold of the Tagus,
Rolling under its shade, become so important, so precious
You have to lie awake, take bribes that you'll have to surrender,
Tossing in gloom, a threat to your mighty patron forever.

"Now let me speak of the race that our rich men dote on most fondly.
These I avoid like the plague, let's have no coyness about it.
Citizens, I can't stand a Greekized Rome. Yet what portion
Of the dregs of our town comes from Achaia only?
Into the Tiber pours the silt, the mud of Orontes,
Bringing its babble and brawl, its dissonant harps and its timbrels,
Bringing also the tarts who display their wares at the Circus.
Here's the place, if your taste is for hatwearing whores, brightly
    colored!
What have they come to now, the simple souls from the country
Romulus used to know? They put on the *trechedipna*
(That might be called, in our tongue, their running-to-dinner outfit),
Pin on their *niketeria* (medals), and smell *ceromatic*
(Attar of wrestler). They come, trooping from Samos and Tralles,
    Adros, wherever that is, Azusa and Cucamonga,
Bound for the Esquiline or the hill we have named for the vineyard,

Termites, into great halls where they hope, some day, to be tyrants.
Desperate nerve, quick wit, as ready in speech as Isaeus,
Also a lot more long-winded. Look over there! See that fellow?
What do you take him for? He can be anybody he chooses,
Doctor of science or letters, a vet or a chiropractor,
Orator, painter, masseur, palmologist, tightrope walker.
If he is hungry enough, your little Greek stops at nothing.
Tell him to fly to the moon, and she runs right off for his space ship.
Who flew first? Some Moor, some Turk, some Croat, or
        some Slovene?
Not on your life, but a man from the very center of Athens.

"Should I not run away from these purple-wearing freeloaders?
Must I wait while they sign their names? Must their couches always
        be softer?
Stowaways, that's how they got here, in the plums and figs from
        Damascus.
I was here long before they were: my boyhood drank in the sky
Over the Aventine hill; I was nourished by Sabine olives.
Agh, what lackeys they are, what sycophants! See how they flatter
Some ignoramus's talk, or the looks of some horrible eyesore,
Saying some Ichabod Crane's long neck reminds them of muscles
Hercules strained when he lifted Antaeus aloft on his shoulders,
Praising some cackling voice that really sounds like a rooster's
When he's pecking a hen. We can praise the same objects that
        they do,
Only, they are believed. Does an actor do any better
Mimicking Thais, Alcestis, Doris without any clothes on?
It seems that a woman speaks, not a mask; the illusion is perfect
Down to the absence of bulge and the little cleft under the belly.
Yet they win no praise at home, for all of their talent.
Why?—Because Greece is a stage, and every Greek is an actor.
Laugh, and he splits his sides; weep, and his tears flow in torrents
Though he's not sad; if you ask for a little more fire in the winter
He will put on his big coat; if you say 'I'm hot,' he starts sweating.
We are not equals at all; he always has the advantage,
Able, by night or day, to assume, from another's expression,
This or that look, prepared to throw up his hands, to cheer loudly
If his friend gives a good loud belch or doesn't piss crooked,
Or if a gurgle comes from his golden cup when inverted
Straight up over his nose—a good deep swig, and no heeltaps!

"Furthermore, nothing is safe from his lust, neither matron nor virgin,
Nor her affianced spouse, or the boy too young for the razor.

If he can't get at these, he would just as soon lay his friend's
  grandma.
(Anything, so he'll get in to knowing the family secrets!)
Since I'm discussing the Greeks, let's turn to their schools and
  professors,
The crimes of the hood and gown. Old Dr. Egnatius, informant,
Brought about the death of Barea, his friend and his pupil,
Born on that riverbank where the pinion of Pegasus landed.
No room here, none at all, for any respectable Roman
Where a Protogenes rules, or a Diphilus, or a Hermarchus,
Never sharing their friends—a racial characteristic!
Hands off! He puts a drop of his own, or his countryside's poison
Into his patron's ear, an ear which is only too willing
And I am kicked out of the house, and all my years of long service
Count for nothing. Nowhere does the loss of a client mean less.

"Let's not flatter ourselves. What's the use of our service?
What does a poor man gain by hurrying out in the nighttime,
All dressed up before dawn, when the praetor nags at his troopers
Bidding them hurry along to convey his respects to the ladies,
Barren, of course, like Albina, before any others can get there?
Sons of men freeborn give right of way to rich man's
Slave; a crack, once or twice, at Calvina or Catiena
Costs an officer's pay, but if you like the face of some floozy
You hardly have money enough to make her climb down from
  her high chair.
Put on the stand, at Rome, a man with a record unblemished,
No more a perjurer than Numa was, or Metellus,
What will they question? His wealth, right away, and possibly, later,
(Only possibly, though) touch on his reputation.
'How many slaves does he feed? What's the extent of his acres?
How big are his platters? How many? What of his goblets and
  wine bowls?
His word is as good as his bond—if he has enough bonds in
  his strongbox.
But a poor man's oath, even if sworn on all altars
All the way from here to the farthest Dodecanese island,
Has no standing in court. What has he to fear from the lightnings
Of the outraged gods? He has nothing to lose; they'll ignore him.
"If you're poor, you're a joke, on each and every occasion.
What a laugh, if your cloak is dirty or torn, if your toga
Seems a little bit soiled, if your shoe has a crack in the leather,
Or if more than one patch attests to more than one mending!
Poverty's greatest curse, much worse than the fact of it, is that

It makes men objects of mirth, ridiculed, humbled, embarrassed.
'Out of the front-row seats!' they cry when you're out of money,
Yield your place to the sons of some pimp, the spawn of some
　　cathouse,
Some slick auctioneer's brat, or the louts some trainer has fathered
Or the well-groomed boys whose sire is a gladiator.
Such is the law of the place, decreed by the nitwitted Otho:
All the best seats are reserved for the classes who have the most money.
Who can marry a girl if he has less money than she does?
What poor man is an heir, or can hope to be? Which of them ever
Rates a political job, even the meanest and lowest?
Long before now, all poor Roman descendants of Romans
Ought to have marched out of town in one determined migration.
Men do not easily rise whose poverty hinders their merit.
Here it is harder than anywhere else: the lodgings are hovels,
Rents out of sight; your slaves take plenty to fill up their bellies
While you make do with a snack.
You're ashamed of your earthenware dishes—
Ah, but that wouldn't be true if you lived content in the country,
Wearing a dark-blue cape, and the hood thrown back on your
　　shoulders.

"In a great part of this land of Italy, might as well face it,
No one puts on a toga unless he is dead. On festival days
Where the theater rises, cut from green turf, and with the great pomp
Old familiar plays are staged again, and a baby,
Safe in his mother's lap, is scared of the grotesque mask,
There you see all dressed alike, the balcony and the front rows,
Even His Honor content with a tunic of simple white.
Here, beyond our means, we have to be smart, and too often
Get our effects with too much, an elaborate wardrobe, on credit!
This is a common vice; we must keep up with the neighbors,
Poor as we are. I tell you, everything here costs you something.
How much to give Cossus the time of day, or receive from Veiento
One quick glance, with his mouth buttoned up for fear he might
　　greet you?
One shaves his beard, another cuts off the locks of his boy friend,
Offerings fill the house, but these, you find, you will pay for.
Put this in your pipe and smoke it—we have to pay tribute
Giving the slaves a bribe for the prospect of bribing their masters.

"Who, in Praeneste's cool, or the wooded Volsinian uplands,
Who, on Tivoli's heights, or a small town like Gabii, say,
Fears the collapse of his house? But Rome is supported on pipestems,

Matchsticks; it's cheaper, so, for the landlord to shore up his ruins,
Patch up the old cracked walls, and notify all the tenants
They can sleep secure, though the beams are in ruins above them.
No, the place to live is out there, where no cry of *Fire*
Sounds the alarm of the night, with a neighbor yelling for water,
Moving his chattels and goods, and the whole third story is smoking.
This you'll never know: for if the ground floor is scared first,
You are the last to burn, up where the eaves of the attic
Keep off the rain, and the doves are brooding over their nest eggs.
Codrus owned one bed, too small for a midget to sleep on.
Six little jugs he had, and a tankard adorning his sideboard,
Under whose marble (clay), a bust or a statue of Chiron,
Busted, lay on its side; an old locker held Greek books
Whose divinest lines were gnawed by the mice, those vandals.
Codrus had nothing, no doubt, and yet he succeeded, poor fellow,
Losing that nothing, his all. And this is the very last straw—
No one will help him out with a meal or loding or shelter.
Stripped to the bone, begging for crusts, he still receives nothing.

"Yet if Asturicus' mansion burns down, what a frenzy of sorrow!
Mothers dishevel themselves, the leaders dress up in black,
Courts are adjourned. We groan at the fall of the city, we hate
The fire, and the fire still burns, and while it is burning,
Somebody rushes up to replace the loss of the marble,
Some one chips in toward a building fund, another gives statues,
Naked and shining white, some masterpiece of Euphranor
Or Polyclitus' chef d'oeuvre; and here's a fellow with bronzes
Sacred to Asian gods. Books, chests, a bust of Minerva,
A bushel of silver coins. *To him that hath shall be given!*
This Persian, childless, of course, the richest man in the smart set,
Now has better things, and more, than before the disaster.
How can we help but think he started the fire on purpose?

"Tear yourself from the games, and get a place in the country!
One little Latian town, like Sora, say, or Frusino,
Offers a choice of homes, at a price you pay here, in one year,
Renting some hole in the wall. Nice houses, too, with a garden,
Springs bubbling up from the grass, no need for a windlass
    or bucket,
Plenty to water your flowers, if they need it, without any trouble.
Live there, fond of your hoe, an independent producer,
Willing and able to feed a hundred good vegetarians.
Isn't it something, to feel, wherever you are, how far off,
You are a monarch? At least, lord of a single lizard.

"Here in town the sick die from insomnia mostly.
Undigested food, on a stomach burning with ulcers,
Brings on listlessness, but who can sleep in a flophouse?
Who but the rich can afford sleep and a garden apartment?
That's the source of infection. The wheels creak by on the narrow
Streets of the wards, the drivers squabble and brawl when
    they're stopped,
More than enough to frustrate the drowsiest son of a sea cow.
When his business calls, the crowd makes way, as the rich man,
Carried high in his car, rides over them, reading or writing,
Even taking a snooze, perhaps, for the motion's composing.
Still, he gets where he wants before we do; for all of our hurry
Traffic gets in our way, in front, around and behind us.
Somebody gives me a shove with an elbow, or two-by-two-four
    scantling.
One clunks my head with a beam, another cracks down with a beer keg.
Mud is thick on my shins, I am trampled by somebody's big feet.
Now what?—a soldier grinds his hobnails into my toes.

"Don't you see the mob rushing along to the handout?
There are a hundred guests, each one with his kitchen servant.
Even Samson himself could hardly carry those burdens,
Pots and pans some poor little slave tries to keep on his head, while
    he hurries
Hoping to keep the fire alive by the wind of his running.
Tunics, new-darned, and ripped to shreds; there's the flash of
    a fir beam
Huge on some great dray, and another carries a pine tree,
Nodding above our heads and threatening death to the people.
What will be left of the mob, if that cart of Ligurian marble
Breaks its axle down and dumps its load on these swarms?
Who will identify limbs or bones? The poor man's cadaver,
Crushed, disappears like his breath. And meanwhile, at home,
    his household
Washes the dishes, and puffs up the fire, with all kinds of a clatter
Over the smeared flesh-scrapers, the flasks of oil, and the towels.
So the boys rush around, while their late master is sitting,
Newly come to the bank of the Styx, afraid of the filthy
Ferryman there, since he has no fare, not even a copper
In his dead mouth to pay for the ride through that muddy whirlpool.

"Look at other things, the various dangers of nighttime.
How high it is to the cornice that breaks, and a chunk beats my
    brains out,

Or some slob heaves a jar, broken or cracked, from a window.
Bang! It comes down with a crash and proves its weight on the
    sidewalk
You are a thoughtless fool, unmindful of sudden disaster,
If you don't make your will before you go out to have dinner.
There are as many deaths in the night as there are open windows
Where you pass by; if you're wise, you will pray, in your
    wretched devotions,
People may be content with no more than emptying slop jars.

"There your hell-raising drunk, who has had the bad luck to kill no one,
Tosses in restless rage, like Achilles mourning Patroclus,
Turns from his face to his back, can't sleep, for only a fracas
Gives him the proper sedation. But any of these young hoodlums,
All steamed up on wine, watches his step when the crimson
Cloak goes by, a lord, with a long, long line of attendants,
Torches and brazen lamps, warning him, *Keep your distance!*
Me, however, whose torch is the moon, or the feeblest candle
Fed by a sputtering wick, he absolutely despises.
Here is how it all starts, the fight, if you think it is fighting
When he throws all the punches, and all I do is absorb them.
He stops. He tells me to stop. I stop. I have to obey him.
What can you do when he's mad and bigger and stronger than you are?
'Where do you come from?' he cries 'you wino, you bean-bloated
    bastard?
Off what shoemaker's dish have you fed on chopped leeks and boiled
    lamb-lip?
What? No answer? Speak up, or take a swift kick in the rear.
Tell me where you hang out—in some praying-house with the
    Jew-boys?
If you try to talk back, or sneak away without speaking,
All the same thing: you're assaulted, and then put under a bail bond
For committing assault. This is a poor man's freedom.
Beaten, cut up by fists, he begs and implores his assailant,
Please, for a chance to go home with a few teeth left in his mouth

"This is not all you must fear. Shut up your house or your store,
Bolts and padlocks and bars will never keep out all the burglars,
Or a holdup man will do you in with a switch blade.
If the guards are strong over Pontine marshes and pinewoods
Near Volturno, the scum of the swamps and the filth of the forest
Swirl into Rome, the great sewer, their sanctuary, their haven.
Furnaces blast and anvils groan with the chains we are forging:
What other use have we for iron and steel? There is danger

We will have little left for hoes and mattocks and ploughshares.
Happy the men of old, those primitive generations
Under the tribunes and kings, when Rome had only one jailhouse!

"There is more I could say, I could give you more of my reasons,
But the sun slants down, my oxen seem to be calling,
My man with the whip is impatient, I must be on my way.
So long! Don't forget me. Whenever you come to Aquino
Seeking relief from Rome, send for me. I'll come over
From my bay to your hills, hiking along in my thick boots
Toward your chilly fields. What's more, I promise to listen
If your satirical verse esteems me worthy the honor."

The Christian Scriptures

In the province of Judea, tucked away in a far corner of the Roman Empire, was born midway through the reign of Caesar Augustus a man whose influence on world history was far to surpass that of the *princeps*—Jesus of Nazareth. The selections that follow from the New Testament contain excerpts illustrating the teachings of Jesus and the early history and theological doctrines of his followers. From the Gospel of St. Matthew comes the Sermon on the Mount, the most complete and one of the most beautiful statements of the religious views of Jesus. The Acts, written by Luke, is a historical book detailing the activities of the founders of the Christian church in the years immediately following the crucifixion, as seen through the eyes of the early church fathers several years later. Of crucial importance to history is the transformation of Christianity from the exclusive possession of an obscure Jewish sect into a message of salvation open to Gentiles as well as to Jews. This was the first step on Christianity's long road to religious domination of the Western world. The selection from Romans contains a statement of Christian doctrine by the apostle Paul (Saul of Tarsus), one of the most influential of all Christian theologians. It was Paul who began the task of developing the teachings of Jesus into an organized and consistent body of theological doctrine.

---

1. In what ways do the ethical standards of the Sermon on the Mount resemble the ethical standards of the Hebrew Scriptures? In what ways are they different?

2. Taking all these selections from the Christian Scriptures together, how would you summarize the Christian message?

MATTHEW 5.1–7.29

5 When Jesus saw the crowds, he went up the mountain; and after he sat down, his disciples came to him. ²Then he began to speak, and taught them, saying:

3 "Blessed are the poor in spirit, for theirs is the kingdom of heaven.

4 "Blessed are those who mourn, for they will be comforted.

5 "Blessed are the meek, for they will inherit the earth.

6 "Blessed are those who hunger and thirst for righteousness, for they will be filled.

7 "Blessed are the merciful, for they will receive mercy.

8 "Blessed are the pure in heart, for they will see God.

9 "Blessed are the peacemakers, for they will be called children of God.

10 "Blessed are those who are persecuted for righteousness' sake, for theirs is the kingdom of heaven.

11 "Blessed are you when people revile you and persecute you and utter all kinds of evil against you falsely on my account. [12] Rejoice and be glad, for your reward is great in heaven, for in the same way they persecuted the prophets who were before you.

13 "You are the salt of the earth; but if salt has lost its taste, how can its saltiness be restored? It is no longer good for anything, but is thrown out and trampled under foot.

14 "You are the light of the world. A city built on a hill cannot be hid. [15]No one after lighting a lamp puts it under the bushel basket, but on the lampstand, and it gives light to all in the house. [16]In the same way, let your light shine before others, so that they may see your good works and give glory to your Father in heaven.

17 "Do not think that I have come to abolish the law or the prophets; I have come not to abolish but to fulfill. [18]For truly I tell you, until heaven and earth pass away, not one letter, not one stroke of a letter, will pass from the law until all is accomplished. [19]Therefore, whoever breaks one of the least of these commandments, and teaches others to do the same, will be called least in the kingdom of heaven; but whoever does them and teaches them will be called great in the kingdom of heaven. [20]For I tell you, unless your righteousness exceeds that of the scribes and Pharisees, you will never enter the kingdom of heaven.

21 "You have heard that it was said to those of ancient times, 'You shall not murder'; and 'whoever murders shall be liable to judgment.' [22]But I say to you that if you are angry with a brother or sister, you will be liable to judgment; and if you insult a brother or sister, you will be liable to the council; and if you say, 'You fool,' you will be liable to the hell of fire. [23]So when you are offering your gift at the altar, if you remember that your brother or sister has something against you, [24]leave your gift there before the altar and go; first be reconciled to your brother or sister, and then come and offer your gift. [25]Come to terms quickly with your accuser while you are on the way to court with him, or your accuser may hand you over to the judge, and the judge to the guard, and you will be thrown into prison. [26]Truly I tell you, you will never get out until you have paid the last penny.

27 "You have heard that it was said, 'You shall not commit adultery.' [28]But I say to you that everyone who looks at a woman with lust has already committed adultery with her in his heart. [29]If your right eye causes you to sin, tear it out and throw it away; it is better for you to lose one of your members than for your whole body to be thrown into hell. [30]And if your right hand causes you to sin, cut it off and throw it away; it is better

for you to lose one of your members than for your whole body to go into hell.

31 "It was also said, 'Whoever divorces his wife, let him give her a certificate of divorce.' [32]But I say to you that anyone who divorces his wife, except on the ground of unchastity, causes her to commit adultery; and whoever marries a divorced woman commits adultery.

33 "Again, you have heard that it was said to those of ancient times, 'You shall not swear falsely, but carry out the vows you have made to the Lord.' [34]But I say to you, Do not swear at all, either by heaven, for it is the throne of God, [35]or by the earth, for it is his footstool, or by Jerusalem, for it is the city of the great King. [36]And do not swear by your head, for you cannot make one hair white or black. [37]Let your word be 'Yes, Yes' or 'No, No'; anything more than this comes from the evil one.

38 "You have heard that it was said, 'An eye for an eye and a tooth for a tooth.' [39]But I say to you, Do not resist an evildoer. But if anyone strikes you on the right cheek, turn the other also; [40]and if anyone wants to sue you and take your coat, give your cloak as well; [41]and if anyone forces you to go one mile, go also the second mile. [42]Give to everyone who begs from you, and do not refuse anyone who wants to borrow from you.

43 "You have heard that it was said. 'You shall love your neighbor and hate your enemy.' [44]But I say to you, Love your enemies and pray for those who persecute you, [45]so that you may be children of your Father in heaven; for he makes his sun rise on the evil and on the good, and sends rain on the righteous and on the unrighteous. [46]For if you love those who love you, what reward do you have? Do not even the tax collectors do the same? [47]And if you greet only your brothers and sisters, what more are you doing than others? Do not even the Gentiles do the same? [48]Be perfect, therefore, as your heavenly Father is perfect.

6 "Beware of practicing your piety before others in order to be seen by them; for then you have no reward from your Father in heaven.

2 "So whenever you give alms, do not sound a trumpet before you, as the hypocrites do in the synagogues and in the streets, so that they may be praised by others. Truly I tell you, they have received their reward. [3]But when you give alms, do not let your left hand know what your right hand is doing, [4]so that your alms may be done in secret; and your Father who sees in secret will reward you.

5 "And whenever you pray, do not be like the hypocrites; for they love to stand and pray in the synagogues and at the street corners, so that they may be seen by others. Truly I tell you, they have received their reward. [6]But whenever you pray, go into your room and shut the door and pray to your Father who is in secret; and your Father who sees in secret will reward you.

7 "When you are praying, do not heap up empty phrases as the Gentiles do; for they think that they will be heard because of their many

words. [8]Do not be like them, for your Father knows what you need before you ask him.

9 "Pray then in this way:

Our Father in heaven,

hallowed be your name.

10 Your kingdom come.

Your will be done,

on earth as it is in heaven.

11 Give us this day our daily bread.

12 And forgive us our debts,

as we also have forgiven

our debtors.

13 And do not bring us to the time of trial,

but rescue us from the evil one.

14 For if you forgive others their trespasses, your heavenly Father will also forgive you; 15but if you do not forgive others, neither will your Father forgive your trespasses.

16 "And whenever you fast, do not look dismal, like the hypocrites, for they disfigure their faces so as to show others that they are fasting. Truly I tell you, they have received their reward. [17]But when you fast, put oil on your head and wash your face, [18]so that your fasting may be seen not by others but by your Father who is in secret; and your Father who sees in secret will reward you.

19 "Do not store up for yourselves treasures on earth, where moth and rust consume and where thieves break in and steal; [20]but store up for yourselves treasures in heaven, where neither moth nor rust consumes and where thieves do not break in and steal. [21]For where your treasure is, there your heart will be also.

22 "The eye is the lamp of the body. So, if your eye is healthy, your whole body will be full of light; [23]but if your eye is unhealthy, your whole body will be full of darkness. If then the light in you is darkness, how great is the darkness!

24 "No one can serve two masters; for a slave will either hate the one and love the other, or be devoted to the one and despise the other. You cannot serve God and wealth.

25 "Therefore I tell you, do not worry about your life, what you will eat or what you will drink, or about your body, what you will wear. Is not life more than food, and the body more than clothing? [26]Look at the birds of the air; they neither sow nor reap nor gather into barns, and yet your heavenly Father feeds them. Are you not of more value than they? [27]And can any of you by worrying add a single hour to your span of life? [28]And why do you worry about clothing? Consider the lilies of the field, how they grow; they neither toil nor spin, [29]yet I tell you, even Solomon in all his glory was not clothed like one of these. [30]But if God so clothes the grass of the field, which

is alive today and tomorrow is thrown into the oven, will he not much more clothe you—you of little faith? [31]Therefore do not worry, saying, 'What will we eat?' or 'What will we drink?' or 'What will we wear?' [32]For it is the Gentiles who strive for all these things; and indeed your heavenly Father knows that you need all these things. [33]But strive first for the kingdom of God and his righteousness, and all these things will be given to you as well.

34 "So do not worry about tomorrow, for tomorrow will bring worries of its own. Today's trouble is enough for today.

7 "Do not judge, so that you may not be judged. [2]For with the judgment you make you will be judged, and the measure you give will be the measure you get. [3]Why do you see the speck in your neighbor's eye, but do not notice the log in your own eye? [4]Or how can you say to your neighbor, 'Let me take the speck out of your eye,' while the log is in your own eye? [5]You hypocrite, first take the log out of your own eye, and then you will see clearly to take the speck out of your neighbor's eye.

6 "Do not give what is holy to dogs; and do not throw your pearls before swine, or they will trample them under foot and turn and maul you.

7 "Ask, and it will be given you; search, and you will find; knock, and the door will be opened for you. [8]For everyone who asks receives, and everyone who searches finds, and for everyone who knocks, the door will be opened. [9]Is there anyone among you who, if your child asks for bread, will give a stone? [10]Or if the child asks for a fish, will give a snake? [11]If you then, who are evil, know how to give good gifts to your children, how much more will your Father in heaven give good things to those who ask him!

12 "In everything do to others as you would have them do to you; for this is the law and the prophets.

13 "Enter through the narrow gate; for the gate is wide and the road is easy that leads to destruction, and there are many who take it. [14]For the gate is narrow and the road is hard that leads to life, and there are few who find it.

15 "Beware of false prophets, who come to you in sheep's clothing but inwardly are ravenous wolves. [16]You will know them by their fruits. Are grapes gathered from thorns, or figs from thistles? [17]In the same way, every good tree bears good fruit, but the bad tree bears bad fruit. [18]A good tree cannot bear bad fruit, nor can a bad tree bear good fruit. [19]Every tree that does not bear good fruit is cut down and thrown into the fire. [20]Thus you will know them by their fruits.

21 "Not everyone who says to me, 'Lord, Lord,' will enter the kingdom of heaven, but only the one who does the will of my Father in heaven. [22]On that day many will say to me, 'Lord, Lord, did we not prophesy in your name, and cast out demons in your name, and do many deeds of power in your name?' [23]Then I will declare to them, 'I never knew you; go away from me, you evildoers.'

24 "Everyone then who hears these words of mine and acts on them will be like a wise man who built his house on rock. [25]The rain fell, the floods came, and the winds blew and beat on that house, but it did not fall, because it had been founded on rock. [26]And everyone who hears these words of mine and does not act on them will be like a foolish man who built his house on sand. [27]The rain fell, and the floods came, and the winds blew and beat against that house, and it fell—and great was its fall!"

28 Now when Jesus had finished saying these things, the crowds were astounded at his teaching, [29]for he taught them as one having authority, and not as their scribes.

ACTS

1 In the first book, Theophilus, I wrote about all that Jesus did and taught from the beginning [2]until the day when he was taken up to heaven, after giving instructions through the Holy Spirit to the apostles whom he had chosen. [3]After his suffering he presented himself alive to them by many convincing proofs, appearing to them during forty days and speaking about the kingdom of God. [4]While staying with them, he ordered them not to leave Jerusalem, but to wait there for the promise of the Father. "This," he said, "is what you have heard from me; [5]for John baptized with water, but you will be baptized with the Holy Spirit not many days from now."

6 So when they had come together, they asked him, "Lord, is this the time when you will restore the kingdom to Israel?" [7]He replied, "It is not for you to know the times or periods that the Father has set by his own authority. [8]But you will receive power when the Holy Spirit has come upon you; and you will be my witnesses in Jerusalem, in all Judea and Samaria, and to the ends of the earth." [9]When he had said this, as they were watching, he was lifted up, and a cloud took him out of their sight. [10]While he was going and they were gazing up toward heaven, suddenly two men in white robes stood by them. [11]They said, "Men of Galilee, why do you stand looking up toward heaven? This Jesus, who has been taken up from you into heaven, will come in the same way as you saw him go into heaven."

2 When the day of Pentecost had come, they were all together in one place. [2]And suddenly from heaven there came a sound like the rush of a violent wind, and it filled the entire house where they were sitting. [3]Divided tongues, as of fire, appeared among them, and a tongue rested on each of them. [4]All of them were filled with the Holy Spirit and began to speak in other languages, as the Spirit gave them ability.

5 Now there were devout Jews from every nation under heaven living in Jerusalem. [6]And at this sound the crowd gathered and was bewildered, because each one heard them speaking in the native language of each. [7]Amazed and astonished, they asked, "Are not all these who are speaking Galileans? [8]And how is it that we hear, each of us, in our own native

language? ⁹Parthians, Medes, Elamites, and residents of Mesopotamia, Judea and Cappadocia, Pontus and Asia, ¹⁰Phrygia and Pamphylia, Egypt and the parts of Libya belonging to Cyrene, and visitors from Rome, both Jews and proselytes, ¹¹Cretans and Arabs—in our own languages we hear them speaking about God's deeds of power." ¹²All were amazed and perplexed, saying to one another, "What does this mean?" ¹³But others sneered and said, "They are filled with new wine."

14 But Peter, standing with the eleven, raised his voice and addressed them, "Men of Judea and all who live in Jerusalem, let this be known to you, and listen to what I say. ¹⁵Indeed, these are not drunk, as you suppose, for it is only nine o'clock in the morning. ¹⁶No, this is what was spoken through the prophet Joel:

'In the last days it will be, God declares,
that I will pour out my Spirit upon all flesh,
and your sons and your daughters shall prophesy,
and your young men shall see visions, and your old men shall
     dream dreams.
18 Even upon my slaves, both men and women,
    in those days I will pour out my Spirit;
    and they shall prophesy.
19 And I will show portents in the heaven above
    and signs on the earth below, blood, and fire, and smoky mist.
20 The sun shall be turned to darkness and the moon to blood.
    before the coming of the Lord's great and glorious day.
21 Then everyone who calls on the name of the Lord shall be saved.'

22 "You that are Israelites, listen to what I have to say: Jesus of Nazareth, a man attested to you by God with deeds of power, wonders, and signs that God did through him among you, as you yourselves know— ²³this man, handed over to you according to the definite plan and foreknowledge of God, you crucified and killed by the hands of those outside the law. ²⁴But God raised him up, having freed him from death, because it was impossible for him to be held in its power. ²⁵For David says concerning him,

'I saw the Lord always before me,
    for he is at my right hand so that I will not be shaken:
26 therefore my heart was glad, and my tongue rejoiced;
    moreover my flesh will live in hope.
27 For you will not abandon my soul to Hades,
    or let your Holy One experience corruption.
28 You have made known to me the ways of life;
    you will make me full of gladness with your presence.

29 "Fellow Israelites, I may say to you confidently of our ancestor David that he both died and was buried, and his tomb is with us to this day. ³⁰Since he was a prophet, he knew that God had sworn with an oath to him

that he would put one of his descendants on his throne. [31]Foreseeing this, David spoke of the resurrection of the Messiah, saying,
'He was not abandoned to Hades,
   nor did his flesh experience corruption.'

32 This Jesus God raised up, and of that all of us are witnesses. [33]Being therefore exalted at the right hand of God, and having received from the Father the promise of the Holy Spirit, he has poured out this that you both see and hear. [34]For David did not ascend into the heavens, but he himself says,
'The Lord said to my Lord,
"Sit at my right hand, [35]until I make your enemies your footstool."'

[36]Therefore let the entire house of Israel know with certainty that God has made him both Lord and Messiah, this Jesus whom you crucified."

37 Now when they heard this, they were cut to the heart and said to Peter and to the other apostles, "Brothers, what should we do?" [38]Peter said to them, "Repent, and be baptized every one of you in the name of Jesus Christ so that your sins may be forgiven; and you will receive the gift of the Holy Spirit. [39]For the promise is for you, for your children, and for all who are far away, everyone whom the Lord our God calls to him." [40]And he testified with many other arguments and exhorted them, saying, "Save yourselves from this corrupt generation." [41]So those who welcomed his message were baptized, and that day about three thousand persons were added.

7 The word of God continued to spread; the number of the disciples increased greatly in Jerusalem, and a great many of the priests became obedient to the faith.

8 Stephen, full of grace and power, did great wonders and signs among the people. [9]Then some of those who belonged to the synagogue of the Freedmen (as it was called), Cyrenians, Alexandrians, and others of those from Cilicia and Asia, stood up and argued with Stephen. [10]But they could not withstand the wisdom and the Spirit with which he spoke. [11]Then they secretly instigated some men to say, "We have heard him speak blasphemous words against Moses and God." [12]They stirred up the people as well as the elders and the scribes; then they suddenly confronted him, seized him, and brought him before the council. [13]They set up false witnesses who said, "This man never stops saying things against this holy place and the law; [14]for we have heard him say that this Jesus of Nazareth will destroy this place and will change the customs that Moses handed on to us." [15]And all who sat in the council looked intently at him, and they saw that his face was like the face of an angel.

7 Then the high priest asked him, "Are these things so?" [2]And Stephen replied: "Brothers and fathers, listen to me. The God of glory appeared to our ancestor Abraham when he was in Mesopotamia, before he lived in Haran.

Most High does not dwell in houses made with human hands; as the prophet says,

49 'Heaven is my throne, and the earth is my footstool.
What kind of house will you build for me, says the Lord,
   or what is the place of my rest?
50 'Did not my hand make all these things?'

51 "You stiff-necked people, uncircumcised in heart and ears, you are forever opposing the Holy Spirit, just as your ancestors used to do. [52]Which of the prophets did your ancestors not persecute? They killed those who foretold the coming of the Righteous One, and now you have become his betrayers and murderers. [53]You are the ones that received the law as ordained by angels, and yet you have not kept it."

54 When they heard these things, they became enraged and ground their teeth at Stephen. [55]But filled with the Holy Spirit, he gazed into heaven and saw the glory of God and Jesus standing at the right hand of God. [56]"Look," he said, "I see the heavens opened and the Son of Man standing at the right hand of God!" [57]But they covered their ears, and with a loud shout all rushed together against him. [58]Then they dragged him out of the city and began to stone him; and the witnesses laid their coats at the feet of a young man named Saul. [59]While they were stoning Stephen, he prayed, "Lord Jesus, receive my spirit." [60]Then he knelt down and cried out in a loud voice, "Lord, do not hold this sin against them." When he had said this, he died. [1]And Saul approved of their killing him.

8 That day a severe persecution began against the church in Jerusalem, and all except the apostles were scattered throughout the countryside of Judea and Samaria. [2]Devout men buried Stephen and made loud lamentation over him. [3]But Saul was ravaging the church by entering house after house; dragging off both men and women, he committed them to prison.

ACTS 9.1–9.22

9 Meanwhile Saul, still breathing threats and murder against the disciples of the Lord, went to the high priest [2]and asked him for letters to the synagogues at Damascus, so that if he found any who belonged to the Way, men or women, he might bring them bound to Jerusalem. [3]Now as he was going along and approaching Damascus, suddenly a light from heaven flashed around him. [4]He fell to the ground and heard a voice saying to him, "Saul, Saul, why do you persecute me?" [5]He asked, "Who are you, Lord?" The reply came, "I am Jesus, whom you are persecuting. [6]But get up and enter the city, and you will be told what you are to do." [7]The men who were traveling with him stood speechless because they heard the voice but saw no one. [8]Saul got up from the ground, and though his eyes were open, he could see nothing; so they led him by the hand and brought him into Damascus. [9]For three days he was without sight, and neither ate nor drank.

10 Now there was a disciple in Damascus named Ananias. The Lord said to him in a vision, "Ananias." He answered, "Here I am, Lord." [11]The Lord said to him, "Get up and go to the street called Straight, and at the house of Judas look for a man of Tarsus named Saul. At this moment he is praying, [12]and he has seen in a vision a man named Ananias come in and lay his hands on him so that he might regain his sight." [13]But Ananias answered, "Lord, I have heard from many about this man, how much evil he has done to your saints in Jerusalem; [14]and here he has authority from the chief priests to bind all who invoke your name." [15]But the Lord said to him, "Go, for he is an instrument whom I have chosen to bring my name before Gentiles and kings and before the people of Israel; [16]I myself will show him how much he must suffer for the sake of my name." [17]So Ananias went and entered the house. He laid his hands on Saul and said, "Brother Saul, the Lord Jesus, who appeared to you on your way here, has sent me so that you may regain your sight and be filled with the Holy Spirit." [18]And immediately something like scales fell from his eyes, and his sight was restored. Then he got up and was baptized, [19]and after taking some food, he regained his strength.

For several days he was with the disciples in Damascus, [20]and immediately he began to proclaim Jesus in the synagogues, saying, "He is the Son of God." [21]All who heard him were amazed and said, "Is not this the man who made havoc in Jerusalem among those who invoked this name? And has he not come here for the purpose of bringing them bound before the chief priests?" [22]Saul became increasingly more powerful and confounded the Jews who lived in Damascus by proving that Jesus was the Messiah.

ACTS 10.1–10.48

10 In Caesarea there was a man named Cornelius, a centurion of the Italian Cohort, as it was called. [2]He was a devout man who feared God with all his household; he gave alms generously to the people and prayed constantly to God. [3]One afternoon at about three o'clock he had a vision in which he clearly saw an angel of God coming in and saying to him, "Cornelius." [4]He stared at him in terror and said, "What is it, Lord?" He answered, "Your prayers and your alms have ascended as a memorial before God. [5]Now send men to Joppa for a certain Simon who is called Peter; [6]he is lodging with Simon, a tanner, whose house is by the seaside." [7]When the angel who spoke to him had left, he called two of his slaves and a devout soldier from the ranks of those who served him, [8]and after telling them everything, he sent them to Joppa.

9 About noon the next day, as they were on their journey and approaching the city, Peter went up on the roof to pray. [10]He became hungry and wanted something to eat; and while it was being prepared, he fell into a trance. [11]He saw the heaven opened and something like a large sheet com-

ing down, being lowered to the ground by its four corners. [12]In it were all kinds of four-footed creatures and reptiles and birds of the air. [13]Then he heard a voice saying, "Get up, Peter; kill and eat." [14]But Peter said, "By no means, Lord; for I have never eaten anything that is profane or unclean." [15]The voice said to him again, a second time, "What God has made clean, you must not call profane." [16]This happened three times, and the thing was suddenly taken up to heaven.

17 Now while Peter was greatly puzzled about what to make of the vision that he had seen, suddenly the men sent by Cornelius appeared. They were asking for Simon's house and were standing by the gate. [18]They called out to ask whether Simon, who was called Peter, was staying there. [19]While Peter was still thinking about the vision, the Spirit said to him, "Look, three men are searching for you. [20]Now get up, go down, and go with them without hesitation: for I have sent them." [21]So Peter went down to the men and said, "I am the one you are looking for; what is the reason for your coming?" [22]They answered, "Cornelius, a centurion, an upright and God-fearing man, who is well spoken of by the whole Jewish nation, was directed by a holy angel to send for you to come to his house and to hear what you have to say." [23]So Peter invited them in and gave them lodging.

The next day he got up and went with them, and some of the believers from Joppa accompanied him. [24]The following day they came to Caesarea. Cornelius was expecting them and had called together his relatives and close friends. [25]On Peter's arrival Cornelius met him, and falling at his feet, worshiped him. [26]But Peter made him get up, saying, "Stand up; I am only a mortal." [27]And as he talked with him, he went in and found that many had assembled; [28]and he said to them, "You yourselves know that it is unlawful for a Jew to associate with or to visit a Gentile; but God has shown me that I should not call anyone profane or unclean. [29]So when I was sent for, I came without objection. Now may I ask why you sent for me?"

30 Cornelius replied, "Four days ago at this very hour, at three o'clock, I was praying in my house when suddenly a man in dazzling clothes stood before me. [31]He said, 'Cornelius, your prayer has been heard and your alms have been remembered before God. [32]Send therefore to Joppa and ask for Simon, who is called Peter; he is staying in the home of Simon, a tanner, by the sea.' [33]Therefore I sent for you immediately, and you have been kind enough to come. So now all of us are here in the presence of God to listen to all that the Lord has commanded you to say."

34 Then Peter began to speak to them: "I truly understand that God shows no partiality, [35]but in every nation anyone who fears him and does what is right is acceptable to him. [36]You know the message he sent to the people of Israel, preaching peace by Jesus Christ—he is Lord of all. [37]That message spread throughout Judea, beginning in Galilee after the baptism that John announced: [38]how God anointed Jesus of Nazareth with the Holy Spirit and with power; how he went about doing good and healing all who

were oppressed by the devil, for God was with him. [39]We are witnesses to all that he did both in Judea and in Jerusalem. They put him to death by hanging him on a tree; [40]but God raised him on the third day and allowed him to appear, [41]not to all the people but to us who were chosen by God as witnesses, and who ate and drank with him after he rose from the dead. [42]He commanded us to preach to the people and to testify that he is the one ordained by God as judge of the living and the dead. [43]All the prophets testify about him that everyone who believes in him receives forgiveness of sins through his name."

44 While Peter was still speaking, the Holy Spirit fell upon all who heard the word. [45]The circumcised believers who had come with Peter were astounded that the gift of the Holy Spirit had been poured out even on the Gentiles, [46]for they heard them speaking in tongues and extolling God. Then Peter said, [47]"Can anyone withhold the water for baptizing these people who have received the Holy Spirit just as we have?" [48]So he ordered them to be baptized in the name of Jesus Christ. Then they invited him to stay for several days.

ROMANS

"There is no one who is righteous, not even one;
11 there is no one who has understanding,
  there is no one who seeks God.
12 All have turned aside, together they have become worthless;
  there is no one who shows kindness, there is not even one."
13 "Their throats are opened graves;
  they use their tongues to deceive."
"The venom of vipers is under their lips."
14 "Their mouths are full of cursing and bitterness."
15 "Their feet are swift to shed blood;
16 ruin and misery are in their paths,
17 and the way of peace they have not known."
18 "There is no fear of God before their eyes."

19 Now we know that whatever the law says, it speaks to those who are under the law, so that every mouth may be silenced, and the whole world may be held accountable to God. [20]For "no human being will be justified in his sight" by deeds prescribed by the law, for through the law comes the knowledge of sin.

21 But now, apart from law, the righteousness of God has been disclosed, and is attested by the law and the prophets, [22]the righteousness of God through faith in Jesus Christ for all who believe. For there is no distinction, [23]since all have sinned and fall short of the glory of God; [24]they are now justified by his grace as a gift, through the redemption that is in Christ Jesus, [25]whom God put forward as a sacrifice of atonement by his blood, effective

through faith. He did this to show his righteousness, because in his divine forbearance he had passed over the sins previously committed; [26]it was to prove at the present time that he himself is righteous and that he justifies the one who has faith in Jesus.

27 Then what becomes of boasting? It is excluded. By what law? By that of works? No, but by the law of faith. [28]For we hold that a person is justified by faith apart from works prescribed by the law. [29]Or is God the God of Jews only? Is he not the God of Gentiles also? Yes, of Gentiles also, [30]since God is one; and he will justify the circumcised on the ground of faith and the uncircumcised through that same faith. [31]Do we then overthrow the law by this faith? By no means! On the contrary, we uphold the law.

ROMANS 5.1–6.23

5 Therefore, since we are justified by faith, we have peace with God through our Lord Jesus Christ, [2]through whom we have obtained access to this grace in which we stand; and we boast in our hope of sharing the glory of God. [3]And not only that, but we also boast in our sufferings, knowing that suffering produces endurance, [4]and endurance produces character, and character produces hope, [5]and hope does not disappoint us, because God's love has been poured into our hearts through the Holy Spirit that has been given to us.

6 For while we were still weak, at the right time Christ died for the ungodly. [7]Indeed, rarely will anyone die for a righteous person—though perhaps for a good person someone might actually dare to die. [8]But God proves his love for us in that while we still were sinners Christ died for us. [9]Much more surely then, now that we have been justified by his blood, will we be saved through him from the wrath of God. [10]For if while we were enemies, we were reconciled to God through the death of his Son, much more surely, having been reconciled, will we be saved by his life. [11]But more than that, we even boast in God through our Lord Jesus Christ, through whom we have now received reconciliation.

12 Therefore, just as sin came into the world through one man, and death came through sin, and so death spread to all because all have sinned— [13]sin was indeed in the world before the law, but sin is not reckoned when there is no law. [14]Yet death exercised dominion from Adam to Moses, even over those whose sins were not like the transgression of Adam, who is a type of the one who was to come.

15 But the free gift is not like the trespass. For if the many died through the one man's trespass, much more surely have the grace of God and the free gift in the grace of the one man, Jesus Christ, abounded for the many. [16]And the free gift is not like the effect of the one man's sin. For the judgment following one trespass brought condemnation, but the free gift following many trespasses brings justification. [17]If, because of the one man's trespass, death exercised dominion through that one, much more surely will those who

receive the abundance of grace and the free gift of righteousness exercise dominion in life through the one man, Jesus Christ.

18 Therefore just as one man's trespass led to condemnation for all, so one man's act of righteousness leads to justification and life for all. [19]For just as by the one man's disobedience the many were made sinners, so by the one man's obedience the many will be made righteous. [20]But law came in, with the result that the trespass multiplied; but where sin increased, grace abounded all the more, [21]so that, just as sin exercised dominion in death, so grace might also exercise dominion through justification leading to eternal life through Jesus Christ our Lord.

6 What then are we to say? Should we continue in sin in order that grace may abound? [2]By no means! How can we who died to sin go on living in it? [3]Do you not know that all of us who have been baptized into Christ Jesus were baptized into his death? [4]Therefore we have been buried with him by baptism into death, so that, just as Christ was raised from the dead by the glory of the Father, so we too might walk in newness of life.

5 For if we have been united with him in a death like his, we will certainly be united with him in a resurrection like his. [6]We know that our old self was crucified with him so that the body of sin might be destroyed, and we might no longer be enslaved to sin. [7]For whoever has died is freed from sin. [8]But if we have died with Christ, we believe that we will also live with him. [9]We know that Christ, being raised from the dead, will never die again; death no longer has dominion over him. [10]The death he died, he died to sin, once for all; but the life he lives, he lives to God. [11]So you also must consider yourselves dead to sin and alive to God in Christ Jesus.

12 Therefore, do not let sin exercise dominion in your mortal bodies, to make you obey their passions. [13]No longer present your members to sin as instruments of wickedness, but present yourselves to God as those who have been brought from death to life, and present your members to God as instruments of righteousness. [14]For sin will have no dominion over you, since you are not under law but under grace.

15 What then? Should we sin because we are not under law but under grace? By no means! [16]Do you not know that if you present yourselves to anyone as obedient slaves, you are slaves of the one whom you obey, either of sin, which leads to death, or of obedience, which leads to righteousness? [17]But thanks be to God that you, having once been slaves of sin, have become obedient from the heart to the form of teaching to which you were entrusted, [18]and that you, having been set free from sin, have become slaves of righteousness. [19]I am speaking in human terms because of your natural limitations. For just as you once presented your members as slaves to impurity and to greater and greater iniquity, so now present your members as slaves to righteousness for sanctification.

20 When you were slaves of sin, you were free in regard to righteousness. [21]So what advantage did you then get from the things of which you

now are ashamed? The end of those things is death. [22]But now that you have been freed from sin and enslaved to God, the advantage you get is sanctification. The end is eternal life. [23]For the wages of sin is death, but the free gift of God is eternal life in Christ Jesus our Lord.

ROMANS 9.1–9.33

9 I am speaking the truth in Christ—I am not lying; my conscience confirms it by the Holy Spirit—[2]I have great sorrow and unceasing anguish in my heart. [3]For I could wish that I myself were accursed and cut off from Christ for the sake of my own people, my kindred according to the flesh. [4]They are Israelites, and to them belong the adoption, the glory, the covenants, the giving of the law, the worship, and the promises; [5]to them belong the patriarchs, and from them, according to the flesh, comes the Messiah, who is over all, God blessed forever. Amen.

6 It is not as though the word of God had failed. For not all Israelites truly belong to Israel, [7]and not all of Abraham's children are his true descendants; but "It is through Isaac that descendants shall be named for you." [8]This means that it is not the children of the flesh who are the children of God, but the children of the promise are counted as descendants. [9]For this is what the promise said, "About this time I will return and Sarah shall have a son." [10]Nor is that all; something similar happened to Rebecca when she had conceived children by one husband, our ancestor Isaac. [11]Even before they had been born or had done anything good or bad (so that God's purpose of election might continue, [12]not by works but by his call) she was told, "The elder shall serve the younger." [13]As it is written,

"I have loved Jacob, but I have hated Esau."

14 What then are we to say? Is there injustice on God's part? By no means! [15]For he says to Moses,

"I will have mercy on whom I have mercy,

and I will have compassion on whom I have compassion."

[16]So it depends not on human will or exertion, but on God who shows mercy. [17]For the scripture says to Pharaoh, "I have raised you up for the very purpose of showing my power in you, so that my name may be proclaimed in all the earth." [18]So then he has mercy on whomever he chooses, and he hardens the heart of whomever he chooses.

19 You will say to me then, "Why then does he still find fault? For who can resist his will?" [20]But who indeed are you, a human being, to argue with God? Will what is molded say to the one who molds it, "Why have you made me like this?" [21]Has the potter no right over the clay, to make out of the same lump one object for special use and another for ordinary use? [22]What if God, desiring to show his wrath and to make known his power, has endured with much patience the objects of wrath that are made for destruction; [23]and what if he has done so in order to make known the riches of his glory for the objects of mercy, which he

has prepared beforehand for glory—[24]including us whom he has called, not from the Jews only but also from the Gentiles? [25]As indeed he says in Hosea,

"Those who were not my people I will call 'my people,'
and her who was not beloved I will call 'beloved.'"

[26]"And in the very place where it was
said to them, 'You are not my people,'
there they shall be called children of the living God."

27 And Isaiah cries out concerning Israel. "Though the number of the children of Israel were like the sand of the sea, only a remnant of them will be saved; [28]for the Lord will execute his sentence on the earth quickly and decisively." [29]And as Isaiah predicted,

"If the Lord of hosts had not left survivors to us,
we would have fared like Sodom
and been made like Gomorrah."

30 What then are we to say? Gentiles, who did not strive for righteousness, have attained it, that is, righteousness through faith; [31]but Israel, who did strive for the righteousness that is based on the law, did not succeed in fulfilling that law. [32]Why not? Because they did not strive for it on the basis of faith, but as if it were based on works. They have stumbled over the stumbling stone, [33]as it is written,

"See, I am laying in Zion a stone that will make people stumble,
a rock that will make them fall,
and whoever believes in him will not be put to shame."

Confucius

To many of us, the words "Confucius say" are the preamble to a witticism, but to billions of Chinese people over thousands of years the sayings of the master have been words of highest wisdom, to be received with respect, if not with reverence. As a result, Confucius has molded the Chinese mind and character in a manner and to an extent that has hardly been equaled by any other single figure in the history of a major civilization.

Although it is difficult to summarize briefly the teachings of Confucius, certain of their basic features are apparent. He was an optimistic moralist; believing people to be fundamentally good, he thought that with proper education and leadership they could realize their potential and achieve the form of life which he described as that of "the superior man." A social order composed of such individuals, including particularly its political leaders, would constitute the ideal society. Although he also believed that such a society is in harmony with the will of heaven, Confucius, unlike many early social philosophers, did not found his ideal society on principles derived from theology. On the contrary, he is well described as a humanist.

Many of the details of the moral and social ideals of Confucius appear in his *Analects*, or "Collection" (of sayings). This collection, which is rambling, ill-arranged, and repetitious, contains twenty "Books," in which, besides the master's sayings, there can be found descriptions of contemporary Chinese society, excursions into past history, stories about various political leaders, and so on.

Confucius (551–479 B.C.) was born of a poor family that apparently had ancestors of substance. Early in life he decided to become a scholar and teacher. He soon gathered a group of disciples about him and, because he believed that society could be reformed only if those who were properly educated held the reins of government, he sought public office and encouraged his students to do so as well. During his career he held a number of government posts, some of consequence. But practical politicians were suspicious of his lofty ideals and he was finally dismissed, to spend the twilight of his career wandering about China, but still teaching.

Near the end of his life he wrote the following succinct autobiography: "At fifteen, I set my heart on learning. At thirty, I was firmly established. At forty, I had no more doubts. At fifty, I knew the will of Heaven.

At sixty, I was ready to listen to it. At seventy, I could follow my heart's desire without transgressing what was right."

The moral teachings of the *Analects*, which Confucius did not actually originate but which he edited and molded to reflect his own ideals, were gathered together, mainly after his death, by his admirers. The selection that follows includes some of his central sayings. These have been rearranged to give them greater coherency, and the topic headings have been added.

---

1. According to Confucius, what is the basis for a stable society?

2. What behaviors or attitudes does Confucius consider virtuous? What is the purpose of being virtuous?

Analects

The Master said, "Is it not pleasant to learn with a constant perseverance and application? Is it not delightful to have friends coming from distant quarters? Is he not a man of complete virtue who feels no discomposure though men may take no note of him?"

Filial Piety

The Master said, "A youth, when at home, should be filial, and, abroad, respectful to his elders. He should be earnest and truthful. He should overflow in love to all, and cultivate the friendship of the good. When he has time and opportunity, after the performance of these things, he should employ them in polite studies."

Mang I asked what filial piety was. The Master said, "It is not being disobedient." Soon after, as Fan Ch'ih was driving him, the Master told him, saying, "Mang'sun asked me what filial piety was, and I answered him,— "not being disobedient." Fan Ch'ih said, "What did you mean?" The Master replied, "That parents, when alive, should be served according to propriety; that, when dead, they should be buried according to propriety; and that they should be sacrificed to according to propriety."

The Master said, "In serving his parents, a son may remonstrate with them, but gently; when he sees that they do not incline to follow his advice, he shows an increased degree of reverence, but does not abandon his purpose; and should they punish him, he does not allow himself to murmur."

Education

The Master said, "If the scholar be not grave, he will not call forth any veneration, and his learning will not be solid."

The Master said, "If a man keeps cherishing his old knowledge, so as continually to be acquiring new, he may be a teacher of others."

The Master said, "The accomplished scholar is not a utensil."

The Master said, "Learning without thought is labor lost; thought without learning is perilous."

The Master said, "Yu, shall I teach you what knowledge is? When you know a thing, to hold that you know it; and when you do not know a thing, to allow that you do not know it;—this is knowledge."

The Master said, "They who know the truth are not equal to those who love it, and they who love it are not equal to those who delight in it."

The Master said, "The scholar who cherishes the love of comfort is not fit to be deemed a scholar."

When the Master went to Wei, Zan Yu acted as driver of his carriage. The Master observed, "How numerous are the people!" Yu said, "Since they are so numerous, what more shall be done for them?" "Enrich them," was the reply. "And when they have been enriched, what more shall be done?" The Master said, "Teach them."

Government

The Master said, "To rule a country of a thousand chariots, there must be reverent attention to business, and sincerity; economy in expenditure, and love for men; and the employment of the people at the proper seasons."

The Master said, "He who exercises government by means of his virtue may be compared to the north polar star, which keeps its place and all the stars turn towards it."

The Master said, "If the people be led by laws, and uniformity sought to be given them by punishment, they will try to avoid the punishment, but have no sense of shame. If they be led by virtue, and uniformity sought to be given them by the rules of propriety, they will have the sense of shame, and moreover will become good."

Chi K'ang asked how to cause the people to reverence their ruler, to be faithful to him, and to go on to nerve themselves to virtue. The Master said, "Let him preside over them with gravity;—then they will reverence him. Let him be filial and kind to all;—then they will be faithful to him. Let him

Trans. James Legge.

advance the good and teach the incompetent;—then they will eagerly seek to be virtuous."

Tsze-kung asked about government. The Master said, "The requisites of government are that there be sufficiency of food, sufficiency of military equipment, and the confidence of the people in their ruler." Tszekung said, "If it cannot be helped, and one of these must be dispensed with, which of the three should be foregone first?" "The military equipment," said the Master. Tsze-kung again asked, "If it cannot be helped, and one of the remaining two must be dispensed with, which of them should be foregone?" The Master answered, "Part with the food. From of old, death has been the lot of all men; but if the people have no faith in their rulers, there is no standing for the State."

Chi K'ang asked Confucius about government, saying, "What do you say to killing the unprincipled for the good of the principled?" Confucius replied, "Sir, in carrying on your government, why should you use killing at all? Let your evinced desires be for what is good, and the people will be good. The relation between superiors and inferiors is like that between the wind and the grass. The grass must bend, when the wind blows across it."

The Master said, "When a prince's personal conduct is correct, the government is effective without the issuing of orders. If his personal conduct is not correct, he may issue orders, but they will not be followed."

Tsze-chang asked Confucius, saying, "In what way should a person in authority act in order that he may conduct government properly?" The Master replied, "Let him honor the five excellent, and banish away the four bad, things;—then may he conduct government properly." Tzse-chang said, "What are meant by the five excellent things?" The Master said, "When the person in authority is beneficent without great expenditure; when he lays tasks on the people without their repining; when he pursues what he desires without being covetous; when he maintains a dignified ease without being proud; when he is majestic without being fierce.". . .

Tsze-chang then asked, "What are meant by the four bad things?" The Master said, "To put the people to death without having instructed them;—this is called cruelty. To require from them, suddenly, the full tale of work, without having given them warning;—this is called oppression. To issue orders as if without urgency, at first, and, when the time comes, to insist on them with severity;—this is called injury. And, generally, in the giving pay or rewards to men, to do it in a stingy way;—this is called acting the part of a mere official."

Religion

The Master said, . . . "He who offends against Heaven has none to whom he can pray."

Chi Lu asked about serving the spirits of the dead. The Master said, "While you are not able to serve men, how can you serve their spirits?" Chi Lu added, "I venture to ask about death." He was answered, "While you do not know life, how can you know about death?"

The Master said, "Alas! there is no one that knows me." Tsze-kung said, "What do you mean by thus saying—that no one knows you?" The Master replied, "I do not murmur against Heaven. I do not grumble against men. My studies lie low, and my penetration rises high. But there is Heaven;—that knows me!"

The Master said, "I would prefer not speaking." Tsze-kung said, "If you, Master, do not speak, what shall we, your disciples, have to record?" The Master said, "Does Heaven speak? The four seasons pursue their courses, and all things are continually being produced, but does Heaven say anything?"

The Master said, "Without recognizing the ordinances of Heaven, it is impossible to be a superior man."

Virtue and Goodness

The Master said, "Fine words and an insinuating appearance are seldom associated with true virtue."

The Master said, "See what a man does. Mark his motives. Examine in what things he rests. How can a man conceal his character?

The Master said, "I do not know how a man without truthfulness is to get on. How can a large carriage be made to go without the cross-bar for yoking the oxen to, or a small carriage without the arrangement for yoking the horses?"

The Master said, . . . "To see what is right and not to do it is want of courage."

The Master said, "If the will be set on virtue, there will be no practice of wickedness."

The Master said, "Riches and honors are what men desire. If virtue cannot be obtained in the proper way, they should not be held. Poverty and meanness are what men dislike. If virtue cannot be obtained in the proper way, they should be avoided."

The Master said, "I have not seen a person who loved virtue, or one who hated what was not virtuous. He who loved virtue, would esteem nothing above it. He who hated what is not virtuous, would practice virtue in such a way that he would not allow anything that is not virtuous to approach his person. Is any one able for one day to apply his strength to virtue? I have not seen the case in which his strength would be insufficient."

The Master said, "A man should say, I am not concerned that I have no place, I am concerned how I may fit myself for one. I am not concerned that I am not known, I seek to be worthy to be known."

The Master said, "When we see men of worth, we should think of equalling them; when we see men of a contrary character, we should turn inwards and examine ourselves."

The Master said, "Virtue is not left to stand alone. He who practices it will have neighbors."

The Master said, "Let the will be set on the path of duty. Let every attainment in what is good be firmly grasped. Let perfect virtue be accorded with. Let relaxation and enjoyment be found in the polite arts."

The Master said, "With coarse rice to eat, with water to drink, and my bended arm for a pillow;—I have still joy in the midst of these things. Riches and honors acquired by unrighteousness are to me as a floating cloud."

The Master said, "Is virtue a thing remote? I wish to be virtuous, and lo! virtue is at hand."

The Master said, "Respectfulness, without the rules of propriety, becomes laborious bustle; carefulness, without the rules of propriety, becomes timidity; boldness, without the rules of propriety, becomes insubordination; straightforwardness, without the rules of propriety, becomes rudeness."

The Master said, "Can men refuse to assent to the words of strict admonition? But it is reforming the conduct because of them which is valuable. Can men refuse to be pleased with words of gentle advice? But it is unfolding their aim which is valuable. If a man be pleased with these words, but does not unfold their aim, and assents to those, but does not reform his conduct, I can really do nothing with him."

The Master said, "Hold faithfulness and sincerity as first principles. Have no friends not equal to yourself. When you have faults, do not fear to abandon them."

The Master said, "The commander of the forces of a large State may be carried off, but the will of even a common man cannot be taken from him."

The Master said, "The wise are free from perplexities; the virtuous from anxiety; and the bold from fear."

The Master said, "To go beyond is as wrong as to fall short."

Chung-kung asked about perfect virtue. The Master said, "It is, when you go abroad, to behave to every one as if you were receiving a great guest; to employ the people as if you were assisting at a great sacrifice; not to do to others as you would not wish done to yourself; to have no murmuring against you in the country, and none in the family."

Fan Ch'ih asked about benevolence. The Master said, "It is to love all men." He asked about knowledge. The Master said, "It is to know all men."

Fan Ch'ih asked about perfect virtue. The Master said, "It is, in retirement, to be sedately grave; in the management of business, to be reverently attentive; in intercourse with others, to be strictly sincere. Though a man go among rude, uncultivated tribes, these qualities may not be neglected."

Tsze-kung asked, saying, "What do you say of a man who is loved by all the people of his neighborhood?" The Master replied, "We may not for that accord our approval of him." "And what do you say of him who is hated by all the people of his neighborhood?" The Master said, "We may not for that conclude that he is bad. It is better than either of these cases that the good in the neighborhood love him, and the bad hate him."

The Master said, "He who speaks without modesty will find it difficult to make his words good."

Some one said, "What do you say concerning the principle that injury should be recompensed with kindness?" The Master said, "With what then will you recompense kindness? Recompense injury with justice, and recompense kindness with kindness."

Tsze-kung asked, saying, "Is there one word which may serve as a rule of practice for all one's life?" The Master said, "Is not RECIPROCITY such a word? What you do not want done to yourself, do not do to others."

The Master said, "Virtue is more to man than either water or fire. I have seen men die from treading on water and fire, but I have never seen a man die from treading the course of virtue."

Confucius said, "There are three friendships which are advantageous, and three which are injurious. Friendship with the upright; friendship with the sincere; and friendship with the man of much observation;—these are advantageous. Friendship with the man of specious airs; friendship with the insinuatingly soft; and friendship with the glib-tongued;—these are injurious."

Confucius said, "There are three things men find enjoyment in which are advantageous, and three things they find enjoyment in which are injurious. To find enjoyment in the discriminating study of ceremonies and music; to find enjoyment in speaking of the goodness of others; to find enjoyment in having many worthy friends;—these are advantageous. To find enjoyment in extravagant pleasures; to find enjoyment in idleness and sauntering; to find enjoyment in the pleasures of feasting;—these are injurious."

Tsze-chang asked Confucius about perfect virtue. Confucius said, "To be able to practice five things everywhere under Heaven constitutes perfect virtue." He begged to ask what they were, and was told, "Gravity, generosity of soul, sincerity, earnestness, and kindness. If you are grave, you will not be treated with disrespect. If you are generous, you will win all. If you are sincere, people will repose trust in you. If you are earnest, you will accomplish much. If you are kind, this will enable you to employ the services of others."

The Superior Man

The Master said, "The superior man, in the world, does not set his mind either for anything, or against anything; what is right he will follow."

The Master said, "The superior man thinks of virtue; the small man thinks of comfort. The superior man thinks of the sanctions of law; the small man thinks of favors which he may receive."

The Master said, "The mind of the superior man is conversant with righteousness; the mind of the mean man is conversant with gain."

The Master said, "The superior man is modest in his speech, but exceeds in his actions."

The Master said, "The superior man in everything considers righteousness to be essential. He performs it according to the rules of propriety. He brings it forth in humility. He completes it with sincerity. This is indeed a superior man.

The Master said, "The superior man is distressed by his want of ability. He is not distressed by men's not knowing him."

The Master said, "The superior man dislikes the thought of his name not being mentioned after his death."

The Master said, "What the superior man seeks, is in himself. What the mean man seeks, is in others."

The Master said, "The superior man is dignified, and does not wrangle. He is sociable, but not a partisan.

The Master said, "The superior man does not promote a man simply on account of his words, nor does he put aside good words because of the man."

Confucius said, "There are three things which the superior man guards against. In youth, when the physical powers are not yet settled, he guards against lust. When he is strong, and the physical powers are full of vigor, he guards against quarrelsomeness. When he is old, and the animal powers are decayed, he guards against covetousness."

Confucius said, "There are three things of which the superior man stands in awe. He stands in awe of the ordinances of Heaven. He stands in awe of great men. He stands in awe of the words of sages. The mean man does not know the ordinances of Heaven, and consequently does not stand in awe of them. He is disrespectful of great men. He makes sport of the words of sages."

Confucius said, "The superior man has nine things which are subjects with him of thoughtful consideration. In regard to the use of his eyes, he is anxious to see clearly. In regard to the use of his ears, he is anxious to hear distinctly. In regard to his countenance, he is anxious that it should be benign. In regard to his demeanor, he is anxious that it should be respectful. In regard to his speech, he is anxious that it should be sincere. In regard to his doing of business, he is anxious that it should be reverently careful. In regard to what he doubts about, he is anxious to question others. When he is angry, he thinks of the difficulties his anger may involve him in. When he sees gain to be got, he thinks of righteousness."

Ssu-ma Chi'en, The Records of the Historian

While Confucius did not find any princes of his day to adopt his ideas, Confucianism would eventually become the official philosophy of classical China under the Han. In 221 B.C. the Ch'in conquered and unified all of Chinese civilization. A short-lived and brutal dynasty, Ch'in were soon replaced by the Han Dynasty (202 B.C. to A.D. 220). The period of the Han Dynasty is often viewed as the Golden Age of Chinese civilization. Indeed, ethnic Chinese still refer to themselves as Han. Yet, the Han themselves sought to recreate a mythical golden age of Chinese civilization. They revived the learning of the ancient philosophers, especially Confucius. They also sponsored a comprehensive dynastic history of China (called the Shih Chi, or Records of the Historian), which would legitimate their dynasty.

According to a distinguished scholar of Chinese history, "The Chinese were the greatest historians of the premodern world. They wrote more history than anyone else, and what they wrote was usually more accurate."[1] The Shih Chi is the best example of premodern Chinese historiography. Begun by the Han Grand Historian Ssu-ma T'an (d. 110 B.C.), his son, Ssuma Chi'en (145–90 B.C.), took over the project and changed it in two significant ways. First, he expanded the breadth of the project to include the whole known world, rather than just the deeds of dynastic rulers. Second, he was the first Chinese historian to use documentary sources, rather than compiling and editing previous chronicles. The Records of the Historian are a collection of treatises, tables, and personal essays by Ssu-ma Chi'en. Not only do they give us an invaluable source for reconstructing classical China, but they also give insight into the personality of a prominent scholar and member of the imperial court. The first selection is Ssu-ma Chi'en's account of his father's last words to him. The second selection deals with the methods Ssu-ma Chi'en used to write his history.

1. What is the purpose of writing history according to Ssu-ma Chi'en? What makes for "good" history?

2. How does this selection reflect Confucian values?

---

[1] Albert Craig, *The Heritage of Chinese Civilization*, Prentice Hall, 2001, p. 44.

Records of the Historian

The Grand Historian [Ssu-ma T'an] grasped my hand and said weeping: "Our ancestors were Grand Historians for the House of Chou. From the most ancient times they were eminent and renowned when in the days of Yü and Hsia they were in charge of astronomical affairs. In later ages our family declined. Will this tradition end with me? If you in turn become Grand Historian, you must continue the work of our ancestors. . . . When you become Grand Historian, you must not forget what I have desired to expound and write. Now filial piety begins with the serving of your parents; next you must serve your sovereign; and finally you must make something of yourself, that your name may go down through the ages to the glory of your father and mother. This is the most important part of filial piety. Everyone praises the Duke of Chou, saying that he was able to expound in word and song the virtues of King Wen and King Wu, publishing abroad the Odes of Chou and Shao; he set forth the thoughts and ideals of T'ai-wang and Wang Chi, extending his words back to King Liu and paying honor to Hou Chi [ancestors of the Chou dynasty]. After the reigns of Yu and Li the way of the ancient kings fell into disuse and rites and music declined. Confucius revived the old ways and restored what had been abandoned, expounding the *Odes* and *History* and making the *Spring and Autumn Annals*. From that time until today men of learning have taken these as their models. It has now been over four hundred years since the capture of the unicorn [481 B.C., end of the Spring and Autumn period]. The various feudal states have merged together, and the old records and chronicles have become scattered and lost. Now the House of Han has arisen and all the world is united under one rule. I have been Grand Historian, and yet I have failed to make a record of all the enlightened rulers and wise lords, the faithful ministers and gentlemen who were ready to die for duty. I am fearful that the historical materials will be neglected and lost. You must remember and think of this!"

I bowed my head and wept, saying: "I, your son, am ignorant and unworthy, but I shall endeavor to set forth in full the reports of antiquity which have come down from our ancestors. I shall not dare to be remiss!"

This our house of Han has succeeded the descendants of the Five Emperors and carried on the task of unification of the Three Dynasties. The ways of Chou fell into disuse and the Ch'in scattered and discarded the old writings and burned and destroyed the *Odes* and the *History*. Therefore the plans and records of the Illustrious Hall and the stone rooms, of the metal caskets and jade tablets, became lost or confused.

Then the Han arose and Hsiao Ho put in order the laws and commandments; Han Hsin set forth the rules of warfare; Chang Ts'ang made the regulations and standards; and Shu-sun T'ung settled questions of rites and ceremonies. At this time the art of letters began again to flourish and advance and the *Odes* and *History* gradually reappeared. From the time when Ts'ao Ts'an put into practice Master Kai's teachings of the Yellow Emperor and Lao Tzu, when Chia Sheng and Ch'ao Ts'o expounded the doctrines of the Legalist philosophers Shen and Shang, and Kung-sun Hung achieved eminence for his Confucian learning, a period of some one hundred years, the books that survived and records of past affairs were all without exception gathered together by the Grand Historian. The Grand Historians, father and son, each in turn held and carried on the position.

• • •

I have sought out and gathered together the ancient traditions of the empire which were scattered and lost. Of the great deeds of kings I have searched the beginnings and examined the ends; I have seen their times of prosperity and observed their decline. Of the affairs that I have discussed and examined, I have made a general survey of the Three Dynasties and a record of the Ch'in and Han, extending in all back as far as Hsien Yüan [the Yellow Emperor] and coming down to the present, set forth in twelve Basic Annals. After this had been put in order and completed, because there were differences in chronology for the same periods and the dates were not always clear, I made the ten Chronological Tables. Of the changes of rites and music, the improvements and revisions of the pitch-pipes and calendar, military power, mountains and rivers, spirits and gods, the relationships between heaven and man, the economic practices handed down and changed age by age, I have made the eight Treatises. As the twenty-eight constellations revolve about the North Star, as the thirty spokes of a wheel come together at the hub, revolving endlessly without stop, so the ministers, assisting like arms and legs, faithful and trustworthy, in true moral spirit serve their lord and ruler: of them I made the thirty Hereditary Houses. Upholding duty, masterful and sure, not allowing themselves to miss their opportunities, they made a name for themselves in the world: of such men I made the seventy Memoirs. In all one hundred and thirty chapters, 526,500 words, this is the book of the Grand Historian, compiled in order to repair omissions and amplify the Six Disciplines. It is the work of one family, designed to supplement the various interpretations of the Six Classics and to put into order the miscellaneous sayings of the hundred schools.

The chronicles of the Five Emperors and the Three Dynasties extend back to high antiquity. For the Yin dynasty and before, we cannot compile any genealogical records of the feudal lords, though from the Chou on down they can usually be constructed. When Confucius arranged the *Spring and Autumn Annals* from the old historical texts, he noted the first year of a reign, the time when the year began, and the day and month for each entry; such was his exactitude. However, when he wrote his prefaces to the *Book of History*, he made only general references and did not mention year and month. Perhaps he had some material, but in many cases there were gaps and it was impossible to record exactly. Therefore, when there was a question of doubt, he recorded it as doubtful.

Hinduism

The *Bhagavad Gita* ("The Song of God"), the best-known work of Indian Hinduism, dates from about the same time as the Christian gospels, or perhaps a bit earlier. Although not considered by Hindus to be a direct revelation to humans from the gods, like the earlier *Vedas*, it is accepted nevertheless as being of divine origin. In it can be found statements of most Hindu religious beliefs; these are set in the context of a poetic story of a great battle being fought between warring noble factions. Among the many cults that fall within the broad expanse of Hinduism, the *Bhagavad Gita* represents in particular that of the hero-god Krishna, who appears as one of the central characters in the drama.

While accepting the main religious beliefs of the Hindu tradition, but decrying its excessive ritualism, the *Bhagavad Gita* makes some significant shifts in emphasis from earlier texts. It modifies the idea that, since the phenomenal world and the life we live are both unreal, the individual should divorce himself from mundane matters to seek union with the supreme Reality. While recognizing the ultimate goal of human life to be escape from endless rebirth through the achievement of Nirvana, it nevertheless maintains that one should participate actively in the affairs of this world, fulfilling the duties of one's station in life. But, in doing so one must strive for selfless action, or action for its own sake, without yearning for the results to which such action will lead. At the same time the *Bhagavad Gita* accepts two other paths to salvation than that of selfless action. One is the way of knowledge, or a recognition that Reality is one and spiritual rather than material. The other is the way of devotion, or belief in a personal God with whom one can have communion and, ultimately, union.

The background to the discussion of Hinduism in the *Bhagavad Gita* is worthy of note. The setting of the poem is sometime near the beginning of the first millennium B.C. Two armies are drawn up for a decisive battle. The commander of one, Prince Arjuna, takes a ride in his chariot before the battle begins, to survey the opposing hosts. To his dismay he sights many of his kinsmen in the enemy ranks, so, reluctant to wage war against them, he asks his chariot-driver, Krishna, what he ought to do. His driver, however, is no ordinary mortal but Lord Krishna, a god who has here taken on human form. He begins by telling Arjuna that he must fight and then explains why he must do so. Then, in answer to a series of further questions that Arjuna puts to him, he elaborates the basic principles of Hinduism.

1. Summarize Krishna's advice to the prince.

2. Does the Bhagavad Gita mandate one code of ethical behavior for all people or different ones for different castes?

Bhagavad Gita

ARJUNA: How can I, in the battle, shoot with shafts
          On Bhishma, or on Drona—O thou Chief!—
          Both worshipful, both honourable men?

          Better to live on beggar's bread
          With those we love alive,
          Than taste their blood in rich feasts spread
          And guiltily survive!
          Ah! were it worse—who knows?—to be
          Victor or vanquished here,
          When those confront us angrily
          Whose death leaves living drear?
          In pity lost, by doubtings tossed,
          My thoughts-distracted-turn
          To Thee, the Guide I reverence most,
          That I may counsel learn:
          I know not what would heal the grief
          Burned into soul and sense,
          If I were earth's unchallenged chief—
          A god—and these gone thence!

SANJAYA: So spake Arjuna to the Lord of Hearts,
          And sighing, "I will not fight!" held silence then.
          To whom, with tender smile,
          While the Prince wept despairing 'twixt those hosts,
          Krishna made answer in divinest verse:

KRISHNA: Thou grievest where no grief should be! thou
              speak'st
          Words lacking wisdom! for the wise in heart
          Mourn not for those that live, nor those that die.
          Nor I, nor thou, nor any one of these,
          Ever was not, nor ever will not be,
          For ever and for ever afterwards.

Trans. E. Arnold

All, that doth live, lives always! To man's frame
As there come infancy and youth and age,
So come there raising-up and layings-down
Of other and of other life-abodes,
Which the wise know, and fear not. This that irks—
Thy sense-life thrilling to the elements—
Bringing thee heat and cold, sorrows and joys,
'Tis brief and mutable! Bear with it, Prince!
As the wise bear. The soul which is not moved,
The soul that with a strong and constant calm
Takes sorrow and takes joy indifferently,
Lives in the life undying! That which is
Can never cease to be; that which is not
Will not exist. To see this truth of both
Is theirs who part essence from accident,
Substance from shadow. Indestructible,
Learn thou! the Life is, spreading life through all;
It cannot anywhere, by any means,
Be anywise diminished, stayed, or changed.
But for these fleeting frames which it informs
With spirit deathless, endless, infinite,
They perish. Let them perish, Prince! and fight!

• • •

Specious, but wrongful deem
The speech of those ill-taught ones who extol
The letter of their Vedas, saying, "This
Is all we have, or need;" being weak at heart
With wants, seekers of Heaven: which comes—they say—
As "fruit of good deeds done;" promising men
Much profit in new births for works of faith;
In various rites abounding; following whereon
Large merit shall accrue towards wealth and power;
Albeit, who wealth and power do most desire
Least fixity of soul have such, least hold
On heavenly meditation. Much these teach,
From Vedas, concerning the "three qualities;"
Free of the "pairs of opposites," and free
From that sad righteousness which calculates;
Self-ruled, Arjuna! simple, satisfied!
Look! like as when a tank pours water forth
To suit all needs, so do these Brahmans draw
Texts for all wants from tank of Holy Writ
But thou, want not! ask not! Find full reward

Of doing right in right! Let right deeds be
Thy motive, not the fruit which comes from them.

• • •

ARJUNA: What is his mark who hath that steadfast heart,
Confirmed in holy meditation? How
Know we his speech, Kesava? Sits he, moves he
Like other men?

KRISHNA: When one, O Pritha's Son!—
Abandoning desires which shake the mind—
Finds in his soul full comfort for his soul,
He hath attained the Yog—that man is such!
In sorrows not dejected, and in joys
Not overjoyed; dwelling outside the stress
Of passion, fear, and anger; fixed in calms
Of lofty contemplation;—such an one
Is Muni, is the Sage, the true Recluse!
He, who to none and nowhere overbound
By ties of flesh, takes evil things and good
Neither desponding nor exulting, such
Bears wisdom's plainest mark! He who shall draw,
As the wise tortoise draws its four feet safe
Under its shield, his five frail senses back
Under the spirit's buckler from the world
Which else assails them, such an one, my Prince!
Hath wisdom's mark! Things that solicit sense
Hold off from the self-governed; nay, it comes,
The appetites of him who lives beyond
Depart,—aroused no more. Yet may it chance,
O Son of Kuntil that a governed mind
Shall some time feel the sense-storms sweep, and wrest
Strong self-control by the roots. Let him regain
His kingdom! let him conquer this, and sit
On Me intent. That man alone is wise
Who keeps the mastery of himself! If one
Ponders on objects of the sense, there springs
Attraction; from attraction grows desire
Desire flames to fierce passion, passion breeds
Recklessness; then the memory—all betrayed—
Lets noble purpose go, and saps the mind,
Till purpose, mind, and man are all undone.
But, if one deals with objects of the sense

Not loving and not hating, making them
Serve his free soul, which rests serenely lord,
Lo! such a man comes to tranquillity;
And out of that tranquillity shall rise
The end and healing of his earthly pains,
Since the will governed sets the soul at peace.
The soul of the ungoverned is not his,
Nor hath he knowledge of himself; which lacked
How grows serenity? and, wanting that,
Whence shall he hope for happiness? The mind
That gives itself to follow shows of sense
Seeth its helm of wisdom rent away,
And, like a ship in waves of whirlwind, drives
To wreck and death. Only with him, great Prince!
Whose senses are not swayed by things of sense—
Only with him who holds his mastery,
Shows wisdom perfect. What is midnight-gloom
To unenlightened souls shines wakeful day
To his clear gaze; what seems as wakeful day
Is known for night, thick night of ignorance,
To his true-seeing eyes. Such is the Saint!
And like the ocean, day by day receiving Floods from all lands,
    which never overflows;
Its boundary-line not leaping, and not leaving,
Fed by the rivers, but unswelled by those;—
So is the perfect one! to his soul's ocean
    The world of sense pours streams of witchery;
They leave him as they find, without commotion,
    Taking their tribute, but remaining free.
Yea! whoso, shaking off the yoke of flesh
Lives lord, not servant, of his lusts; set free
From pride, from passion, from the sin of "Self,"
Toucheth tranquillity! O Pritha's Son!
That is the state of Brahm! There rests no dread
When that last step is reached! Live where he will,
Die when he may, such passeth from all 'plaining,
To blest Nirvana, with the Gods, attaining.

$$\bullet\ \bullet\ \bullet$$

ARJUNA: Yet, Krishna! at the one time thou dost laud
    Surcease of works, and, at another time,
    Service through work. Of these twain plainly tell
    Which is the better way?

KRISHNA: To cease from works
          Is well, and to do works in holiness
          Is well; and both conduct to bliss supreme;
          But of these twain the better way is his
          Who working piously refraineth not.

          That is the true Renouncer, firm and fixed,
          Who—seeking nought, rejecting nought—dwells proof
          Against the "opposites."[1]
          O valiant Prince!
          In doing, such breaks lightly from all deed:
          'Tis the new scholar talks as they were two,
          This Sankhya and this Yoga: wise men know
          Who husbands one plucks golden fruit of both!
          The region of high rest which Sankhyans reach
          Yogins attain. Who sees these twain as one
          Sees with clear eyes! Yet such abstraction, Chief!
          Is hard to win without much holiness.
          Whoso is fixed in holiness, self-ruled,
          Pure-hearted, lord of senses and of self,
          Lost in the common life of all which lives—
          A "Yogayukt"—he is a Saint who wends
          Straightway to Brahm. Such an one is not touched
          By taint of deeds. "Nought of myself I do"
          Thus will he think—who holds the truth of truths—
          In seeing, hearing, touching, smelling; when
          He eats, or goes, or breathes; slumbers or talks,
          Holds fast or loosens, opes his eyes or shuts;
          Always assured "This is the sense-world plays
          With senses." He that acts in thought of Brahm,
          Detaching end from act, with act content,
          The world of sense can no more stain his soul
          Than waters mar th' enamelled lotus-leaf.
          With life, with heart, with mind,—nay, with the help
          Of all five senses—letting selfhood go—
          Yogins toil ever towards their souls' release.
          Such votaries, renouncing fruit of deeds,
          Gain endless peace: the unvowed, the passion-bound,
          Seeking a fruit from works, are fastened down.
          The embodied sage, withdrawn within his soul,
          At every act sits godlike in "the town

---

[1]That is, "joy and sorrow, success and failure, heat and cold," etc.

Which hath nine gateways,"[2] neither doing aught
Nor causing any deed. This world's Lord makes
Neither the work, nor passion for the work,
Nor lust for fruit of work; the man's own self
Pushes to these!

• • •

The world is overcome—aye! even here!
By such as fix their faith on Unity.
The sinless Brahma dwells in Unity,
And they in Brahma. Be not over-glad
Attaining joy, and be not over-sad
Encountering grief, but, stayed on Brahma, still
Constant let each abide! The sage whose soul
Holds off from outer contacts, in himself
Finds bliss; to Brahma joined by piety,
His spirit tastes eternal peace. The joys
Springing from sense-life are but quickening wombs
Which breed sure griefs: those joys begin and end!
The wise mind takes no pleasure, Kunti's Son!
In such as those! But if a man shall learn,
Even while he lives and bears his body's chain,
To master lust and anger, he is blest!
He is the *Yukta*; he hath happiness,
Contentment, light, within: his life is merged
In Brahma's life; he doth Nirvana touch!
Thus go the Rishis unto rest, who dwell
With sins effaced, with doubts at end, with hearts
Governed and calm. Glad in all good they live,
Nigh to the peace of God; and all those live
Who pass their days exempt from greed and wrath,
Subduing self and senses, knowing the Soul!

The Saint who shuts outside his placid soul
All touch of sense, letting no contact through;
Whose quiet eyes gaze straight from fixed brows,
Whose outward breath and inward breath are drawn
Equal and slow through nostrils still and close;
That one—with organs, heart, and mind constrained,
Bent on deliverance, having put away
Passion, and fear, and rage;—hath, even now,

[2]*i.e.*, the body.

Obtained deliverance, ever and ever freed.
Yea! for he knows Me Who am He that heeds
The sacrifice and worship, God revealed;
And He who heeds not, being Lord of Worlds,
Lover of all that lives, God unrevealed,
Wherein who will shall find surety and shield!

● ● ●

Sequestered should he sit,
Steadfastly meditating, solitary,
His thoughts controlled, his passions laid away,
Quit of belongings. In a fair, still spot
Having his fixed abode,—not too much raised,
Nor yet too low,—let him abide, his goods
A cloth, a deerskin, and the Kusa-grass.
There, setting hard his mind upon The One,
Restraining heart and senses, silent, calm,
Let him accomplish Yoga, and achieve
Pureness of soul, holding immovable
Body and neck and head, his gaze absorbed
Upon his nose-end, rapt from all around,
Tranquil in spirit, free of fear, intent
Upon his Brahmacharya vow, devout,
Musing on Me, lost in the thought of Me.
That Yojin, so devoted, so controlled,
Comes to the peace beyond,—My peace, the peace
Of high Nirvana!
But for earthly needs
Religion is not his who too much fasts
Or too much feasts, nor his who sleeps away
An idle mind; nor his who wears to waste
His strength in vigils. Nay, Arjuna! call
That the true piety which most removes
Earth-aches and ills, where one is moderate
In eating and in resting, and in sport;
Measured in wish and act; sleeping betimes,
Waking betimes for duty.
When the man,
So living, centres on his soul the thought
Straitly restrained—untouched internally
By stress of sense—then is he *Yukta*. See!
Steadfast a lamp burns sheltered from the wind;
Such is the likeness of the Yogi's mind

Shut from sense-storms and burning bright to Heaven.
When mind broods placid, soothed with holy wont;
When Self contemplates self, and in itself
Hath comfort; when it knows the nameless joy
Beyond all scope of sense, revealed to soul—
Only to soul! and, knowing, wavers not,
True to the farther Truth; when, holding this,
It deems no other treasure comparable,
But, harboured there, cannot be stirred or shook
By any gravest grief, call that state "peace,"
That happy severance Yoga; call that man
The perfect Yogin!
Steadfastly the will
Must toil thereto, till efforts end in ease,
And thought has passed from thinking. Shaking off
All longings bred by dreams of fame and gain,
Shutting the doorways of the senses close
With watchful ward; so, step by step, it comes
To gift of peace assured and heart assuaged,
When the mind dwells self-wrapped, and the soul broods
Cumberless. But, as often as the heart
Breaks—wild and wavering—from control, so oft
Let him re-curb it, let him rein it back
To the soul's governance; for perfect bliss
Grows only in the bosom tranquillised,
The spirit passionless, purged from offence,
Vowed to the Infinite. He who thus vows
His soul to the Supreme Soul, quitting sin,
Passes unhindered to the endless bliss
Of unity with Brahma.

• • •

ARJUNA: And what road goeth he who, having faith,
      Fails, Krishna! in the striving; falling back
      From holiness, missing the perfect rule?
      Is he not lost, straying from Brahma's light,
      Like the vain cloud, which floats 'twixt earth and heaven
      When lightning splits it, and it vanisheth?
      Fain would I hear thee answer me herein,
      Since, Krishna! none save thou can clear the doubt.

KRISHNA: He is not lost, thou Son of Pritha! No!
      Nor earth, nor heaven is forfeit, even for him,

Because no heart that holds one right desire
Treadeth the road of loss! He who should fail,
Desiring righteousness, cometh at death
Unto the Region of the Just; dwells there
Measureless years, and being born anew,
Beginneth life again in some fair home
Amid the mild and happy. It may chance
He doth descend into a Yogin house
On Virtue's breast; but that is rare! Such birth
Is hard to be obtained on this earth, Chief!
So hath he back again what heights of heart
He did achieve, and so he strives anew
To perfectness, with better hope, dear Prince!
For by the old desire he is drawn on
Unwittingly; and only to desire
The purity of Yoga is to pass
Beyond the *Sabdabrahm*, the spoken Ved.
But, being Yogi, striving strong and long,
Purged from transgressions, perfected by births
Following on births, he plants his feet at last
Upon the farther path. Such an one ranks
Above ascetics, higher than the wise,
Beyond achievers of vast deeds!

                                                    • • •

Learn now, dear Prince! how, if thy soul be set
Ever on Me—still exercising Yog,
Still making Me thy Refuge—thou shalt come
Most surely unto perfect hold of Me.
I will declare to thee that utmost lore,
Whole and particular, which, when thou knowest,
Leaveth no more to know here in this world.

Of many thousand mortals, one, perchance,
Striveth for Truth; and of those few that strive—
Nay, and rise high—one only—here and there—
Knoweth Me, as I am, the very Truth.

Earth, water, flame, air, ether, life, and mind,
And individuality—those eight
Make up the showing of Me, Manifest.

These be my lower Nature; learn the higher,
Whereby, thou Valiant One! this Universe

Is, by its principle of life, produced;
Whereby the worlds of visible things are born
As from a *Yoni*. Know! I am that womb:
I make and I unmake this Universe:
Than me there is no other Master, Prince!
No other Maker! All these hang on me
As hangs a row of pearls upon its string.
I am the fresh taste of the water; I
The silver of the moon, the gold o' the sun,
The word of worship in the Veds, the thrill
That passeth in the ether, and the strength
Of man's shed seed. I am the good sweet smell
Of the moistened earth, I am the fire's red light,
The vital air moving in all which moves,
The holiness of hallowed souls, the root
Undying, whence hath sprung whatever is;
The wisdom of the wise, the intellect
Of the informed, the greatness of the great,
The splendour of the splendid. Kunti's Son!
These am I, free from passion and desire;
Yet am I right desire in all who yearn,
Chief of the Bharatas! for all those moods,
Soothfast, or passionate, or ignorant,
Which Nature frames, deduce from me; but all
Are merged in me—not I in them!

• • •

ARJUNA: Who is that BRAHMA? What that Soul of Souls,
The ADHYATMAN? What, Thou Best of All!
Thy work, the KARMA? Tell me what it is
Thou namest ADHIBHUTA? What again
Means ADHIDAIVA? Yea, and how it comes
Thou canst be ADHIYAJNA in thy flesh?
Slayer of Madhu! Further, make me know
How good men find thee in the hour of death?

KRISHNA: I BRAHMA am! the One Eternal GOD
And ADHYATMAN is My Being's name,
The Soul of Souls! What goeth forth from Me,
Causing all life to live, is KARMA called:
And, Manifested in divided forms,
I am the ADHIBHUTA, Lord of Lives;
And ADHIDAIVA, Lord of all the Gods,
Because I am PURUSHA, who begets.

And ADHIYAJNA, Lord of Sacrifice,
I—speaking with thee in this body here—
Am, thou embodied one! (for all the shrines
Flame unto Me!) And, at the hour of death,
He that hath meditated Me alone,
In putting off his flesh, comes forth to Me,
Enters into My Being—doubt thou not!
But, if he meditated otherwise
At hour of death, in putting off the flesh,
He goes to what he looked for, Kunti's Son!
Because the Soul is fashioned to its like.

Have Me, then, in thy heart always! and fight!
Thou too, when heart and mind are fixed on Me,
Shalt surely come to Me!

•••

By Me the whole vast Universe of things
Is spread abroad;—by Me, the Unmanifest!
In Me are all existences contained;
Not I in them!

Yet they are not contained,
Those visible things! Receive and strive to embrace
The mystery majestical! My Being—
Creating all, sustaining all–still dwells
Outside of all!

See! as the shoreless airs
Move in the measureless space, but are not space,
[And space were space without the moving airs];
So all things are in Me, but are not I.

At closing of each Kalpa, Indian Prince!
All things which be back to My Being come:
At the beginning of each Kalpa, all
Issue new-born from Me.
By Energy And help of Prakriti, my outer Self,
Again, and yet again, I make go forth
The realms of visible things—without their will—
All of them—by the power of Prakriti.
Yet these great makings, Prince! involve Me not,
Enchain Me not! I sit apart from them,
Other, and Higher, and Free; nowise attached!

Thus doth the stuff of worlds, moulded by Me,
Bring forth all that which is, moving or still,
Living or lifeless! Thus the worlds go on!
The minds untaught mistake Me, veiled in form;—
Naught see they of My secret Presence, nought
Of My hid Nature, ruling all which lives.
Vain hopes pursuing, vain deeds doing; fed
On vainest knowledge, senselessly they seek
An evil way, the way of brutes and fiends.
But My Mahatmas, those of noble soul
Who tread the path celestial, worship Me
With hearts unwandering,—knowing Me the Source,
Th' Eternal Source, of Life. Unendingly
They glorify Me; seek Me; keep their vows
Of reverence and love, with changeless faith
Adoring Me. Yea, and those too adore,
Who, offering sacrifice of wakened hearts,
Have sense of one pervading Spirit's stress,
One Force in every place, though manifold!
I am the Sacrifice! I am the Prayer!
I am the Funeral-Cake set for the dead!
I am the healing herb! I am the ghee,
The Mantra, and the flame, and that which burns!
I am—of all this boundless Universe—
The Father, Mother, Ancestor, and Guard!
The end of Learning! That which purifies
In lustral water! I am OM! I am
Rig-Veda, Sama-Veda, Yajur-Ved;
The Way, the Fosterer, the Lord, the Judge,
The Witness; the Abode, the Refuge-House,
The Friend, the Fountain and the Sea of Life
Which sends, and swallows up; Treasure of Worlds
And Treasure-Chamber! Seed and Seed-Sower,
Whence endless harvests spring! Sun's heat is mine;
Heaven's rain is mine to grant or to withhold;
Death am I, and Immortal Life I am, Arjuna!

••••

But to those blessed ones who worship Me,
Turning not otherwise, with minds set fast,
I bring assurance of full bliss beyond.

Nay, and of hearts which follow other gods
In simple faith, their prayers arise to me,

O Kunti's Son! though they pray wrongfully;
For I am the Receiver and the Lord
Of every sacrifice, which these know not
Rightfully; so they fall to earth again!
Who follow gods go to their gods; who vow
Their souls to Pitris go to Pitris; minds
To evil Bhuts given o'er sink to the Bhuts;
And whoso loveth Me cometh to Me.

• • •

KRISHNA: So be it! Kuru Prince! I will to thee unfold
Some portions of My Majesty, whose powers are manifold!
I am the Spirit seated deep in every creature's heart;
From Me they come; by Me they live; at My word they depart!
Vishnu of the Adityas I am, those Lords of Light;
Maritchi of the Maruts, the Kings of Storm and Blight;
By day I gleam, the golden Sun of burning cloudless Noon;
By Night, amid the asterisms I glide, the dappled Moon!
Of Vedas I am Sama-Veda, of gods in Indra's Heaven
Vasava; of the faculties to living beings given
The mind which apprehends and thinks; of Rudras Sankara;
Of Yakshas and of Rakshasas, Vittesh; and Pavaka
Of Vasus, and of mountain-peaks Meru; Vrihas-Pati
Know Me 'mid planetary Powers; 'mid Warriors heavenly
Skanda; of all the water-floods the Sea which drinketh each,
And Bhrigu of the holy Saints, and OM of sacred speech;
Of prayers the prayer ye whisper; of hills Him-ala's snow,
And Aswattha, the fig-tree, of all the trees that grow;
Of the Devarshis, Narada; and Chitrarath of them
That sing in Heaven, and Kapila of Munis, and the gem
Of flying steeds, Uchehaisravas, from Amrit-wave which burst;
Of elephants Airavata; of males the Best and First;
Of weapons Heav'n's hot thunderbolt; of cows white Kamadhuk,
From whose great milky udder-teats all hearts' desires are strook;
Vasuki of the serpent-tribes, round Mandara en-twined;
And thousand-fanged Ananta, on whose broad coils reclined
Leans Vishnu; and of water-things Varuna; Aryam
Of Pitris, and, of those that judge, Yama the Judge I am;
Of Daityas dread Prahlada; of what metes days and years,
Time's self I am; of woodland-beasts—buffaloes, deers, and bears—
The lordly-painted tiger, of birds the vast Garud,
The whirlwind 'mid the winds; 'mid chiefs Rama with blood imbrued,
Makar 'mid fishes of the sea, and Ganges 'mid the streams;

Yea! First, and Last, and Centre of all which is or seems
I am, Arjuna! Wisdom Supreme of what is wise,
Words on the uttering lips I am, and eyesight of the eyes,
And "A" of written characters, Dwandwa of knitted speech,
And Endless Life, and boundless Love, whose power sustaineth each;
And bitter Death which seizes all, and joyous sudden Birth,
Which brings to light all beings that are to be on earth;
And of the viewless virtues, Fame, Fortune, Song am I,
And Memory, and Patience; and Craft, and Constancy:
Of Vedic hymns the Vrihatsam, of metres Gayatri,
Of months the Margasirsha, of all the seasons three
The flower-wreathed Spring; in dicer's-play the conquering Double-Eight;
The splendour of the splendid, and the greatness of the great,
Victory I am, and Action! and the goodness of the good,
And Vasudev of Vrishni's race, and of this Pandu brood
Thyself!—Yea, my Arjuna! thyself; for thou art Mine!
Of poets Usana, of saints Vyasa, sage divine;
The policy of conquerors, the potency of kings,
The great unbroken silence in learning's secret things;
The lore of all the learned, the seed of all which springs.
Living or lifeless, still or stirred, whatever beings be,
None of them is in all the worlds, but it exists by Me!
Nor tongue can tell, Arjuna! nor end of telling come
Of these My boundless glories, whereof I teach thee some;
For wheresoe'er is wondrous work, and majesty, and might,
From Me hath all proceeded. Receive thou this aright!
Yet how shouldst thou receive, O Prince! the vastness of this word?
I, who am all, and made it all, abide its separate Lord!

• • •

ARJUNA: Lord! of the men who serve Thee—true in heart—
As God revealed; and of the men who serve,
Worshipping Thee Unrevealed, Unbodied, Far,
Which take the better way of faith and life?

KRISHNA: Whoever serve Me—as I show Myself—
Constantly true, in full devotion fixed,
Those hold I very holy. But who serve— Worshipping Me The One,
The Invisible,
The Unrevealed, Unnamed, Unthinkable,
Uttermost, All-pervading, Highest, Sure—
Who thus adore Me, mastering their sense,
Of one set mind to all, glad in all good,

These blessed souls come unto Me. Yet, hard
The travail is for such as bend their minds
To reach th' Unmanifest. That viewless path
Shall scarce be trod by man bearing the flesh!
But whereso any doeth all his deeds
Renouncing self for Me, full of Me, fixed
To serve only the Highest, night and day
Musing on Me—him will I swiftly lift
Forth from life's ocean of distress and death,
Whose soul clings fast to Me. Cling thou to Me!
Clasp Me with heart and mind! so shalt thou dwell
Surely with Me on high. But if thy thought
Droops from such height; if thou be'st weak to set
Body and soul upon Me constantly,
Despair not! give Me lower service! seek
To reach Me, worshipping with steadfast will;
And, if thou canst not worship steadfastly,
Work for Me, toil in works pleasing to Me!
For he that laboureth right for love of Me
Shall finally attain! But, if in this
Thy faint heart fails, bring Me thy failure! find
Refuge in Me! let fruits of labour go,
Renouncing hope for Me, with lowliest heart,
So shalt thou come; for, though to know is more
Than diligence, yet worship better is
Than knowing, and renouncing better still.
Near to renunciation—very near—
Dwelleth Eternal Peace!
Who hateth nought
Of all which lives, living himself benign,
Compassionate, from arrogance exempt,
Exempt from love of self, unchangeable
By good or ill; patient, contented, firm
In faith, mastering himself, true to his word,
Seeking Me, heart and soul; vowed unto Me,—
That man I love! Who troubleth not his kind,
And is not troubled by them; clear of wrath,
Living too high for gladness, grief, or fear,
That man I love! Who, dwelling quieteyed,
Stainless, serene, well-balanced, unperplexed,
Working with Me, yet from all works detached,
That man I love! Who, fixed in faith on Me,
Dotes upon none, scorns none; rejoices not,
And grieves not, letting good or evil hap

Light when it will, and when it will depart,
That man I love! Who, unto friend and foe
Keeping an equal heart, with equal mind
Bears shame and glory; with an equal peace
Takes heat and cold, pleasure and pain; abides
Quit of desires, hears praise or calumny
In passionless restraint, unmoved by each;
Linked by no ties to earth, steadfast in Me,
That man I love! But most of all I love
Those happy ones to whom 'tis life to live
In single fervid faith and love unseeing,
Drinking the blessed Amrit of my Being!

ARJUNA: Now would I hear, O gracious Kesava!
Of Life which seems, and Soul beyond, which sees,
And what it is we know—or think to know.

KRISHNA: Yea! Son of Kunti! for this flesh ye see
Is *Kshetra*, is the field where Life disports;
And that which views and knows it is the Soul,
Kshetrajna. In all "fields," thou Indian prince!
I am *Kshetrajna*. I am what surveys!
Only that knowledge knows which knows the known
By the knower! What it is, that "field" of life,
What qualities it hath, and whence it is,
And why it changeth, and the faculty
That wotteth it, the mightiness of this,
And how it wotteth—hear these things from Me!

The elements, the conscious life, the mind,
The unseen vital force, the nine strange gates
Of the body, and the five domains of sense;
Desire, dislike, pleasure and pain, and thought
Deep-woven, and persistency of being;
These all are wrought on Matter by the Soul!

Humbleness, truthfulness, and harmlessness,
Patience and honour, reverence for the wise,
Purity, constancy, control of self,
Contempt of sense-delights, self-sacrifice,
Perception of the certitude of ill
In birth, death, age, disease, suffering, and sin;
Detachment, lightly holding unto home,
Children, and wife, and all that bindeth men;

An ever-tranquil heart in fortunes good
And fortunes evil, with a will set firm
To worship Me—Me only! ceasing not;
Loving all solitudes, and shunning noise
Of foolish crowds; endeavours resolute
To reach perception of the Utmost Soul,
And grace to understand what gain it were
So to attain,—this is true Wisdom, Prince!
And what is otherwise is ignorance!

Now will I speak of knowledge best to know—
That Truth which giveth man Amrit to drink,
The Truth of HIM, the Para-Brahm, the All,
The Uncreated; not *Asat*, not *Sat*,
Not Form, nor the Unformed; yet both, and more;—
Whose hands are everywhere, and everywhere
Planted His feet, and everywhere His eyes
Beholding, and His ears in every place
Hearing, and all His faces everywhere
Enlightening and encompassing His worlds.
Glorified in the senses He hath given,
Yet beyond sense He is; sustaining all,
Yet dwells He unattached: of forms and modes
Master, yet neither form nor mode hath He;
He is within all beings—and without—
Motionless, yet still moving; not discerned
For subtlety of instant presence; close
To all, to each; yet measurelessly far!
Not manifold, and yet subsisting still
In all which lives; for ever to be known
As the Sustainer, yet, at the End of Times,
He maketh all to end—and re-creates.
The Light of Lights He is, in the heart of the Dark
Shining eternally. Wisdom He is
And Wisdom's way, and Guide of all the wise,
Planted in every heart.
So have I told
Of Life's stuff, and the moulding, and the lore
To comprehend. Whoso, adoring Me,
Perceiveth this, shall surely come to Me!

Know thou that Nature and the Spirit both
Have no beginning! Know that qualities
And changes of them are by Nature wrought;

That Nature puts to work the acting frame,
But Spirit doth inform it, and so cause
Feeling of pain and pleasure. Spirit, linked
To moulded matter, entereth into bond
With qualities by Nature framed, and, thus
Married to matter, breeds the birth again
In good or evil *yonis.*[3]
Yet is this—
Yea! in its bodily prison!—Spirit pure.
Spirit supreme; surveying, governing,
Guarding, possessing; Lord and Master still
PURUSHA, Ultimate, One Soul with Me.

Whoso thus knows himself, and knows his soul
PURUSHA working through the qualities
With Nature's modes, the light hath come for him!
Whatever flesh he bears, never again
Shall he take on its load. Some few there be
By meditation find the Soul in Self
Self-schooled; and some by long philosophy
And holy life reach thither; some by works:
Some, never so attaining, hear of light
From other lips, and seize, and cleave to it
Worshipping; yea! and those—to teaching true—
Overpass Death!

• • •

For in this world
Being is twofold: the Divided, one;
The Undivided, one. All things that live
Are "the Divided." That which sits apart,
"The Undivided."

Higher still is He,
The Highest, holding all, whose Name is LORD,
The Eternal, Sovereign, First! Who fills all worlds,
Sustaining them. And—dwelling thus beyond
Divided Being and Undivided—I
Am called of men and Vedas, Life Supreme,
The PURUSHOTTAMA.

[3]Wombs.

Who knows Me thus,
With mind unclouded, knoweth all, dear Prince!
And with his whole soul ever worshippeth Me.

Now is the sacred, secret Mystery
Declared to thee! Who comprehendeth this
Hath wisdom!

KRISHNA: Fearlessness, singleness of soul, the will
Always to strive for wisdom; opened hand
And governed appetites; and piety,
And love of lonely study; humbleness,
Uprightness, heed to injure nought which lives,
Truthfulness, slowness unto wrath, a mind
That lightly letteth go what others prize;
And equanimity, and charity
Which spieth no man's faults; and tenderness
Towards all that suffer; a contended heart,
Fluttered by no desires; a bearing mild,
Modest, and grave, with manhood nobly mixed,
With patience, fortitude, and purity;
An unrevengeful spirit, never given
To rate itself too high;—such be the signs,
O Indian Prince! of him whose feet are set
On that fair path which leads to heavenly birth!

Deceitfulness, and arrogance, and pride,
Quickness to anger, harsh and evil speech,
And ignorance, to its own darkness blind,—
These be the signs, My Prince! of him whose birth
Is fated for the regions of the vile.

The Heavenly Birth brings to deliverance,
So should'st thou know! The birth with Asuras
Brings into bondage. Be thou joyous, Prince!
Whose lot is set apart for heavenly Birth.

Two stamps there are marked on all living men,
Divine and Undivine; I spake to thee
By what marks thou shouldst know the Heavenly Man,
Hear from me now of the Unheavenly!

They comprehend not, the Unheavenly,
How Souls go forth from Me; nor how they come

Back unto Me: nor is there Truth in these,
Nor purity, nor rule of Life. "This world
Hath not a Law, nor Order, nor a Lord,"
So say they: "nor hath risen up by Cause
Following on Cause, in perfect purposing,
But is none other than a House of Lust."
And, this thing thinking, all those ruined ones—
Of little wit, dark-minded—give themselves
To evil deeds, the curses of their kind.
Surrendered to desires insatiable,
Full of deceitfulness, folly, and pride,
In blindness cleaving to their errors, caught
Into the sinful course, they trust this lie
As it were true—this lie which leads to death—
Finding in Pleasure all the good which is,
And crying "Here it finisheth!"

Ensnared
In nooses of a hundred idle hopes,
Slaves to their passion and their wrath, they buy
Wealth with base deeds, to glut hot appetites;
"Thus much, to-day," they say, "we gained! thereby
Such and such wish of heart shall have its fill;
And this is ours! and th' other shall be ours!
To-day we slew a foe, and we will slay
Our other enemy to-morrow! Look!
Are we not lords? Make we not goodly cheer?
Is not our fortune famous, brave, and great?
Rich are we, proudly born! What other men
Live like to us? Kill, then, for sacrifice!
Cast largesse, and be merry!" So they speak
Darkened by ignorance; and so they fall—
Tossed to and fro with projects, tricked, and bound
In net of black delusion, lost in lusts—
Down to foul Naraka. Conceited, fond,
Stubborn and proud, dead-drunken with the wine
Of wealth, and reckless, all their offerings
Have but a show of reverence, being not made
In piety of ancient faith. Thus vowed
To self-hood, force, insolence, feasting, wrath,
These My blasphemers, in the forms they wear
And in the forms they breed, my foemen are,
Hateful and hating; cruel, evil, vile,
Lowest and least of men, whom I cast down

Again, and yet again, at end of lives,
Into some devilish womb, whence—birth by birth—
The devilish wombs re-spawn them, all beguiled;
And, till they find and worship Me, sweet Prince!
Tread they that Nether Road.

The Doors of Hell
Are threefold, whereby men to ruin pass,—
The door of Lust, the door of Wrath, the door
Of Avarice. Let a man shun those three!

• • •

Whoso performeth—diligent, content—
The work allotted him, whate'er it be,
Lays hold of perfectness! Hear how a man
Findeth perfection, being so content:
He findeth it through worship—wrought by work—
Of HIM that is the Source of all which lives,
Of HIM by Whom the universe was stretched.

Better thine own work is, though done with fault,
Than doing others' work, ev'n excellently.
He shall not fall in sin who fronts the task
Set him by Nature's hand! Let no man leave
His natural duty, Prince! though it bear blame!
For every work hath blame, as every flame
Is wrapped in smoke! Only that man attains
Perfect surcease of work whose work was wrought
With mind unfettered, soul wholly subdued
Desires forever dead, results renounced.

Learn from me, Son of Kunti! also this,
How one, attaining perfect peace, attains
BRAHM, the supreme, the highest height of all!

Devoted—with a heart grown pure, restrained
In lordly self-control, foregoing wiles
Of song and senses, freed from love and hate,
Dwelling 'mid solitudes, in diet spare,
With body, speech, and will tamed to obey,
Ever to holy meditation vowed,
From passions liberate, quit of the Self,
Of arrogance, impatience, anger, pride;
Freed from surroundings, quiet, lacking nought—

Such an one grows to oneness with the BRAHM;
Such an one, growing one with BRAHM, serene,
Sorrows no more, desires no more; his soul,
Equally loving all that lives, loves well
Me, Who have made them, and attains to Me.
By this same love and worship doth he know
Me as I am, how high and wonderful,
And knowing, straightway enters into Me.
And whatsoever deeds he doeth—fixed
In Me, as in his refuge—he hath won
Forever and forever by My grace
Th' Eternal Rest!

Buddhism

Unlike Hinduism, which developed gradually over several centuries through the fusion of the religious myths of the early, indigenous population of India with those of the Aryan invaders, Buddhism owes its origin to the career of one person—Siddhartha Gautama (563?–483? B.C.), who later came to be called the Buddha (the "Enlightened One"). Also unlike Hinduism, which has largely remained a religion of India, Buddhism spread throughout the rest of Asia, and beyond, to become one of history's great world religions. Nevertheless, Buddhism, although it arose in part as a reaction against traditional Hinduism, shares several of the features, in a modified form, of the older religion.

Gautama, the founder of Buddhism, was born in northern India, the son of a local chieftain. Although innumerable legends have grown up about him, the facts apparently are that, as a young man, he became disillusioned with life, as he was living it, and decided to seek salvation through enlightenment. He pursued his goal (it is said for six years), first through philosophical meditation and then through asceticism and the mortification of his body. But neither method produced the result he sought. Finally, in desperation, he sat down under a fig tree (later famous as the "Bo-tree") and reviewed his past, unsuccessful endeavors. There the realization struck him that his efforts must be self-defeating because they were the result of his own desires. From this it followed that he must abandon desires altogether, if he was to gain true peace of mind and blessedness. Here was his great Enlightenment; he became the Buddha. Returning from this experience to the town of Benares, he accosted five ascetics with whom he had previously been living. In a deer park nearby he preached his first sermon to them.

Gautama spent the remainder of his life teaching, preaching, and organizing his growing band of disciples. Each initiate of the Buddhist order subscribed to the following confession: "I take refuge in the Buddha, I take refuge in the Law of Truth, I take refuge in the Order." However, about a century after Gautama's death, a schism developed within the faith, with the result that historically Buddhism can be divided into two large branches. First is what is known as Theravada Buddhism, the more conserative branch, which has attempted to adhere as closely as possible to the fundamental doctrines of the founder. The second is Mahayana Buddhism. Its main doctrinal difference from Theravada

Trans. T. W. Rhys Davids.

Buddhism is the belief in a multiplicity of Buddhas (known as Bodhisattvas), both actual and potential, who delay entering Nirvana in order to help others. This change has had great practical effects because it gives assurance to the faithful that there will always be a power in the universe to ameliorate their sufferings and guarantee their salvation.

The first of the following selections is from the Buddha's Deer Park Sermon, as it was later recorded. It contains statements of three basic concepts of the Buddhist faith—the Four Noble Truths, the Noble Eight-fold Path, and the Middle Way. The second, longer selection also, according to tradition, repeats the words of the Buddha himself. The title may be translated in a variety of ways; a good rendition is *The Path of Virtue*. The work itself consists mainly of a discussion of Buddhist morality; its main goal is to draw distinctions between an evil and a good way of life. More particularly, the author instructs novices in the requirements they must fulfill to become worthy Buddhist monks, wearing "the yellow gown."

The third selection is a collection of edicts by the Theravadan Buddhist Indian ruler Ashoka. The last selection is an excerpt from a Mahayana treatise produced in China that shows the intercultural nature of Buddhism, as well as its intellectual diversity.

---

1.   According to the Buddha, what is the essential problem of human existence? What is the solution?

2.   Ashoka wished to be (or at least present himself as) the model Buddhist ruler. What did he think that meant? What activities did he emphasize to prove his dedication to Buddhism?

3.   Compare and contrast Mahayana (Greater Vehicle) teachings with the teachings attributed to the Buddha himself.

The Foundation of the Kingdom of Righteousness

Reverence to the Blessed One, the Holy One, the Fully-Enlightened One.

Thus have I heard. The Blessed One was once staying at Benares, at the hermitage called Migadâya. And there the Blessed One addressed the company of the five Bhikkhus [monks], and said:

'There are two extremes, O Bhikkhus, which the man who has given up the world ought not to follow—the habitual practice, on the one hand, of those things whose attraction depends upon the passions, and especially of sensuality—a low and pagan way (of seeking satisfaction) unworthy, unprofitable, and fit only for the worldly-minded—and the habitual practice, on the other hand, of asceticism (or self-mortification), which is painful, unworthy, and unprofitable.

'There is a middle path, O Bhikkhus, avoiding these two extremes, discovered by the Tathâgata [Buddha]—a path which opens the eyes, and bestows understanding, which leads to peace of mind, to the higher wisdom, to full enlightenment, to Nirvana.

'What is that middle path, O Bhikkhus, avoiding these two extremes, discovered by the Tathâgata—that path which opens the eyes, and bestows understanding, which leads to peace of mind, to the higher wisdom, to full enlightenment, to Nirvana? Verily! it is this noble eightfold path; that is to say:

'Right views;
Right aspirations;
Right speech;
Right conduct;
Right livelihood;
Right effort;
Right mindfulness; and
Right contemplation.

'This, O Bhikkhus, is that middle path, avoiding these two extremes, discovered by the Tathâgata—that path which opens the eyes, and bestows understanding, which leads to peace of mind, to the higher wisdom, to full enlightenment, to Nirvana.

'Now this, O Bhikkhus, is the noble truth concerning suffering.

'Birth is attended with pain, decay is painful, disease is painful, death is painful. Union with the unpleasant is painful, painful is separation from the pleasant; and any craving that is unsatisfied, that too is painful. In brief, the five aggregates which spring from attachment (the conditions of individuality and their cause) are painful.

'This then, O Bhikkhus, is the noble truth concerning suffering.

'Now this, O Bhikkhus, is the noble truth concerning the origin of suffering.

'Verily, it is that thirst (or craving), causing the renewal of existence, accompanied by sensual delight, seeking satisfaction now here, now there—that is to say, the craving for the gratification of the passions, or the craving for (a future) life, or the craving for success (in this present life).

'This then, O Bhikkhus, is the noble truth concerning the origin of suffering.

'Now this, O Bhikkhus, is the noble truth concerning the destruction of suffering.

Trans. F. Max Müller.

'Verily, it is the destruction, in which no passion remains, of this very thirst; the laying aside of, the getting rid of, the being free from, the harbouring no longer of this thirst.

'This then, O Bhikkhus, is the noble truth concerning the destruction of suffering.

'Now this, O Bhikkhus, is the noble truth concerning the way which leads to the destruction of sorrow. Verily! it is this noble eightfold path.'

Dhammapada

Chapter I

THE TWIN VERSES

All that we are is the result of what we have thought: it is founded on our thoughts, it is made up of our thoughts. If a man speaks or acts with an evil thought . . . , pain follows him, as the wheel follows the foot of the ox that draws the carriage.

All that we are is the result of what we have thought: it is founded on our thoughts, it is made up of our thoughts. If a man speaks or acts with a pure thought, happiness follows him, like a shadow that never leaves him.

'He abused me, he beat me, he defeated me, he robbed me,'—in those who harbour such thoughts hatred will never cease.

'He abused me, he beat me, he defeated me, he robbed me,'—in those who do not harbour such thoughts hatred will cease.

For hatred does not cease by hatred at any time: hatred ceases by love, this is an old rule.

The world does not know that we must all come to an end here;—but those who know it, their quarrels cease at once.

He who lives looking for pleasures only, his senses uncontrolled, immoderate in his food, idle, and weak, Mâra (the tempter) will certainly overthrow him, as the wind throws down a weak tree.

He who lives without looking for pleasures, his senses well controlled, moderate in his food, faithful and strong, him Mâra will certainly not overthrow, any more than the wind throws down a rocky mountain.

He who wishes to put on the yellow dress without having cleansed himself from sin, who disregards also temperance and truth, is unworthy of the yellow dress.

But he who has cleansed himself from sin, is well grounded in all virtues, and regards also temperance and truth, he is indeed worthy of the yellow dress.

They who imagine truth in untruth, and see untruth in truth, never arrive at truth, but follow vain desires.

They who know truth in truth, and untruth in untruth, arrive at truth, and follow true desires.

As rain breaks through an illthatched house, passion will break through an unreflecting mind.

As rain does not break through a well-thatched house, passion will not break through a well-reflecting mind.

The evil-doer mourns in this world, and he mourns in the next; he mourns in both. He mourns and suffers when he sees the evil of his own work.

The virtuous man delights in this world, and he delights in the next; he delights in both. He delights and rejoices, when he sees the purity of his own work.

The evil-doer suffers in this world, and he suffers in the next; he suffers in both. He suffers when he thinks of the evil he has done; he suffers more when going on the evil path.

The virtuous man is happy in this world, and he is happy in the next; he is happy in both. He is happy when he thinks of the good he has done; he is still more happy when going on the good path.

The thoughtless man, even if he can recite a large portion (of the law), but is not a doer of it, has no share in the priesthood, but is like a cowherd counting the cows of others.

The follower of the law, even if he can recite only a small portion (of the law), but, having forsaken passion and hatred and foolishness, possesses true knowledge and serenity of mind, he, caring for nothing in this world or that to come, has indeed a share in the priesthood.

Chapter III

THOUGHT

As a fletcher makes straight his arrow, a wise man makes straight his trembling and unsteady thought, which is difficult to guard, difficult to hold back,

As a fish taken from his watery home and thrown on the dry ground, our thought trembles all over in order to escape the dominion of Mâra (the tempter).

It is good to tame the mind, which is difficult to hold in and flighty, rushing wherever it listeth; a tamed mind brings happiness.

Let the wise man guard his thoughts, for they are difficult to perceive, very artful, and they rush wherever they list: thoughts well guarded bring happiness.

Those who bridle their mind which travels far, moves about alone, is without a body, and hides in the chamber (of the heart), will be free from the bonds of Mâra (the tempter).

If a man's thoughts are unsteady, if he does not know the true law, if his peace of mind is troubled, his knowledge will never be perfect.

If a man's thoughts are not dissipated, if his mind is not perplexed, if he has ceased to think of good or evil, then there is no fear for him while he is watchful.

Knowing that this body is (fragile) like a jar, and making this thought firm like a fortress, one should attack Mâra (the tempter) with the weapon of knowledge, one should watch him when conquered, and should never rest.

Before long, alas! this body will lie on the earth, despised, without understanding, like a useless log.

Whatever a hater may do to a hater, or an enemy to an enemy, a wrongly directed mind will do us greater mischief.

Not a mother, not a father will do so much, nor any other relative; a well-directed mind will do us greater service.

Chapter V

THE FOOL

Long is the night to him who is awake; long is a mile to him who is tired; long is life to the foolish who do not know the true law.

If a traveller does not meet with one who is his better, or his equal, let him firmly keep to his solitary journey; there is no companionship with a fool.

'These sons belong to me, and this wealth belongs to me,' with such thoughts a fool is tormented. He himself does not belong to himself; how much less sons and wealth?

The fool who knows his foolishness, is wise at least so far. But a fool who thinks himself wise, he is called a fool indeed.

If a fool be associated with a wise man even all his life, he will perceive the truth as little as a spoon perceives the taste of soup.

If an intelligent man be associated for one minute only with a wise man, he will soon perceive the truth, as the tongue perceives the taste of soup.

Fools of little understanding have themselves for their greatest enemies, for they do evil deeds which must bear bitter fruits.

That deed is not well done of which a man must repent, and the reward of which he receives crying and with a tearful face.

No, that deed is well done of which a man does not repent, and the reward of which he receives gladly and cheerfully.

As long as the evil deed done does not bear fruit, the fool thinks it is like honey: but when it ripens, then the fool suffers grief.

Let a fool month after month eat his food (like an ascetic) with the tip of a blade of Kusa grass, yet is he not worth the sixteenth particle of those who have well weighed the law.

An evil deed, like newly drawn milk, does not turn (suddenly); smouldering, like fire covered by ashes, it follows the fool.

Chapter VI

THE WISE MAN

If you see an intelligent man who tells you where true treasures are to be found, who shows what is to be avoided, and administers reproofs, follow that wise man; it will be better, not worse, for those who follow him.

Let him admonish, let him teach, let him forbid what is improper!—he will be beloved of the good, by the bad he will be hated.

Do not have evil-doers for friends, do not have low people for friends: have virtuous people for friends, have for friends the best of men.

He who drinks in the law lives happily with a serene mind: the sage rejoices always in the law, as preached by the elect (Ariyas).

Well-makers lead the water (wherever they like); fletchers bend the arrow; carpenters bend a log of wood; wise people fashion themselves.

As a solid rock is not shaken by the wind, wise people falter not amidst blame and praise.

Wise people, after they have listened to the laws, become serene, like a deep, smooth, and still lake.

Good people walk on whatever befall, the good do not prattle, longing for pleasure; whether touched by happiness or sorrow wise people never appear elated or depressed.

If, whether for his own sake, or for the sake of others, a man wishes neither for a son, nor for wealth, nor for lordship, and if he does not wish for his own success by unfair means, then he is good, wise, and virtuous.

Chapter IX

EVIL

If a man would hasten towards the good, he should keep his thought away from evil; if a man does what is good slothfully, his mind delights in evil.

If a man commits a sin, let him not do it again; let him not delight in sin: pain is the outcome of evil.

If a man does what is good, let him do it again; let him delight in it: happiness is the outcome of good.

Even an evil-doer sees happiness as long as his evil deed has not ripened; but when his evil deed has ripened, then does the evil-doer see evil.

Even a good man sees evil days, as long as his good deed has not ripened; but when his good deed has ripened, then does the good man see happy days.

Let no man think lightly of evil, saying in his heart, It will not come nigh unto me. Even by the falling of water-drops a water-pot is filled; the fool becomes full of evil, even if he gather it little by little.

Let no man think lightly of good, saying in his heart. It will not come nigh unto me. Even by the falling of water-drops a water-pot is filled; the wise man becomes full of good, even if he gather it little by little.

Let a man avoid evil deeds, as a merchant, if he has few companions and carries much wealth, avoids a dangerous road; as a man who loves life avoids poison.

He who has no wound on has hand, may touch poison with his hand; poison does not affect one who has no wound; nor is there evil for one who does not commit evil.

If a man offend a harmless, pure, and innocent person, the evil falls back upon that fool, like light dust thrown up against the wind.

Some people are born again; evil-doers go to hell; righteous people go to heaven; those who are free from all worldly desires attain Nirvana.

Chapter XIII

THE WORLD

Do not follow the evil law! Do not live on in thoughtlessness! Do not follow false doctrine! Be not a friend of the world.

Rouse thyself! do not be idle! Follow the law of virtue! The virtuous rests in bliss in this world and in the next.

Follow the law of virtue; do not follow that of sin. The virtuous rests in bliss in this world and in the next.

Look upon the world as a bubble, look upon it as a mirage: the king of death does not see him who thus looks down upon the world.

Come, look at this glittering world, like unto a royal chariot; the foolish are immersed in it, but the wise do not touch it.

He who formerly was reckless and afterwards became sober, brightens up this world, like the moon when freed from clouds.

He whose evil deeds are covered by good deeds, brightens up this world, like the moon when freed from clouds.

This world is dark, few only can see here; a few only go to heaven, like birds escaped from the net.

The swans go on the path of the sun, they go through the ether by means of their miraculous power; the wise are led out of this world, when they have conquered Mâra and his train.

If a man has transgressed one law, and speaks lies, and scoffs at another world, there is no evil he will not do.

The uncharitable do not go to the world of the gods; fools only do not praise liberality; a wise man rejoices in liberality, and through it becomes blessed in the other world.

Better than sovereignty over the earth, better than going to heaven, better than lordship over all worlds, is the reward of the first step in holiness.

Chapter XIV

THE BUDDHA

He whose conquest is not conquered again, into whose conquest no one in this world enters, by what track can you lead him, the Awakened, the Omniscient, the trackless?

He whom no desire with its snares and poisons can lead astray, by what track can you lead him, the Awakened, the Omniscient, the trackless?

Even the gods envy those who are awakened and not forgetful, who are given to meditation, who are wise, and who delight in the repose of retirement (from the world).

Difficult (to obtain) is the conception of men, difficult is the life of mortals, difficult is the hearing of the True Law, difficult is the birth of the Awakened (the attainment of Buddhahood).

Not to commit any sin, to do good, and to purify one's mind, that is the teaching of (all) the Awakened.

The Awakened call patience the highest penance, long-suffering the highest Nirvana; for he is not an anchorite who strikes others, he is not an ascetic who insults others.

Not to blame, not to strike, to live restrained under the law, to be moderate in eating, to sleep and sit alone, and to dwell on the highest thoughts,— this is the teaching of the Awakened.

There is no satisfying lusts, even by a shower of gold pieces; he who knows that lusts have a short taste and cause pain, he is wise;

Even in heavenly pleasures he finds no satisfaction, the disciple who is fully awakened delights only in the destruction of all desires.

Men, driven by fear, go to many a refuge, to mountains and forests, to groves and sacred trees.

But that is not a safe refuge, that is not the best refuge; a man is not delivered from all pains after having gone to that refuge.

He who takes refuge with Buddha, the Law, and the Church; he who, with clear understanding, sees the four holy truths:—

Viz, pain, the origin of pain, the destruction of pain, and the eight-fold holy way that leads to the quieting of pain;—

That is the safe refuge, that is the best refuge; having gone to that refuge, a man is delivered from all pain.

A supernatural person (a Buddha) is not easily found, he is not born everywhere. Wherever such a sage is born, that race prospers.

Happy is the arising of the awakened, happy is the teaching of the True Law, happy is peace in the church, happy is the devotion of those who are at peace.

He who pays homage to those who deserve homage, whether the awakened (Buddha) or their disciples, those who have overcome the host (of evils), and crossed the flood of sorrow, he who pays homage to such as have found deliverance and know no fear, his merit can never be measured by anybody.

Chapter XVI

PLEASURE

He who gives himself to vanity, and does not give himself to meditation, forgetting the real aim (of life) and grasping at pleasure, will in time envy him who has exerted himself in meditation.

Let no man ever look for what is pleasant, or what is unpleasant. Not to see what is pleasant is pain, and it is pain to see what is unpleasant.

Let, therefore, no man love anything; loss of the beloved is evil. Those who love nothing, and hate nothing, have no fetters.

From pleasure comes grief, from pleasure comes fear; he who is free from pleasure knows neither grief nor fear.

From affection comes grief, from affection comes fear; he who is free from affection knows neither grief nor fear.

From lust comes grief, from lust comes fear; he who is free from lust knows neither grief nor fear.

From love comes grief, from love comes fear; he who is free from love knows neither grief nor fear.

From greed comes grief, from greed comes fear; he who is free from greed knows neither grief nor fear.

He who possesses virtue and intelligence, who is just, speaks the truth, and does what is his own business, him the world will hold dear.

Chapter XVII

ANGER

Let a man leave anger, let him forsake pride, let him overcome all bondage! No sufferings befall the man who is not attached to name and form, and who calls nothing his own.

He who holds back rising anger like a rolling chariot, him I call a real driver; other people are but holding the reins.

Let a man overcome anger by love, let him overcome evil by good; let him overcome the greedy by liberality, the liar by truth!

Speak the truth, do not yield to anger; give, if thou art asked for little; by these three steps thou wilt go near the gods.

The sages who injure nobody, and who always control their body, they will go to the unchangeable place (Nirvana), where, if they have gone, they will suffer no more.

Those who are ever watchful, who study day and night, and who strive after Nirvana their passions will come to an end.

This is an old saying, O Atula, this is not only of to-day: 'They blame him who sits silent, they blame him who speaks much, they also blame him who says little; there is no one on earth who is not blamed.'

There never was, there never will be, nor is there now, a man who is always blamed, or a man who is always praised.

But he whom those who discriminate praise continually day after day, as without blemish, wise, rich in knowledge and virtue, who would dare to blame him like a coin made of gold from the Gambû river? Even the gods praise him, he is praised even by Brahman.

Beware of bodily anger, and control thy body! Leave the sins of the body, and with thy body practice virtue!

Beware of the anger of the tongue, and control thy tongue! Leave the sins of the tongue, and practise virtue with thy tongue!

Beware of the anger of the mind, and control thy mind! Leave the sins of the mind, and practise virtue with thy mind!

The wise who control their body, who control their tongue, the wise who control their mind, are indeed well controlled.

Chapter XVIII

IMPURITY

Thou art now like a sere leaf, the messengers of death have come near to thee; thou standest at the door of thy departure, and thou hast no provision for thy journey.

Make thyself an island, work hard, be wise! When thy impurities are blown away, and thou art free from guilt, thou wilt enter into the heavenly world of the elect.

Thy life has come to an end, thou art come near to death, there is no resting-place for thee on the road, and thou hast no provision for thy journey.

Make thyself an island, work hard, be wise! When thy impurities are blown away, and thou art free from guilt, thou wilt not enter again into birth and decay.

Let a wise man blow off the impurities of his self, as a smith blows off the impurities of silver, one by one, little by little, and from time to time.

As the impurity which springs from the iron, when it springs from it, destroys it; thus do a transgressor's own works lead him to the evil path.

The taint of prayers is non-repetition; the taint of houses, non-repair; the taint of the body is sloth; the taint of a watchman, thoughtlessness.

Bad conduct is the taint of woman, greediness the taint of a benefactor; tainted are all evil ways, in this world and in the next.

But there is a taint worse than all taints,—ignorance is the greatest taint. O mendicants! throw off that taint, and become taintless!

Life is easy to live for a man who is without shame, a crow hero, a mischief-maker, an insulting, bold, and wretched fellow.

But life is hard to live for a modest man, who always looks for what is pure, who is disinterested, quiet, spotless, and intelligent.

He who destroys life, who speaks untruth, who in this world takes what is not given him, who goes to another man's wife;

And the man who gives himself to drinking intoxicating liquors, he, even in this world, digs up his own root.

O man, know this, that the unrestrained are in a bad state; take care that greediness and vice do not bring thee to grief for a long time!

The world gives according to their faith or according to their pleasure: if a man frets about the food and the drink given to others, he will find no rest either by day or by night.

He in whom that feeling is destroyed, and taken out with the very root, finds rest by day and by night.

There is no fire like passion, there is no shark like hatred, there is no snare like folly, there is no torrent like greed.

The fault of others is easily perceived, but that of oneself is difficult to perceive; a man winnows his neighbour's faults like chaff, but his own fault he hides, as a cheat hides the bad die from the gambler.

Chapter XXII

THE DOWNWARD COURSE

He who says what is not, goes to hell; he also who, having done a thing, says I have not done it. After death both are equal, they are men with evil deeds in the next world.

Many men whose shoulders are covered with the yellow gown are ill-conditioned and unrestrained; such evil-doers by their evil deeds go to hell.

Better it would be to swallow a heated iron ball, like flaring fire, than that a bad unrestrained fellow should live on the charity of the land.

Four things does a reckless man gain who covets his neighbour's wife,— a bad reputation, an uncomfortable bed, thirdly, punishment, and lastly, hell.

There is bad reputation, and the evil way (to hell), there is the short pleasure of the frightened in the arms of the frightened, and the king imposes heavy punishment; therefore let no man think of his neighbour's wife.

As a grass-blade, if badly grasped, cuts the arm, badly-practised asceticism leads to hell.

An act carelessly performed, a broken vow, and hesitating obedience to discipline, all this brings no great reward.

If anything is to be done, let a man do it, let him attack it vigorously! A careless pilgrim only scatters the dust of his passions more widely.

An evil deed is better left undone, for a man repents of it afterwards; a good deed is better done, for having done it, one does not repent.

Like a well-guarded frontier fort, with defences within and without, so let a man guard himself. Not a moment should escape, for they who allow the right moment to pass, suffer pain when they are in hell.

They who are ashamed of what they ought not to be ashamed of, and are not ashamed of what they ought to be ashamed of, such men, embracing false doctrines, enter the evil path.

They who fear when they ought not to fear, and fear not when they ought to fear, such men, embracing false doctrines, enter the evil path.

They who forbid when there is nothing to be forbidden, and forbid not when there is something to be forbidden, such men, embracing false doctrines, enter the evil path.

They who know what is forbidden as forbidden, and what is not forbidden as not forbidden, such men, embracing the true doctrine, enter the good path.

Chapter XXIV

THIRST

The thirst of a thoughtless man grows like a creeper; he runs from life to life, like a monkey seeking fruit in the forest.

Whomsoever this fierce thirst overcomes, full of poison, in this world, his sufferings increase like the abounding Bîrana grass.

He who overcomes this fierce thirst, difficult to be conquered in this world, sufferings fall off from him, like water-drops from a lotus leaf.

This salutary word I tell you, 'Do ye, as many as are here assembled, dig up the root of thirst, as he who wants the sweet-scented Usîra root must dig up the Bîrana grass, that Mâra (the tempter) may not crush you again and again, as the stream crushes the reeds.'

As a tree, even though it has been cut down, is firm so long as its root is safe, and grows again, thus, unless the feeders of thirst are destroyed, this pain (of life) will return again and again.

He whose thirst running towards pleasure is exceeding strong in the thirty-six channels, the waves will carry away that misguided man, viz, his desires which are set on passion.

The channels run everywhere, the creeper (of passion) stands sprouting; if you see the creeper springing up, cut its root by means of knowledge.

A creature's pleasures are extravagant and luxurious; sunk in lust and looking for pleasure, men undergo (again and again) birth and decay.

Men, driven on by thirst, run about like a snared hare; held in fetters and bonds, they undergo pain for a long time, again and again.

Men, driven on by thirst, run about like a snared hare; let therefore the mendicant drive out thirst, by striving after passionlessness for himself.

He who having got rid of the forest (of lust) (i.e. after having reached Nirvana) gives himself over to forestlife (i.e. to lust), and who, when removed from the forest (i.e. from lust), runs to the forest (i.e. to lust), look at that man! though free, he runs into bondage.

Wise people do not call that a strong fetter which is made of iron, wood, or hemp; far stronger is the care for precious stones and rings, for sons and a wife.

That fetter wise people call strong which drags down, yields, but is difficult to undo; after having cut this at last, people leave the world, free from cares, and leaving desires and pleasures behind.

Those who are slaves to passions, run down with the stream (of desires), as a spider runs down the web which he has made himself; when they have cut this, at last, wise people leave the world, free from cares, leaving all affection behind.

Give up what is before, give up what is behind, give up what is in the middle, when thou goest to the other shore of existence; if thy mind is altogether free, thou wilt not again enter into birth and decay.

If a man is tossed about by doubts, full of strong passions, and yearning only for what is delightful, his thirst will grow more and more, and he will indeed make his fetters strong.

If a man delights in quieting doubts, and, always reflecting, dwells on what is not delightful (the impurity of the body, etc.), he certainly will remove, nay, he will cut the fetter of Mâra.

He who has reached the consummation, who does not tremble, who is without thirst and without sin, he has broken all the thorns of life: this will be his last body.

From the Thirteenth Rock Edict

When the king, Beloved of the Gods and of Gracious Mien, had been consecrated eight years Kalinga was conquered, 150,000 people were deported, 100,000 were killed, and many times that number died. But after the conquest of Kalinga, the Beloved of the Gods began to follow Righteousness (Dharma), to love Righteousness, and to give instruction in Righteousness. Now the Beloved of the Gods regrets the conquest of Kalinga, for when an independent country is conquered people are killed, they die, or are deported, and that the Beloved of the Gods finds very painful and grievous. And this he finds even more grievous—that all the inhabitants—brāhmans, ascetics, and other sectarians, and householders who are obedient to superiors, parents, and elders, who treat friends, acquaintances, companions, relatives, slaves, and servants with respect, and are firm in their faith—all suffer violence, murder, and separation from their loved ones. Even those who are fortunate enough not to have lost those near and dear to them are afflicted at the misfortunes of friends, acquaintances, companions, and relatives. The participation of all men in common suffering is grievous to the Beloved of the Gods. Moreover there is no land, except that of the Greeks, where groups of brāhmans and ascetics are not found, or where men are not members of one sect or another. So now, even if the number of those killed and captured in the conquest of Kalinga had been a hundred or a thousand times less, it would be grievous to the Beloved of the Gods. The Beloved of the Gods will forgive as far as he can, and he even conciliates the forest tribes of his dominions; but he warns them that there is power even in the remorse of the Beloved of the Gods, and he tells them to reform, lest they be killed.

For all beings the Beloved of the Gods desires security, self-control, calm of mind, and gentleness. The Beloved of the Gods considers that the greatest victory is the victory of Righteousness; and this he has won here (in India) and even five hundred leagues beyond his frontiers in the realm of the Greek king Antiochus, and beyond Antiochus among the four kings Ptolemy, Antigonus, Magas, and Alexander. Even where the envoys of the Beloved of the Gods have not been sent men hear of the way in which he follows and teaches Righteousness, and they too follow it and will follow it. Thus he achieves a universal conquest, and conquest always gives a feeling of pleasure; yet it is but a slight pleasure, for the Beloved of the Gods only looks on that which concerns the next life as of great importance.

I have had this inscription of Righteousness engraved that all my sons and grandsons may not seek to gain new victories, that in whatever victories they may gain they may prefer forgiveness and light punishment, that they may consider the only [valid] victory the victory of Righteousness, which is of value both in this world and the next, and that all their pleasure may be in Righteousness. . . .

From a minor Rock Edict (Maski Version)

Thus speaks Ashoka, the Beloved of the Gods. For two and a half years I have been an open follower of the Buddha, though at first I did not make much progress. But for more than a year now I have drawn closer to the [Buddhist] Order, and have made much progress. In India the gods who formerly did not mix with men now do so. This is the result of effort, and may be obtained not only by the great, but even by the small, through effort—thus they may even easily win heaven.

Father and mother should be obeyed, teachers should be obeyed: pity . . . should be felt for all creatures. These virtues of Righteousness should be practiced. . . . This is an ancient rule, conducive to long life.

Now when he goes on tour ... he interviews and gives gifts to brāhmans and ascetics; he interviews and gives money to the aged; he interviews the people of the provinces, and instructs and questions them on Righteousness; and the pleasure which the Beloved of the Gods derives therefrom is as good as a second revenue.

Even when they have to be done [to conform to custom and keep up appearances] such ceremonies are of little use. But the ceremonies of Righteousness are of great profit—these are the good treatment of slaves and servants, respect for elders, self-mastery in one's relations with living beings, gifts to brāhmans and ascetics, and so on. But for their success everyone—fathers, mothers, brothers, masters, friends, acquaintances, and neighbors—must agree—"These are good! These are the ceremonies that we should perform for success in our undertakings ... and when we have succeeded we will perform them again!" Other ceremonies are of doubtful utility—one may achieve one's end through them or one may not. Moreover they are only of value in this world, while the value of the ceremonies of Righteousness is eternal, for even if one does not achieve one's end in this world one stores up boundless merit in the other, while if one achieves one's end in this world the gain is double.

From the Seventh Pillar Edict

In the past kings sought to make the people progress in Righteousness, but they did not progress. ... And I asked myself how I might uplift them through progress in Righteousness. ... Thus I decided to have them instructed in Righteousness, and to issue ordinances of Righteousness, so that by hearing them the people might conform, advance in the progress of Righteousness, and themselves make great progress. ... For that purpose many officials are employed among the people to instruct them in Righteousness and to explain it to them. ...

Moreover I have had banyan trees planted on the roads to give shade to man and beast; I have planted mango groves, and I have had ponds dug and shelters erected along the roads at every eight kos. Everywhere I have had wells dug for the benefit of man and beast. But this benefit is but small, for in many ways the kings of olden time have worked for the welfare of the world; but what I have done has been done that men may conform to Righteousness.

All the good deeds that I have done have been accepted and followed by the people. And so obedience to mother and father, obedience to teachers, respect for the aged, kindliness to brāhmans and ascetics, to the poor and weak, and to slaves and servants, have increased and will continue to increase. ... And this progress of Righteousness among men has taken place in two manners, by enforcing conformity to Righteousness, and by exhortation. I have enforced the law against killing certain animals and many others, but the greatest progress of Righteousness among men comes from exhortation in favor of noninjury to life and abstention from killing living beings.[12]

I have done this that it may endure . . . as long as the moon and sun, and that my sons and my great-grandsons may support it; for by supporting it they will gain both this world and the next.

Tao-Ch'o

COMPENDIUM ON THE HAPPY LAND

The refutation of the misunderstanding of the characterlessness of the Great Vehicle consists of two parts. First is a summary statement of origination, the purpose of which is to enable scholars of later generations to understand right and wrong clearly, to depart from the crooked and face toward the straight. Second is a clarification of right, with reference to the attachments, and consequent refutation. . . .

Question: There are some persons who say that the Great Vehicle is characterless, that it takes no thought of "that" or "this." If one vows to be reborn in the Pure Land, then one is clinging to a characteristic, which ever increases one's impurities and fetters. Why should one seek after this?

Answer: If one reckons thus, it must be said not to be so. Why? The preaching of the Law by all the Buddhas must be accompanied by two conditions. Firstly, it must depend upon the true principles of the Dharma-Nature. Secondly, it must harmonize with the Twofold Truth. Some people claim that the Greater Vehicle, being free of any false conceptions, is based only on the Dharma-Nature, but they malign the Great Vehicle by saying that there is no condition on which to seek it. This does not harmonize with the Twofold Truth. One who views it in this way falls into the trap of the Emptiness which annihilates. . . .

Question: According to the holy doctrine of the Great Vehicle, if the bodhisattva evinces toward the beings a loving view or great compassion, he should immediately resist it. Now the bodhisattva encourages all beings to be reborn in the Pure Land. Is this not a combining with love, a grasping at character? Or does he escape defiling attachments [in spite of this]?

Answer: The efficacy of the dharmas practiced by the bodhisattva is of two kinds. Which are they? One is perception of the understanding of Emptiness and Perfect Wisdom. The second is full possession of great compassion. In the case of the former, by virtue of his practice of the understanding of Emptiness and Perfect Wisdom, though he may enter into the cycles of life and death of the six stages of existence, he is not fettered by their grime or contamination. In the case of the latter, by virtue of his compassionate mindfulness of the beings, he does not dwell in Nirvāna. The bodhisattva, though he dwells in the midst of the Two-fold Truth, is ever able subtly to reject existence and nonexistence, to strike the mean in his acceptances and rejections and not to run counter to the principles of the Great Way.

Refutation of the notion that there are no dharmas outside of the Mind consists of two parts. First is the refutation of the feelings that reckon thus; second is an interpretation in questions and answers.

Question: There are some who say: "The realm of purity which one contemplates is restricted to the inner mind. The Pure Land is all-pervasive; the mind, if pure, is identical with it. Outside of the Mind there are no dharmas. What need is there to enter the West[ern Paradise]?"

Answer: Only the Pure Land of the Dharma-Nature dwells in principle in empty all-pervasion and is in substance unrestricted. This is the birth of no-birth, into which the superior gentlemen may enter. . . . There are the middle and lower classes [of bodhisattvas], who are not yet able to overcome the world of characters, and who must rely on the circumstance of faith in the Buddha to seek rebirth in the Pure Land. Though they reach that Land, they still dwell in a Land of characters. It is also said: "If one envelops conditions and follows the origin, this is what is meant by 'no dharmas outside the Mind.' But if one distinguishes the Twofold Truth to clarify the doctrine, then the Pure Land does not conflict with the existence of dharmas outside the Mind." Now let us interpret through question and answer.

Question: A while ago, when you said that the "birth of no-birth" is something into which only superior gentlemen can enter, while the middle and inferior ones cannot, were you merely creating this interpretation by fitting the doctrine to the man, or is there also proof of this in the Sacred Doctrine?

Answer: According to the *Treatise of the Perfection of Wisdom*: "The bodhisattvas who have newly aroused their minds [to the ultimate goal of Buddhahood] are by receptivity and understanding soft and weak. Though one may say that they have aroused their minds, most of them vow to be reborn in the Pure Land. For what reason is this so? They are like a child which, if not close to the loving care of its father and mother, may descend into a pit, or fall into a well, or suffer calamity at the hands of fire or snake and the like, or may be deprived of milk and die, but which must rely on the care and nurture of its father and mother in order to grow and be able to carry on the heritage of the family. So also is the bodhisattva. If he can arouse his bodhi-mind, pray much for rebirth in the Pure Land, approach the Buddhas, and advance the Dharma-Body, only then can he properly carry on the household heritage of the bodhisattva and in all ten directions ferry the beings over. For the sake of this benefit, most of them vow for rebirth in the Pure Land."

Fourth is the refutation of the notion that one should vow to be reborn in this filthy land, not in that Pure Land.

Question: There are some who say that one vows to be reborn in this filthy land in order to convert the beings by one's teaching, and that one does not vow to go to the Pure Land to be reborn. How is this?

Answer: Of such persons also there is a certain group. Why? If the body resides in [an estate from which there is] no backsliding, or beyond, in order to convert the sundry evil beings it may dwell in contamination without becoming contaminated or encounter evil without being transformed, just as the swan and the duck may enter the water but the water cannot wet them. Such persons as these can dwell in filth and extricate the beings from their suffering. But if the person is in truth an ordinary man, I only fear that his own conduct is not yet established, and that if he encounters suffering he will immediately change. He who wishes to save him will perish together with him. For example, if one forces a chicken into the water, how can one not get wet?

Fifth is the refutation of the proposition that those who are reborn in the Pure Land mostly take pleasure in clinging to enjoyment.

Question: There are some who say: "Within the Pure Land there are only enjoyable things. Much pleasure in clinging to enjoyment hinders and destroys the practice of the Way. Why should one vow to go thither and be reborn?"

Answer: Since it is called "Pure Land," it means that there are no impurities in it. If one speaks of "clinging to enjoyment," this refers to lust and the afflictions. If so, why call it pure?

Question: The scriptures of the Great Vehicle say that the way of karma is like a scale, the heavier side showing its influence first. How can beings who throughout their lives until this day, whether for a hundred years or for ten, have practiced all evils, how can they, when they approach their end, meet a benevolent person and after ten uninterrupted moments of thought [of the Buddha, etc.] be enabled to go thither to be reborn? If this is so, how can one believe what is said about the heavier side showing its influence first?

Answer: You say that the evil karma of one lifetime is heavy, while you suppose the good of ten moments of thought in the life of an inferior man to be light. Let us now compare their relative lightness and heaviness on the basis of principle precisely to make clear that what matters lies in the mind, in the conditions and one's determination, and not in the distance or length of time involved. In what sense is it in the mind? By that we mean that when such a man commits a sin the sin is born from a vain and perverse mind, while these ten moments of thought are born from hearing the dharma of real character from a benevolent man who by resorting to expedient means comforts him. In the one case it is reality, and in the other it is vanity. How can they be equated? Why do we say this? Suppose a room has been dark for a thousand years. If light enters it for but a moment, it will be clear and bright. How could one say that the darkness, having been in the room for a thousand years, cannot be eliminated? . . . This is what is meant by "in the mind." Secondly, in what sense do we mean "in conditions"? We mean that when that man commits sin, his sin is born from false notions, from among beings who suffer the retribution of the afflictions. But now these ten moments of thought are born out of a mind of supreme faith, out of the name of Amita the Thus-Come-One, a true and pure name of infinite merits. It is as if a man were to be struck by a poisoned arrow, which pierced his sinews and broke his bone, and were immediately to have the arrow removed and the poison cleared away by the mere act of hearing the sound of a drum advertising a remedy. How could one say that, though the arrow was deep and the poison dangerous, he was not able, as soon as he heard the sound of the drum, to pull out the arrow and clear away the poison? This is what is meant by "in conditions." Thirdly, in what sense do we mean "one's determination"? When that man commits sin, the sin is born from a mind that fears consequences and has interruptions, while these ten moments of thought arise from a mind that has neither consequences nor interruptions. This is what is meant by "determination."

Question: If I wish now to practice diligently the concentration of the mindfulness of the Buddha, I do not know what the character and form of this mindfulness look like.

Answer: Suppose a man in an empty and distant place encounters a bandit who, drawing his sword, comes forcefully and directly to kill him. This man runs straight on, looking ahead to cross a river. But before reaching the river he would have the following thoughts: "When I reach the river bank, shall I take off my clothes and cross or wear them and float? To take them off and cross I fear there may not be time. If I wear them and float, then I fear that my life will not be saved." At such a time he has only the single thought of a means to cross the river, and no other thoughts would be mingled with it. So also is the practitioner. When he is contemplating Amita Buddha, he is like the man contemplating the crossing. The thought is continuous, no others being mingled with it. He may contemplate the Buddha's Dharma-Body, or he may contemplate the Buddha's supernatural might, or he may contemplate the Buddha's wisdom, or he may contemplate the Buddha's hair-mark, or he may contemplate the goodness of the Buddha's character, or he may contemplate the Buddha's original vow. In the same way he may recite the name of the Buddha. If one is able to concentrate on it wholeheartedly, continuously and without interruption, one will certainly be reborn in the Buddha's presence.

Question: The *Scripture of the Buddha of Limitless Life* says: "If the beings of the ten directions shall with intense belief and desire for as much as ten moments wish to be reborn in my Land, and if then they should not be reborn there, may I never attain enlightenment." Now there are men in the world who hear this holy teaching and who in their present life never arouse their minds to it, but wait until the end approaches and then wish to practice such contemplation. What do you say of such cases?

Answer: Such cases are not true. Why? The scriptures say: "Ten continuous moments may seem not to be difficult. However, the minds of ordinary men are like a zephyr, their consciousness is more capricious than a monkey's. It runs through the six objects of sensual perception without rest." Everyone should arouse his faith and first conquer his own thoughts, so that through the accumulated practice it will become his nature and the roots of goodness become firm. As the Buddha proclaimed to the great king, if men accumulate good conduct, at death they will have no evil thoughts, just as, when a tree is first bent in a certain direction, when it falls it will follow that bent. Once the sword and the wind arrive, and a hundred woes concentrate upon the body, if the practice is not there to begin with, how can contemplation be consummated? Everyone should form a bond with three or five comrades to enlighten one another. When life's end faces them, they should enlighten one another, recite Amita Buddha's name to one another, and pray for rebirth in Paradise in such a way that voice succeeds upon voice until the ten moments of thought are completed. It is as, when a wax seal has been impressed in clay, after the wax has been destroyed, the imprint remains. When this life is cut off, one is reborn immediately in the Comfortable and Pleasant Land. At the time one enters completely into the cluster of right contemplation. What more is there to worry about? Everyone should weigh this great blessing. Why should one not conquer one's own thoughts ahead of time?

THINKING ACROSS CULTURES

1. Compare and contrast the ideal ruler according to Plato, Confucius, and Ashoka.

2. Both Christianity and Buddhism propose to identify and solve the problems of human existence. Compare and contrast these two world religions on these points.

3. Both Christianity and Buddhism were able to flourish outside of the cultures in which they originated. What features of each religion do you think made that possible?

4. How would Aristotle describe the Chinese state? What kind of government did it have according to Aristotle's taxonomy? How would he describe the relationship among individual, family, and state in classical China?

5. How would Ssu-ma Chi'en have described Ashoka? Would he have approved of his rule or not?

6. What three or four adjectives would you use to describe each of the three major classical civilizations represented in this section (China, India, Mediterranean)?

POST-CLASSICAL WORLD

Until recently, many scholars have seen the fifth through fifteenth centuries as a period of decline, a middle age between the glories of the classical past and the progress of the modern period. This point of view presupposes two biases. First, the traditional interpretation deals mostly with the cultures that followed the Roman Empire. It fails to take into account the cultures that were influenced by classical Chinese or Indian civilizations. Second, it assumes that any deviation from the classical models created by Greece and Rome are failures and signs of cultural degradation. Since you are reading this book as part of a world history course, we will assume that we need not justify abandoning the first bias. As for the second, historians should not examine cultures to see how well they preserved a classical past, or by how well they anticipated modern accomplishments. While the cultures that succeeded the classical civilizations looked to their predecessors for many of the foundational aspects of civilization, for the most part they were not failed imitators. In most cases, civilizations of this period did not merely *adopt* important aspects of previous civilizations, but *adapted* them to there own social and cultural circumstances. Because of the importance of the classical heritage to the civilizations of this period, the historian Peter Stearns calls this period "post-classical," and, for want of a better term, so will we.

The Greco-Roman civilization centered on the Mediterranean Sea was succeeded by three distinct civilizations. The most direct heir to the heritage of the classical Mediterranean was the Byzantine Empire of the Eastern Mediterranean. The term "Byzantine" is a modern one used to refer to the eastern Roman Empire after the collapse of the western provinces to Germanic invaders and immigrants. Christian and Greek-speaking, the rulers referred to themselves (and were referred to by other rulers) as Roman emperors. The Byzantine Empire slowly contracted until Muslim Turks captured the capital, Constantinople, in 1453.

The Islamic civilization that supplanted the Byzantines is the second successor civilization. Beginning early in the seventh century a robust culture began to develop in the hot desert sands of Arabia. It owed its origin to Muhammad the prophet, the founder of the Muslim faith. Following Muhammad's death, the Muslims quickly expanded their power and influence so that within about three hundred years they controlled an area greater in extent than the Roman Empire. Even during the lifetime of Muhammad (570–632), they had gained control over the entire Arabian peninsula. From there they expanded in all directions, moving into Asia Minor (modern Turkey), Persia (modern Iran and Iraq), and Egypt by the middle of the seventh century, then pushing westward across northern Africa toward the Atlantic coast and eastward, first into Afghanistan, and then into the Indus valley of India.

The conquest of northern Africa brought the Muslims to the Strait of Gibraltar, which they crossed at the beginning of the eighth century, quickly occupying most of the Iberian peninsula then crossing the Pyrenees to begin a northward probe into France. But they had finally reached the limit of their military resources. They were defeated in a crucial encounter by a Frankish force under the leadership of Charles Martel in 732 near the city of Tours and had to retreat back into Spain. There they remained in control, but against increasing pressure from local rulers, who gradually pushed them southward until finally, in 1492, they were forced from their last Spanish stronghold of Granada.

It is not easy to explain how the Muslims were able to conquer such vast areas so quickly. But two factors certainly contributed to their success. First, their armies were imbued with the enthusiasm of their religious faith, which they believed they had a mission to propagate, by arms if necessary. Second, their foes, for the most part, were ill-prepared and ill-equipped, so often offered little more than token opposition to their forces.

Besides their extensive military exploits, Muslims made important contributions in a wide variety of fields. Baghdad, on the Tigris River, became their cultural center; here they founded a university in the eleventh century. But well before that time Muslim scientists and scholars were active. Islamic scholars were able to draw on the heritage of both the classical Mediterranean and ancient Persia as material for their own intellectual culture. Later, as Islam expanded, Muslims came into contact with the heirs of classical India and China. Islamic civilization became the center for advances in science and medicine during this period. Probably the greatest impetus to this activity came from their translation of the great works of the ancient Greeks into the Arabic language, which was accomplished in the ninth century. In medicine the writings of the Greek, Galen, became the foundation for the important work of people such as Ibn Sina, or Avicenna (980–1037), who compiled a great medical encyclopedia. Astronomy, based on Ptolemy, was developed, with observatories at Damascus and Baghdad. Although the growth of this science was a result, in part, of the need for navigational aids, another strong force was its utility, here as in other cultures, in the "science" of astrology, or the prediction of the future. One important scientific development, not derived from Greece but from India, needs special mention—Arabic numerals, including the use of "zero." This proved a great advance over anything that Greece and Rome had done and marked a milestone in the history of mathematics. The Muslims also produced a major historian, Ibn Khaldun (1332–1406), who wrote a *Universal History*. In philosophy they were inspired by the great works of the classical Greeks but faced the problem of how to fit such speculations into the framework of their Muslim faith. Ibn Rushd, or Averroes (1126–1198), devoted much of his effort to the reconciliation of reason with faith. Al-Farabi (c. 870–950), by contrast, was a rationalist, who was more concerned with providing a reconciliation between Plato and Aristotle. Although the Muslim empire began to disintegrate as early as the ninth century, the cultural unity provided by the Muslim faith has continued to persist. Islam is the second largest religion practiced in the world today. Also, the accomplishments of the Muslim scientists and scholars were gradually to find their way into Western Europe, with significant effects.

The third civilization to form after the disintegration of the classical Mediterranean world, arose slowly in the rather backward, abandoned western provinces of the Roman Empire. Germanic tribes had immigrated, both peacefully and otherwise, into the western provinces of the Roman Empire beginning in the third century. By the sixth century, the Roman Empire had contracted to the East and the former western provinces became unstable kingdoms governed by Germanic nobility, along with what Roman aristocracy remained. Gradually, this area of Western Europe developed an identity over against its Greek-speaking Christian and Arabic-speaking Muslim neighbors. Traditionally called Medieval Europe, a more useful name might be Latin Christendom. While most Europeans of this period were illiterate and probably not very well Christianized, the elites of this civilization adopted Latin (the language of the Romans) as the de facto language of government and learning as well as a form of Christianity different from the Byzantines, which eventually centered on the authority of the bishop of Rome, or Pope. Beginning with the brief political unification of the region under the Frankish king Charlemagne, and culminating in the universities and noble courts of Europe in the thirteenth century, educated and high-ranking members of this society saw themselves as a culture unified by the application of Roman political theory and Latin Christianity. Charlemagne is an excellent example of this. A Frankish king, he looked to both Roman and Christian models for his rule. He sponsored the study of both pagan and Christian classics. When members of his court adopted "nicknames" from the classical past, he was referred to as David, God's chosen and the most important king in the Hebrew Scriptures. Finally, he was crowned emperor of the Romans as a symbol of his unification of the area that once comprised the western provinces of the Roman Empire. Although Charlemagne's empire did not survive his death, the precedent was established. Western Europe would look to the classical Mediterranean, particularly the later, Christianized Roman Empire for its culture.

In the eleventh century, demographic and political factors were initiating a more permanent development in Latin Christian civilization. Increasing political stability, economic growth, the formation of cities and new centers of learning combined to form the beginnings of a European society that would eventually dominate the world in the modern period. Increasing contact was made with the more advanced Byzantine and Arabic civilizations contributing to the economic and cultural flowering of Latin Christendom in this period. Sometimes this contact was peaceful, as in the intellectual exchanges among scholars on the frontiers in Spain and Sicily. Other times the contact was violent, as in the military conflicts between the Latin Christians and Muslims in Spain (known in the West as the *reconquista*) or the Middle East (known in the West as the Crusades). By the thirteenth century, Latin Christendom was a significant civilization in its own right, with universities producing scholars such as Thomas Aquinas and engaging in trade throughout the known world through merchants such as Marco Polo.

As impressive as the achievements of Latin Christendom were by the thirteenth century, Marco Polo's travels to Asia revealed that Western Europe was still a small and peripheral civilization. In China, the centuries between the fifth and fifteenth were, on the whole, a time of stability, punctuated by periods of turmoil. The wealth, power, and sophistication of dynasties such as the T'ang (618–907) and the Sung (960–1279) gave no reason for the Chinese to reconsider their claim as the "Middle Kingdom," the center of the world. In the thirteenth century, a new political force entered the Chinese scene, coming from the north and west. The Mongols, under the great warrior, Genghis Kahn (d. 1227) began to penetrate into northern China (as well as eastern Europe). Under his grandson, Kublai Khan, who reigned from the capital city of Cambaluc (Beijing), the remainder of China fell under Mongol rule. Even under Mongol domination, Chinese civilization retained its cultural and economic power. In the following century, Mongol control of China eventually weakened until in 1368 they were driven out and the Ming Dynasty came into power. This dynasty was to rule China until 1644.

Much of the stability of Chinese political life resulted from the organization of its government. Although the emperor ruled, the administration of the country was in the hands of a corps of bureaucrats, called mandarins. Recruited mainly from the class of landed gentry, they gained office through passing a set of examinations based on their knowledge of Chinese classics. These famous examinations, for which aspirants had to prepare for many years, were instituted as far back as the Han and continued for two thousand years, until the early twentieth century.

China, because of her fertile river valleys, has always been a land of farmers but, because of the population density, the farms have been small. In early times, only grains such as millet could be grown in the northern Yellow River valley, while rice prospered farther south in the Yangtze valley. During the Sui Dynasty, these two valleys were linked by construction of the Grand Canal. Transportation by barge traffic greatly encouraged trade and commerce, leading to economic prosperity and a steadily increasing population.

Concurrently, other forms of technology were developed. Prosperity led to the use of money and the manufacture of paper to that of paper money. The invention of printing in the eighth century came centuries before its introduction in Europe. The same is true of gunpowder, which the Chinese were using in the tenth century. By the fifteenth century, the Chinese were the most advanced civilization in the world.

The ability of post-classical China to both preserve and expand on its classical heritage is only one aspect of its importance in this period. During this period, other civilizations were arising in East Asia in places such as Vietnam, Korea, and Japan. In each case, their immense, sophisticated, and ancient neighbor would profoundly affect them. Let us use Japan as an example.

Just across the East China Sea from the Chinese coast lie the islands of Japan. Although they had lived on the islands at least since Neolithic times, the Japanese did not develop an advanced civilization until very late. The beginnings came around the first century A.D. (roughly three thousand years later than China) when warrior clans from Korea began to infiltrate the land. About the fourth century, one of these clans gained ascendancy over the others and its chief became the source for the imperial family, which was to rule Japan thereafter. The latter half of the sixth century marked the real beginnings of Japanese civilization, as the mature culture of China began to penetrate the islands, particularly through the agency of proselytizing Chinese Buddhist monks. Although much of the later culture of Japan is, as a result, derivative from that of China, it developed its own, distinctive Japanese character.

After a centralized government based on the Chinese model with the emperor at its head proved unsuccessful, Japan, from the twelfth century, developed a feudal form of society. Although the emperor continued to reign, he had little real power. Instead, effective control was in the hands of a hierarchy of warrior-knights, known as *samurai*, at whose head was a chief warrior, the *shogun*. This peculiarly Japanese system of government by feudal warriors with a symbolic emperor was to remain much the same until the nineteenth century. But, for several centuries during the post-classical epoch, until the Tokugawa Shogunate crushed all opposition at the end of the sixteenth century, no single shogun succeeded in gaining full control of Japan. Instead there was almost constant warfare as various contenders, with their categories of warrior-knights, struggled for supremacy. One event of military significance that was to have historical effects many centuries later occurred during this time. In 1281, Kublai Khan, having brought all of China under his dominion, decided to invade Japan, so he dispatched a large fleet carrying an army across the sea. Before the Chinese could mount their invasion, however, a typhoon struck and destroyed their fleet. To this storm the Japanese gave the name "Divine Wind," or *kamikaze*.

The third classical civilization, India, was sustained through this period and spread to Southeast Asia. Classical Indian culture was preserved and expanded on in the southern part of the subcontinent. In the north, Muslim invaders oppressed the indigenous Hindus, but interaction between Indian and Islamic elements produced a unique and vibrant elite culture. In Southeast Asia, Indian civilization spread through the adoption of political systems and through religion. The Khmers of Cambodia adopted the Hinduism of the Indian advisors who helped them rule an empire. The Burmese—and, through them, the Thai—became the most significant bastions of traditional Buddhism after the religion faded in its homeland.

The post-classical period also saw the development of civilizations independent of the early classical civilizations in the Americas and sub-Saharan Africa. In Africa, for instance, several powerful empires arose during this period, generally centered in the northwestern part of the continent. The most important were the Ghana empire, which reached its height in the eleventh century; the Mali empire, which flourished in the thirteenth and fourteenth centuries and whose beginning is described in the epic *Sundiata*; and the Songhai empire of the fifteenth and sixteenth centuries.

St. Augustine

For three hundred years after the death of Jesus, the Christian churches were engaged in a continuing struggle. Early in the fourth century, under the emperors Galerius and Constantine (himself a convert), Christianity was recognized and tolerated; later in the century, under Theodosius, it was proclaimed the official religion of the Roman Empire.

But the problems of the churches were far from over, for a host of controversies now arose within the ranks of the Christians themselves. The most serious dispute was over questions of doctrine. Innumerable sects, each preaching its special version of Christian doctrine and combating the views of the others, were scattered throughout the empire. Clearly, if Christianity was to survive, some order had to be brought out of such theological chaos. Into this scene of confusion stepped Augustine (354–430), the most important of Christian theologians. Highly intelligent, firmly devoted to his conception of the truth, and possessed of unusual administrative ability, Augustine was admirably fitted for the task of developing a theological doctrine for the Christian religion and then making that doctrine prevail.

After having been attracted as a youth to various pagan cults, Augustine was converted to Christianity in 386 through the influence of Ambrose, bishop of Milan. Following his conversion, Augustine devoted most of the rest of his life to formulating and disseminating what he believed to be the true Christian doctrine. The main features of this doctrine are given in the following selection from *The Enchiridion* ("Manual"). The central concept, as with St. Paul, is original sin, but with Augustine the theory becomes systematically articulated. Once he had worked out his doctrine completely, Augustine was in a good position to brand opposing theories as heresies. He devoted much of his time, thought, and energy, especially in later life, to doctrinal controversies in an effort to purge Christian theology of all heretical elements. He was singularly successful in this endeavor, and orthodox Christianity (even with the later additions made by Thomas Aquinas and others) has remained basically Augustinian.

---

1. According to Augustine, what has disrupted the relationship between God and man? How is this relationship restored?

2. In what sense is man free, according to Augustine?

The Enchiridion

God's Judgments Upon Fallen Men and Angels. The Death of the Body is Man's Peculiar Punishment

... Now the evils I have mentioned are common to all who for their wickedness have been justly condemned by God, whether they be men or angels. But there is one form of punishment peculiar to man—the death of the body. God had threatened him with this punishment of death if he should sin, leaving him indeed to the freedom of his own will, but yet commanding his obedience under pain of death; and He placed him amid the happiness of Eden, as it were in a protected nook of life, with the intention that, if he preserved his righteousness, he should thence ascend to a better place.

Through Adam's Sin His Whole Posterity were Corrupted, and were Born Under the Penalty of Death, which He had Incurred

Thence, after his sin, he was driven into exile, and by his sin the whole race of which he was the root was corrupted in him, and thereby subjected to the penalty of death. And so it happens that all descended from him, and from the woman who had led him into sin, and was condemned at the same time with him,—being the offspring of carnal lust on which the same punishment of disobedience was visited,—were tainted with the original sin, and were by it drawn through divers errors and sufferings into that last and endless punishment which they suffer in common with the fallen angels, their corrupters and masters, and the partakers of their doom. And thus "by one man sin entered into the world, and death by sin; and so death passed upon all men, for that all have sinned." By "the world" the apostle,[1] of course, means in this place the whole human race.

The State of Misery to Which Adam's Sin Reduced Mankind, and the Restoration Effected through the Mercy of God

Thus, then, matters stood. The whole mass of the human race was under condemnation, was lying steeped and wallowing in misery, and was being tossed from one form of evil to another, and, having joined the faction of the fallen angels, was paying the well-merited penalty of that impious rebellion. For whatever the wicked freely do through blind and unbridled

---

[1]St. Paul—*Ed.*
"The Enchiridion," in *The Works of Aurelius Augustine*, ed. M. Dods. Vol. IX.

lust, and whatever they suffer against their will in the way of open punishment, this all evidently pertains to the just wrath of God. But the goodness of the Creator never fails either to supply life and vital power to the wicked angels (without which their existence would soon come to an end); or, in the case of mankind, who spring from a condemned and corrupt stock, to impart form and life to their seed, to fashion their members, and through the various seasons of their life, and in the different parts of the earth, to quicken their senses, and bestow upon them the nourishment they need. For He judged it better to bring good out of evil, than not to permit any evil to exist. And if He had determined that in the case of men, as in the case of the fallen angels, there should be no restoration to happiness, would it not have been quite just, that the being who rebelled against God, who in the abuse of his freedom spurned and transgressed the command of his Creator when he could so easily have kept it, who defaced in himself the image of his Creator by stubbornly turning away from His light, who by an evil use of his free-will broke away from his wholesome bondage to the Creator's laws,—would it not have been just that such a being should have been wholly and to all eternity deserted by God, and left to suffer the everlasting punishment he had so richly earned? Certainly so God would have done, had He been only just and not also merciful, and had He not designed that His unmerited mercy should shine forth the more brightly in contrast with the unworthiness of its objects.

Men are not Saved by Good Works, nor by the Free Determination of Their Own Will, but by the Grace of God through Faith

But this part of the human race to which God has promised pardon and a share in His eternal kingdom, can they be restored through the merit of their own works? God forbid. For what good work can a lost man perform, except so far as he has been delivered from perdition? Can they do anything by the free determination of their own will? Again I say, God forbid. For it was by the evil use of his free-will that man destroyed both it and himself. For, as a man who kills himself must, of course, be alive when he kills himself, but after he has killed himself ceases to live, and cannot restore himself to life; so, when man by his own free-will sinned, then sin being victorious over him, the freedom of his will was lost. "For of whom a man is overcome, of the same is he brought in bondage." This is the judgment of the Apostle Peter. And as it is certainly true, what kind of liberty, I ask, can the bond-slave possess, except when it pleases him to sin? For he is freely in bondage who does with pleasure the will of his master. Accordingly, he who is the servant of sin is free to sin. And hence he will not be free to do right, until, being freed from sin, he shall begin to be the servant of righteousness. And this is true liberty, for he has pleasure in the righteous deed; and it is at the same time a holy bondage, for he is obedient to the will of God. But whence comes this liberty to do right to the man who is in bondage and sold under sin, except he be redeemed by Him who has said, "If the Son shall make you free, ye shall be free indeed"? And before this redemption is wrought in a man, when he is not yet free to do what is right, how can he talk of the freedom of his will and his good works, except he be inflated by that foolish pride of boasting which the apostle restrains when he says, "By grace are ye saved, through faith"?

Faith Itself is the Gift of God; and Good Works will not be Wanting in Those Who Believe

And lest men should arrogate to themselves the merit of their own faith at least, not understanding that this too is the gift of God, this same apostle, who says in another place that he had "obtained mercy of the Lord to be faithful," here also adds: "and that not of yourselves; it is the gift of God: not of works, lest any man should boast." And lest it should be thought that good works will be wanting in those who believe, he adds further: "For we are His workmanship, created in Christ Jesus unto good works, which God hath before ordained that we should walk in them." We shall be made truly free, then, when God fashions us, that is, forms and creates us anew, not as men—for He has done that already—but as good men, which His grace is now doing, that we may be a new creation in Christ Jesus, according as it is said: "Create in me a clean heart, O God." For God had already created his heart, so far as the physical structure of the human heart is concerned; but the psalmist prays for the renewal of the life which is still lingering in his heart.

The Freedom of the Will is Also the Gift of God, for God Worketh in Us Both to Will and to do

And further, should any one be inclined to boast, not indeed of his works, but of the freedom of his will, as if that first merit belong to him, this very liberty of good action being given to him as a reward he had earned, let him listen to this same preacher of grace, when he says: "For it is God which worketh in you, both to will and to do of His own good pleasure"; and in another place: "So, then, it is not of him that willeth, nor of him that runneth, but of God that showeth mercy." Now as, undoubtedly, if a man is of the age to use his reason, he cannot believe, hope, love, unless he will to do so, nor obtain the prize of the high calling of God unless he voluntarily run for it; in what sense is it "not of him that willeth, nor of him that runneth, but of God that showeth mercy," except that, as it is written, "The preparation of the heart is from the Lord"? Otherwise, if it is said, "it is not of him that willeth nor of him that runneth, but of God that showeth mercy," because it is of both, that is, both of the will of man and of the mercy of God, so that we are to understand the saying, "It is not of him that willeth, nor of him that runneth, but of God that showeth mercy," as if it meant the will of man alone is not sufficient, if the mercy of God go not with it—then it will follow that the mercy of God alone is not sufficient, if the will of man go not with it; and therefore, if we may rightly say, "it is not of man that willeth, but of God that showeth mercy," because the will of man by itself is not enough, why may we not also rightly put it in the converse way: "It is not of God that showeth mercy, but of man that willeth," because the mercy of God by itself does not suffice? Surely, if no Christian will dare to say this, "It is not of God that showeth mercy, but of man that willeth," lest he should openly contradict the apostle, it follows that the true interpretation of the saying, "It is not of him that willeth, nor of him that runneth, but of God that showeth mercy," is that the whole work belongs to God, who both makes the will of man righteous, and thus prepares it for assistance, and assists it when it is prepared. For the man's righteousness of will precedes many of God's gifts, but not all and it must itself be included among those which it does not precede. We read in Holy Scripture, both that God's mercy "shall prevent me," and that His mercy "shall follow me." It prevents the unwilling to make him willing; it follows the willing to make his will effectual. Why are we taught to pray for our enemies, who are plainly unwilling to lead a holy life, unless that God may work willingness in them? And why are we ourselves taught to ask that we may receive, unless that He who has created in us the wish, may Himself satisfy the wish? We pray, then, for our enemies, that the mercy of God may prevent them, as it has prevented us: we pray for ourselves that His mercy may follow us.

Men, Being by Nature the Children of Wrath, Needed a Mediator. In What Sense God is Said to be Angry

And so the human race was lying under a just condemnation, and all men were the children of wrath. Of which wrath it is written: "All our days are passed away in Thy wrath; we spend our years as a tale that is told." Of which wrath also Job says: "Man that is born of a woman is of few days, and full of trouble." Of which wrath also the Lord Jesus says: "He that believeth on the Son hath everlasting life: and he that believeth not the Son shall not see life; but the wrath of God abideth on him." He does not say it will come, but it "abideth on him." For every man is born with it; wherefore the apostle says: "We were by nature the children of wrath, even as others." Now, as men were lying under this wrath by reason of their original sin, and as this original sin was the more heavy and deadly in proportion to the number and magnitude of the actual sins which were added to it, there was need for a Mediator, that is, for a reconciler, who, by the offering of one sacrifice, of which all the sacrifices of the law and the prophets were types, should take away this wrath. Wherefore the apostle says: "For if, when we were enemies, we were reconciled to God by the death of His Son, much more, being reconciled, we shall be saved by His life." Now when God is said to be angry, we do not attribute to Him such a disturbed feeling as exists in the mind of an angry man; but we call His just displeasure against sin by the name "anger," a word transferred by analogy from human emotions. But our being reconciled to God through a Mediator, and receiving the Holy Spirit, so that we who were enemies are made sons ("For as many as are led by the Spirit of God, they are the sons of God"): this is the grace of God through Jesus Christ our Lord.

Christ, who was Himself Free From Sin, was made Sin for Us, that We might be Reconciled to God

Begotten and conceived, then, without any indulgence of carnal lust, and therefore bringing with Him no original sin, and by the grace of God joined and united in a wonderful and unspeakable way in one person with the Word, the Only-begotten of the Father, a son by nature, not by grace, and therefore having no sin of His own; nevertheless, on account of the likeness of sinful flesh in which He came, He was called sin, that He might be sacrificed to wash away sin. For, under the Old Covenant, sacrifices for sin were called sins. And He, of whom all these sacrifices were types and shadows, was Himself truly made sin. Hence the apostle, after saying, "We pray you in Christ's stead, be ye reconciled to God," forthwith adds: "for He hath made Him to be sin for us who knew no sin; that we might be made the righteousness of God in Him." He does not say, as some incorrect copies read, "He who knew no sin did sin for us," as if Christ had Himself sinned for our sakes; but he says, "Him who knew no sin," that is, Christ God, to whom we are to be reconciled, "hath made to be sin for us," that is, hath made Him a sacrifice for our sins, by which we might be reconciled to God. He, then being made sin, just as we are made righteousness (our righteousness being not our own, but God's, not in ourselves, but in Him); He being made sin, not His own, but ours, not in Himself, but in us, showed, by the likeness of sinful flesh in which He was crucified, that though sin was not in Him, yet that in a certain sense He died to sin, by dying in the flesh which was the likeness of sin; and that although He himself had never lived the old life of sin, yet by His resurrection He typified our new life springing up out of the old death in sin.

By the Sacrifice of Christ All Things are Restored, and Peace is Made Between Earth and Heaven

And, of course, the holy angels, taught by God, in the eternal contemplation of whose truth their happiness consists, know how great a number of the human race are to supplement their ranks, and fill up the full tale of their citizenship. Wherefore the apostle says, that "all things are gathered together in one in Christ, both which are in heaven and which are on earth." The things which are in heaven are gathered together when what was lost there-form in the fall of the angels is restored from among men; and the things which are on earth are gathered together, when those who are predestined to eternal life are redeemed from their old corruption. And thus, through that single sacrifice in which the Mediator was offered up, the one sacrifice of which the many victims under the law were types, heavenly things are brought into peace with earthly things, and earthly things with heavenly. Wherefore, as the same apostle says: "For it pleased the Father that in Him should all fulness dwell: and, having made peace through the blood of His cross, by Him to reconcile all things to Himself: by Him, I say, whether they be things in earth or things in heaven."

Predestination to Eternal Life is Wholly of God's Free Grace

And, moreover, who will be so foolish and blasphemous as to say that God cannot change the evil wills of men, whichever, whenever and wheresoever He chooses, and direct them to what is good? But when He does this, He does it of mercy; when He does it not, it is of justice that He does it not; for "He hath mercy on whom He will have mercy, and whom He will He hardeneth." And when the apostle said this, he was illustrating the grace of God, in connection with which he had just spoken of the twins in the womb of Rebecca, "who being not yet born, neither having done any good or evil, that the purpose of God according to election might stand, not of works, but of Him that calleth, it was said unto her, 'The elder shall serve the younger.'" And in reference to this matter he quotes another prophetic testimony: "Jacob have I loved, but Esau have I hated." But perceiving how what he had said might affect those who could not penetrate by their understanding the depth of this grace: "What shall we say then?" he says: "Is there unrighteousness with God? God forbid." For it seems unjust that, in the absence of any merit or demerit from good or evil works, God should love the one and hate the other. Now, if the apostle had wished us to understand that there were future good works of the one, and evil works of the other, which of course God foreknew, he would never have said, "not of works," but, "of future works," and in that way would have solved the difficulty, or rather there would then have been no difficulty to solve. As it is, however, after answering, "God forbid"; that is, God forbid that there should be unrighteousness with God; he goes on to prove that there is no unrighteousness in God's doing this, and says: "For he saith to Moses, I will have mercy on whom I will have mercy, and I will have compassion on whom I will have compassion." Now who but a fool would think that God was unrighteous, either in inflicting penal justice on those who earned it, or in extending mercy to the unworthy? Then he draws his conclusion: "So then it is not of him that willeth, nor of him that runneth, but of God that showeth mercy." Thus both the twins were born children of wrath, not on account of any works of their own, but because they were bound in the fetters of that original condemnation which came through Adam. But He who said, "I will have mercy on whom I will have mercy," loved Jacob of His undeserved grace, and hated Esau of His deserved judgement. And as this judgment was due to both, the former learnt from the case of the latter that the fact of the same punishment not falling upon himself gave him no room to glory in any merit of his own, but only in the riches of the divine grace; because "it is not of him that willeth, nor of him that runneth, but of God that showeth mercy." And indeed the whole face, and, if I may use the expression, every lineament of the countenance of Scripture conveys by a very profound analogy this wholesome warning to every one who looks carefully into it, that he who glories should glory in the Lord.

As God's Mercy is Free, So His Judgments are Just, and Cannot be Gainsaid

Now after commending the mercy of God, saying, "So it is not of him that willeth, nor of him that runneth, but of God that showeth mercy," that he might commend His Justice also (for the man who does not obtain mercy finds, not iniquity, but justice, there being no iniquity with God), he immediately adds: "For the scripture saith unto Pharaoh, 'Even for this same purpose have I raised thee up, that I might show my power in thee, and that my name might be declared throughout all the earth.'" And then he draws a conclusion that applies to both, that is, both to His mercy and His justice: "Therefore hath He mercy on whom He will have mercy, and whom He will He hardeneth." "He hath mercy" of His great goodness, "He hardeneth" without any injustice; so that neither can he that is pardoned glory in any merit of his own, nor he that is condemned complain of anything but his own demerit. For it is grace alone that separates the redeemed from the lost, all having been involved in one common perdition through their common origin. Now if any one, on hearing this, should say, "Why doth He yet find fault? for who hath resisted His will?" as if a man ought not to be blamed for being bad, because God hath mercy on whom He will have mercy, and whom He will He hardeneth, God forbid that we should be ashamed to answer as we see the apostle answered: "Nay, but, O man, who are thou that repliest against God? Shall the thing formed say to Him that formed it, Why hast Thou made me thus? Hath not the potter power over the clay, of the same lump to make one vessel unto honour, and another unto dishonour?" Now some foolish people think that in this place the apostle had no answer to give; and for want of a reason to render, rebuked the presumption of his interrogator. But there is great weight in this saying: "Nay, but, O man, who are thou?" and in such a matter as this it suggests to a man in a single word the limits of his capacity, and at the same time does in reality convey an important reason. For if a man does not understand these matters, who is he that he should reply against God? And if he does understand them, he finds no further room for reply. For then he perceives that the whole human race was condemned in its rebellious head by a divine judgment so just, that if not a single member of the race had been redeemed, no one could justly have questioned the justice of God; and that it was right that those who are redeemed should be redeemed in such a way as to show, by the greater number who are unredeemed and left in their just condemnation, what the whole race deserved, and whither the deserved judgment of God would lead even the redeemed, did not His undeserved mercy interpose, so that every mouth might be stopped of those who wish to glory in their own merits, and that he that glorieth might glory in the Lord.

There is No Ground in Scripture for the Opinion of Those Who Deny the Eternity of Future Punishments

It is in vain, then, that some, indeed very many, make moan over the eternal punishment, and perpetual, unintermitted torments of the lost, and say they do not believe it shall be so; not, indeed, that they directly oppose themselves to Holy Scripture, but, at the suggestion of their own feelings, they soften down everything that seems hard, and give a milder turn to statements which they think are rather designed to terrify than to be received as literally true. For "Hath God," they say, "forgotten to be gracious? hath He in anger shut up His tender mercies?" Now, they read this in one of the holy psalms. But without doubt we are to understand it as spoken of those who are elsewhere called "vessels of mercy," because even they are freed from misery not on account of any merit of their own, but solely through the pity of God. Or, if the men we speak of insist that this passage applies to all mankind, there is no reason why they should therefore suppose that there will be an end to the punishment of those of whom it is said, "These shall go away into everlasting punishment"; for this shall end in the same manner and at the same time as the happiness of those of whom it is said, "but the righteous unto life eternal." But let them suppose, if the thought gives them pleasure, that the pains of the damned are, at certain intervals, in some degree assuaged. For even in this case the wrath of God, that is, their condemnation (for it is this, and not any disturbed feeling in the mind of God that is called his wrath), abideth upon them; that is, His wrath, though it still remains, does not shut up His tender mercies; though His tender mercies are exhibited, not in putting an end to their eternal punishment, but in mitigating, or in granting them a respite from, their torments; for the psalm does not say, "to put an end to His anger," or, "when His anger is passed by," but "in His anger." Now, if this anger stood alone, or if it exited in the smallest conceivable degree, yet to be lost out of the kingdom of God, to be an exile from the city of God, to be alienated from the life of God, to have no share in that great goodness which God hath laid up for them that fear Him, and hath wrought out for them that trust in Him, would be a punishment so great, that, supposing it to be eternal, no torments that we know of, continued through as many ages as man's imagination can conceive, could be compared with it.

The Death of the Wicked Shall be Eternal in the Same Sense As the Life of The Saints

This perpetual death of the wicked, then, that is, their alienation from the life of God, shall abide for ever, and shall be common to them all, whatever men, prompted by their human affections, may conjecture as to a variety of punishments, or as to a mitigation or intermission of their woes; just as the eternal life of the saints shall abide for ever, and shall be common to them all, whatever grades of rank and honour there may be among those who shine with an harmonious effulgence.

Muhammad

Although of more recent origin than the others, Islam is one of the great world religions; today the number of its adherents is comparable to that of Christianity. The word "Islam" itself means submission or surrender, and a Muslim, or follower of Islam, is one who surrenders or submits himself to the will of Allah (God).

Islam had its beginnings on the Arab peninsula in the seventh century A.D. Its founder, Muhammad (c. 571–632), was orphaned in early childhood and grew up in poverty. As he matured he became increasingly estranged from the polytheistic religion of his native city of Mecca, with its worship of idols and its practice of female infanticide. He began to absent himself from Mecca for protracted periods, retiring to a cave in the mountains to meditate. There, one night, he had a vision in which the angel Gabriel appeared before him, telling him he was a messenger, transmitting to him the word of God. On later occasions Gabriel reappeared with more messages, which Muhammad memorized and repeated to his disciples. These were collected together and became the Koran (or Qur'an). Opposed by the traditional religious functionaries in Mecca, Muhammad was forced to flee for his life to the city of Medina, where he consolidated his forces, finally returning in triumph to Mecca. By the time of his death in 632, Muhammad and Islam had achieved both religious and political control over Arabia.

The Qur'an is the sacred book of Islam; it is held by Muslims to be the infallible word of God, directly revealed to Muhammad. Although it was written in part during the prophet's lifetime it was completed and arranged in its present form shortly after his death. The Islamic creed rests on two central articles of faith. The first is "There is no god but God (Allah)." Thus Islam is a strict monotheism; as such it rejects not only the traditional Arabian polytheism that it supplanted but the trinitarianism of Christianity as well. The second article of faith is "Muhammad is the messenger, or prophet, of Allah." Islam recognizes other important prophets, like Abraham, Moses, and Jesus, and frequent references to them appear in the Qur'an, but it insists that Muhammad is the ultimate, authoritative prophet. Yet he is a human and not a divine being. Although Muslims believe that on one occasion Muhammad actually ascended to the throne of God and conversed with him, he lived and died as an ordinary mortal.

As an elaborated religion the Muslim faith rests on "Five Pillars," which are obligatory on its adherents: (1) Repetition of the creed "There is no god but Allah, and Muhammad is the prophet of Allah"; (2) prayer, normally done five times daily while bowing toward Mecca; (3) alms-giving, for the support of the poor and needy; (4) the fast, for a full day during the sacred month of Ramadan; and (5) the pilgrimage, to Mecca, which every Muslim is expected to make once in a lifetime.

To one outside of the Muslim community the organization of the Qur'an may appear baffling because it seems to lack any recognizable logical coherence. To give the Qur'an's message greater structure and continuity, the contents of the selection that follows have been rearranged. The numbers of the "Suras" or chapters of the Koran from which the excerpts have been taken are given in parentheses at the end of each quotation. Also, headings describing the contents of each of these have been added.

1. Summarize the message of the Qur'an. How is it similar to, or different from, the central message of the Christian Scriptures? The Hebrew Scriptures?

2. What sort of social structures (class, gender, ethnicity, etc.) are assumed in the Qur'an?

The Qur'an

Preamble

In the Name of God, The Compassionate, the Merciful

Praise be to God, Lord of the worlds!
The compassionate, the merciful!
King on the day of reckoning!
Thee *only* do we worship, and to Thee do we cry for help.
Guide Thou us on the straight path,
The path of those to whom Thou hast been gracious;—with whom
    thou are not angry, and who go not astray. (1)

God

He is God alone;
God the eternal!

Trans. J. M. Rodwell.

He begetteth not, and He is not begotten;
And there is none like unto Him. (112)

Muhammad the Prophet

Muhammad is not more than an apostle; other apostles have already passed away before him. If he die, therefore, or be slain, will ye turn upon your heels? But he who turneth on his heels shall not injure God at all, and God will certainly reward the thankful! (3)

The Qur'an

This Book is without a doubt a revelation sent down from the Lord of the Worlds.

Will they say, he [Muhammad] hath forged it? Nay, it is the truth from thy Lord that thou mayest warn a people to whom no warner hath come before thee, that haply they may be guided.

God it is who hath created the heavens and the earth and all that is between them in six days, then ascended his throne. Save Him ye have no patron, and none to plead for you. Will ye not then reflect?

From the heaven to the earth He governeth all things; hereafter shall they come up to him on a day, whose length shall be a thousand of such years as ye reckon.

This is He who knoweth the unseen and the seen; the Mighty, the Merciful. Who hath made everything which he hath created most good; and began the creation of man with clay;

Then ordained his progeny from germs of life, from sorry water;

Then shaped him and breathed of His Spirit into him, and gave you hearing and seeing and hearts: What little thanks do ye return? (32)

By the star when it setteth,
Your compatriot [Muhammad] erreth not, nor is he led astray,
Neither speaketh he from mere impulse.
The Koran is no other than a revelation revealed to him.
One terrible in power [Gabriel] taught it him,
Endued with wisdom. With even balance stood he
In the highest part of the horizon;
Then came he nearer and approached,
And was at the distance of two bows, or even closer,—
And he revealed to his servant what he revealed. (53)

God's Creation and Creatures

Verily God causeth the grain and the date stone to put forth. He bringeth forth the living from the dead, and dead from the living! This is God! Why, then, are ye turned aside from Him?

He causeth the dawn to appear, and hath ordained the night for rest, and the sun and the moon for computing time! The ordinance of the Mighty, the Wise!

And it is He who hath ordained the stars for you that ye may be guided thereby in the darknesses of the land and of the sea! Clear have we made our signs to men of knowledge.

And it is He who hath produced you from one man, and hath provided for you an abode and resting place! Clear have we made our signs for men of insight.

And it is He who sendeth down rain from heaven; and we bring forth by it the buds of all the plants, and from them bring we forth the green foliage, and the close growing grain, and palm trees with sheaths of clustering dates, and gardens of grapes, and the olive and the pomegranate, like and unlike. Look ye on their fruits when they fruit and ripen. Truly herein are signs unto people who believe. (6)

Now of fine clay have we created man;

Then we placed him a moist germ, in a safe abode;

Then made we the moist germ a clot of blood; then made the clotted blood into a piece of flesh; then made the piece of flesh into bones; and we clothed the bones with flesh; then brought forth man of yet another make— Blessed therefore be God, the most excellent of makers—

Then after this ye shall surely die;

Then shall ye be waked up on the day of resurrection.

And we have created over you seven heavens:—and we are not careless of the creation.

And we send down water from the heaven in its due degree, and we cause it to settle on the earth;—and we have power for its withdrawal;—

And by it we cause gardens of palm trees, and vineyards to spring forth for you, in which ye have plenteous fruits, and whereof ye eat;

And the tree that groweth up on Mount Sinai; which yieldeth oil and a juice for those who eat.

And there is a lesson for you in the cattle. We give you to drink of what is in their bellies, and many advantages do ye derive from them, and for food they serve you;

And on them and on ships are ye borne. (23)

Nay! but it (the Qur'an) is a warning;

(And whoso is willing beareth it in mind)

Written on honored pages,
Exalted, purified,
By the hands of scribes, honored, righteous.
Cursed be man! What hath made him unbelieving?
Of what thing did God create him?
Out of moist germs,
He created him and fashioned him,
Then made him an easy passage from the womb,
Then causeth him to die and burieth him;
Then, when he pleaseth, will raise him again to life.
Aye! but man hath not yet fulfilled the bidding of his Lord.
Let man look at his food;
It was We who rained down the copious rains,
Then cleft the earth with clefts,
And caused the upgrowth of the grain,
And grapes and healing herbs,
And the olive and the palm,
And enclosed gardens thick with trees,
And fruits and herbage,
For the service of yourselves and of your cattle. (80)

God's Providence

And with Him are the keys of the secret things; none knoweth them but He. He knoweth whatever is on the land and in the sea; and no leaf falleth but He knoweth it; neither is there a grain in the darknesses of the earth, nor a thing green or sere, but it is noted in a distinct writing.

It is He who taketh your souls at night, and knoweth what ye have merited in the day; then he awaketh any one of you, our messengers take his soul, and fail not.

Then are they returned to God their Lord, the True. Is not judgment His? (6)

Thus unto thee as unto those who preceded thee doth God, the Mighty, the Wise, reveal!

All that is in the heavens and all that is in the earth is His, and He is the High, the Great!

Ready are the heavens to cleave asunder from above for very awe, and the angels celebrate the praise of their Lord, and ask forgiveness for the dwellers on earth. Is not God the Indulgent, the Merciful?

But whoso take aught beside Him as lords—God watcheth them! But thou hast them not in thy charge.

It is thus moreover that we have revealed to thee an Arabic Qur'an, that thou mayest warn the mother city [Mecca] and all around it, and that thou mayest warn them of that day of the Gathering, of which there is no doubt—when part shall be in Paradise and part in the flame.

Had God so pleased, He had made them one people and of one creed, but He bringeth whom He will within His mercy; and as for the doers of evil, no patron, no helper shall there be for them.

Will they take other patrons than Him? But God is man's only Lord. He quickeneth the dead, and He is mighty over all things.

And whatever the subject of your disputes, with God doth its decision rest. This is God, my Lord; in Him do I put my trust, and to Him do I turn in penitence.

Creator of the heavens and of the earth! He giveth with open hand, or sparingly, to whom He will; He knoweth all things.

To you hath He prescribed the faith which He commanded unto Noah, and which we have revealed to thee, and which we commanded unto Abraham and Moses and Jesus, saying, "Observe this faith, and be not divided into sects therein." Intolerable to those who worship idols jointly with God is that faith to which thou dost call them. Whom He pleaseth will God choose for it, and whosoever shall turn to Him in penitence will He guide to it. (42)

Eschatology

By the night when she spreads her veil;
By the day when it brightly shineth;
By Him who made male and female;
At different ends truly do ye aim!
But as to him who giveth alms and feareth God,
And yieldeth assent to the good,
To him will we make easy the path to happiness.
But as to him who is covetous and bent on riches,
And calleth the good a lie,
To him will we make easy the path to misery,
And what shall his wealth avail him when he goeth down?
Truly man's guidance is with Us,
And ours, the future and the past.
I warn you therefore of the flaming fire;
None shall be cast to it but the most wretched,—
Who hath called the truth a lie and turned his back.
But the God-fearing shall escape it,—
Who giveth away his substance that he may become pure;
And who offereth not favors to any one for the sake of recompense,
But only as seeking the face of his Lord the Most High.
And surely in the end he shall be well content. (92)

Of what ask they of one another?
Of the great news.
The theme of their disputes.
Nay! they shall certainly know its truth!
Again. Nay! they shall certainly know it.
Have we not made the earth a couch?
And the mountains its tent-stakes?
We have created you of two sexes,
And ordained you sleep for rest,
And ordained the night as a mantle,
And ordained the day for gaining livelihood.
And built above you seven solid heavens,
And placed therein a burning lamp;
And we send down water in abundance from the rain-clouds,
That we may bring forth by it corn and herbs,
And gardens thick with trees.
Lo! the day of Severance is fixed;
The day when there shall be a blast on the trumpet, and ye shall come
    in crowds,
And the heaven shall be opened and be full of portals,
And the mountains shall be set in motion, and melt into thin vapor.
Hell truly shall be a place of snares,
The home of transgressors,
To abide therein ages.
No coolness shall they taste therein nor any drink,
Save boiling water and running sores;
Meet recompense!
For they looked not forward to their account;
And they gave the lie to our signs, charging them with falsehood.
But we noted and wrote down all.
"Taste this then, and we will give you increase of nought
    but torment."
But for the God-fearing is a blissful abode,
Enclosed gardens and vineyards;
And damsels with swelling breasts, their peers in age,
And a full cup.
There shall they hear no vain discourse nor any falsehood;
A recompense from thy Lord—sufficing gift!—

Lord of the heavens and of the earth, and of all that between them
lieth—the God of Mercy! But not a word shall they obtain from Him.

On the day whereon the Spirit and the Angels shall be ranged in order,
they shall not speak; save he whom the God of Mercy shall permit, and who
shall say that which is right.

This is the sure day. Whoso then will, let him take the path of return to his Lord.

Verily, we warn you of a chastisement close at hand.

The day on which a man shall see the deeds which his hands have sent before him; and when the unbeliever shall say, "Oh! would I were dust!" (78)

O children of Adam! There shall come to you apostles from among yourselves, rehearsing my signs to you; and whoso shall fear God and do good works, no fear shall be upon them, neither shall they be put to grief.

But they who charge our signs with falsehood, and turn away from them in their pride, shall be inmates of the fire; for ever shall they abide therein. And who is worse than he who deviseth a lie of God, or treateth our signs as lies? To them shall a portion here below be assigned in accordance with the Book of our decrees, until the time when our messengers, as they receive their souls, shall say, "Where are they on whom ye called beside God?" They shall say, "Gone from us." And they shall witness against themselves that they were infidels.

He shall say, "Enter ye into the Fire with the generations of Djinn and men who have preceded you. So oft as a fresh generation entereth, it shall curse its sister, until when they have all reached it, the last comers shall say to the former, "O our Lord! these are they who led us astray; assign them therefore a double torment of the fire." He will say, "Ye shall all have double." But of this are ye ignorant.

And the former of them shall say to the latter, "What advantage have ye over us? Taste ye therefore the torment for that which ye have done."

Verily, they who have charged our signs with falsehood and have turned away from them in their pride, heaven's gates shall not be opened to them, nor shall they enter Paradise, until the camel passeth through the eye of the needle. After this manner will we recompense the transgressors.

They shall make their bed in hell, and above them shall be coverings of fire! And this way will we recompense the evil doers.

But as to those who have believed and done the things which are right (we will lay on no one a burden beyond his power)—these shall be inmates of Paradise, for ever shall they abide therein.

And we will remove whatever rancor was in their bosoms; rivers shall roll at their feet, and they shall say, "Praise be to God who hath guided us hither! We had not been guided had not God guided us! Of a surety the apostles of our Lord came to us with truth." And a voice shall cry to them, "This is Paradise, of which, as the meed of your works, ye are made heirs."

And the inmates of Paradise shall cry to the inmates of the fire, "Now have we found what our Lord promised us to be true. Have ye too found what your Lord promised you to be true?" And they shall answer, "Yes." And a herald shall proclaim between them, "The curse of God be upon the evil doers.

"Who turn men aside from the way of God, and seek to make it crooked, and who believe not in the life to come!"

And between them shall be a partition, and on the wall Al Araf [between heaven and hell] shall be men who will know all, by their tokens, and they shall cry to the inmates of Paradise, "Peace be on you!" but they shall not yet enter it, although they long to do so.

And when their eyes are turned towards the inmates of the fire they shall say, "O our Lord! place us not with the offending people."

And they who upon Al Araf shall cry to those whom they shall know by their tokens, "Your amassings and your pride have availed you nothing.

"Are these they on whom ye sware God would not bestow mercy? Enter ye into Paradise! where no fear shall be upon you, neither shall ye be put to grief."

And the inmates of the fire shall cry to the inmates of Paradise, "Pour upon us some water, or of the refreshments God hath given you." They shall say, "Truly God hath forbidden both to unbelievers, who made their religion a sport and pastime, and whom the life of the world hath deceived." This day therefore will we forget them. . . . (71)

Moral Precepts

Kill not your children for fear of want; for them and for you will we provide. Verily, the killing them is a great wickedness.

Have nought to do with adultery; for it is a foul thing and an evil way.

Neither slay any one whom God hath forbidden you to slay, unless for a just cause; and whosoever shall be slain wrongfully, to his heir have we given powers; but let him not outstep bounds in putting the manslayer to death, for he too, in his turn, will be assisted and avenged.

And touch not the substance of the orphan, unless in an upright way, till he attain his age of strength. And perform your covenant; verily the covenant shall be inquired of.

And give full measure when you measure, and weigh with just balance. This will be better, and fairest for settlement.

And follow not that of which thou hast no knowledge; because the hearing and the sight and the heart—each of these shall be inquired of.

And walk not proudly on the earth, for thou canst not cleave the earth, neither shalt thou reach to the mountains in height. (17)

There is no piety in turning your faces toward the east or the west, but he is pious who believeth in God, and the last day, and the angels, and the scriptures, and the prophets; who for the love of God disburseth his wealth to his kindred, and to the orphans, and the needy, and the wayfarer, and those who ask, and for ransoming; who observeth prayer, and payeth the legal alms, and who is of those who are faithful to their engagements when they have engaged in them, and patient under ills and hardships, and in time of trouble. These are they who are just, and these are they who fear the Lord.

O believers! retaliation for blood-shedding is prescribed to you; the free man for the free, and the slave for the slave, and the woman for the woman. But he to whom his brother shall make any remission is to be dealt with equitably, and to him should he pay a fine with liberality.

This is a relaxation from your Lord and a mercy. For him who after shall transgress a sore punishment!

But in this law of retaliation is your security for life, O men of understanding! to the intent that ye may fear God.

It is prescribed to you, when any one of you is at the point of death, if he leave goods, that he bequeath equitably to his parents and kindred. This is binding on those who fear God. But as for him who after he hath heard the bequest shall change it, surely the wrong of this shall be on those who change it; verily, God heareth, knoweth.

But he who feareth from the testator any mistake or wrong, and shall make a settlement between the parties—that shall be no wrong in him; verily, God is Lenient, Merciful.

O believers! a Fast is prescribed to you as it was prescribed to those before you, that ye may fear God, for certain days.

But he among you who shall be sick, or on a journey shall fast that same number of other days; and as for those who are able to keep it and yet break it, the expiation of this shall be the maintenance of a poor man. And he who of his own accord performeth a good work shall derive good from it, and good shall it be for you to fast—if ye knew it.

As to the month Ramadhan in which the Qur'an was sent down to be man's guidance, and an explanation of that guidance, and of that illumination, as soon as any one of you observeth the moon, let him set about the fast; but he who is sick, or upon a journey, shall fast a like number of other days. God wisheth you ease, but wisheth not your discomfort and that you fulfil the number of days, and that you glorify God for his guidance, and that you be thankful.

And when my servants ask thee concerning me, then will I be nigh unto them. I will answer the cry of him that crieth, when he crieth unto me; but let them hearken unto me, and believe in me, that they may proceed aright.

You are allowed on the night of the fast to approach your wives; they are your garment and ye are their garment. God knoweth that ye defraud yourselves therein, so He turneth unto you and forgiveth you! Now, therefore, go in unto them with full desire for that which God hath ordained for you; and eat and drink until ye can discern a white thread from a black thread by the daybreak, then fast strictly till night, and go not in unto them, but rather pass the time in the Mosque.

• • •

The likeness of those who expend their wealth for the cause of God is that of a grain of corn which produceth seven ears, and in each ear a hundred grains; and God will multiply to whom He pleaseth. God is Liberal, Knowing!

They who expend their wealth for the cause of God, and never follow what they have laid out with reproaches or harm, shall have their reward with their Lord; no fear shall come upon them, neither shall they be put to grief.

A kind speech and forgiveness is better than alms followed by injury. God is Rich, Clement.

O ye who believe! make not your alms void by reproaches and injury, like him who spendeth his substance to be seen of men, and believeth not in God and in the latter day. The likeness of such an one is that of a rock with a thin soil upon it, on which a heavy rain falleth but leaveth it hard. No profit from their works shall they be able to gain; for God guideth not the unbelieving people.

And the likeness of those who expend their substance from a desire to please God, and for the stablishing of their souls, is as a garden on a hill, on which the heavy rain falleth, and it yieldeth its fruits twofold; and even if a heavy rain fall not on it, yet is there a dew. God beholdeth your actions.

• • •

Ye may divorce your wives twice. Keep them honorably or put them away with kindness. But it is not allowed you to appropriate to yourselves aught of what ye have given to them, unless both fear that they cannot keep within the bounds set up by God. And if ye fear that they cannot observe the ordinances of God, no blame shall attach to either of you for what the wife shall herself give for her redemption. These are the bounds of God; therefore overstep them not, for whoever oversteppeth the bounds of God, they are evildoers.

But if the husband divorce her a third time, it is not lawful for him to take her again, until she shall have married another husband; and if he also divorce her, then shall no blame attach to them if they return to each other, thinking that they can keep within the bounds fixed by God. (2)

O men! fear your Lord, who hath created you of one man (soul), and of him created his wife, and from these twain hath spread abroad so many men and women. And fear ye God, in whose name ye ask mutual favors,—and reverence the wombs that bare you. Verily is God watching over you!

And give to the orphans their property; substitute not worthless things of your own for their valuable ones, and devour not their property after adding it to your own, for this is a great crime.

And if ye are apprehensive that ye shall not deal fairly with orphans, then of other women who seem good in your eyes, marry but two, or three, or four; and if ye still fear that ye shall not act equitably, then one only; or the slaves whom ye have acquired. This will make justice on your part easier. Give women their dowry freely; but if of themselves they give up aught thereof to you, then enjoy it as convenient, and profitable.

And entrust not to the incapable the substance which God hath placed with you for their support; but maintain them therewith, and clothe them, and speak to them with kindly speech.

• • •

And if ye be desirous to exchange one wife for another, and have given one of them a talent, make no deduction from it. Would ye take it by slandering her, and with manifest wrong?

How, moreover, could ye take it, when one of you hath gone in unto the other, and they have received from you a strict bond of union?

And marry not women whom your fathers have married; for this is a shame, and hateful, and an evil way:—though what is past may be allowed.

Forbidden to you are your mothers, and your daughters, and your sisters, and your aunts, both on the father and mother's side, and your nieces on the brother and sister's side, and your foster-mothers, and your foster-sisters, and the mothers of your wives, and your step-daughters who are your wards, born of your wives to whom ye have gone in; (but if ye have not gone in unto them, it shall be no sin in you to marry them); and the wives of your sons who proceed out of your loins; and ye may not have two sisters, except where it is already done. Verily, God is Indulgent, Merciful!

Forbidden to you also are married women, except those who are in your hands as slaves. This is the law of God for you. And it is allowed you, beside this, to seek out wives by means of your wealth, with modest conduct, and without fornication. And give those with whom ye have cohabited their dowry. This is the law. But it shall be no crime in you to make agreements over and above the law.

• • •

Men are superior to women on account of the qualities with which God hath gifted the one above the other, and on account of the outlay they make from their substance for them. Virtuous women are obedient, careful, during the husband's absence, because God hath of them been careful. But chide those for whose refractoriness ye have cause to fear; remove them into beds apart, and scourge them. But if they are obedient to you, then seek not occasion against them. (4)

Warfare

Fight for the cause of God against those who fight against you; but commit not the injustice of attacking them first. God loveth not such injustice.

And kill them wherever ye shall find them, and eject them from whatever place they have ejected you; for civil discord is worse than carnage. Yet attack them not at the sacred Mosque, unless they attack you therein; but if they attack you, slay them. Such is the reward of the infidels.

But if they desist, then verily God is Gracious, Merciful.

Fight therefore against them until there be no more civil discord, and the only worship be that of God. But if they desist, then let there be no hostility, save against the wicked. (2)

Christians and Jews

We believe in God, and in what hath been sent down to us, and what hath been sent down to Abraham, and Ismael, and Isaac, and Jacob, and the tribes, and in what was given to Moses, and Jesus, and the Prophets, from their Lord. We make no difference between them. And to Him are we resigned (Muslims).

Whoso desireth any other religion than Islam, that religion shall never be accepted from him, and in the next world he shall be among the lost. (3)

Verily, they who believe (Muslims), and they who follow the Jewish religion, and the Christians, and the Sabeites—whoever of these believeth in God and the last day, and doeth that which is right, shall have their reward with their Lord. Fear shall not come upon them, neither shall they be grieved. (2)

Make war upon such of those to whom the Scriptures have been given as believe not in God, or in the last day, and who forbid not that which God and His Apostle have forbidden, and who profess not the profession of the truth, until they pay tribute out of hand, and they be humbled.

The Jews say, "Ezra is a son of God," and the Christians say, "The Messiah is a son of God." Such the sayings in their mouths! They resemble the saying of the infidels of old! God do battle with them! How are they misguided!

They take their teachers, and their monks, and the Messiah, son of Mary, for Lords beside God, though bidden to worship one God only. There is no God but He! Far from His glory be what they associate with Him! (9)

al-Farabi

One of the most important Muslim thinkers during the Golden Age of Islam was Abu Nasr Muhammad al-Farabi (c. 870–950). Of Turkish descent, al-Farabi was born in Turkestan, in the interior of southern Asia. For most of his life he lived in the city of Baghdad, where he became a student of philosophy, taught by Christians steeped in the classical Greek tradition as it had been developed during the Hellenistic age and later in the school of Alexandria in Egypt. Although he was a noted philosopher in his own time, al-Farabi shunned fame and publicity, preferring to live a secluded and austere life.

The influence of classical Greek philosophy on al-Farabi, particularly of Plato, Aristotle, and the neo-Platonists, is evident throughout his writings, including his book *The Perfect State*. Although the title of this work indicates its subject to be politics, al-Farabi turns to his description of the ideal state only in Chapter 15, after he has grounded his views in a full theory both of metaphysics (including theology and natural science) and psychology, employing arguments from analogy as the basis for his political conclusions. His use of this kind of philosophical generalization and integration reveals the influence of Aristotle, as does the opening paragraph of the following selection, in which he reiterates the Aristotelian view that "man is a political animal." In his description of the ideal ruler, whom al-Farabi conceives to be a philosopher-king, can be found a strong echo of the central theme of Plato's *Republic*.

But al-Farabi's thought was not just derivative from the Greeks. As a Muslim he added a further dimension to the philosopher-king concept. The ideal ruler must also be a prophet. Not only is such a ruler an individual of high intelligence but one of an intellect of "divine quality" who can look into the future and warn "of things to come."

---

1. To what extent has al-Farabi adopted the philosophy of the Classical Mediterranean?

2. To what extent does this selection reflect Islamic ideas and assumptions?

The Perfect State

Section V

CHAPTER 15. PERFECT ASSOCIATIONS AND PERFECT RULER; FAULTY ASSOCIATIONS

1.   In order to preserve himself and to attain his highest perfections every human being is by his very nature in need of many things which he cannot provide all by himself; he is indeed in need of people who each supply him with some particular need of his. Everybody finds himself in the same relation to everybody in this respect. Therefore man cannot attain the perfection, for the sake of which his inborn nature has been given to him, unless many (societies of) people who co-operate come together who each supply everybody else with some particular need of his, so that as result of the contribution of the whole community all the things are brought together which everybody needs in order to preserve himself and to attain perfection. Therefore human individuals have come to exist in great numbers, and have settled in the inhabitable (inhabited?) region of the earth, so that human societies have come to exist in it, some of which are perfect, others imperfect.

2.   There are three kinds of perfect society, great, medium and small. The great one is the union of all the societies in the inhabitable world; the medium one the union of one nation in one part of the inhabitable world; the small one the union of the people of a city in the territory of any nation whatsoever. Imperfect are the union of people in a village, the union of people in a quarter, then the union in a street, eventually the union in a house, the house being the smallest union of all. Quarter and village exist both for the sake of the city, but the relation of the village to the city is one of service whereas the quarter is related to the city as a part of it; the street is a part of the quarter, the house a part of the street. The city is a part of the territory of a nation, the nation a part of all the people of the inhabitable world.

3.   The most excellent good and the utmost perfection is, in the first instance, attained in a city, not in a society which is less complete than it. But since good in its real sense is such as to be attainable through choice and will, and evils are also due to will and choice only, a city may be established to enable its people to co-operate in attaining some aims that are evil. Hence felicity is not attainable in every city. The city, then, in which people aim through association at co-operating for the things by which felicity in its real and true sense can be attained, is the excellent city, and the society in which there is a co-operation to acquire felicity is the excellent society; and the

Al-Farabi on the Perfect State, trans. Richard Walzer (Oxford: Clarendon Press, 1985). Reprinted by permission of Oxford University Press.

nation in which all of its cities co-operate for those things through which felicity is attained is the excellent nation. In the same way, the excellent universal state will arise only when all the nations in it co-operate for the purpose of reaching felicity.

4.   The excellent city resembles the perfect and healthy body, all of whose limbs co-operate to make the life of the animal perfect and to preserve it in this state. Now the limbs and organs of the body are different and their natural endowments and faculties are unequal in excellence, there being among them one ruling organ, namely the heart, and organs which are close in rank to that ruling organ, each having been given by nature a faculty by which it performs its proper function in conformity with the natural aim of that ruling organ. Other organs have by nature faculties by which they perform their functions according to the aims of those organs which have no intermediary between themselves and the ruling organ; they are in the second rank. Other organs, in turn, perform their functions according to the aim of those which are in the second rank, and so on until eventually organs are reached which only serve and do not rule at all.

The same holds good in the case of the city. Its parts are different by nature, and their natural dispositions are unequal in excellence: there is in it a man who is the ruler, and there are others whose ranks are close to the ruler, each of them with a disposition and a habit through which he performs an action in conformity with the intention of that ruler; these are the holders of the first ranks. Below them are people who perform their actions in accordance with the aims of those people; they are in the second rank. Below them in turn are people who perform their actions according to the aims of the people mentioned in the second instance, and the parts of the city continue to be arranged in this way, until eventually parts are reached which perform their actions according to the aims of others, while there do not exist any people who perform their actions according to their aims; these, then, are the people who serve without being served in turn, and who are hence in the lowest rank and at the bottom of the scale.

But the limbs and organs of the body are natural, and the dispositions which they have are natural faculties, whereas, although the parts of the city are natural, their dispositions and habits, by which they perform their actions in the city, are not natural but voluntary—notwithstanding that the parts of the city are by nature provided with endowments unequal in excellence which enable them to do one thing and not another. But they are not parts of the city by their inborn nature alone but rather by the voluntary habits which they acquire such as the arts and their likes; to the natural faculties which exist in the organs and limbs of the body correspond the voluntary habits and dispositions in the parts of the city.

5.   The ruling organ in the body is by nature the most perfect and most complete of the organs in itself and in its specific qualification, and it also has the best of everything of which another organ has a share as well; beneath it,

in turn, are other organs which rule over organs inferior to them, their rule being lower in rank than the rule of the first and indeed subordinate to the rule of the first; they rule and are ruled.

In the same way, the ruler of the city is the most perfect part of the city in his specific qualification and has the best of everything which any-body else shares with him; beneath him are people who are ruled by him and rule others.

The heart comes to be first and becomes then the cause of the existence of the other organs and limbs of the body, and the cause of the existence of their faculties in them and of their arrangement in the ranks proper to them, and when one of its organs is out of order, it is the heart which provides the means to remove that disorder. In the same way the ruler of this city must come to be in the first instance, and will subsequently be the cause of the rise of the city and its parts and the cause of the presence of the voluntary habits of its parts and of their arrangement in the ranks proper to them; and when one part is out of order he provides it with the means to remove its disorder.

The parts of the body close to the ruling organ perform of the natural functions, in agreement—by nature—with the aim of the ruler, the most noble ones; the organs beneath them perform those functions which are less noble, and eventually the organs are reached which perform the meanest functions. In the same way the parts of the city which are close in authority to the ruler of the city perform the most noble voluntary actions, and those below them less noble actions, until eventually the parts are reached which perform the most ignoble actions. The inferiority of such actions is some-times due to the inferiority of their matter, although they may be extremely useful—like the action of the bladder and the action of the lower intestine in the body; sometimes it is due to their being of little use; at other times it is due to their being very easy to perform. This applies equally to the city and equally to every whole which is composed by nature of well ordered coher-ent parts: they have a ruler whose relation to the other parts is like the one just described.

6.   This applies also to all existents. For the relation of the First Cause to the other existents is like the relation of the king of the excellent city to its other parts. For the ranks of the immaterial existents are close to the First. Beneath them are the heavenly bodies, and beneath the heavenly bodies the material bodies. All these existents act in conformity with the First Cause, follow it, take it as their guide and imitate it; but each existent does that according to its capacity, choosing its aim precisely on the strength of its established rank in the universe: that is to say the last follows the aim of that which is slightly above it in rank, equally the second existent, in turn, follows what is above itself in rank, and in the same way the third existent has an aim which is above it. Eventually existents are reached which are linked with the First Cause without any intermediary whatsoever. In accord-ance with this order of rank all the existents permanently follow the aim of

the First Cause. Those which are from the very outset provided with all the essentials of their existence are made to imitate the First (Cause) and its aim from their very outset, and hence enjoy eternal bliss and hold the highest ranks; but those which are not provided from the outset with all the essentials of their existence, are provided with a faculty by which they move towards the expected attainment of those essentials and will then be able to follow the aim of the First (Cause). The excellent city ought to be arranged in the same way: all its parts ought to imitate in their actions the aim of their first ruler according to their rank.

7. The ruler of the excellent city cannot just be any man, because rulership requires two conditions: (a) he should be predisposed for it by his inborn nature, (b) he should have acquired the attitude and habit of will for rulership which will develop in a man whose inborn nature is predisposed for it. Nor is every art suitable for rulership; most of the arts, indeed, are rather suited for service within the city, just as most men are by their very nature born to serve. Some of the arts rule certain (other) arts while serving others at the same time, whereas there are other arts which, not ruling anything at all, only serve. Therefore the art of ruling the excellent city cannot just be any chance art, nor due to any chance habit whatever. For just as the first ruler in a genus cannot be ruled by anything in that genus—for instance the ruler of the limbs cannot be ruled by any other limb, and this holds good for any ruler of any composite whole—so the art of the ruler in the excellent city of necessity cannot be a serving art at all and cannot be ruled by any other art, but his art must be an art towards the aim of which all the other arts tend, and for which they strive in all the actions of the excellent city.

8. That man is a person over whom nobody has any sovereignty whatsoever. He is a man who has reached his perfection and has become actually intellect and actually being thought (intelligized), his representative faculty having by nature reached its utmost perfection in the way stated by us; this faculty of his is predisposed by nature to receive, either in waking life or in sleep, from the Active Intellect the particulars, either as they are or by imitating them, and also the intelligibles, by imitating them. His Passive Intellect will have reached its perfection by [having apprehended] all the intelligibles, so that none of them is kept back from it, and it will have become actually intellect and actually being thought. Indeed any man whose Passive Intellect has thus been perfected by [having apprehended] all the intelligibles and has become actually intellect and actually being thought, so that the intelligible in him has become identical with that which thinks in him, acquires an actual intellect which is superior to the Passive Intellect and more perfect and more separate from matter (immaterial?) than the Passive Intellect. It is called the 'Acquired Intellect' and comes to occupy a middle position between the Passive Intellect and the Active Intellect, nothing else being between it and the Active Intellect. The Passive Intellect is thus like matter and substratum for the Acquired

Intellect, and the Acquired Intellect like matter and substratum for the Active Intellect, and the rational faculty, which is a natural disposition, is a matter underlying the Passive Intellect which is actually intellect.

9.   The first stage, then, through which man becomes man is the coming to be of the receptive natural disposition which is ready to become actually intellect; this disposition is common to all men. Between this disposition and the Active Intellect are two stages, the Passive Intellect which has become actually intellect, and [the rise of] the Acquired Intellect. There are thus two stages between the first stage of being a man and the Active Intellect. When the perfect Passive Intellect and the natural disposition become one thing in the way the compound of matter and form is one—and when the form of the humanity of this man is taken as identical with the Passive Intellect which has become actually intellect, there will be between this man and the Active Intellect only one stage. And when the natural disposition is made the matter of the Passive Intellect which has become actually intellect, and the Passive Intellect the matter of the Acquired Intellect, and the Acquired Intellect the matter of the Active Intellect, and when all this is taken as one and the same thing, then this man is the man on whom the Active Intellect has descended.

10.   When this occurs in both parts of his rational faculty, namely the theoretical and the practical rational faculties, and also in his representative faculty, then it is this man who receives Divine Revelation, and God Almighty grants him Revelation through the mediation of the Active Intellect, so that the emanation from God Almighty to the Active Intellect is passed on to his Passive Intellect through the mediation of the Acquired Intellect, and then to the faculty of representation. Thus he is, through the emanation from the Active Intellect to his Passive Intellect, a wise man and a philosopher and an accomplished thinker who employs an intellect of divine quality, and through the emanation from the Active Intellect to his faculty of representation a visionary prophet: who warns of things to come and tells of particular things which exist at present.

11.   This man holds the most perfect rank of humanity and has reached the highest degree of felicity. His soul is united as it were with the Active Intellect, in the way stated by us. He is the man who knows every action by which felicity can be reached. This is the first condition for being a ruler. Moreover, he should be a good orator and able to rouse [other people's] imagination by well chosen words. He should be able to lead people well along the right path to felicity and to the actions by which felicity is reached. He should, in addition, be of tough physique, in order to shoulder the tasks of war.

This is the sovereign over whom no other human being has any sovereignty whatsoever; he is the Imām; he is the first sovereign of the excellent city, he is the sovereign of the excellent nation, and the sovereign of the universal state.

12. But this state can only be reached by a man in whom twelve natural qualities are found together, with which he is endowed by birth. (1) One of them is that he should have limbs and organs which are free from deficiency and strong, and that they will make him fit for the actions which depend on them; when he intends to perform an action with one of them, he accomplishes it with ease. (2) He should by nature be good at understanding and perceiving everything said to him, and grasp it in his mind according to what the speaker intends and what the thing itself demands. (3) He should be good at retaining what he comes to know and see and hear and apprehend in general, and forget almost nothing. (4) He should be well provided with ready intelligence and very bright; when he sees the slightest indication of a thing, he should grasp it in the way indicated. (5) He should have a fine diction, his tongue enabling him to explain to perfection all that is in the recess of his mind. (6) He should be fond of learning and acquiring knowledge, be devoted to it and grasp things easily, without finding the effort painful, nor feeling discomfort about the toil which it entails. (7) He should by nature be fond of truth and truthful men and hate falsehood and liars. (8) He should by nature not crave for food and drink and sexual intercourse, and have a natural aversion to gambling and hatred of the pleasures which these pursuits provide. (9) He should be proud of spirit and fond of honour, his soul being by his (?) nature above everything ugly and base, and rising naturally to the most lofty things. (10) Dirham and dīnār and the other worldly pursuits should be of little amount in his view. (11) He should by nature be fond of justice and of just people, and hate oppression and injustice and those who practice them, giving himself and others their due, and urging people to act justly and showing pity to those who are oppressed by injustice; he should lend his support to what he considers to be beautiful and noble and just; he should not be reluctant to give in nor should he be stubborn and obstinate if he is asked to do justice; but he should be reluctant to give in if he is asked to do injustice and evil altogether. (12) He should be strong in setting his mind firmly upon the thing which, in his view, ought to be done, and daringly and bravely carry it out without fear and weak-mindedness.

13. Now it is difficult to find all these qualities united in one man, and, therefore, men endowed with this nature will be found one at a time only, such men being altogether very rare. Therefore if there exists such a man in the excellent city who, after reaching maturity, fulfils the six aforementioned conditions—or five of them if one excludes the gift of visionary prophecy through the faculty of representation—he will be the sovereign. Now when it happens that, at a given time, no such man is to be found but there was previously an unbroken succession of sovereigns of this kind, the laws and the customs which were introduced will be adopted and eventually firmly established.

The next sovereign, who is the successor of the first sovereigns, will be someone in whom those [twelve] qualities are found together from the time of his birth and his early youth and who will, after reaching his maturity, be distinguished by the following six qualities: (1) He will be a philosopher. (2) He will know and remember the laws and customs (and rules of conduct) with which the first sovereigns had governed the city, conforming in all his actions to all their actions. (3) He will excel in deducing a new law by analogy where no law of his predecessors has been recorded, following for his deductions the principles laid down by the first Imāms. (4) He will be good at deliberating and be powerful in his deductions to meet new situations for which the first sovereigns could not have laid down any law; when doing this he will have in mind the good of the city. (5) He will be good at guiding the people by his speech to fulfil the laws of the first sovereigns as well as those laws which he will have deduced in conformity with their principles after their time. (6) He should be of tough physique in order to shoulder the tasks of war, mastering the serving as well as the ruling military art.

14.   When one single man who fulfils all these conditions cannot be found but there are two, one of whom is a philosopher and the other fulfils the remaining conditions, the two of them will be the sovereigns of this city.

But when all these six qualities exist separately in different men, philosophy in one man and the second quality in another man and so on, and when these men are all in agreement, they should all together be the excellent sovereigns.

But when it happens, at a given time, that philosophy has no share in the government, though every other condition may be present in it, the excellent city will remain without a king, the ruler actually in charge of this city will not be a king, and the city will be on the verge of destruction; and if it happens that no philosopher can be found who will be attached to the actual ruler of the city, then, after a certain interval, this city will undoubtedly perish.

Futo No Yasumaro

The *Kojiki, or Records of Ancient Matters*, filled as it is with inconsistencies and anomalies, is a document that is next to impossible for us today to disentangle, let alone comprehend. But it is of great historical importance because it is the earliest attempt made by the Japanese to give a written account of their beginnings, including the birth of the islands themselves and the descent of the imperial rulers. It would be gratuitous to suggest, as its author Yasumaro presumably believed, that the episodes he describes constitute authentic history, for they obviously are an amalgam of mythology and fantasy. Yet they provide us with valuable insights not only into ways of early thinking but also, in the special case of Japan, into a set of beliefs that has persisted in the national consciousness for millennia.

The history of the composition of the *Kojiki* is worthy of note. In the seventh century A.D., as Yasumaro explains in his preface, the Emperor Temmu decided, probably following the precedent of China, to produce an accurate history of early Japan and the imperial line. So he appointed a young man of exceptional memory to carry out the project. But the emperor died before the task was completed and it was not renewed until the following century under the Empress Gemmyo, who commissioned Yasumaro to put the *Records* in writing, an undertaking he completed in a few months.

The selection that follows details the generation and activities of the innumerable gods who preceded human occupation of Japan, as well as of the origin of the Japanese islands themselves. Passages have been chosen in an attempt to provide a maximum amount of coherence to an often-unintelligible sequence of events. Many of the gods named are of relatively minor significance except for the fact that they indicate that the early Japanese were prepared to deify almost everything. Of particular significance is the description near the end of the generation of the early leaders of Japan, who culminated in the imperial line, from gods descended from heaven. The myth of the divine descent of the emperors persisted throughout Japanese history until 1946 when Emperor Hirohito, bowing to pressure from the American army of occupation, acknowledged in an official proclamation to his people that he was not really a divine descendant of the sun goddess but only an ordinary human being.

It should be noted that the *Kojiki* is of relatively late origin historically. As the first written records of early Japanese "history," thus an important symbol of the beginnings of that civilization, it appeared around a thousand years after the classics of ancient Chinese civilization.

1. How are the gods depicted in this text? What are their functions?

2. This text was created to legitimize the authority of the imperial dynasty. How does it do that? How is this approach different from Chinese writings with the same purpose?

The Kojiki or Records of Ancient Matters

Preface

•••

The Heavenly Sovereign [Emperor Temmu] commanded, saying "I hear that the chronicles of the emperors and likewise the original words in the possession of the various families deviate from exact truth, and are most amplified by empty falsehoods. If at the present time these imperfections be not amended, ere many years shall have elapsed, the purport of this, the great basis of the country, the grand foundation of the monarchy, will be destroyed. So now I desire to have the chronicles of the emperors selected and recorded, and the old words examined and ascertained, falsehoods being erased and truth determined, in order to transmit the latter to after ages." At that time there was a retainer whose surname was Hiyeda and his personal name Are. He was twenty-eight years old, and of so intelligent a disposition that he could repeat with his mouth whatever met his eyes, and record in his heart whatever struck his ears. Forthwith Are was commanded to learn by heart the genealogies of the emperors, and likewise the words of former ages. Nevertheless, time elapsed and the age changed, and the thing was not yet carried out.

Prostrate I consider how Her Majesty the Empress [Gemmyo], having obtained Unity, illumines the empire. . . . Regretting the errors in the old words, and wishing to correct the misstatements in the former chronicles, She, on the eighteenth day of the ninth moon of the fourth year of Wado [A.D. 711], commanded me Yasumaro to select and record the old words learnt by heart by Hiyeda no Are according to the Imperial Decree, and dutifully to lift them up to Her.

In reverent obedience to the contents of the Decree, I have made a careful choice. . . . Altogether the things recorded commence with the separation of Heaven and Earth, and conclude with the august reign at Woharida [in 628, when Empress Sui-ko died]. . . . Altogether I have written three volumes, which I reverently and respectfully present. I Yasumaro, with true trembling and true fear, bow my head, bow my head.

Trans. Basil Hall Chamberlain.

Reverently presented by the Court Noble Futo no Yasumaro, an Officer of the Upper Division of the First Class of the Fifth Rank and of the Fifth Order of Merit, on the 28th day of the first moon of the fifth year of Wado [March 10, 712].

Section I. The Beginning of Heaven and Earth*

The names of the Deities** that were born in the Plain of High Heaven when the Heaven and Earth began were the Deity Master-of-the-August-Centre-of-Heaven, next the High-August-Producing-Wondrous-Deity, next the Divine-Producing-Wondrous-Deity. These three Deities were all Deities born alone, and hid their persons [i.e., died]. The names of the Deities that were born next from a thing that sprouted up like unto a reed-shoot when the earth, young and like unto floating oil, drifted about medusa-like, were the Pleasant-Reed-Shoot-Prince-Elder-Deity, next the Heavenly-Eternally-Standing-Deity. These two Deities were likewise born alone, and hid their persons.

Section II. The Seven Divine Generations

The names of the Deities that were born next were the Earthly-Eternally-Standing-Deity, next the Luxuriant-Integrating-Master-Deity. These two Deities were likewise Deities born alone, and hid their persons. The names of the Deities that were born next were the Deity Mud-Earth-Lord, next his younger sister the Deity Mud-Earth-Lady, next the Germ-Integrating-Deity, next his younger sister the Life-Integrating-Deity, next the Deity Elder-of-the-Great-Place, next his younger sister the Deity Elder-Lady-of-the-Great-Place, next the Deity Perfect-Exterior, next his younger sister the Deity Oh-Awful-Lady, next the Deity Male-Who-Invites [also named Izanagi], next his younger sister the Deity Female-Who-Invites [also named Izanami]. From the Earthly-Eternally-Standing-Deity down to the Deity Female-Who-Invites [Izanami] in the previous list are what are termed the Seven Divine Generations.

Section III. The Island of Onogoro

Hereupon all the Heavenly Deities commanded the two Deities His Augustness Izanagi and Her Augustness Izanami, ordering them to "make, consolidate, and give birth to this drifting land [Japan]." Granting to them

---

*Section titles have been added by the translator.
**The Japanese word *kami*, here and later translated as "deity" or "god," actually has a broader meaning; it can refer to anything superior, particularly to a superior being.

a heavenly jewelled spear, they thus deigned to charge them. So the two Deities, standing upon the Floating Bridge of Heaven, pushed down the jewelled spear and stirred with it, whereupon when they had stirred the brine till it went curdle-curdle, and drew the spear up, the brine that dripped down from the end of the spear was piled up and became an island. This is the Island of Onogoro [a Japanese islet].

Section IV. Courtship of the Deities the Male-Who-Invites and the Female-Who-Invites

Having descended from Heaven onto this island, they saw to the erection of a heavenly august pillar, they saw to the erection of a hall of eight fathoms. [They then produced a child.] This child they placed in a boat of reeds, and let it float away. Next they gave birth to the Island of Aha [another islet]. . . .

Section V. Birth of the Eight Great Islands

Hereupon the two Deities took counsel, saying: "The children to whom we have now given birth are not good. It will be best to announce this in the august place of the Heavenly Deities." They ascended forthwith to Heaven and inquired of Their Augustnesses the Heavenly Deities. Then the Heavenly Deities commanded and found out by grand divination, and ordered them, saying: "They were not good because the woman spoke first. Descend back again and amend your words." So thereupon descending back, they again went round the heavenly august pillar as before. Thereupon his Augustness Izanagi spoke first: "Ah! what a fair and lovely maiden!" Afterwards his younger sister Her Augustness Izanami spoke: "Ah! what a fair and lovely youth!" [They gave birth to another child.] Next they gave birth to the Island of Futa-na in Iyo. This island has one body and four faces, and each face has a name. So the Land of Iyo is called Lovely-Princess, the Land of Sanuki is called Prince-Good-Boiled-Rice, the Land of Aha is called the Princess-of-Great-Food, the Land of Tosa is called Brave-Good-Youth. Next they gave birth to the Islands of Mitsu-go near Oki, another name for which islands is Heavenly-Great-Heart-Youth. Next they gave birth to the island of Tsukushi. This island likewise has one body and four faces, and each face has a name. So the Land of Tsukushi is called White-Sun-Youth, the Land of Toyo is called Luxuriant-Sun-Youth, the Land of Hi is called Brave-Sun-Confronting-Luxuriant-Wondrous-Lord-Youth, the Land of Kumaso is called Brave-Sun-Youth. Next they gave birth to the Island of Iki, another name for which is Heaven's-One-Pillar. Next they gave birth to the Island of Tsu, another name for which is Heavenly-Handnet-Good-Princess. Next they gave birth to the Island of Sado. Next they gave birth to Great-Yamato-the-Luxuriant-Island-of-the-Dragon-Fly, another name for which is Heavenly-August-Sky-Luxuriant-Dragon-Fly-Lord-Youth. The name of "Land-of-the-Eight-Great-Islands" therefore originated in these eight islands having been born first. [They then completed giving birth to the islands of Japan.]

Section VI. Birth of the Various Deities

When they had finished giving birth to countries, they began afresh giving birth to Deities. [There follows a long list of deities to whom Izanagi and Izanami give birth, and who in turn give birth to further deities, and so on. Many of these deities have names descriptive of natural phenomena like rocks, wind, sea, autumn, trees, mountains, and moors.]

Section VII. Retirement of Her Augustness the Princess-Who-Invites

Through giving birth to this child her august private parts were burnt, and she [Izanami] sickened and lay down. . . . So the Deity Izanami, through giving birth to the Deity-of-Fire, at length divinely retired [died]. The total number of islands given birth to jointly by the two Deities Izanagi and Izanami was fourteen, and of Deities thirty-five.

So then His Augustness Izanagi said: "Oh! Thine Augustness my lovely younger sister! Oh! that I should have exchanged thee for this single child!" And as he crept round her august pillow, and as he crept round her august feet and wept, there was born from his august tears the Deity that dwells at Konomoto near Unewo on Mount Kagu, and whose name is the Crying-Weeping-Female-Deity. So he buried the divinely retired Deity Izanami on Mount Hiba at the boundary of the Land of Idzumo and the Land of Hahaki.

• • •

Section IX. The Land of Hades

Thereupon His Augustness Izanagi, wishing to meet and see his younger sister Her Augustness Izanami, followed after her to the Land of Hades. So when from the palace she raised the door and came out to meet him, His Augustness Izanagi spoke, saying: "Thine Augustness my lovely younger sister! the lands that I and thou made are not yet finished making, so come back." Then Her Augustness Izanami answered, saying: "Lamentable indeed that thou camest not sooner! I have eaten of the furnace of Hades. Nevertheless, as I reverence the entry here of Thine

Augustness my lovely elder brother, I wish to return. Moreover I will discuss it particularly with the Deities of Hades. Look not at me!" Having thus spoken, she went back inside the palace; and as she tarried there very long, he could not wait. So having taken and broken off one of the end-teeth of the multitudinous and close-toothed comb stuck in the august left bunch of his hair, he lit one light and went in and looked. Maggots were swarming, and she was rotting, and in her head dwelt the Great-Thunder, in her breast dwelt the Fire-Thunder, in her belly dwelt the Black-Thunder, in her private parts dwelt the Cleaving-Thunder, in her left hand dwelt the Young-Thunder, in her right hand dwelt the Earth-Thunder, in her left foot dwelt the Rumbling-Thunder, in her right foot dwelt the Couchant-Thunder—altogether eight Thunder-Deities had been born and dwelt there. Hereupon His Augustness Izanagi, overawed at the sight, fled back, whereupon his younger sister Her Augustness Izanami said: "Thou hast put me to shame," and at once sent the Ugly-Female-of-Hades to pursue him. So His Augustness Izanagi took his black august headdress and cast it down, and it instantly turned into grapes. While she picked them up and ate them, he fled on; but as she still pursued him, he took and broke the multitudinous and close-toothed comb in the right bunch of his hair and cast it down, and it instantly turned into bamboo-sprouts. While she pulled them up and ate them, he fled on. Again later his younger sister sent the eight Thunder-Deities with a thousand and five hundred warriors of Hades to pursue him. So he, drawing the ten-grasp sabre that was augustly girded on him, fled forward brandishing it in his back hand; and as they still pursued, he took, on reaching the base of the Even Pass of Hades, three peaches that were growing at its base, and waited and smote his pursuers therewith, so that they all fled back. Then His Augustness Izanagi announced to the peaches: "Like as ye have helped me, so much ye help all living people in the Central Land of Reed-Plains [Japan] when they shall fall into troublous circumstances and be harassed!"—and he gave to the peaches the designation of Their Augustnesses Great-Divine-Fruit. Last of all his younger sister Her Augustness Izanami came out herself in pursuit. So he drew a thousand-draught rock, and with it blocked up the Even Pass of Hades, and placed the rock in the middle; and they stood opposite to one another and exchanged leave-takings; and Her Augustness Izanami said: "My lovely elder brother, thine Augustness! If thou do like this, I will in one day strangle to death a thousand of the folks of thy land." Then His Augustness Izanagi replied: "My lovely younger sister, Thine Augustness! If *thou* do this *I* will in one day set up a thousand and five hundred parturition-houses. In this manner each day a thousand people would surely die, and each day a thousand and five hundred people would surely be born." So Her Augustness Izanami is called the Great-Deity-of-Hades. Again it is said that, owing to her having pursued and reached her elder brother, she is called the Road-Reaching-Great-Diety. Again the rock with which he blocked up the Pass of Hades is called the Great-Deity-of-the-Road-Turning-Back, and again it is called the Blocking-Great-Deity-of-the-Door-of-Hades. . . .

Section X. The Purification of the August Person

Therefore the Great Deity Izanagi said: "Nay! hideous! I have come to a hideous and polluted land, I have! So I will perform the purification of my august person." So he went out to a plain covered with bushclover at a small river mouth near Tachibana in Himuka [probably on Honshu] in the island of Tsukushi and purified and cleansed himself. [Izanagi removes his clothing and begins to bathe; as by-products of these activities he creates a sizeable number of diverse deities, of which only the last three are significant.] The name of the Deity that was born as he thereupon washed his left august eye was the Heaven-Shining-Great-August-Deity. The name of the Deity that was next born as he washed his right august eye was His Augustness Moon-Night-Possessor. The name of the Deity that was next born as he washed his august nose was His Brave-Swift-Impetuous-Male-Augustness (or Susanoo). . . .

Section XI. Investiture of the Three Deities, The Illustrious August Children

At this time His Augustness Izanagi greatly rejoiced, saying: "I, begetting child after child, have at my final begetting gotten three illustrious children," with which words, at once jinglingly taking off and shaking the jewel-string forming his august necklace, he bestowed it on the Heaven-Shining-Great-August-Deity, saying: "Do Thine Augustness rule the Plain-of-High-Heaven." With this charge he bestowed it on her. Now the name of this august necklace was the August-Storehouse-Shelf-Deity. Next he said to His Augustness Moon-Night-Possessor: "Do Thine Augustness rule the Dominion of the Night." Thus he charged him. Next he said to Susanoo: "Do Thine Augustness rule the Sea-Plain."

Section XII. The Crying and Weeping of His Impetuous-Male-Augustness

So while the other two Deities each assumed his and her rule according to the command with which their father had deigned to charge them, Susanoo did not assume the rule of the dominion with which he had been charged, but cried and wept till his eight-grasp beard reached to the pit of his stomach. The fashion of his weeping was such as by his weeping to wither the green mountains into withered mountains and by his weeping to dry up all the rivers and seas. For this reason the sound of bad Deities was like unto the flies in the fifth moon as they all swarmed, and in all things every portent of woe arose. So the Great August Deity Izanagi said to Susanoo: "How is it that, instead of ruling the land with which I charged thee, thou dost wail and weep?" He replied, saying: "I wail because I wish to depart to my deceased mother's land, to the Nether Distant Land [Hades]." Then the Great August Deity Izanagi was very angry and said: "If that be so, thou shalt not dwell in this land," and forthwith expelled him with a divine expulsion. . . .

Section XIII. The August Oath

So thereupon Susanoo said: "If that be so, I will take leave of the Heaven-Shining-Great-August-Deity, and depart." With these words he forthwith went up to Heaven, whereupon all the mountains and rivers shook, and every land and country quaked. So the Heaven-Shining-Great-August-Deity, alarmed at the noise, said: "The reason of the ascent hither of His Augustness my elder brother is surely no good intent. It is only that he wishes to wrest my land from me." And she forthwith, unbinding her august hair, twisted it into august bunches, and both into the left and into the right august bunch, as likewise into her august head-dress and likewise on to her left and her right august arm, she twisted an augustly complete string of curved jewels eight feet long, of five hundred jewels, and, slinging on her back a quiver holding a thousand arrows, and adding thereto a quiver holding five hundred arrows, she likewise took and slung at her side a mighty and high-sounding elbow-pad, and brandished and stuck her bow upright so that the top shook, and she stamped her feet into the hard ground up to her opposing thighs, kicking away the earth like rotten snow, and stood valiantly like unto a mighty man, and waiting, asked: "Wherefore ascendest thou hither?"

Then Susanoo replied, saying: "I have no evil intent. It is only that when the Great-August-Deity our father spoke, deigning to inquire the cause of my wailing and weeping, I said: 'I wail because I wish to go to my deceased mother's land,' whereupon the Great-August-Deity said: 'Thou shalt not dwell in this land,' and deigned to expel me with a divine expulsion. It is therefore solely with the thought of taking leave of thee and departing, that I have ascended hither. I have no strange intentions" [The two deities then engage in a contest of producing children, the sun goddess begetting five male deities and Susanoo begetting three female deities.]

Section XV. The August Ravages of His
Impetuous-Male-Augustness

Then Susanoo said to the Heaven-Shining-Great-August-Deity: "Owing to
the sincerity of my intentions I have, in begetting children, gotten delicate
females. Judging from this, I have undoubtedly gained the victory." With
these words, and impetuous with victory, he broke down the divisions of the
ricefields laid out by the Heaven-Shining-Great-August-Deity, filled up the
ditches, and moreover strewed excrements in the palace where she partook
of the great food. So, though he did thus, the Heaven-Shining-Great-August-
Deity upbraided him not, but said: "What looks like excrements must be
something that His Augustness mine elder brother has vomited through
drunkenness. Again, as to his breaking down the divisions of the rice-fields
and filling up the ditches, it must be because he grudges the land they
occupy that His Augustness mine elder brother acts thus." But notwithstanding these apologetic words, he still continued his evil acts, and was
more and more violent. As the Heaven-Shining-Great-August-Deity sat in
her awful [sacred] weaving-hall seeing to the weaving of the august
garments of the Deities, he broke a hole in the top of the weaving-hall, and
through it let fall a heavenly piebald horse which he had flayed. . . .

Section XVI. The Door of The Heavenly Rock Dwelling

So thereupon the Heaven-Shining-Great-August-Deity, terrified at the sight,
closed behind her the door of the Heavenly Rock-Dwelling, made it fast, and
retired. Then the whole Plain of High Heaven was obscured and all the Central
Land of Reed-Plains [Japan] darkened. Owing to this, eternal night prevailed.
Hereupon the voices of the myriad Deities were like unto the flies in the fifth
moon as they swarm and a myriad portents of woe arose. Therefore did
the eight hundred myriad Deities assemble in a divine assembly in the bed of
the Tranquil River of Heaven, and bid the Deity Thought-Includer, child of the
High-August-Producing-Wondrous-Deity, think of a plan, assembling the
long-singing birds of eternal night and making them sing, taking the hard rocks
of Heaven from the river-bed of the Tranquil River of Heaven, and taking the
iron from the Heavenly Metal-Mountains, calling in the smith Ama-tsu-ma-ra,
charging Her Augustness I-shi-ko-ri-do-me to make a mirror, and charging His
Augustness Jewel-Ancestor to make an augustly complete string of curved
jewels eight feet long, of five hundred jewels, and summoning His Augustness
Heavenly-Beckoning-Ancestor-Lord and His Augustness Grand-Jewel, and
causing them to pull out with a complete pulling the shoulderblade of a true
stag from the Heavenly Mount Kagu, and take cherrybark from the Heavenly
Mount Kagu, and perform divination, and pulling up by pulling its roots a true
Cleyera japonica with five hundred branches from the Heavenly Mount Kagu,

and taking and putting upon its upper branches the augustly complete string of curved jewels eight feet long, of five hundred jewels, and taking and tying to the middle branches the mirror eight feet long, and taking and hanging upon its lower branches the white pacificatory offerings and the blue pacificatory offerings, His Augustness Grand-Jewel taking these divers things and holding them together with the grand august offerings, and His Augustness Heavenly-Beckoning-Ancestor-Lord prayerfully reciting grand liturgies, and the Heavenly-Hand-Strength-Male-Deity standing hidden beside the door, and Her Augustness Heavenly-Alarming-Female hanging round her the heavenly clubmoss from the Heavenly Mount Kagu as a sash, and making the heavenly spindle-tree her headdress, and binding the leaves of the bamboo-grass of the Heavenly Mount Kagu in a posy for her hands, laying a sounding-board before the door of the Heavenly Rock-Dwelling, and stamping till she made it resound and doing as if possessed by a Deity, and pulling out the nipples of her breasts, pushing down her skirt-string to her private parts. Then the Plain of High Heaven shook, and the eight hundred myriad Deities laughed together. Hereupon the Heaven-Shining-Great-August-Deity was amazed, and, slightly opening the door of the Heavenly Rock-Dwelling, spoke thus from the inside: "Me-thought that owing to my retirement the Plain of Heaven would be dark, and likewise the Central Land of Reed-Plains would all be dark: how then is it that the Heavenly-Alarming-Female makes merry, and that likewise the eight hundred myriad Deities all laugh?" Then the Heavenly-Alarming-Female spoke, saying: "We rejoice and are glad because there is a Deity more illustrious than Thine Augustness." While she was thus speaking, His Augustness Heavenly-Beckoning-Ancestor-Lord and His Augustness Grand-Jewel pushed forward the mirror and respectfully showed it to the Heaven-Shining-Great-August-Deity, whereupon the Heaven-Shining-Great-August-Deity, more and more astonished, gradually came forth from the door and gazed upon it, whereupon the Heavenly-Hand-Strength-Male-Deity, who was standing hidden, took her august hand and drew her out, and then His Augustness Grand-Jewel drew the bottom-tied rope along at her august back, and spoke, saying: "Thou must not go back further in than this!" So when the Heaven-Shining-Great-August-Deity had come forth, both the Plain of High Heaven and the Central-Land-of-Reed-Plains of course again became light.

● ● ●

Section XXXIII. The August Descent from Heaven of His Augustness the August Grandchild

Then the Heaven-Shining-Great-August-Deity and the High-Integrating-Deity commanded and charged the Heir Apparent His Augustness Truly-Conqueror-I-Conquer-Shift-Heavenly-Great-Great-Ears saying: "The Brave-Awful-Possessing-Male-Deity says that he has now finished pacifying the Central Land of Reed-Plains. So do thou, in accordance with our gracious charge, descend to and dwell in and rule over it." Then the Heir Apparent His Augustness Truly-Conqueror-I-Conquer-Conquering-Swift-Heavenly-Great-Great-Ears replied, saying: "While I have been getting ready to descend, there has been born to me a child whose name is His Augustness Heaven-Plenty-Earth-Plenty-Heaven's-Sun-Height-Prince-Rice-ear-Ruddy-Plenty. This child should be sent down." Therefore, in accordance with these words, they laid their command on His Augustness Prince-Rice-ear-Ruddy-Plenty, deigning to charge him with these words: "This Luxuriant Reed-Plain-Land-of-Fresh-Rice-ears [Japan] is the land over which thou shalt rule." So he replied: "I will descend from Heaven according to your commands."

Then . . . they sent him down from Heaven. Thereupon they joined to him the eight-feet-long curved jewels and mirror that had allured the Heaven-Shining-Great-August-Deity from the Rock-Dwelling and also the Herb-Quelling-Great-Sword, and likewise the Deity Thought-Includer, the Hand-Strength-Male-Deity, and the Deity Heavenly-Rock-Door-Opener of Eternal Night, and charged him thus: "Regard this mirror exactly as if it were our august spirit, and reverence it as if reverencing us." Next did they say: "Let the Deity Thought-Includer take in hand our affairs, and carry on the government." These two Deities are worshipped at the temple of Isuzu [at Ise]. The next, the Deity of Luxuriant-Food, is the Deity dwelling in the outer temple of Watarahi. The next, the Deity Heavenly-Rock-Door-Opener, another name for whom is the Wondrous-Rock-True-Gate-Deity, and another name for whom is the Luxuriant-Rock-True-Gate-Deity—this Deity is the Deity of the August Gate [of the Imperial Palace]. The next, the Deity Hand-Strength-Male dwells in Sanagata. Now His Augustness the Heavenly-Beckoning-Ancestor-Lord is the ancestor of the Nakatomi Chieftains, His Augustness Grand Jewel is the ancestor of the Imibe Headmen, Her Augustness the Heavenly-Alarming-Female is the ancestress of the Duchesses of Saru, Her Augustness I-shi-ko-ri-do-me is the ancestress of the Mirror-Making Chieftains, His Augustness-Jewel-Ancestor is the ancestor of the Jewel-Ancestor Chieftains.

St. Benedict

St. Benedict (c. 480(?)–543(?)) established a monastic order and built a monastery on top of Monte Cassino, in central Italy, which flourished for about fifteen hundred years. During World War II, the monastery was occupied by the German army and subsequently bombed to rubble by Allied planes; it can still be seen on top of the mountain, above the town of Cassino.

The selection that follows is taken from the beginning of St. Benedict's *Rule*, a guidebook for those wishing to enter the Benedictine order. Clearly exhibiting the fervid piety of the early medieval Christians, it was widely studied throughout the Middle Ages. St. Benedict's interpretation of Christianity exerted a profound influence not only on the thinking but also on the lives of medieval Christians. The Benedictine order, like the Franciscan, developed into one of the major institutions of the Catholic Church, of which it is still a part.

1. What is the purpose of the monastic life?

2. Describe the perfect monk.

Rule of St. Benedict

LISTEN, my son, to the precepts of your master, and incline the ear of your heart: willingly receive and faithfully fulfil the admonition of your loving father, that you may return by the toil of obedience to Him from whom you had departed through the sloth of disobedience. To you, therefore, my words are now addressed, whoever you are that (renouncing your own desires) are taking up the strong and bright weapons of obedience, in order to fight for the Lord Christ, our true King. In the first place, whatever good work you begin to do, beg of Him with most earnest prayer to complete it; that He who has now been good enough to count us in the number of His children may not at any time have to grieve over our evil deeds. For we must always so serve Him with the gifts with which He has endowed us that He will never as an angry Father disinherit His children, and never as a dread Master, incensed by our sins, deliver us to eternal punishment as most wicked servants who were unwilling to follow Him to glory.

Trans. Richard Crotty (Nedlands: The University of Western Australia Press, 1963).

Let us then at long last arise, since Scripture stirs us up saying: It is high time for us to awake from sleep. And, our eyes being open to the deifying light, let us hear with attentive ears the Divine Voice warning us, daily crying out: Would you but listen to His voice today! Do not harden your hearts. And again: He that hath ears to hear, let him hear what the Spirit says to Christian communities. And what does He say? Come, my children (He says), listen to Me; I will teach you to be God-fearing folk. Run while you have the light of life, lest the darkness of death overtake you.

And the Lord, seeking His own workman in the multitude of people to whom He thus cries out, says again: Who is the man who wants life, and desires success? And if you, hearing this, answer that you do, God says to you: If you want true, everlasting life, keep your tongue from evil, and your lips from deceit; turn from evil and do good; seek peace, and pursue it. And when you have done these things, My eyes will look favourably on you, and My ears will be open to your prayers; and before you call upon Me, I shall say unto you: Behold, I am here. What can be sweeter to us, dearest brethren, than this voice of the Lord inviting us? See how the Lord, in His loving-kindness, shows us the way of life.

Having our loins girded, therefore, with faith and the performance of good works, let us walk in His paths by the guidance of the Gospel, so that we may deserve to see Him who has called us into His kingdom. And if we wish to dwell in the tabernacle of His kingdom, be sure we shall not reach it unless we run to it by our good deeds. But let us ask the Lord, in the words of the prophet: Lord, who shall dwell in Your tabernacle? Who shall find rest upon your holy hill? Having asked this question, brethren, let us listen to the Lord answering and showing us the way to His tabernacle in these words: He that lives a pure life and practises virtue, he that is honest at heart and does not deceive with his tongue, he that does not defraud or slander his neighbour. He that has brought Satan and his malice to nought, casting him out of his heart with all his suggestions, taken his temptations, newly born as yet, and dashed them upon the rock that is Christ. Such God-fearing men are not made proud by their own good works: knowing that the good which is in them comes not from themselves but from the Lord, they magnify Him for what He accomplishes in them, saying with the prophet: Not unto us, Lord, not unto us, but unto Your Name give the glory. Just as the apostle Paul took no credit to himself for his preaching, but said: By the grace of God I am what I am. And the same apostle says elsewhere: He who boasts should make his boast in the Lord.

Hence also the Lord says in the Gospel: He that hears these instructions of mine and carries them out is like a wise man who built his house upon rock; the floods came and the winds blew and beat upon that house, but it did not fall, because it was founded upon rock. And the Lord, in fulfilment of these words, is waiting daily for us to make due response by deeds to His holy warnings. So the number of our days is increased, with a view to the mending of our evil ways, as the apostle says: Do you not know that the patience of God is inviting you to repentance? For in His love the Lord says: I desire not the death of the sinner, but that he be converted, and live.

So, brethren, since we have asked the Lord who are to inhabit His tabernacle, He has told us the duties of an inhabitant: if only we can fulfil those duties! Our hearts and bodies, therefore, must be made ready for the holy warfare which consists of obedience to His commands; and let us ask God to supply by the help of His grace what we cannot do by nature. And if we want to attain eternal life, escaping the penalties of hell, then while there is yet time, while we are still in the flesh and able to fulfil all these things before darkness and death come upon us, let us hasten to do now what will benefit us in eternity.

We must establish, therefore, a school of the Lord's service, in the arrangement of which we hope to order nothing that is harsh or burdensome. But if it does turn out that equity itself, for the amendment of vices or the safeguarding of charity, should dictate some element of strictness, do not thereupon yield to fear and turn aside from a way of salvation whose beginning is inevitably difficult. But as we make progress in our way of life and in faith, our heart becomes more courageous, and with ineffable sweetness of love we run in the way of God's commandments; so that, never departing from His guidance, persevering in His teaching in a monastery until death, we may share by patience in the sufferings of Christ, so as to deserve also to reign with Him in heaven.

Chapter I. On the Various Kinds of Monks

It is clear that there are four kinds of monks. The first are the Cenobites: those who perform their service in monasteries, under a rule and an abbot. The second are the Anchorites, i.e. the Hermits: not in the first fervour of Religious life, but after long probation in a monastery, they have learned by the help and experience of others to fight against the devil, and going forth well equipped from the ranks of their brethren to the lonely combat of the desert, are not anxious now in being without the support of others, fighting single-handed, with God's aid, against vices of flesh or spirit.

A third kind of monks, but a detestable kind, are the Sarabaites. They have not been tried or taught by the experience of living under a rule, as gold is tried in a furnace; but, being as soft as lead, are still loyal to the world in practice, though by their tonsure they make an obviously false claim of loyalty to God. In twos or threes or even singly without a shepherd, not enclosed in the Lord's sheep-folds but in their own, they make a law for themselves of their own pleasure and desires: whatever they think fit, whatever it pleases them to do, that they call holy; and what they do not desire, that they think unlawful.

The fourth kind of monks are those called Gyrovagues, who spend all their lives wandering about various provinces, staying in different monasteries for three or four days at a time, perpetual vagrants, always unsettled, given up to their own wills and to the snares of gluttony, worse in every way than the Sarabaites. Of the wretched way of life of all these it is better to say nothing than to speak. Leaving them aside, then, let us with God's help set about laying down a rule for the strong breed of Cenobites.

Chapter II. What Kind of Man The Abbot Ought To Be

An Abbot who is worthy to rule over a monastery ought always to remember what he is called, and be superior in deed as well as in name. For he is believed to be the representative of Christ in a monastery, since he is called by a name of His, as the Apostle says: You have received the spirit of adoption, which makes you sons, crying Abba (Father). So the Abbot ought not to reach or arrange or command anything contrary to the law of God; but let his commands and teaching be as a leaven of God-given holiness introduced into the minds of his disciples. Let the Abbot be ever mindful that at the dread judgment of God an account will have to be given both of his own teaching and of the obedience of his disciples. Let him be assured that any failure of the flock discovered by the Head of the Household will be a heavy load of guilt laid upon the shepherd. On the other hand, if he has bestowed all pastoral diligence on a restless and disobedient flock, and taken all possible care to mend their corrupt ways, then it is equally clear that their shepherd will go free at the Lord's judgment, saying to Him with the prophet: I have not hidden Your just dealing in my heart, I have made known Your faithfulness and saving power; but adding that they looked down on and despised him. Then, finally, for souls that refused his care punishment shall prevail: death itself.

So when anyone takes the name of Abbot he ought to rule his disciples by teaching them in two different ways; that is, he should let all that is good and holy be seen in his deeds even more than in his words: declaring to the intelligent disciples by words, but to the hard-hearted and simple-minded by his exemplary deeds what it is that the Lord commands. Whatever he has taught his disciples to be contrary to God's law, let him indicate by his example that it is not to be done; lest while preaching to others he himself become reprobate; and lest God finally say to him in his sins: How is it that you can repeat My commandments by rote, and boast of My covenant with you, and all the while have no love for the amendment of your ways, casting every warning of Mine to the winds? And: You who saw the speck of dust in your brother's eye, did you not see the beam in your own?

Let him have no human preferences in the monastery. Let not one be loved more than another unless he be found better than others in good works or obedience. Let not one who is classified as well-born be put before one who was formerly a slave, unless some other and reasonable cause exist for doing so. If, in the Abbot's judgment, justice requires it, let him make such a promotion, and from any class whatever: otherwise let the monks keep their own places, because, whether slave-born or free, we are all one in Christ, and undertake one and the same service in the army of the one Lord; there are no human preferences with God. Only for one reason are we preferred by Him: if we be found to surpass others in good works and humility. So the Abbot should show equal love to all; and let the same discipline be meted out to them, according to the deserts of each.

In his teaching, the Abbot ought always to observe the rule of the Apostle, which runs: Bring home wrong-doing, comfort the waverer, rebuke the sinner; in other words: there is a time for everything, let your regime be a blend of gentleness and severity, show now the rigour of a master, now the loving affection of a father. That is to say, the Abbot must rebuke the undisciplined and restless, and exhort the obedient, gentle and patient to advance in virtue; and such as are negligent and contemptuous of authority we bid him reprove and correct. Let him not shut his eyes to the faults of offenders; but rather, as soon as they manifest their presence, let him root them out, as he has authority for that (the fate of Heli, priest of Shiloh, is worth remembering). The sensible ones, and those of rather good disposition, at a first or second offence are to be corrected only with words, but such as are impudent, hard of heart and proud, or disobedient, should be chastised with bodily stripes at the first sign of sin. Let the Abbot remember what is written: A fool is not amended by mere words; and: Strike your son with the rod, and you will deliver his soul from death.

The Abbot ought always to remember what he is, and what he is called, knowing that more is expected of him to whom more is entrusted; and he must realize how difficult and arduous a task he is undertaking, that of ruling souls and of being at the service of a variety of characters. Let him accommodate himself to the peculiarities and mentality of each, winning some by kindness, others by reproof, others again by persuasion, in such a way that he may not only keep intact the flock committed to him, but also rejoice over an increase in their numbers and virtue.

Above all, let him not overlook or undervalue the spiritual needs of his charges, taking too much care of fleeting, material and perishable things; rather let him always consider that he has undertaken to govern souls and will have to answer for them. And that there may be no talk of the possibility of want, let him recall the text: Make it your first care to find the Kingdom of God and His approval, and all these things shall be yours without the asking. And again: Those who fear God never go wanting. And let him realize that preparation is necessary, in the case of a ruler of souls, for rendering an account of them. Whatever the number of brethren under his care, let him be well assured that on the Day of Judgment he must account to the Lord for all these souls, and of course for his own as well. And so, ever in fear of the future examination of the shepherd on the state of the flock entrusted to him, ever careful about other men's accounts, he will take exceptional care over his own. So, while correcting others by his warnings, he too will be cured of his defects.

Einhard

Charlemagne (c. 742–814) was a remarkable man. Although only semiliterate himself, he was a patron of learning, as well as of the arts. He made his capital at Aachen (Aix-la-Chapelle) a cultural center by establishing a palace school there to train both the clergy and the sons of the nobles of his court. He appointed, as director of the school, the English teacher and scholar, Alcuin of York, who was probably the outstanding intellectual of his time. He also brought together a number of other scholars from around Europe, among them Einhard.

Einhard (c. 770–844) was born in what is now southern Germany, of a wealthy family. After studying at the Abbey of Fulda, he went to Aachen as a student of Alcuin in the palace school. He remained in Aachen for nearly forty years, becoming a close friend and advisor of Charlemagne. An individual of many talents, Einhard not only continued the tradition of his mentor, Alcuin, as a teacher but also engaged in diplomatic missions for his lord. In addition he employed his skills as an architect to design the royal palace at Aachen, much of which still stands. But his major contribution to history was his biography of Charlemagne. Even after the death of the emperor in 814, Einhard remained in Aachen, continuing his position as advisor to the next monarch, Louis the Pious. It was during these years that he wrote his famous biography. He finally left the royal household in 830 and retired to a rural location in southern Germany where he founded an abbey.

Einhard's is not a disinterested biography, for the author's admiration for Charlemagne is evident throughout. Still it gives us an informative, if brief, description of the emperor and his times. Einhard used the classical biographer, Suetonius, for his literary model, copying his style and even reproducing the language of his *Life of Augustus, Life of Charlemagne*.

---

1. According to Einhard, what made Charlemagne a great ruler?

2. Describe Charlemagne's relationship to the Roman church.

The Life of Charlemagne

Prologue

After I had made up my mind to describe the life and habits and, above all, the deeds of my lord and patron, the illustrious and deservedly famous King Charles, I set about doing so as succinctly as possible. I have tried not to omit anything that has come to my notice, and at the same time not to be long-winded and offend those discerning readers who object to the very idea of a modern history. But I also wanted to keep my new work from displeasing those who disapprove even of the masterpieces of the wisest and most learned authors of antiquity. To be sure, I am fully aware that there are many men of letters who do not regard contemporary matters so far beneath their notice as to treat them with contempt and consider them fit only to sink into silence and oblivion. On the contrary, the enthusiasm for things past leads some writers to recount the famous deeds of other men as best they can, and in this way they hope to insure that their own names will be remembered by posterity.

Be this as it may, none of these possible objections can prevent me from writing on the subject, since I am convinced that no one can describe these events better than I can. For I was there when they took place and I know them as an eyewitness, so to speak. Furthermore, I am not entirely sure if they will be recorded by anyone else. And so I thought it would be better to write down what I had to say even at the risk of duplicating what others might write, rather than to allow the illustrious life of the greatest king of the age and his famous deeds, unmatched by his contemporaries, to disappear forever into forgetfulness.

Besides, there was another reason, important enough in itself, I think, to make me compose this book: namely, that Charles educated me and gave me his lifelong friendship and that of his children from the time I came to the court. In this way he attached me to his person and made me so devoted to him in life and death that I might well be called ungrateful if I were to forget everything he did for me and never say a word about his great and magnificent generosity, I, who owe him so much; indeed, that would mean allowing his life to remain unremembered and unpraised, as though he had never lived! To be sure, my abilities, feeble and inadequate as they are—nonexistent even—are incapable of portraying his life as it really ought to be portrayed. Even the eloquence of a Cicero would not have been up to that.

Here, then, is the book containing the life story of a truly great man. You will marvel at his deeds, and probably also at the presumption of a barbarous Frank for imagining that he could write tastefully and elegantly

Einhard, *The Life of Charlemagne*, trans. E. S. Firchow and E. H. Zeydel (Coral Gables: University of Miami Press, 1972). Used by permission of University of Miami Press.

in Latin. For I am not much versed in the Roman tongue. Then, too, you will perhaps be amazed at my temerity in ignoring the words of Cicero when, speaking of Latin writers, he said in the first book of his *Tusculan Disputations* that "whoever puts his thoughts in writing and can not arrange and state them clearly, and delight the reader with a pleasant style, makes a complete mockery of the writer's craft." This remark of the famous orator might have kept me from writing if I had not already made up my mind to brave the judgment of the world and take a chance with my feeble talents. I thought this would be better than to allow the memory of so great a man to perish out of petty concern for my own reputation.

1. The Merovingians

The family of the Merovingians from which the Franks customarily chose their kings is believed to have ruled until the time of King Hilderich. Hilderich was deposed, tonsured, and sent to a monastery by the command of the Roman Pope Stephen. Although the royal line apparently ended only with him, it had long before ceased to matter and possessed no more except the empty title of king. The real wealth and power of the kingdom were in the hands of the prefects of the palace, the so-called majordomos, and their word was law. The king had no choice but to sit on the throne with flowing hair and full beard, content with his title and the semblance of sovereignty. He would listen to messengers coming from all around and, as they left, give them replies as though they were his own, but in reality, they had been dictated to him or even forced on him.

Except for the empty title of king and an intermittent allowance which the prefect of the palace gave or did not give him at his pleasure, the king owned nothing but a single estate, and that was not a very lucrative one. He lived on it and had a few servants there performing the most necessary duties and making a show of obsequiousness. Wherever he had to go, he went like a farmer in a cart drawn by a span of oxen with a carter driving them. That is how he went to the palace and how he went to the meetings of his people, which took place yearly for the good of the realm. And in the same way he returned home. But the administration of the state and all internal and external business was carried out by the prefect of the palace.

2. Charles' Ancestors

When Hilderich was deposed, the office of majordomo was already hereditarily held by Pepin, the father of King Charles. For Pepin's father, Charles [Charles Martel—*Ed.*], had in his time crushed the rebels who were trying to take over all of Franconia. He had also defeated the Saracens so badly in two great battles, when they attempted to occupy Gaul, that they had to return to Spain. One of these battles had taken place in Aquitaine near Poitiers [in 732—*Ed.*], the other on the Berre River not far from Narbonne. This same Charles had in turn received the office of majordomo from his father Pepin and had administered it extremely well. It was customary for the people to bestow such an honor only on men of noble birth and great wealth.

When Pepin, the father of King Charles, held this office, bequeathed by his grandfather and father to him and to his brother Carloman, the two of them shared it quite amicably for several years, nominally under King Hilderich. But then for some unknown reason Carloman abandoned the burdensome government of the temporal kingdom—possibly because he longed for a more contemplative life—and went into retirement in Rome. There, giving up his worldly garb, he became a monk and built a monastery on Mt. Soracte near the church of St. Sylvester. For a number of years he enjoyed his longed-for seclusion, along with a few monks who had accompanied him. But when a great many noble Franks came on pilgrimages to Rome to fulfill vows and insisted on paying homage to their former lord, it was impossible for him to get any peace, which he cherished more than anything else, and he decided to move elsewhere. When he saw that the crowds of intruders were interfering with his resolve to be alone, he left the mountain and went away to the province of Samnium, to the monastery of St. Benedict on Monte Cassino, where he spent the rest of his life in prayer.

3. Charles Becomes King

Pepin, no longer majordomo but king by authority of the Roman pontiff, ruled alone over the Franks for fifteen years or more. For nine unbroken years he fought against Waifar, duke of Aquitaine, and then, at the end of the war, he died of dropsy in Paris. His sons Charles and Carloman survived him, and on them, by the will of Providence, the succession devolved. In solemn assembly the Franks appointed them kings on condition that they share the realm equally, Charles ruling the part which had belonged to their father Pepin, Carloman the part formerly controlled by his uncle Carloman. Both accepted these conditions and each one took over that section of the divided kingdom which he had received according to the agreement.

But peace between the two brothers was maintained only with the greatest difficulty since many of Carloman's followers plotted to break up the partnership. A few even tried to provoke a war with their intrigues. The outcome, however, showed that there was more imagined than real danger. When Carloman died, his wife and sons fled to Italy with the most important members of their court. Without any apparent reason she spurned her brother-in-law and placed herself and her children under the protection of Desiderius, king of the Lombards. Carloman had succumbed to an illness after ruling jointly for two years, and at his death Charles was unanimously proclaimed king of the Franks.

4. Plan of this Work

Because nothing has been recorded in writing about Charles' birth,[1] infancy, or even boyhood, and because no survivor has been found who claims to know of these matters, I consider it foolish to write about them. So I have decided to skip what we know nothing about and proceed to recount and describe Charles' exploits, habits, and other facts of his life. First I want to tell of his deeds at home and abroad, then describe his habits and interests, his rulership and finally his death, omitting nothing that is worth mentioning or necessary to know.

5. War in Aquitaine

Of all the wars Charles waged, the first was the Aquitainian campaign, begun but not finished by his father. Charles believed that it would soon be over. He asked his brother, who was still living at the time, to help him. But although his brother disappointed him and failed to provide the promised support, Charles completed the undertaking with great vigor. He was unwilling to give up what he had begun or to abandon a task once taken on until he had carried out his plans and brought them to a happy conclusion by force of perseverance and steadfastness. He even compelled Hunold, who after Waifar's death had tried to seize Aquitaine and revive a war that was almost finished, to leave the country and flee to the land of the Basques. But Charles gave him no respite. He crossed the Garonne River, built Fort Fronsac, and through diplomatic channels let the Basque Duke Lupus know that he had better return the fugitive speedily or he would come and get Hunold by force. Lupus thought better of it and not only handed over Hunold but also submitted himself and the province he ruled to the jurisdiction of Charles.

6. War with the Lombards

When the affairs of Aquitaine had been settled and the war ended, and after his brother had died, Charles undertook a campaign against the Lombards at the request and pleading of Bishop Hadrian of Rome. His father had once

[1]The conjectural date of Charlemagne's birth is April 2, 742.—*Ed.*

before fought the Lombards, that time in response to the entreaties of Pope Stephen. Pepin had done so under great difficulties, for certain nobles with whom he usually consulted had opposed his wishes so strongly that they openly declared they would desert the king and go home. Nevertheless, arms were taken up against King Aistulf at that time and the war brought to a speedy end. But although the reasons for this conflict seem to have been similar and indeed the same in both Charles' and Pepin's case, the difficulties of seeing it through and settling it varied in each instance. Pepin, after a few days' siege at Pavia, forced Aistulf to give hostages and to return to the Romans the cities and fortresses he had taken. He also made Aistulf swear a sacred oath that he would not try to regain what he had surrendered. Charles, on the other hand, pursued the war more single-mindedly and did not rest until he had forced King Desiderius to surrender unconditionally after weakening him in a lengthy siege. He also ordered Desiderius' son Adalgis, who was the favorite of his people, to leave the kingdom and Italy and to restore everything he had taken from the Romans. Charles then prevented Rotgaud, the duke of Friuli, from starting a revolt. After that he subjected all of Italy to his rule and made his son Pepin king of the conquered Italian territories.

At this point I should describe how difficult it was for Charles to cross the Alps on the way to Italy and how the Franks toiled when crossing the trackless mountain ridges, the rocky cliffs, and the sharp peaks reaching to the sky. But I have decided to describe in this work Charles' way of life rather than the outcome of the wars he waged. Suffice it to say that the end of the campaign resulted in the subjugation of Italy, the deportation of Desiderius into permanent exile, the expulsion of his son Adalgis from Italy, and the restoration of the possessions taken by the Lombard kings to Pope Hadrian of Rome.

7. War with the Saxons

Then the Saxon war—which had merely been interrupted—was taken up again. The Franks have never been involved in any struggle that was more prolonged, more bitter, or more laborious. For the Saxons—like almost all of the nations inhabiting Germania—are savage by nature, given to the cult of demons, and hostile to our religion. They do not find it dishonorable to violate or break divine or human laws. Hardly a day passed without incidents threatening the peace. The border between our land and theirs runs almost entirely through plains, with the exception of a few areas where large forests or mountain ridges provide the territories with natural boundaries. Thus, murder, robbery, and arson never ceased on both sides. Eventually the Franks became so enraged that it no longer seemed enough to retaliate and so they decided to wage open war. Accordingly, war was declared and fought by both parties with great ferocity. It continued for thirty-three years and cost the Saxons far more than the Franks. To be sure, it could have been concluded sooner if the treachery of the Saxons had allowed it. For it is difficult to say how many times they surrendered to the king and promised to do what they were ordered, how often and without delay they furnished hostages that were demanded, and how often they received legates. Many times they were so badly defeated and weakened that they vowed to give up their cult of demons and indicated their willingness to submit to the Christian faith. But just as they were often ready to do this, just as often were they in a hurry to break their promises. Thus, I cannot say with certainty which of these courses of action they more truthfully favored. It is a fact, however, that after the beginning of the war against the Saxons hardly a year passed without some vacillation on their part. And yet the king in his high purpose and unswerving constancy both in success and failure was not to be frustrated by their fickleness, nor could he be made to abandon what he had begun. He never allowed any of them who perpetrated such perfidy to go unpunished. In these instances he either led an army personally or sent one with his counts to avenge the crimes and mete out proper punishment. After he had defeated all of those who had been offering resistance, he subjected them to his power. Then he took ten thousand Saxons who lived on both banks of the Elbe river, with their wives and children, and resettled them in various contingents here and there throughout Gaul and Germania. And so the war which had dragged on for so many years was concluded under the conditions which the king imposed and the Saxons accepted. The conditions were that they give up the cult of demons, abandon the religious practices of their ancestors, adopt the sacraments of the Christian faith and religion, and become a single nation with the Franks.

8. War with the Saxons (Continued)

Although this struggle had gone on for many years, the king himself fought the enemy not more than twice during the period, and this within a single month with only a few days intervening: once at the mountain Osning, in a place called Detmold, and once at the river Hase. The enemies were so routed and defeated in these two battles that they subsequently never dared to provoke the king again or to resist him when he approached, unless they were protected by fortifications. In these fights many noblemen and leaders in highest positions were killed, both among the Franks and Saxons. Finally, the strife ended in the thirty-third year. But meanwhile so many other great wars had been declared against the Franks in various parts of the world and were taken up under the king's guidance that anyone considering the matter might justifiably wonder whether Charles' endurance in time of trouble or his good fortune is more to be admired. The Saxon war had begun two years before the Italian, and, although it was carried on without interruption, none of the other pressing duties were set aside nor other equally difficult struggles dropped for its sake. For the king surpassed everyone in his time in prudence and nobility of mind, and he turned down nothing that had to be undertaken or carried out. He did not shy at the difficulties or fear the dangers involved because he had learned to accept and endure everything in accordance with its nature. Neither in adversity did he yield nor was he misled by good fortune when it beckoned deceptively during times of great success.

9. Expedition to Spain

While Charles was engaged in the strenuous and almost incessant struggle with the Saxons and after he had built fortifications at strategic points along the frontier, he decided to invade Spain with as large an army as he could raise. He crossed the Pyrenees successfully and accepted the surrender of all the towns and castles on his way. Finally, he turned back with his forces safe and intact, but when recrossing the mountains he was made to feel the treachery of the Basques. In a densely wooded area well suited for ambush the Basques had prepared to attack the army from the top of the highest mountain. As the troops were proceeding in a long column through the narrow mountain passes, the Basques descended on the baggage train and the protecting rear guard and forced them into the valley. In the ensuing battle the Basques slaughtered them to a man. They seized the baggage and, under cover of the growing darkness, quickly scattered in all directions. In this encounter the Basques had the advantage of light weapons and a favorable terrain; the Franks on the other hand were hampered by their heavy equipment and the unevenness of the battle ground. Ekkehard, the royal steward, Anshelm, the count of the Palace, and Roland the Margrave of Brittany, as well as many others were killed in the engagement.[2] Unfortunately, the incident could not be avenged since the enemies disappeared without a trace after the attack and there were no signs where they might be found.

10. Submission of the Bretons and Beneventians

Charles also conquered the Bretons, who lived in a certain remote part of Gaul along the west coast and were not subject to him. He sent an expedition against them, which forced them to give hostages and made them promise to do what was expected of them.

---

[2]The Battle of Roncesvalles (778), described in the *Song of Roland.—Ed.*

Then he entered Italy with an army and, marching through Rome, went as far as Capua, a city in Campania. There he set up a camp and threatened to take up arms against the Beneventians unless they surrendered. Aregis, the duke of Benevento, prevented this by sending his sons Rumold and Grimold with a large sum of money asking the king to accept them as hostages. He promised that he and his people would do as Charles demanded, on the condition that he would not be forced to appear before the king in person. Charles was more concerned about the good of the people than about the duke's stubbornness, and so he accepted the hostages and agreed that, in view of the large gift of money, the duke should not be compelled to come. He kept one of the two sons of Aregis, not yet of age, as a hostage and sent the older one back to his father. Charles also dispatched legates to receive oaths of loyalty from the Beneventians and from Aregis himself. After that he returned to Rome, spent several days there in worship at the holy places, and finally went back to Gaul.

11. Tassilo and the War with the Beneventians

All at once a war broke out in Bavaria which was, however, swiftly concluded. It was caused by the pride and folly of Duke Tassilo. At the urging of his wife, who was a daughter of King Desiderius and who imagined that she could avenge her father's exile through her husband, he made an alliance with the Huns, the neighbors of the Bavarians to the east. According to its terms, Tassilo not only refused to do the king's bidding but also tried his best to challenge him to war. The dauntless king could not tolerate this outrageous insolence. He therefore collected his troops from all over and personally marched to Bavaria with a large army. He reached the river Lech, which separates the Bavarians from the Alemanni, and established his camp there. Before invading the province, however, he decided to find out about the plans of the duke by sending messengers to him. Tassilo realized that there was no point for him or his people to act stubbornly, and so he presented himself to the king to ask for forgiveness. He furnished the hostages that were demanded, among them also his son Theodo, and swore an oath that he would never again be persuaded by anyone to be disobedient to Charles. Thus a speedy end was made to the war which at first had threatened to become one of major proportions. Tassilo, however, was later summoned to the court and not permitted to return. His province was from that time on ruled not by one duke but by several counts.

12. War with the Slavs

After these problems had been solved arms were taken up against the Slavs, who were known to us as Wiltzes but who call themselves Welatabi in their own language. The Saxons fought as auxiliaries in this war, together with other peoples who followed the standards of the king. To be sure, their loyalty was more perfunctory than real. The conflict was caused by the Wiltzes, who were constantly invading and harassing the Abodrites—long-time allies of the Franks—and could not be intimidated by warnings.

A gulf of undetermined length stretches from the western Ocean toward the East, nowhere exceeding a hundred miles across, though narrower at many points [the Baltic Sea—*Ed*.]. Numerous nations live around its shores. The Danes, for instance, and the Swedes, whom we call Norsemen, occupy the northern shore and all the islands along it. The southern shore, on the other hand, is inhabited by Slavs, Estes, and various other nationalities. Among these are the Wiltzes whom Charles was attacking now. In a single campaign led by himself, he crushed and conquered them so effectively that they never again dared to refuse his order.

13. War with the Huns

Next to the Saxon the war which now followed was the most important of them all: it was directed against the Avars or Huns. Charles undertook it with greater energy and far better equipment than any other before. He made one expedition himself to Pannonia—the Huns were occupying this province at that time—and the execution of the rest of the campaign he assigned to his son Pepin and to his provincial prefects, counts, and representatives. Although the war was carried on most vigorously, it ended only in the eighth year. The deserted palace of the Khan as well as the way in which Pannonia was divested of all its population so that not even a trace of human habitation now remains, testify to the many battles fought and the great amount of blood shed there. The entire Hunnish nobility perished during these struggles and their glory vanished. All the money and treasures they had collected over many years were taken away. There is in memory of man no war ever fought against the Franks in which they became richer and accumulated greater wealth. Indeed, although up to that time the Huns had almost seemed to be paupers, so much gold and silver were found in their palace, and so much precious loot captured in the battles, that one can say with good reason: the Franks justly took away from the Huns what the latter had previously unjustly acquired from other peoples.

Only two leaders of the Franks perished in this campaign. Duke Eric of Friuli was killed through the treachery of the townspeople in the seaport town of Tarsatica in Liburnia. Gerold, the prefect of Bavaria, was slain by an unidentified person in Pannonia when he was about to join the attack against the Huns and was marshaling his lines on horseback. He died together with two others who accompanied him while he was exhorting his soldiers one by one to muster their courage for the battle. Otherwise the conflict was practically bloodless and its outcome highly advantageous for the Franks, although because of its magnitude, it lasted for a long time.

14. War with the Danes

At long last the Saxon war, too, came to a proper conclusion befitting its long duration. The following wars in Bohemia and Linonia were bound to be brief. Under the leadership of the young King Charles they were quickly settled. Charles' last campaign was directed against those Norsemen who are called Danes. They first were engaged in piracy; later they invaded and devastated the coasts of Gaul and Germania with a rather large fleet. Godofrid, their king, was so filled with vain ambition that he saw himself as the future master over all of Germania. Already he regarded Frisia and Saxony as his own provinces and had subjugated his neighbors, the Abodrites, forcing them to pay tribute. Furthermore, he bragged that in a short time he would be coming with a very large force to the king's court at Aachen. However empty his boasts were, some people thought that he was about to do something of this kind. But he was prevented by sudden death from carrying out his plans. He was assassinated by his own guard, and this ended his life and the war he had begun.

15. Conquest

These were the wars which the mighty King Charles planned so carefully and executed so brilliantly in various parts of the world during his reign of forty-seven years. As a result the kingdom of the Franks, which was already great and powerful when Charles inherited it from his father Pepin, was almost doubled in size. Formerly, the Frankish territory had encompassed only that part of Gaul lying between the Rhine and the Loire, the ocean and the Balearic Sea, as well as that part of Germania inhabited by the so-called East Franconians and bordering on Saxony and the Danube, the Rhine and the Saale—a river separating the Thuringians from the Sorbs—and, finally, the land of the Alemanni and Bavarians.

Through the wars described above Charles conquered first Aquitaine, then Gascony and the entire Pyrenees region as far south as the Ebro River. This river originates in Navarre and flows through the most fertile plains of Spain, emptying into the Balearic Sea beneath the walls of the city of Tortosa. Charles also added to his territory all of Italy from Aosta to Lower Calabria, where the border runs between the Beneventians and the Greeks—an area extending over more than a thousand miles. Furthermore, he incorporated

Saxony—no small part of Germania and considered equal in length and twice the width of Franconia—and both Upper and Lower Pannonia, as well as Dacia on the other side of the Danube, Istria, Liburnia, and Dalmatia. Only the coastal towns of the latter countries he left to the emperor of Constantinople out of friendship and in consideration of a treaty he had made with him. Finally, Charles subjugated and forced to pay tribute all of the barbarian and savage nations who inhabit Germania between the Rhine and the Vistula rivers, the ocean and the Danube. They speak almost the same language but have very different customs and habits. The most important of these tribes are the Wiltzes, Sorbs, Abodrites, and Bohemians. With these he was forced to fight, but others, by far the greater number, surrendered without a struggle.

16. Foreign Relations

Charles also increased the glory of his empire by establishing friendly relations with many kings and peoples. An example is his close friendship with King Alfons of Galicia and Asturias, who always insisted on calling himself Charles' vassal when sending him letters or ambassadors. Charles also secured the favor of the Scottish kings by his great generosity, so that they always referred to him as their master and called themselves his subjects and servants. To this day there exist letters sent by them which clearly express these feelings.

With King Harun of Persia, who ruled almost all of the Orient except India, he was on such friendly terms that Harun preferred Charles' goodwill to the friendship of all other kings and potentates on earth and considered Charles alone worthy of his respect and homage. At one time the king of the Franks sent messengers with offerings to the most Holy Sepulcher, the site of the Resurrection of our Lord and Savior. When they appeared before Harun to relay their master's wishes, the king not only permitted them to carry out their mission but also gave Charles the jurisdiction over their holy and blessed place. On their return Harun sent along his own messengers with precious gifts, garments, spices, and other riches of the Orient. A few years earlier Charles had asked him for an elephant and Harun had sent him the only one he owned.

The three emperors of Constantinople, Nicephorus, Michael, and Leo, all sought Charles' friendship and alliance and sent numerous legations to his court. Only when Charles assumed the title of emperor did they begin to distrust him out of fear that he would seize their lands. To allay these fears and make sure that there would be no occasion for further trouble, Charles at once concluded a firm treaty with them. But the Greeks and the Romans remained suspicious of Frankish power. Hence a Greek proverb; "Have a Frank as a friend, but not as a neighbor."

17. Public Works

No matter how much time and effort Charles spent on planning and carrying out campaigns to enlarge his realm and subjugate foreign nations, he still was able to begin work on a number of public projects designed to help and beautify his kingdom. Some of them he actually managed to complete. The Basilica of the Holy Mother of God in Aachen, a triumph of the arts in construction, is quite rightly considered among the most remarkable of these. So, too, the bridge spanning the Rhine at Mainz, which is a full five hundred paces long, since the river is that wide at this point [2250 feet—*Ed.*]. The bridge was destroyed by fire and was not rebuilt because Charles died a year later. He had intended to replace the wooden structure with one of stone. He also began building two magnificent palaces, one near the city of Mainz close to his estate at Ingelheim, the other in Nymwegen on the Waal River, which flows south of the island of the Batavians. But his chief concern was for the churches. When he discovered one in any part of his kingdom that was old and ready to collapse he charged the responsible bishops and priests with restoring it. And he made sure that his instructions were carried out by having his agents check up on them.

He also set up a navy to withstand the attacks of the Norsemen and had the necessary ships built on the rivers which flow from Gaul and Germania into the North Sea. Since the Norsemen were continuously invading and devastating the Gallic and Germanic coasts, he placed guards and fortifications in all harbors and large estuaries where ships could enter. In this way he prevented the enemy from landing and looting. He did the same in the south along the shores of Narbonensis, Septimania, and Italy as far south as Rome to ward off the Moors who had just begun to take up piracy. As a consequence Italy was hardly touched during his reign except for the Etruscan town of Civita Vecchia, which was treacherously captured and plundered by the Moors. Gaul and Germania were likewise spared except for a few Frisian islands along the Germanic coast which were laid waste by Norsemen.

18. Private Life

This is how Charles enlarged and defended his empire and at the same time made it beautiful. My subject from this point on will be his intellectual abilities and his extraordinary steadfastness both in success and in adversity; and, further, whatever else concerns his private and domestic life.

After the death of his father, Charles ruled the kingdom together with his brother. Everyone was surprised that he bore the latter's animosity and envy with so much patience that he could never be provoked to anger by him. At his mother's request he married a daughter of the Lombard king Desiderius but repudiated her for unknown reasons after one year. Then he married Hildegard, who came from a very noble Swabian family. With her he had three sons, Charles, Pepin, and Louis, and as many daughters, Rotrud, Bertha, and Gisela. He had three more daughters, Theoderada, Hiltrud, and Rotheid, two of them with his [third] wife Fastrada, who came from Eastern Franconia and was therefore Germanic, the third by a concubine whose name I cannot recall at the moment. When Fastrada died he took Liutgard to wife, who was from Alemannia and with whom he had no children. After her death he had four concubines: Madelgard, who bore him a daughter by the name of Rothild; Gerswinda from Saxony, with whom he had another daughter called Adeltrud; Regnia, who gave him two sons, Drogo and Hugo; and Adelind, who had Theoderic.

His mother Berthrada spent her old age in great honor in his house. He always treated her with the greatest respect; only when he divorced the daughter of King Desiderius, whom he had married to please her, was there any disagreement between them. Berthrada died soon after Hildegard, but she had lived long enough to see three grandsons and three granddaughters in the house of her son. Charles buried her with highest honors in the church of St. Denis, where his father had been laid to rest.

Like his mother, he treated his only sister Gisela, who had entered a convent as a young girl, with the greatest affection. She died a few years before he did in the convent where she had spent most of her life.

19. Private Life (Continued)

For the education of his children Charles made the following provisions: his sons as well as his daughters were to be instructed first in those liberal arts in which he took most interest himself. As soon as the boys were old enough they had to learn how to ride, hunt, and handle weapons in Frankish style. The girls had to get used to carding wool and to the distaff and the spindle. To prevent their becoming bored and lazy he gave orders for them to be taught to engage in these and all other virtuous activities. Of his children, only two sons and one daughter died before him: Charles, who was the oldest; Pepin, whom he had made king of Italy; and his oldest daughter Rotrud, who had been engaged to marry the emperor Constantine of Greece. Pepin was survived by one son, called Bernhard, and five daughters: Adelheid, Atula, Guntrada, Bertheid, and Theoderada. How much Charles cared for his grandchildren was proved after their father's death: he made Bernhard Pepin's successor and raised the five girls together with his own daughters. When his two sons and daughter died, Charles reacted to their deaths with much less equanimity than might have been expected of so strong-minded a man. Because of his deepseated devotion to them he broke down in tears. Also, when he was told of the death of the Roman Pope Hadrian, who was one of his best friends, he wept as much as if he had lost a brother or a favorite son. For Charles was by nature a man who had a great gift for friendship, who made friends easily and never wavered in his loyalty to them. Those whom he loved could rely on him absolutely.

He supervised the upbringing of his sons and daughters very carefully. When he was at home he never ate his meals without them and when he went away, he always took them along. At such times his sons rode by his side and his daughters followed close behind, protected by a bodyguard of hand-picked men. Although the girls were very beautiful and he loved them dearly, it was odd that he did not permit any of them to get married either to a man of his own nation or to a foreigner. Rather, he kept all of them with him until his death, saying that he could not live without their company. And on account of this, he had to suffer a number of unpleasant experiences, however lucky he was in every other respect. But he never let on that he had heard of any suspicions regarding their chastity or any rumors about them.

20. Conspiracies Against Charles

By one of the concubines he had a son whom I have not mentioned along with the others. His name was Pepin and he had a handsome face but was hunch-backed. While his father was wintering in Bavaria during the war against the Huns, Pepin pretended to be ill and became involved with some Frankish nobles in a plot against his father. He had been lured into it by empty promises that they would make him king. But the scheme was discovered and the traitors punished. Pepin was tonsured and allowed, on his own free will, to enter the monastery of Pruem, where he spent the rest of his life as a monk.

But even before this there had been a great conspiracy in Germania against Charles. All of the guilty ones were exiled; some of them only after being blinded, but the others were not harmed physically. Only three were killed because they had drawn their swords and tried to resist being taken prisoners. After they had slaughtered a number of men, they were killed themselves since there was no other way to subdue them. It was generally felt that Queen Fastrada's cruelty was responsible for these uprisings. And in both cases the reason they were aimed at Charles was because he apparently acquiesced in his wife's cruelty and seemed to have lost a good deal of his usual kindness and easy disposition. But for the rest, he was deeply loved and respected by everyone at home and abroad during all of his life, and no one ever accused him of being unnecessarily harsh.

21. Treatment of Foreigners

Charles liked foreigners and made every effort to see that they were well received. Often there were so many of them in his palace and kingdom that they were quite rightly considered a nuisance. But, magnanimous as he was, he was never bothered by such annoyances. For he felt that he would be rewarded for his troubles if they praised his generosity and gave him a good reputation.

22. Personal Appearance

Charles had a big and powerful body and was tall but well-proportioned. That his height was seven times the length of his own feet is well known. He had a round head, his eyes were unusually large and lively, his nose a little longer than average, his gray hair attractive, and his face cheerful and friendly. Whether he was standing or sitting his appearance was always impressive and dignified. His neck was somewhat short and thick and his stomach protruded a little, but this was rendered inconspicuous by the good proportion of the rest of his body. He walked firmly and his carriage was manly, yet his voice, though clear, was not as strong as one might have expected from someone his size. His health was always excellent except during the last four years of his life, when he frequently suffered from attacks of fever. And at the end he also limped with one foot. All the same, he continued to rely on his own judgment more than on that of his physicians, whom he almost hated because they ordered him to give up his customary roast meat and eat only boiled meat instead.

According to Frankish custom, he rode and hunted a great deal. There is probably no nation on earth that can match the Franks in these skills. Charles was also fond of the steam of natural hot springs. He swam a great deal and did it so well that no one could compete with him. This was why he built the palace in Aachen and spent there the last years of his life without interruption until he died. He invited not only his sons but also his nobles and friends, sometimes even his retinue and body-guard, to bathe with him, so that frequently there would be more than a hundred people in the baths.

23. Dress

He wore the national dress of the Franks. The trunk of his body was covered with a linen shirt, his thighs with linen pants. Over these he put a tunic trimmed at the border with silk. The legs from the knee down-ward were wound with leggings, fastened around the calves with laces, and on his feet he wore boots. In winter he protected his shoulders and chest with a vest made of otter skins or marten fur, and over that he wrapped a blue cloak. He always carried a sword strapped to his side, and the hilt and belt thereof were made either of gold or silver. Only on special holidays or when ambassadors from foreign nations were to be received did he sometimes carry a jewel-studded saber. He disliked foreign clothes no matter how beautiful they were, and would never allow himself to be dressed in them. Only in Rome was he seen on two occasions in a long tunic, chlamys, and Roman shoes: the first time at the entreaty of Pope Hadrian and the second by request of his successor Leo. On high festival days he wore a suit of golden cloth and boots ornamented with jewels. His cloak was fastened by a golden brooch, and on his head he carried a diadem of gold, embellished with gems. On the other days, however, his dress was not much different from that of the common people.

24. Habits

Charles was a moderate eater and drinker, especially the latter, because he abominated drunkenness in any man, particularly in himself and in his associates. But he could not easily abstain from eating and often complained that fasting was bad for his health. He rarely gave banquets and then only on special feast days for large numbers of guests. His daily dinner consisted of four courses, besides the roast which the hunters used to bring in on spits and which he loved more than any other food. During the meal he either listened to music or to someone reading aloud. Stories and the deeds of the old heroes were recited to him. He also enjoyed the books of St. Augustine, especially *The City of God*.

He was so temperate in drinking wine or other beverages that he rarely drank more than three times during a meal. After his midday meal in the summer he would eat some fruit and take another drink, then remove his clothes and shoes, just as he did at night, and rest for two to three hours. His sleep at night would usually be interrupted four or five times, and as soon as he awoke, he got up. While he was being dressed and having his shoes put on, he would invite his friends to come into the room. If the count of the palace told him of some dispute which could not be settled without his decision, he ordered the litigants brought before him at once and, just as though he were sitting in a court of justice, would hear the case and pronounce judgment. At the same time he would give instructions on what had to be transacted that day, or what his ministers were to be charged with doing.

25. Studies

Charles was a gifted speaker. He spoke fluently and expressed whatever he had to say with great clarity. Not only was he proficient in his mother tongue but he also took trouble to learn foreign languages. He spoke Latin as well as his own language, but Greek he understood better than he could speak it. At times he was so eloquent that he almost seemed verbose. He was zealous in his cultivation of the liberal arts, and respected and honored highly those who taught them. He learned grammar from the Deacon Peter of Pisa, who was then already an old man. Another deacon, Albinus, surnamed Alcuin,[3] a man of Saxon origin who came from Britain and was the greatest scholar of his time, taught him the other subjects. Under his direction, the king spent a great deal of time and effort studying rhetoric, logic, and especially astronomy. He learned how to calculate and with great diligence and curiosity investigated the course of the stars. He also tried his hand at writing and to this end always kept writing tablets and notebooks under his pillow in bed in order to practice during spare moments. But since he had only started relatively late in life, he never became very accomplished in this art.

26. Piety

The king practiced the Christian religion, in which he had been raised since childhood, with the greatest piety and devotion. That is why he built the beautiful basilica in Aachen and decorated it with gold and silver, candelabras, lattices, and portals of solid bronze. Since he was unable to get the columns and marble for the structure from anywhere else, he had them brought from Rome and Ravenna.

As long as his health permitted, the king attended church regularly in the morning and evening and took part in the late-night hours and morning mass. He was especially concerned that everything done in church should be carried out with the greatest possible dignity. Often he admonished the sacristans to see to it that nothing unseemly or unclean was brought into the church or left there. He gave many sacred vessels of gold and silver and so many priestly vestments that when services were held not even the door-keepers—the humblest in ecclesiastical rank—had to perform their duties in everyday clothes.

Charles also worked very hard at improving the quality of liturgical reading and chanting of the psalms. He himself was well versed in both, although he would never read in public or sing, except in a low voice and together with the congregation.

27. Generosity

Charles was especially interested in helping the poor, and his generosity was of the kind for which the Greeks use the word *eleemosyna* (alms). But his charity was not limited to his own country and kingdom, for wherever he

---

[3]Alcuin of York (735–804).—*Ed.*

heard of Christians living in poverty, he would send them money out of compassion for their wretched lot, even overseas, to Syria and Egypt, as well as to Africa, Jerusalem, Alexandria, and Carthage. This was also the chief reason why he cultivated friendships with kings across the seas, so that the Christians living in need under their jurisdiction would receive some aid and succor.

Of all sacred and hallowed places, he loved the Cathedral of the Holy Apostle Peter in Rome most of all. He endowed its treasure room with great quantities of gold, silver, and precious stones. He sent its pontiffs many, indeed innumerable, gifts. During his entire reign nothing seemed more important to him than to exert himself to restore the city of Rome to its old splendor and to have the Cathedral of St. Peter not only secured and defended but, through his generosity, adorned and enriched beyond all other churches. Although he favored this church so much, he only visited it four times during his reign of forty-seven years, there to fulfill his vows and offer his prayers.

28. Charles Becomes Emperor

But there were also other reasons for Charles' last visit to Rome. The Romans had forced Pope Leo, on whom they had inflicted various injuries, like tearing out his eyes and cutting out his tongue, to beg for the king's assistance. Charles therefore went to Rome to put order into the confused situation and reestablish the status of the Church. This took the whole winter. It was on this occasion that he accepted the titles of Emperor and Augustus, which at first he disliked so much that he said he would never have entered the church even on this highest of holy days[4] if he had beforehand realized the intentions of the Pope. Still, he bore with astonishing patience the envy his imperial title aroused in the indignant Eastern Roman emperors. He overcame their stubborn opposition with magnanimity—of which he unquestionably had far more than they did—and sent frequent embassies to them, always calling them his brothers in his letters.

29. Reforms

After Charles had accepted the imperial title he noticed that there were many flaws in the legal code of his people, for the Franks have two separate sets of laws differing markedly in many details. He planned to fill in the gaps, to reconcile discrepancies, and to correct what was wrongly and improperly stated.

[4]Charlemagne was crowned Emperor on Christmas day, 800.—*Ed.*

But he was unable to get very much done, except for making a very few additions and even those incomplete. Even so, he did order all the unwritten laws of the nations under his rule collected and written down. He also had the same done for the very old heathen songs which tell of the deeds and wars of former kings, so that they might be preserved for posterity. In addition, he began a grammar of his native language.

Charles gave Frankish names to the months. Before that the Franks had used partly Latin, partly barbarian names for them. He also invited appropriate designations for the twelve winds for which there had previously been barely four words. As for the months, he called January uuintarmanoth, February hornung, March lenzinmanoth, April ostarmanoth, May uuinnemanoth, June brachmanoth, July heuuimanoth, August aranmanoth, September uuitumanoth, October uuindumemanoth, November herbistmanoth, and December heilagmanoth. To the winds he gave the following names: the east wind (subsolanus) he called ostroniuuint, the southeaster (eurus) ostsundroni, the south-southeaster (euroauster) sundostroni, the south wind (auster) sundroni, the south-south-wester (austroafricus) sunduuestroni, the southwester (africus) uuestsundroni, the west wind (zephyrus) uuestroni, the north-wester (chorus) uuestnordroni, the north-northwester (circius) norduuestroni, the north wind (septentrio) nordroni, the northeaster (aquilo) nordostroni, and the north-north-easter (vulturnus) ostnordroni.

30. Coronation of Louis and Charles' Death

At the end of his life, when he was already beset by illness and old age, Charles summoned Louis, the king of Aquitaine and Hildegard's only surviving son, to his presence. He invited all of the Frankish nobles to a solemn assembly, in which with their consent he appointed Louis coregent over the entire realm and heir to the imperial title. He crowned his son himself by placing the diadem on his head and ordering that he be addressed Emperor and Augustus. His decision was received by all those present with great acclaim since it seemed to be divinely inspired for the good of the kingdom. It increased his reputation as a ruler and instilled considerable respect among foreign nations. After Charles had sent his son back to Aquitaine, he started out as usual for the hunt paying no heed to his advanced age. Thus occupied, he spent what was left of the autumn not far from Aachen and returned to the palace at approximately the beginning of November. While he was wintering there he was attacked by a high fever during the month of January and had to retire to bed. As he always did when he had a temperature, he began to diet in the belief that he could cure or at least alleviate his illness by abstaining from food. In addition to the fever he developed a pain in his side, which the Greeks call pleurisy, but he kept fasting and did not take any sustenance except for an occasional drink. On the seventh day after he had taken to bed he received the Holy Communion and died on 28 January between eight and nine o'clock in the morning. Charles was then in the seventy-second year of his life and in the forty-seventh year of his reign.

31. Burial

His body was washed and prepared for burial in the usual way, then brought to the basilica and buried amid the great lamentations of the entire population. At first there was uncertainty about where he should be laid to rest because he had never given any instructions on this point during his lifetime. Finally everyone agreed that there could be no more appropriate place than the basilica which he had built at his own expense in this city out of love for God and our Lord Jesus Christ and in honor of the Holy and Immaculate Virgin. He was interred there on the same day he died. Above his grave a gilded arch was raised with his image and an inscription reading as follows: "In this tomb lies the body of Charles, the great Christian Emperor, who gloriously increased the kingdom of the Franks and ruled successfully for forty-seven years. He died in his seventies in the seventh year of the indiction, on January 28th in the year of our Lord 814."

32. Omens of Death

There were many omens indicating the approach of his death, so that not only others but even himself took note of the forewarnings. During the last three years of his life there were frequent eclipses of the sun and moon, and black spots were seen on the face of the sun for seven days. On Ascension Day the portico between the cathedral and the palace which he had built with immense effort suddenly came crashing down in complete ruin. The wooden bridge across the Rhine at Mainz, which had taken ten years of hard work to build and which was so cleverly constructed that it seemed as if it would last forever, this bridge accidentally caught fire and burnt to ashes in three hours, so that not a single plank remained except what was under water. During his last campaign in Saxony against Godofrid, the king of the Danes, Charles all at once saw a ball of brilliant fire falling from the sky and flashing from right to left through the clear atmosphere. He had just left his camp before sunrise to start out on the march. While everybody was looking and wondering what this sign meant, his horse fell headfirst and threw him to the ground so violently that the clasp on his cloak broke and his sword belt burst. The attendants who were near him and rushed to his aid helped him up without his weapons and cloak. The lance which he had been holding tightly in his hand was thrown a distance of more than twenty feet.

In addition to all this there were numerous earth tremors in his palace in Aachen, and in the houses which Charles visited the wooden beams in the ceilings creaked constantly. Furthermore, lightning had struck the basilica in which he was later to be buried and the golden ball which decorated the gable was destroyed and hurled onto the roof of the bishop's house next to the church. In the same basilica there was an inscription written in red ochre naming its builder and running along the edge of the circular space which surrounds the interior part of the building between the upper and lower arches. Its last words read: "Karolus Princeps." Several people noticed that during the last year of his life, only a few months before he died, the letters of the word "Princeps" had become so blurred that they could hardly be deciphered.

But Charles took no notice of these omens; in any case he acted as if they had nothing whatever to do with him.

33. Last Will

Charles had decided to draw up a will in which he wanted to make his daughters and illegitimate children heirs to some part of his estate. Since he started too late, however, he was unable to complete it. Nevertheless, three years before his death he made a division of his treasures, money, clothing, and other movable property in the presence of his friends and attendants. He called on them to bear witness that the apportionment which he had planned should be executed faithfully after his death. He had a brief statement prepared summarizing what he wanted done with the property he had divided. This document reads as follows: "In the name of the Almighty Lord God, the Father, the Son, and the Holy Ghost. Here is a description of the division which was made by the most glorious and pious Lord Charles, Emperor and Augustus, in the eight hundred and eleventh year after the incarnation of our Lord Jesus Christ, during the forty-third year of his reign over the Franks, in the thirty-sixth year of his rule over Italy, in the eleventh year of his imperial sovereignty, and in the fourth indiction. After much pious and prudent deliberation and with the help of God, he has decided to distribute the valuables and money which on this day are on deposit in his treasury. In doing so he wished above all to ensure that in his case the distribution of alms, which among Christians is traditionally made from their own personal belongings, would be carried out in an orderly and reasonable fashion. He also wanted to be certain that his heirs should understand quite clearly and definitely what was to be theirs, so that they could divide up the inheritance properly without any litigation or dispute. Such being his intention and purpose, he first divided all his tangible and movable possessions, consisting of gold and of silver, precious stones and royal vestments, deposited in his treasury on the stipulated day into three main parts. One part he left intact; the other two he subdivided into twenty-one smaller portions, the reason for this being that, as is well known, there are twenty-two capital cities in his realm. One of these portions shall be given for charitable purposes to each of the cities by his heirs and friends. The archbishop responsible for the diocese shall receive the portion and divide it with his suffragans in such a manner that one-third is kept for his church and two-thirds is given to the suffragans. These twenty-one portions into which two-thirds of his property were subdivided to correspond to the number of capital cities in the kingdom have been carefully separated and set aside in individual coffers on which the names of the cities of destination are written. The cities to which these alms and gifts are to be given are as follows: Rome, Ravenna, Milan, Cividale del Friuli, Grado, Cologne, Mainz, Salzburg, Trier, Sens, Besançon, Lyons, Rouen, Rheims, Arles, Vienne, Moûtiers-en-Tarantaise, Embrun, Bordeaûx, Tours, and Bourges.

"The third main part which is to be preserved intact shall be dealt with in the following manner: while both of the above-mentioned parts are to be divided in the way stated and are to be kept under seal, the third part is to be used for the defrayment of the daily expenses by the owner and will constitute property of which he cannot be deprived by any sworn obligation whatsoever. This provision shall remain in force for as long as he lives or for as long as he judges that he has need of it. After his death or voluntary withdrawal from the secular world the said part is to be divided into four shares. One of these shall be added to the above-mentioned twenty-one portions; the second share is to go to his sons and daughters and their sons and daughters and shall be distributed in a just and equitable way; the third shall be devoted to the poor in the customary Christian manner; the fourth is to be similarly parceled out in form of a pension, in the name of Christian charity, among the male and female servants of the Palace.

"To this third main part of his fortune, which like the rest consists of gold and silver, he desires that there be added all vessels and utensils made of bronze, iron, and other metal, together with his weapons, clothes, and other movable property, whether valuable or not, and for whatever use intended, such as curtains, coverlets, tapestries, woolens, leather goods, pack saddles, and whatever else might be found that day in the treasury or in his wardrobe. In this way the shares of the third part will be enlarged and the alms distributed among a greater number of people.

"Further, he has given orders that the chapel, that is to say the furnishings which he has donated and collected, or inherited from his father, be kept intact and not be subject to any kind of division. Should there, however, be any vessels, books, or other objects of which it is certainly known that they were not given to the chapel by him, then any person desiring them may buy them, provided a fair price is paid. In the same way he decreed that the large collection of books in his library may be bought by persons who want them and will pay a just price for them. The proceeds shall go to the poor.

"Among his other treasures and valuables there are known to be three silver tables and one of unusual size and weight made of gold. He has stipulated and decreed that one of them, square in shape and decorated with a plan of the city of Constantinople, be sent to Rome to the Cathedral of the Holy Apostle Peter along with the other gifts thereto intended. The second table, round in shape and engraved with a picture of the city of Rome, shall be given to the bishopric of the church of Ravenna. The third, far superior to the others, both in beauty of craftsmanship and in weight, consists of three concentric circles on which a map of the entire world is skillfully traced in great detail. This table together with the golden one, called the fourth, shall be added to the third main part of his fortune, which he has allotted to his heirs and to those who are to receive alms.

"These arrangements and stipulations were done in the presence of the following bishops, abbots, and counts who were able to attend on that day, and whose names are herein recorded:

Bishops

Hildebald	John
Richolf	Theodolf
Arno	Jesse
Wolfar	Heito
Bernoin	Waltgaud
Laidrad	

Abbots

Fridugis	Angilbert
Adalung	Irmino

Counts

Walach	Unruoch
Meginher	Burchard
Otolf	Meginhard
Stephan	Hatto
Richwin	Bero
Edo	Hildegern
Ercanger	Hroccolf."
Gerold	

After Charles' death, his son Louis, who succeeded him by divine ordination, examined this document and had its provisions carried out as speedily as possible and with the utmost scrupulousness.

The Crusades

The Crusades, the series of offensives by Western European armies beginning in 1095 to control the Eastern Mediterranean, are usually described as a religious conflict between Christianity and Islam. This is true, but far too simplistic. Between the seventh and ninth centuries, Muslim Arabic and Persian forces had conquered most of North Africa and Eastern Mediterranean at the expense of the Christian, Greek-speaking, Byzantine Empire. By the eleventh century, however, the Byzantines and the Arabic and Persian Muslims coexisted with only occasional conflict. Both Greek and Latin Christians were allowed to visit the holy sites in and around Jerusalem, and there were significant intellectual and cultural contacts among Muslim, Greek Christian, and Latin Christian elites, based on their shared heritage from Classical Mediterranean civilizations.

The conflicts that became known as the Crusades were partly the result of the continued spread of Latin Christian and Islamic civilizations. The documents of the time do not commonly refer to the combatants in the Crusades as Christians and Muslims, but as Franks and Turks. The Franks were one of the Germanic tribes that took advantage of the weakness of the later Roman Empire. In the fifth century, they took control of the Roman province of Gaul (modern France) and converted to orthodox Christianity. By the time of the Crusades, the term "Frank" was used by Greek and Arabic writers to refer to the Latin Christian warrior nobility of Western Europe. While many members of this class were committed Christians, some seemed to ignore the teachings of the church. None, however, gave up their warrior ethos. While the aggressive tendencies of the "Franks" were often directed against Muslims and justified in religious terms in places like Spain and Sicily, fellow Christians in places such as the British Isles or Southern Italy were also targets. In fact, the Western European nobility spent even more energy and blood fighting among themselves than they did against outsiders. For the Roman church and the highest level of Western Europe nobility, the challenge of the eleventh century was how to stabilize and further civilize this military class. Far to the East, Islamic civilization also was facing upheaval from newly converted and thinly civilized groups. In the tenth century, many of the Turkish-speaking tribes in Central Asia converted to Islam. Like the Franks, they had been warlike, tribal nomads before their conversion. They embraced their new faith with fervor, but also like the Franks, did not give up their military culture. With the zealousness typical of new converts, they saw the sophisticated Arabic and Persian Muslims as decadent, and often heretical. By the eleventh century, the Turks had gone from being slaves and mercenaries in the Middle East, to the new rulers. Although their quarrel was almost entirely with other Muslims, the conflict in the Muslim territories in the Middle East spilled over into Byzantine lands. The Byzantine emperor responded with force and was defeated by the Turks in 1071 at the Battle of Manzikert. The introduction of Latin Christian soldiers into this conflict springs from the twin problems of internal violence in Latin Christianity and the threat of the Christian Byzantine Empire being conquered by Muslim forces. The first Crusade, called by Pope Urban II in 1092, was a possible solution to both problems. Urban's articulation of a just war against the Muslim Turks offered a legitimate use of violence to Western European warriors. At the very least, it would direct their violence outside of Europe. Also, sending military support to Byzantines would both protect a Christian empire and serve as a context to heal the split between Greek and Latin Christians. None of these objectives were accomplished by the Crusades. The crusaders often conducted themselves with violence unusual even then. European Jews were slaughtered *en route*. Once in the Middle East they made no distinction between Muslim Turks and the Greek Christians they were sent to liberate. They claimed their conquests for themselves, not for the Byzantine emperor whom they supposedly served. In 1204 Latin Christian armies even conquered the Byzantine Empire for themselves. And while the territories that the Crusaders conquered lasted little more than a century, the ill will has lasted until this day.

The first selection is an account of Urban's preaching of the First Crusade in the French town of Clermont in 1092. This account is by Fulcher of Chartres, a priest who was present at Clermont and served as a chaplain to the northern French contingent in the crusading army. The second two selections are descriptions of one prominent crusader, Bohemund. One of the accounts is by Anna Comnena, a Byzantine princess who saw the crusaders as a child in the imperial court of her father. Bohemund had previously been an enemy of the Byzantine's in Southern Italy. Bohemund is also described by an anonymous French chronicler. Finally, there is a description of the Franks by a Muslim nobleman.

---

1. On what basis does Urban distinguish between legitimate and illegitimate uses of violence?

2. You have descriptions of the crusaders from European, Byzantine, and Muslim perspectives. From these biased and contradictory sources, describe the crusaders as objectively as possible.

In the year 1095 from the Lord's Incarnation, with Henry reigning in Germany as so-called emperor, and with Philip as king in France, manifold evils were growing in all parts of Europe because of wavering faith. In Rome ruled Pope Urban II, a man distinguished in life and character, who always strove wisely and actively to raise the status of the Holy Church above all things.

He saw that the faith of Christianity was being destroyed to excess by everybody, by the clergy as well as by the laity. He saw that peace was altogether discarded by the princes of the world, who were engaged in incessant warlike contention and quarreling among themselves. He saw the wealth of the land being pillaged continuously. He saw many of the vanquished, wrongfully taken prisoner and very cruelly thrown into foulest dungeons, either ransomed for a high price or, tortured by the triple torments of hunger, thirst, and cold, blotted out by a death hidden from the world. He saw holy places violated; monasteries and villas burned. He saw that no one was spared of any human suffering, and that things divine and human alike were held in derision.

He heard, too, that the interior regions of Romania, where the Turks ruled over the Christians, had been perniciously subjected in a savage attack. Moved by long-suffering compassion and by love of God's will, he descended the mountains to Gaul, and in Auvergne he called for a council to congregate from all sides at a suitable time at a city called Clermont. Three hundred and ten bishops and abbots, who had been advised beforehand by messengers, were present.

Then, on the day set aside for it, he called them together to himself and, in an eloquent address, carefully made the cause of the meeting known to them. In the plaintive voice of an aggrieved Church, he expressed great lamentation, and held a long discourse with them about the raging tempests of the world, which have been mentioned, because faith was undermined.

One after another, he beseechingly exhorted them all, with renewed faith, to spur themselves in great earnestness to overcome the Devil's devices and to try to restore the Holy Church, most unmercifully weakened by the wicked, to its former honorable status.

"Most beloved brethren," he said, "by God's permission placed over the whole world with the papal crown. I, Urban, as the messenger of divine admonition, have been compelled by an unavoidable occasion to come here to you servants of God. I desired those whom I judged to be stewards of God's ministries to be true stewards and faithful, with all hypocrisy rejected.

"But with temperance in reason and justice being remote, I, with divine aid, shall strive carefully to root out any crookedness or distortion which might obstruct God's law. For the Lord appointed you temporarily as stewards over His family to serve it nourishment seasoned with a modest savor. Moreover, blessed will you be if at last the Overseer find you faithful.

"You are also called shepherds; see that you are not occupied after the manner of mercenaries. Be true shepherds, always holding your crooks in your hands; and sleeping not. guard on every side the flock entrusted to you.

"For if through your carelessness or negligence, some wolf seizes a sheep, you doubtless will lose the reward prepared for you by our Lord. Nay, first most cruelly beaten by the whips of the lictors, you afterwards will be angrily cast into the keeping of a deadly place.

"Likewise, according to the evangelical sermon, you are the 'salt of the earth.' But if you fail, it will be disputed wherewith it was salted. O how much saltiness, indeed, is necessary for you to salt the people in correcting them with the salt of wisdom, people who are ignorant and panting with desire after the wantonness of the world; so that, unsalted, they might not be rotten with sins and stink whenever the Lord might wish to exhort them.

"For if because of the sloth of your management, He should find in them worms, that is, sin, straightway, He will order that they, despised, be cast into the dungheap. And because you could not make restoration for such a great loss, He will banish you, utterly condemned in judgment, from the familiarity of His love.

"It behooves saltiness of this kind to be wise, provident, temperate, learned, peace-making, truth-seeking, pious, just, equitable, pure. For how will the unlearned be able to make men learned, the intemperate make temperate, the impure make them pure? If one despises peace, how will he appease? Or if one has dirty hands, how will he be able to wipe the filth off another one defiled? For it is read, 'If the blind lead the blind, both shall fall into a ditch.'

"Set yourselves right before you do others, so that you can blamelessly correct your subjects. If you wish to be friends of God, gladly practise those things which you feel will please Him.

"Especially establish ecclesiastical affairs firm in their own right, so that no simoniac heresy will take root among you. Take care lest the vendors and moneychangers, flayed by the scourges of the Lord, be miserably driven out into the narrow streets of destruction.

"Uphold the Church in its own ranks altogether free from all secular power. See that the tithes of all those who cultivate the earth are given faithfully to God; let them not be sold or held back.

"Let him who has seized a bishop be considered an outlaw. Let him who has seized or robbed monks, clerics, nuns and their servants, pilgrims, or merchants, be excommunicated. Let the robbers and burners of homes and their accomplices, banished from the Church, be smitten with excommunication.

"It must be considered very carefully, as Gregory says, by what penalty he must be punished who seizes other men's property, if he who does not bestow his own liberally is condemned to Hell. For so it happened to the rich man in the well-known Gospel, who on that account was not punished because he had taken away the property of others, but because he had misused that which he had received.

"And so by these iniquities, most beloved, you have seen the world disturbed too long; so long, as it was told to us by those reporting, that perhaps because of the weakness of your justice in some parts of your provinces, no one dares to walk in the streets with safety, lest he be kidnapped by robbers by day or thieves by night, either by force or trickery, at home or outside.

"Wherefore the Truce, as it is commonly called, now for a long time established by the Holy Fathers, must be renewed. In admonition. I entreat you to adhere to it most firmly in your own bishopric. But if anyone affected by avarice or pride breaks it of his own free will, let him be excommunicated by God's authority and by the sanction of the decrees of this Holy Council."

Bohemund: The *Gesta* Version

When the Emperor heard that the most honorable man, Bohemund, had come to him, he commanded that he be received with honor and carefully lodged outside the city. When he had been so lodged, the evil Emperor sent for him to come to speak with him in secret. Thither, also, came Duke Godfrey with his brother, and at length the Count of St. Gilles approached the city. Then the Emperor in anxious and fervid rage was pondering some way by which they might seize these knights of Christ adroitly and by fraud. But Divine Grace disclosing (his plans), neither time nor place was found by him, or his men, to do them ill. At last, all the noble leaders who were at Constantinople were assembled. Fearing lest they should be deprived of their country, they decided in their counsels and ingenious calculations that our dukes, counts, or all the leaders, ought to make an oath of fealty to the Emperor. These absolutely refused and said: "It is indeed unworthy of us, and, furthermore, it seems to us unjust to swear an oath to him." Perchance we shall yet often be deceived by our leaders. In the end, what were they to do? They say that under the force of necessity they humiliated themselves, willy-nilly, to the will of the most unjust Emperor. To that most mighty man Bohemund, however, whom he greatly feared because in times past he (Bohemund) had often driven him from the field with his army, the Emperor said that, if he willingly took the oath to him, he would give him, in return, land in extent from Antioch fifteen days journey, and eight in width. And he (the Emperor) swore to him in such wise that, if he loyally observed that oath, he would never pass beyond his own land. Knights, so brave and so sturdy, why did they do this? For the reason that they were constrained by much necessity. The Emperor also gave to all our men a pledge of security. He likewise took oath that he, together with his army, would come with us, by land and by sea; that he would afford us faithfully a market by land and sea, and that he would diligently make good our losses; in addition, that he did not wish, and would not permit, any of our pilgrims to be disturbed or come to grief on their way to the Holy Sepulchre.

Bohemund: The Version of Anna Comnena

But when Bohemund had arrived at Apri with his companions, realizing both that he was not of noble birth, and that for lack of money he had not brought with him a large enough army, he hastened, with only ten Gauls, ahead of the other counts and arrived at Constantinople. He did this to win the favor of the Emperor for himself, and to conceal more safely the plans which he was concocting against him. Indeed, the Emperor, to whom the schemes of the man were known, for he had long since become acquainted with the hidden and deceitful dealings of this same Bohemund, took great pains to arrange it so that before the other counts should come he would speak with him alone. Thus having heard what Bohemund had to say, he hoped to persuade him to cross before the others came, lest, joined with them after their coming, he might pervert their minds.

When Bohemund had come to him, the Emperor greeted him with gladness and inquired anxiously about the journey and where he had left his companions. Bohemund responded to all these things as he thought best for his own interests, affably and in a friendly way, while the Emperor recalled in a familiar talk his bold undertakings long ago around Durazzo and Larissa and the hostilities between them at that time. Bohemund answered. "Then I confess I was your enemy, then I was hostile. But, behold, I now stand before you like a deserter to the ranks of the enemy! I am a friend of your Majesty." The Emperor proceeded to scrutinize the man, considering him cautiously and carefully and drawing out what was in his mind. As soon as he saw that Bohemund was ready to consent to swear an oath of fealty to him, he said, "You must be tired from the journey and should retire to rest. We will talk tomorrow about anything else."

So Bohemund departed to Cosmidion, where hospitality was prepared for him, and he found a table richly laden with an abundance of food and condiments of all kinds. Then the cooks came and showed him the uncooked flesh of animals and birds, saying: "We have prepared this food which you see on the table according to our skill and the custom of this region; but if, perchance, these please you less, here is food, still uncooked, which can be prepared just as you order." The Emperor, because of his almost incredible tact in handling men, had commanded that this be done and said by them. For, since he was especially expert in penetrating the secrets of minds and in discovering the disposition of a man, he very readily understood that Bohemund was of a shrewd and suspicious nature: and he foresaw what happened. For, lest Bohemund should conceive any suspicion against him, the Emperor had ordered that raw meats be placed before him, together with the cooked, thus easily removing suspicion. Neither did his conjecture fail, for the very shrewd Bohemund took the prepared food, without even touching it with the tips of his fingers, or tasting it, and immediately turned around, concealing, nevertheless, the suspicion which occurred to him by the following ostentatious show of liberality. For under the pretext of courtesy he distributed all the food to those standing around; in reality, if one understood rightly, he was dividing the cup of death among them. Nor did he conceal his cunning, so much did he hold his subjects in contempt; for he this day used the raw meat which had been offered to him and had it prepared by his own cooks after the manner of his country. On the next day he asked his men whether they were well. Upon their answering in the affirmative, that they were indeed very well, that not even one felt even the least indisposed, he disclosed his secret in his reply: "Remembering a war, once carried on by me against the Emperor, and that strife. I feared lest perchance he had intended to kill me by putting deadly poison in my food."

Such a man was Bohemund. Never, indeed, have I seen a man so dishonest. In everything, in his words as well as in his deeds, he never chose the right path; and when anyone deviates from the moderation of virtue, it makes little difference to whatsoever extreme he goes, for he is always far from honesty.

For the rest, the Emperor then summoned Bohemund and exacted from him the usual oath of the Latins. The latter, knowing well his own resources, and realizing that he was neither of noble birth nor well supplied by fortune with wealth, for he had no great force, but only a moderate number of Gauls with him, and being, besides, dishonest in character, readily submitted himself to the will of the Emperor.

After this, the Emperor saw to it that a room in the palace was so filled with a collection of riches of all kinds that the very floor was covered with costly raiment, and with gold and silver coins, and certain other less valuable things, so much so that one was not able even to walk there, so hindered was he by the abundance of these things. The Emperor ordered the guide suddenly and unexpectedly to open the doors, thus revealing all this to Bohemund. Amazed at the spectacle, Bohemund exclaimed: "If such riches were mine, long ago I would have been lord of many lands!" The guide answered, "And all these things the Emperor bestows upon you today as a gift." Most gladly Bohemund received them and with many gracious thanks he left, intending to return to his rest in the inn. But changing his mind when they were brought to him, he, who a little before had admired them, said: "Never can I let myself be treated with such ignominy by the Emperor. Go, take those things and carry them back to him who sent them." The Emperor, knowing the base fickleness of the Latins, quoted this common saying, "Let the evil return to its author." Bohemund having heard this, and seeing that the messengers were busily bringing these things back to him, decided anew about the goods which he had sent back with regret, and, like a polypus, changed in a moment, he now showed a joyous countenance to the bearers. For he was quick, and a man of very dishonest disposition, as much surpassing in malice and intrepidity all the Latins who had crossed over as he was inferior to them in power and wealth. But even though he thus excelled all in great cunning, the inconstant character of the Latins was also in him. Verily, the riches which he spurned at first, he now gladly accepted. For when this man of evil design had left his country in which he possessed no wealth at all (under the pretext, indeed, of adoring at the Lord's Sepulchre, but in reality endeavoring to acquire for himself a kingdom), he found himself in need of much money, especially, indeed, if he was to seize the Roman power. In this he followed the advice of his father and, so to speak, was leaving no stone unturned.

Moreover, the Emperor, who understood fully his wicked intention and perverse mind, skillfully managed carefully to remove whatever might further Bohemund's ambitious designs. Wherefore, Bohemund, seeking a home for himself in the East and using Cretan scheming against Cretans, did not obtain it. For the Emperor feared lest, after obtaining power, he would use it to place the Latin counts under obligation to him, finally thus accomplishing easily what he wished. But since he did not want Bohemund to surmise that he was already discovered, the Emperor misled him by this hope: "Not yet," he said, "has the time come for the thing which you say; but after a little it shall come about by your fortitude and trust in me."

After the Emperor had bestowed upon the Gauls promises, gifts, and honors of every kind, the next day he solemnly took his seat on the imperial throne. Summoning Bohemund and all the counts, he talked about the things which would happen to them on the journey. He wanted, likewise, to show what methods and means of warfare the Turks were wont to employ, and to give directions how the line of battle should be drawn up against them, how ambushes should be set, and how they ought not to follow the fleeing Turks too far. And so, both by gifts of money and by flattering speeches, he soothed the rude nature of the people, and, after giving useful advice, he persuaded them to pass over the sea. . . .

Memoirs of Us-Amah Ibn-Munqidh

Their lack of sense.—Mysterious are the works of the Creator, the author of all things! When one comes to recount cases regarding the Franks, he cannot but glorify Allah (exalted is he!) and sanctify him, for he sees them as animals possessing the virtues of courage and fighting, but nothing else; just as animals have only the virtues of strength and carrying loads. I shall now give some instances of their doings and their curious mentality.

In the army of King Fulk, son of Fulk, was a Frankish reverend knight who had just arrived from their land in order to make the holy pilgrimage and then return home. He was of my intimate fellowship and kept such constant company with me that he began to call me "my brother." Between us were mutual bonds of amity and friendship. When he resolved to return by sea to his homeland, he said to me:

My brother, I am leaving for my country and I want thee to send with me thy son (my son, who was then fourteen years old, was at that time in my company) to our country, where he can see the knights and learn wisdom and chivalry. When he returns, he will be like a wise man.

Thus there fell upon my ears words which would never come out of the head of a sensible man; for even if my son were to be taken captive, his captivity could not bring him a worse misfortune than carrying him into the lands of the Franks. However, I said to the man:

By thy life, this has exactly been my idea. But the only thing that prevented me from carrying it out was the fact that his grandmother, my mother, is so fond of him and did not this time let him come out with me until she exacted an oath from me to the effect that I would return him to her.

Thereupon he asked, "Is thy mother still alive?" "Yes." I replied. "Well," said he, "disobey her not."

Their curious medication.—A case illustrating their curious medicine is the following:

The lord of al-Munaytirah wrote to my uncle asking him to dispatch a physician to treat certain sick persons among his people. My uncle sent him a Christian physician named Thābit. Thābit was absent but ten days when he returned. So we said to him, "How quickly hast thou healed thy patients!" He said:

They brought before me a knight in whose leg an abscess had grown; and a woman afflicted with imbecility. To the knight I applied a small poultice until the abscess opened and became well; and the woman I put on diet and made her humor wet. Then a Frankish physician came to them and said, "This man knows nothing about treating them." He then said to the knight, "Which wouldst thou prefer, living with one leg or dying with two?" The latter replied, "Living with one leg." The physician said, "Bring me a strong knight and a sharp ax." A knight came with the ax. And I was standing by. Then the physician laid the leg of the patient on a block of wood and bade the knight strike his leg with the ax and chop it off at one blow. Accordingly he struck it—while I was looking on—one blow, but the leg was not severed. He dealt another blow, upon which the marrow of the leg flowed out and the patient died on the spot. He then examined the woman and said, "This is a woman in whose head there is a devil which has possessed her. Shave off her hair." Accordingly they shaved it off and the woman began once more to eat their ordinary diet — garlic and mustard. Her imbecility took a turn for the worse. The physician then said, "The devil has penetrated through her head." He therefore took a razor, made a deep cruciform incision on it, peeled off the skin at the middle of the incision until the bone of the skull was exposed and rubbed it with salt. The woman also expired instantly. Thereupon I asked them whether my services were needed any longer, and when they replied in the negative I returned home, having learned of their medicine what I knew not before.

I have, however, witnessed a case of their medicine which was quite different from that.

The king of the Franks had for treasurer a knight named Bernard [*barnād*], who (may Allah's curse be upon him!) was one of the most accursed and wicked among the Franks. A horse kicked him in the leg, which was subsequently infected and which opened in fourteen different places. Every time one of these cuts would close in one place, another would open in another place. All this happened while I was praying for his perdition. Then came to him a Frankish physician and removed from the leg all the ointments which were on it and began to wash it with very strong vinegar. By this treatment all the cuts were healed and the man became well again. He was up again like a devil.

Another case illustrating their curious medicine is the following:

In Shayzar we had an artisan named abu-al-Fath, who had a boy whose neck was afflicted with scrofula. Every time a part of it would close, another part would open. This man happened to go to Antioch on business of his, accompanied by his son. A Frank noticed the boy and asked his father about him. Abu-al-Fath replied, "This is my son." The Frank said to him, "Wilt thou swear by thy religion that if I prescribe to thee a medicine which will cure thy boy, thou wilt charge nobody fees for prescribing it thyself? In that case, I shall prescribe to thee a medicine which will cure the boy." The man took the oath and the Frank said:

Take uncrushed leaves of glasswort, burn them, then soak the ashes in olive oil and sharp vinegar. Treat the scrofula with them until the spot on which it is growing is eaten up. Then take burnt lead, soak it in ghee butter [*samn*] and treat him with it. That will cure him.

The father treated the boy accordingly, and the boy was cured. The sores closed and the boy returned to his normal condition of health.

I have myself treated with this medicine many who were afflicted with such disease, and the treatment was successful in removing the cause of the complaint.

Newly arrived Franks are especially rough: One insists that Usāmah should pray eastward.—Everyone who is a fresh emigrant from the Frankish lands is ruder in character than those who have become acclimatized and have held long association with the Moslems. Here is an illustration of their rude character.

Whenever I visited Jerusalem I always entered the Aqsa Mosque, beside which stood a small mosque which the Franks had converted into a church. When I used to enter the Aqsa Mosque, which was occupied by the Templars [*al-dāwiyyah*], who were my friends, the Templars would evacuate the little adjoining mosque so that I might pray in it. One day I entered this mosque, repeated the first formula, "Allah is great," and stood up in the act of praying, upon which one of the Franks rushed on me, got hold of me and turned my face eastward saying, "This is the way thou shouldst pray!" A group of Templars hastened to him, seized him and repelled him from me. I resumed my prayer. The same man, while the others were otherwise busy, rushed once more on me and turned my face eastward, saying, "This is the way thou shouldst pray!" The Templars again came in to him and expelled him. They apologized to me, saying, "This is a stranger who has only recently arrived from the land of the Franks and he has never before seen anyone praying except eastward." Thereupon I said to myself, "I have had enough prayer." So I went out and have ever been surprised at the conduct of this devil of a man, at the change in the color of his face, his trembling and his sentiment at the sight of one praying towards the *qiblah*.

Another wants to show to a Moslem God as a child.—I saw one of the Franks come to al-Amīr Mu'īn-al-Dīn (may Allah's mercy rest upon his soul!) when he was in the Dome of the Rock and say to him, "Dost thou want to see God as a child?" Mu'īn-al-Dīn said, "Yes." The Frank walked ahead of us until he showed us the picture of Mary with Christ (may peace be upon him!) as an infant in her lap. He then said, "This is God as a child." But Allah is exalted far above what the infidels say about him!

Franks lack jealousy in sex affairs.—The Franks are void of all zeal and jealousy. One of them may be walking along with his wife. He meets another man who takes the wife by the hand and steps aside to converse with her while the husband is standing on one side waiting for his wife to conclude the conversation. If she lingers too long for him, he leaves her alone with the conversant and goes away.

Here is an illustration which I myself witnessed:

When I used to visit Nāblus, I always took lodging with a man named Mu'izz, whose home was a lodging house for the Moslems. The house had windows which opened to the road, and there stood opposite to it on the other side of the road a house belonging to a Frank who sold wine for the merchants. He would take some wine in a bottle and go around announcing it by shouting, "So and so, the merchant, has just opened a cask full of this wine. He who wants to buy some of it will find it in such and such a place." The Frank's pay for the announcement made would be the wine in that bottle. One day this Frank went home and found a man with his wife in the same bed. He asked him, "What could have made thee enter into my wife's room?" The man replied, "I was tired, so I went in to rest." "But how," asked he, "didst thou get into my bed?" The other replied, "I found a bed that was spread, so I slept in it." "But," said he, "my wife was sleeping together with thee!" The other replied, "Well, the bed is hers. How could I therefore have prevented her from using her own bed?" "By the truth of my religion," said the husband, "if thou shouldst do it again, thou and I would have a quarrel." Such was for the Frank the entire expression of his disapproval and the limit of his jealousy.

Another illustration:

We had with us a bath-keeper named Sālim, originally an inhabitant of al-Ma'arrah, who had charge of the bath of my father (may Allah's mercy rest upon his soul!). This man related the following story:

I once opened a bath in al-Ma'arrah in order to earn my living. To this bath there came a Frankish knight. The Franks disapprove of girding a cover around one's waist while in the bath. So this Frank stretched out his arm and pulled off my cover from my waist and threw it away. He looked and saw that I had recently shaved off my pubes. So he shouted, "Sālim!" As I drew near him he stretched his hand over my pubes and said, " Sālim, good! By the truth of my religion, do the same for me." Saying this, he lay on his back and I found that in that place the hair was like his beard. So I shaved it off. Then he passed his hand over the place and, finding it smooth, he said, " Sālim, by the truth of my religion, do the same to madame [*al-dāma*]" (*al-dāma* in their language means the lady), referring to his wife. He then said to a servant of his, "Tell madame to come here." Accordingly the servant went and brought her and made her enter the bath. She also lay on her back. The knight repeated, "Do what thou hast done to me." So I shaved all that hair while her husband was sitting looking at me. At last he thanked me and handed me the pay for my service.

Consider now this great contradiction! They have neither jealousy nor zeal but they have great courage, although courage is nothing but the product of zeal and of ambition to be above ill repute.

Magna Carta

What was Magna Carta? Historically it has come to be regarded as a document that guarantees the legal rights of free men, thus as a foundation for a democratic social order. This conclusion is based on Article 39, which states that a free man will not be prosecuted, except through lawful means and the judgment of his peers. But this Article, however important, is only one of sixty-three of which the Great Charter is composed. The others say little about such fundamental human rights but rather are devoted mainly to feudal liberties and obligations in thirteenth-century England. A recognition of this fact should help us to focus our attention on the central significance of the document, at least as it was conceived by those who were responsible for its writing.

Magna Carta was the consequence of a dispute that had been developing over a period of years between the monarchs and the barons of England. From the time of the Norman conquest in 1066 succeeding English kings had embarked on a practice of consolidating administration and, as a result, power around the throne. Such a policy, of course, worked to the disadvantage of the barons who, in their reaction against these royal encroachments, claimed that they constituted violations of the feudal contract. Thus Magna Carta reveals much about feudal society, and the customary and legal relationships between individuals and classes, as these existed in the England of that time.

The dispute between king and barons intensified after the accession of King John to the throne in 1199. Much of the blame for this development lay with John himself, for he succeeded in making himself unpopular with almost every segment of his population. He alienated many of the clergy by his quarrels with Pope Innocent III; he discouraged the military class by his armed incursions into France, which led to defeat; he enraged the London merchants by imposing an ever-increasing tax burden on them; and he kept infringing on the feudal rights and privileges of the baronial class. In all of this he displayed himself as an insensitive autocrat.

The selection that follows contains about half of the Magna Carta; from it one can get a good grasp of the charter's general nature. Although it may appear from the flavor of the language employed that John is graciously granting royal favors to his subjects, it must be remembered that these concessions were forced from him by his rebellious barons.

1.   What rights and obligations does the king have?

2.   What rights and obligations do subjects have?

Magna Carta

John, by the grace of God, King of England, Lord of Ireland, Duke of Normandy and Aquitaine, and Count of Anjou: To the Archbishops, Bishops, Abbots, Earls, Barons, Justiciaries, Foresters, Sheriffs, Reeves, Ministers, and all Bailiffs and others, his faithful subjects, Greeting. Know ye that in the presence of God, and for the health of Our soul, and the souls of Our ancestors and heirs, to the honor of God, and the exaltation of Holy Church, and amendment of Our kingdom, by the advice of Our reverend Fathers, Stephen, Archbishop of Canterbury, Primate of all England, and Cardinal of the Holy Roman Church; Henry, Archbishop of Dublin; William of London, Peter of Winchester, Jocelin of Bath and Glastonbury, Hugh of Lincoln, Walter of Worcester, William of Coventry, and Benedict of Rochester, Bishops; Master Pandulph, the Pope's subdeacon and familiar; Brother Aymeric, Master of the Knights of the Temple in England; and the noble persons, William Marshal, Earl of Pembroke: William, Earl of Salisbury; William, Earl of Warren; William, Earl of Arundel; Alan de Galloway, Constable of Scotland; Warin FitzGerald, Peter Fitz-Herbert, Hubert de Burgh, Seneschal of Poitou, Hugh de Neville, Matthew Fitz-Herbert, Thomas Basset, Alan Basset, Philip Daubeny, Robert de Roppelay, John Marshal, John Fitz-Hugh, and others, Our liegemen:

1.   We have, in the first place, granted to God, and by this Our present Charter confirmed for Us and Our heirs forever—That the English Church shall be free and enjoy her rights in their integrity and her liberties untouched. And that We will this so to be observed appears from the fact that We of Our own free will, before the outbreak of the dissensions between Us and Our barons, granted, confirmed, and procured to be confirmed by Pope Innocent III the freedom of elections, which is considered most important and necessary to the English Church, which Charter We will both keep Ourself and will it to be kept with good faith by Our heirs forever. We have also granted to all the free men of Our kingdom, for Us and Our heirs forever, all the liberties underwritten, to have and to hold to them and their heirs of Us and Our heirs.

2.   If any of Our earls, barons, or others who hold of Us in chief by knight's service shall die, and at the time of his death his heir shall be of full age and owe a relief [a form of tax], he shall have his inheritance by ancient

Magna Carta, trans. A. E. Dick Howard (Charlottesville: The University Press of Virginia, 1964). Reprinted with permission of the University Press of Virginia.

relief; to wit, the heir or heirs of an earl of an entire earl's barony, £100; the heir or heirs of a baron of an entire barony, £100; the heir or heirs of a knight of an entire knight's fee, 100s. at the most; and he that owes less shall give less, according to the ancient custom of fees.

3. If, however, any such heir shall be under age and in ward, he shall, when he comes of age, have his inheritance without relief or fine.

4. The guardian of the land of any heir thus under age shall take therefrom only reasonable issues, customs, and services, without destruction or waste of men or property; and if We shall have committed the wardship of any such land to the sheriff or any other person answerable to Us for the issues thereof, and he commit destruction or waste, We will take an amends from him, and the land shall be committed to two lawful and discreet men of that fee, who shall be answerable for the issues to Us or to whomsoever We shall have assigned them. And if We shall give or sell the wardship of any such land to anyone, and he commit destruction or waste upon it, he shall lose the wardship, which shall be committed to two lawful and discreet men of that fee, who shall, in like manner, be answerable unto Us as has been aforesaid.

5. The guardian, so long as he shall have the custody of the land, shall keep up and maintain the houses, parks, fishponds, pools, mills, and other things pertaining thereto, out of the issues of the same, and shall restore the whole to the heir when he comes of age, stocked with ploughs and tillage, according as the season may require and the issues of the land can reasonably bear.

6. Heirs shall be married without loss of station, and the marriage shall be made known to the heir's nearest of kin before it be contracted.

7. A widow, after the death of her husband, shall immediately and without difficulty have her marriage portion and inheritance. She shall not give anything for her marriage portion, dower, or inheritance which she and her husband held on the day of his death, and she may remain in her husband's house for forty days after his death, within which time her dower shall be assigned to her.

8. No widow shall be compelled to marry so long as she has a mind to live without a husband, provided, however, that she give security that she will not marry without Our assent, if she holds of Us, or that of the lord of whom she holds, if she holds of another.

9. Neither We nor Our bailiffs shall seize any land or rent for any debt so long as the debtor's chattels are sufficient to discharge the same; nor shall the debtor's sureties be distrained so long as the debtor is able to pay the debt. If the debtor fails to pay, not having the means to pay, then the sureties shall answer the debt, and, if they desire, they shall hold the debtor's lands and rents until they have received satisfaction of the debt which they have paid for him, unless the debtor can show that he has discharged his obligation to them.

10. If anyone who has borrowed from the Jews any sum of money, great or small, dies before the debt has been paid, the heir shall pay no interest on the debt so long as he remains under age, of whomsoever he may

hold. If the debt shall fall into Our hands, We will take only the principal sum named in the bond.

• • •

12. No scutage [a payment in place of a personal service—*Ed.*] or aid shall be imposed in Our kingdom unless by common counsel thereof, except to ransom Our person, make Our eldest son a knight, and once to marry Our eldest daughter, and for these only a reasonable aid shall be levied. So shall it be with regard to aids from the City of London.

13. The City of London shall have all her ancient liberties and free customs, both by land and water. Moreover, We will and grant that all other cities, boroughs, towns, and ports shall have all their liberties and free customs.

14. For obtaining the common counsel of the kingdom concerning the assessment of aids (other than in the three cases aforesaid) or of scutage, We will cause to be summoned, severally by Our letters, the archbishops, bishops, abbots, earls, and great barons. We will also cause to be summoned, generally, by Our sheriffs and bailiffs, all those who hold lands directly to Us, to meet on a fixed day, but with at least forty days' notice, and at a fixed place. In all letters of such summons We will explain the cause thereof. The summons being thus made, the business shall proceed on the day appointed, according to the advice of those who shall be present, even though not all the persons summoned have come.

15. We will not in the future grant permission to any man to levy an aid upon his free men, except to ransom his person, make his eldest son a knight, and once to marry his eldest daughter, and on each of these occasions only a reasonable aid shall be levied.

16. No man shall be compelled to perform more service for a knight's fee or other free tenement than is due therefrom.

17. Common Pleas shall not follow Our Court, but shall be held in some certain place.

• • •

20. A free man shall be amerced [fined] for a small fault only according to the measure thereof, and for a great crime according to its magnitude, saving his position; and in like manner a merchant saving his trade, and a villein [serf] saving his tillage, if they should fall under Our mercy. None of these amercements shall be imposed except by the oath of honest men of the neighborhood.

21. Earls and barons shall be amerced only by their peers, and only in proportion to the measure of the offense.

22. No amercement shall be imposed upon a clerk's [clergyman's] lay property, except after the manner of the other persons aforesaid, and without regard to the value of his ecclesiastical benefice.

• • •

28.　No constable or other of Our bailiffs shall take corn or other chattels of any man without immediate payment, unless the seller voluntarily consents to postponement of payment.

29.　No constable shall compel any knight to give money in lieu of castle-guard when the knight is willing to perform it in person or (if reasonable cause prevents him from performing it himself) by some other fit man. Further, if We lead or send him into military service, he shall be quit of castle-guard for the time he shall remain in service by Our command.

30.　No sheriff or other of Our bailiffs, or any other man, shall take the horses or carts of any free man for carriage without the owner's consent.

•••

31.　Neither We nor Our bailiffs will take another man's wood for Our castles or for any other purpose without the owner's consent.

•••

35.　There shall be one measure of wine throughout Our kingdom, and one of ale, and one measure of corn, to wit, the London quarter, and one breadth of dyed cloth, russets, and haberjets, to wit, two ells within the selvages. As with measures so shall it also be with weights.

•••

38.　In the future no bailiff shall upon his own unsupported accusation put any man to trial without producing credible witnesses to the truth of the accusation.

39.　No free man shall be taken, imprisoned, disseised [dispossessed], outlawed, banished, or in any way destroyed, nor will We proceed against him or prosecute him, except by the lawful judgment of his peers and by the law of the land.

40.　To no one will We sell, to none will We deny or delay, right or justice.

41.　All merchants shall have safe conduct to go and come out of and into England, and to stay in and travel through England by land and water for purposes of buying and selling, free of illegal tolls, in accordance with ancient and just customs, except, in time of war, such merchants as are of a country at war with Us. If any such be found in Our dominion at the outbreak of war, they shall be attached, without injury to their persons or goods, until it be known to Us or Our Chief Justiciary how our merchants are being treated in the country at war with Us, and if Our merchants be safe there, then theirs shall be safe with Us.

42.　In the future it shall be lawful (except for a short period in time of war, for the common benefit of the realm) for anyone to leave and return to our kingdom safely and securely by land and water, saving his fealty to Us. Excepted are those who have been imprisoned or outlawed according to the law of the land, people of the country at war with Us, and merchants, who shall be dealt with as aforesaid.

• • •

52.   If anyone has been disseised or deprived by Us, without the legal judgment of his peers, of lands, castles, liberties, or rights, We will immediately restore the same, and if any dispute shall arise thereupon, the matter shall be decided by judgment of the twenty-five barons mentioned below in the clause for securing the peace. With regard to all those things, however, of which any man was disseised or deprived, without the legal judgment of his peers, by King Henry Our Father or Our Brother King Richard, and which remain in Our hands or are held by others under Our warranty, We shall have respite during the term commonly allowed to the Crusaders, except as to those matters on which a plea had arisen, or an inquisition had been taken by Our command, prior to Our taking the Cross. Immediately after Our return from Our pilgrimmage, or if by chance We should remain behind from it, We will at once do full justice.

• • •

54.   No one shall be arrested or imprisoned upon a woman's appeal for the death of any person other than her husband.

55.   All fines unjustly and unlawfully given to Us, and all amercements levied unjustly and against the law of the land, shall be entirely remitted or the matter settled by judgment of the twenty-five barons of whom mention is made below in the clause for securing the peace, or the majority of them, together with the aforesaid Stephen, Archbishop of Canterbury, if he himself can be present, and any others whom he may wish to bring with him for the purpose; if he cannot be present, the business shall nevertheless proceed without him. If any one or more of the said twenty-five barons be interested in a suit of this kind, he or they shall be set aside, as to this particular judgment, and another or others, elected and sworn by the rest of said barons for this occasion only, be substituted in his or their stead.

• • •

60.   All the customs and liberties aforesaid, which We have granted to be enjoyed, as far as in Us lies, by Our people throughout Our kingdom, let all Our subjects, whether clerks or laymen, observe, as far as in them lies, toward their dependents.

61.   Whereas We, for the honor of God and the amendment of Our realm, and in order the better to allay the discord arisen between Us and Our barons, have granted all these things aforesaid, We, willing that they be forever enjoyed wholly and in lasting strength, do give and grant to Our subjects the following security, to wit, that the barons shall elect any twenty-five barons of the kingdom at will, who shall, with their utmost power, keep,

hold, and cause to be kept the peace and liberties which We have granted unto them and by this Our present Charter have confirmed, so that if We, Our Justiciary, bailiffs, or any of Our ministers offend in any respect against any man, or shall transgress any of these articles of peace or security, and the offense be brought before four of the said twenty-five barons, these four barons shall come before Us, or Our Chief Justiciary if We are out of the kingdom, declaring the offense, and shall demand speedy amends for the same. If We, or, in case of Our being out of the kingdom, Our Chief Justiciary fail to afford redress within the space of forty days from the time the case was brought before Us or, in the event of Our having been out of the kingdom, Our Chief Justiciary, the aforesaid four barons shall refer the matter to the rest of the twenty-five barons, who, together with the commonalty of the whole country, shall distrain and distress Us to the utmost of their power, to wit, by capture of Our castles, lands, and possessions and by all other possible means, until compensation be made according to their decision, saving Our person and that of Our Queen and children; as soon as redress has been had, they shall return to their former allegiance. Anyone in the kingdom may take oath that, for the accomplishment of all the aforesaid matters, he will obey the orders of the said twenty-five barons and distress Us to the utmost of his power; and We give public and free leave to everyone wishing to take such oath to do so, and to none will we deny the same. Moreover, all such of Our subjects who shall not of their own free will and accord agree to swear to the said twenty-five barons, to distrain and distress Us together with them, We will compel to do so by Our command in the manner aforesaid. If any one of the twenty-five barons shall die or leave the country or be in any way hindered from executing the said office, the rest of the said twenty-five barons shall choose another in his stead, at their discretion, who shall be sworn in like manner as the others. In all cases which are referred to the said twenty-five barons to execute, and in which a difference shall arise among them, supposing them all to be present, or in which not all who have been summoned are willing or able to appear, the verdict of the majority shall be considered as firm and binding as if the whole number should have been of one mind. The aforesaid twenty-five shall swear to keep faithfully all the aforesaid articles, and, to the best of their power, to cause them to be kept by others. We will not procure, either by Ourself or any other, anything from any man whereby any of these concessions or liberties may be revoked or abated. If any such procurement be made, let it be null and void; it shall never be made use of either by Us or by any other.

62. We have also wholly remitted and pardoned all ill-will, wrath, and malice which has arisen between Us and Our subjects, both clergy and laymen, during the disputes, to and with all men. Morover, We have fully remitted and, as far as in Us lies, wholly pardoned to and with all, clergy and laymen, all trespasses made in consequence of the said disputes from Easter in the sixteenth year of Our reign till the restoration of peace. Over and

above this, We have caused to be made in their behalf letters patent by testimony of Stephen, Archbishop of Canterbury, Henry, Archbishop of Dublin, the Bishops above-mentioned, and Master Pandulph, for the security and concessions aforesaid.

63. Wherefore We will, and firmly charge, that the English Church shall be free, and that all men in Our kingdom shall have and hold all the aforesaid liberties, rights, and concessions, well and peaceably, freely, quietly, fully, and wholly, to them and their heirs, of Us and Our heirs, in all things and places forever, as is aforesaid. It is moreover sworn, as well on Our part as on the part of the barons, that all these matters aforesaid shall be kept in good faith and without deceit. Witness the above-named and many others. Given by Our hand in the meadow which is called Runnymede, between Windsor and Staines, on the fifteenth day of June in the seventeenth year of Our reign.

St. Thomas Aquinas

St. Thomas Aquinas (1225–1274), was one of the greatest synthesizers in European thought. The task he undertook was to reconcile the philosophy of Aristotle, rediscovered by European scholars through their contacts with the Muslims in Spain and elsewhere, with Christian theology. During a relatively short lifetime, he succeeded in combining these two disparate elements into a single system capable in principle of explaining everything in the universe that people could know. Questions have been raised about the logical consistency of the Thomistic synthesis, but, whether successful or not, it still stands as a substantial intellectual achievement.

Beyond their general historical importance, the writings of Thomas have a special significance in the history of Catholicism. Although Thomas was opposed during his lifetime by various religious leaders because of his heavy reliance on the pagan Aristotle, and although his writings were even condemned at several theological centers in the years immediately after his death, within a century his system was generally accepted as the basis for orthodox Roman Catholic philosophy. The authoritativeness of Thomistic doctrine was formally recognized by the church in 1879 in the encyclical *Aeterni Patris* of Pope Leo XIII, which ordered all Catholic schools to teach Thomas's position as the true philosophy. Leo's order was reiterated in 1923 by Pius X, who wrote, "The following canon of the church's code should be held as a sacred command: In the study of rational philosophy and theology and in the instruction of students the professor should follow entirely the method, doctrine and principles of the Angelic Doctor [Thomas], and hold them religiously."

Of noble Italian lineage, Thomas decided early in life to become a Dominican monk, much to the displeasure of his family. As a student, he was nicknamed "the dumb ox" because of his quietness and ponderous bulk. Later, as a teacher at the University of Paris, he was so popular that it was difficult to find a hall large enough to accommodate the students who flocked to his lectures.

The selection that follows illustrates Thomas's attempt to establish the consonance between the philosophers' quest for truth based on reason and the Christians' acceptance of divine truth based on revelation. It is clear from the nature of his argument that, however much we should rely on reason, in the final analysis revelation is the arbiter of truth.

1. What aspects of Classical Mediterranean philosophy has Thomas adopted?

2. According to Thomas, what is the relationship between faith and reason?

Summa Contra Gentiles

Chapter III

IN WHAT WAY IT IS POSSIBLE TO MAKE KNOWN THE DIVINE TRUTH

Since, however, not every truth is to be made known in the same way, and it is the part of an educated man to seek for conviction in each subject, only so far as the nature of the subject allows, as the Philosopher[1] most rightly observes as quoted by Boethius, it is necessary to show first of all in what way it is possible to make known the aforesaid truth.

Now in those things which we hold about God there is truth in two ways. For certain things that are true about God wholly surpass the capability of human reason, for instance that God is three and one: while there are certain things to which even natural reason can attain, for instance that God is, that God is one, and others like these, which even the philosophers proved demonstratively of God, being guided by the light of natural reason.

That certain divine truths wholly surpass the capability of human reason, is most clearly evident. For since the principle of all the knowledge which the reason acquires about a thing, is the understanding of that thing's essence, because according to the Philosopher's teaching the principle of a demonstration is *what a thing is*, it follows that our knowledge about a thing will be in proportion to our understanding of its essence. Wherefore, if the human intellect comprehends the essence of a particular thing, for instance a stone or a triangle, no truth about that thing will surpass the capability of human reason. But this does not happen to us in relation to God, because the human intellect is incapable by its natural power of attaining to the comprehension of His essence: since our intellect's knowledge, according to the mode of the present life, originates from the senses: so that things which are not objects of sense cannot be comprehended by the human intellect, except in so far as knowledge of them is gathered from sensibles. Now sensibles cannot lead our intellect to see in them what God is, because they are effects unequal to the power of their cause. And yet our intellect is led by

---

[1][Aristotle—*Ed.*]

The "Summa Contra Gentiles" of St. Thomas Aquinas, trans. Fathers of the English Dominican Province (New York: Benziger Brothers, Inc., 1924). Courtesy of Benziger Publishing Co.

sensibles to the divine knowledge so as to know about God that He is, and other such truths, which need to be ascribed to the first principle. Accordingly some divine truths are attainable by human reason, while others altogether surpass the power of human reason.

Again. The same is easy to see from the degrees of intellects. For if one of two men perceives a thing with his intellect with greater subtlety, the one whose intellect is of a higher degree understands many things which the other is altogether unable to grasp; as instanced in a yokel who is utterly incapable of grasping the subtleties of philosophy. Now the angelic intellect surpasses the human intellect more than the intellect of the cleverest philosopher surpasses that of the most uncultured. For an angel knows God through a more excellent effect than does man, for as much as the angel's essence, through which he is led to know God by natural knowledge, is more excellent than sensible things, even than the soul itself, by which the human intellect mounts to the knowledge of God. And the divine intellect surpasses the angelic intellect much more than the angelic surpasses the human. For the divine intellect by its capacity equals the divine essence, wherefore God perfectly understands of Himself what He is, and He knows all the things that can be understood about Him: whereas the angel knows not what God is by his natural knowledge, because the angel's essence, by which he is led to the knowledge of God, is an effect unequal to the power of its cause. Consequently an angel is unable by his natural knowledge to grasp all that God understands about Himself: nor again is human reason capable of grasping all that an angel understands by his natural power. Accordingly just as a man would show himself to be a most insane fool if he declared the assertions of a philosopher to be false because he was unable to understand them, so, and much more, a man would be exceedingly foolish, were he to suspect of falsehood the things revealed by God through the ministry of His angels, because they cannot be the object of reason's investigations.

Furthermore. The same is made abundantly clear by the deficiency which every day we experience in our knowledge of things. For we are ignorant of many of the properties of sensible things, and in many cases we are unable to discover the nature of those properties which we perceive by our senses. Much less therefore is human reason capable of investigating all the truths about the most sublime existence.

With this the saying of the Philosopher is in accord where he says that *our intellect in relation to those primary things which are most evident in nature is like the eye of a bat in relation to the sun.*

To this truth Holy Writ also bears witness. For it is written (Job xi. 7): *Peradventure thou wilt comprehend the steps of God and wilt find out the Almighty perfectly?* and (xxxvi. 26) *Behold God is great, exceeding our knowledge,* and (I Cor. xiii. 9): *We know in part.*

Therefore all that is said about God, though it cannot be investigated by reason, must not be forthwith rejected as false, as the Manicheans and many unbelievers have thought.

Chapter IV

THAT THE TRUTH ABOUT DIVINE THINGS WHICH IS ATTAINABLE BY REASON IS FITTINGLY PROPOSED TO MAN AS AN OBJECT OF BELIEF

While then the truth of the intelligible things of God is twofold, one to which the inquiry of reason can attain, the other which surpasses the whole range of human reason, both are fittingly proposed by God to man as an object of belief. We must first show this with regard to that truth which is attainable by the inquiry of reason, lest it appears to some, that since it can be attained by reason, it was useless to make it an object of faith by supernatural inspiration. Now three disadvantages would result if this truth were left solely to the inquiry of reason. One is that few men would have knowledge of God: because very many are hindered from gathering the fruit of diligent inquiry, which is the discovery of truth, for three reasons. Some indeed on account of an indisposition of temperament, by reason of which many are naturally indisposed to knowledge: so that no efforts of theirs would enable them to reach to the attainment of the highest degree of human knowledge, which consists in knowing God. Some are hindered by the needs of household affairs. For there must needs be among men some that devote themselves to the conduct of temporal affairs, who would be unable to devote so much time to the leisure of contemplative research as to reach the summit of human inquiry, namely the knowledge of God. And some are hindered by laziness. For in order to acquire the knowledge of God in those things which reason is able to investigate, it is necessary to have a previous knowledge of many things: since almost the entire consideration of philosophy is directed to the knowledge of God: for which reason metaphysics, which is about divine things, is the last of the parts of philosophy to be studied. Wherefore it is not possible to arrive at the inquiry about the aforesaid truth except after a most laborious study: and few are willing to take upon themselves this labour for the love of a knowledge, the natural desire for which has nevertheless been instilled into the mind of man by God.

The second disadvantage is that those who would arrive at the discovery of the aforesaid truth would scarcely succeed in doing so after a long time. First, because this truth is so profound, that it is only after long practice that the human intellect is enabled to grasp it by means of reason. Secondly, because many things are required beforehand, as stated above. Thirdly, because at the time of youth, the mind, when tossed about by the various movements of the passions, is not fit for the knowledge of so sublime a truth, whereas *calm gives prudence and knowledge*, as stated in 7 *Phys.* Hence mankind would remain in the deepest darkness of ignorance, if the path of reason were the only available way to the knowledge of God: because the knowledge of God which especially makes men perfect and good, would be acquired only by the few, and by these only after a long time.

The third disadvantage is that much falsehood is mingled with the investigations of human reason, on account of the weakness of our intellect in forming its judgments, and by reason of the admixture of phantasms. Consequently many would remain in doubt about those things even which are most truly demonstrated, through ignoring the force of the demonstration: especially when they perceive that different things are taught by the various men who are called wise. Moreover among the many demonstrated truths, there is sometimes a mixture of falsehood that is not demonstrated, but assumed for some probable or sophistical reason which at times is mistaken for a demonstration. Therefore it was necessary that definite certainty and pure truth about divine things should be offered to man by the way of faith.

Accordingly the divine clemency has made this salutary commandment, that even some things which reason is able to investigate must be held by faith: so that all may share in the knowledge of God easily, and without doubt or error.

Hence it is written (Eph. iv. 17, 18): That *henceforth you walk not as also the Gentiles walk in the vanity of their mind, having their understanding darkened*; and (Isa. liv. 13): *All thy children shall be taught of the Lord*.

Chapter V

THAT THOSE THINGS WHICH CANNOT BE INVESTIGATED BY REASON ARE FITTINGLY PROPOSED TO MAN AS AN OBJECT OF FAITH

It may appear to some that those things which cannot be investigated by reason ought not to be proposed to man as an object of faith: because divine wisdom provides for each thing according to the mode of its nature. We must therefore prove that it is necessary also for those things which surpass reason to be proposed by God to man as an object of faith.

For no man tends to do a thing by his desire and endeavour unless it be previously known to him. Wherefore since man is directed by divine providence to a higher good than human frailty can attain in the present life, as we shall show in the sequel, it was necessary for his mind to be bidden to something higher than those things to which our reason can reach in the present life, so that he might learn to aspire, and by his endeavors to tend to something surpassing the whole state of the present life. And this is especially competent to the Christian religion, which alone promises goods spiritual and eternal: for which reason it proposes many things surpassing the thought of man: whereas the old law which contained promises of temporal things, proposed few things that are above human inquiry. It was with this motive that the philosophers, in order to wean men from sensible pleasures to virtue, took care to show that there are other goods of greater account than those which appeal to the senses, the taste of which things affords much greater delight to those who devote themselves to active or contemplative virtues.

Again it is necessary for this truth to be proposed to man as an object of faith in order that he may have truer knowledge of God. For then alone do we know God truly, when we believe that He is far above all that man can possibly think of God, because the divine essence surpasses man's natural knowledge, as stated above. Hence by the fact that certain things about God are proposed to man, which surpass his reason, he is strengthened in his opinion that God is far above what he is able to think.

There results also another advantage from this, namely, the checking of presumption which is the mother of error. For some there are who presume so far on their wits that they think themselves capable of measuring the whole nature of things by their intellect, in that they esteem all things true which they see, and false which they see not. Accordingly, in order that man's mind might be freed from this presumption, and seek the truth humbly, it was necessary that certain things far surpassing his intellect should be proposed to man by God.

Yet another advantage is made apparent by the words of the Philosopher (10 *Ethic*). For when a certain Simonides maintained that man should neglect the knowledge of God, and apply his mind to human affairs, and declared that *a man ought to relish human things, and a mortal, mortal things*: the Philosopher contradicted him, saying that *a man ought to devote himself to immortal and divine things as much as he can*. Hence he says (11 *De Anima.*) that though it is but little that we perceive of higher substances, yet that little is more loved and desired than all the knowledge we have of lower substances. He says also (2 *De Coelo et Mundo*) that when questions about the heavenly bodies can be answered by a short and probable solution, it happens that the hearer is very much rejoiced. All this shows that however imperfect the knowledge of the highest things may be, it bestows very great perfection on the soul: and consequently, although human reason is unable to grasp fully things that are above reason, it nevertheless acquires much perfection, if at least it hold things, in any way whatever, by faith.

Wherefore it is written (Eccles, iii. 25): *Many things are shown to thee above the understanding of men*, and (I Cor. ii. 10, 11): *The things . . . that are of God no man knoweth, but the Spirit of God: but to us God hath revealed them by His Spirit.*

Chapter VI

THAT IT IS NOT A MARK OF LEVITY TO ASSENT TO THE THINGS THAT ARE OF FAITH, ALTHOUGH THEY ARE ABOVE REASON

Now those who believe this truth, *of which reason affords a proof*, believe not lightly, as though *following foolish fables* (2 Pet. i. 16). For divine Wisdom Himself, Who knows all things most fully, designed to reveal to man *the secrets of God's wisdom*: and by suitable arguments proves His presence, and the truth of His doctrine and inspiration, by performing works surpassing the capability of the whole of nature, namely, the wondrous healing of the sick, the raising of the dead to life, a marvellous control over the heavenly bodies, and what excites yet more wonder, the inspiration of human minds, so that unlettered and simple persons are filled with the Holy Ghost, and in one instant are endowed with the most sublime wisdom and eloquence. And after considering these arguments, convinced by the strength of the proof, and not by the force of arms, nor by the promise of delights, but—and this is the greatest marvel of all—amidst the tyranny of persecutions, a countless crowd of not only simple but also of the wisest men, embraced the Christian faith, which inculcates things surpassing all human understanding, curbs the pleasures of the flesh, and teaches contempt of all worldly things. That the minds of mortal beings should assent to such things, is both the greatest of miracles, and the evident work of divine inspiration, seeing that they despise visible things and desire only those that are invisible. And that this happened not suddenly nor by chance, but by the disposition of God, is shown by the fact that God foretold that He would do so by the manifold oracles of the prophets, whose books we hold in veneration as bearing witness to our faith. This particular kind of proof is alluded to in the words of Heb. ii, 3, 4: *Which*, namely the salvation of mankind, *having begun to be declared by the Lord, was confirmed with us by them that heard Him, God also bearing witness by signs and wonders, and divers . . . distributions of the Holy Ghost.*

Now such a wondrous conversion of the world to the Christian faith is a most indubitable proof that such signs did take place, so that there is no need to repeat them, seeing that there is evidence of them in their result. For it would be the most wondrous signs of all if without any wondrous signs the world were persuaded by simple and lowly men to believe things so arduous, to accomplish things so difficult, and to hope for things so sublime. Although God ceases not even in our time to work miracles through His saints in confirmation of the faith.

On the other hand those who introduced the errors of the sects proceeded in contrary fashion, as instanced by Mohammed, who enticed people with the promise of carnal pleasures, to the desire of which the concupiscence of the flesh instigates. He also delivered commandments in keeping with his promises, by giving the reins to carnal pleasure, wherein it is easy for carnal men to obey: and the lessons of truth which he inculcated were only such as can be easily known to any man of average wisdom by his natural powers: yea, rather the truths which he taught were mingled by him with many fables and most false doctrines. Nor did he add any signs of supernatural agency, which alone are a fitting witness to divine inspiration, since a visible work that can be from God alone, proves the teacher of truth to be invisibly inspired: but he asserted that he was sent in the power of arms, a sign that is not lacking even to robbers and tyrants. Again, those who believed in him from the outset were not wise men practised in things divine and human, but beastlike men who dwelt in the wilds, utterly ignorant of all divine teaching; and it was by a multitude of such men and the force of arms that he impelled others to submit to his law.

Lastly, no divine oracles or prophets in a previous age bore witness to him; rather he did corrupt almost all the teaching of the Old and New Testaments by a narrative replete with fables, as one may see by a perusal of his law. Hence by a cunning device, he did not commit the reading of the Old and New Testament Books to his followers, lest he should thereby be convicted of falsehood. Thus it is evident that those who believe his words believe lightly.

Chapter VII

THAT THE TRUTH OF REASON IS NOT IN OPPOSITION TO THE TRUTH OF THE CHRISTIAN FAITH

Now though the aforesaid truth of the Christian faith surpasses the ability of human reason, nevertheless those things which are naturally instilled in human reason cannot be opposed to this truth. For it is clear that those things which are implanted in reason by nature, are most true, so much so that it is impossible to think them to be false. Nor is it lawful to deem false that which is held by faith, since it is so evidently confirmed by God. Seeing then that the false alone is opposed to the true, as evidently appears if we examine their definitions, it is impossible for the aforesaid truth of faith to be contrary to those principles which reason knows naturally.

Again. The same thing which the disciple's mind receives from its teacher is contained in the knowledge of the teacher, unless he teach insincerely, which it were wicked to say of God. Now the knowledge of naturally known principles is instilled into us by God, since God Himself is the author of our nature. Therefore the divine Wisdom also contains these principles. Consequently whatever is contrary to these principles, is contrary to the divine Wisdom; wherefore it cannot be from God. Therefore those things which are received by faith from divine revelation cannot be contrary to our natural knowledge.

Moreover. Our intellect is stayed by contrary arguments, so that it cannot advance to the knowledge of truth. Wherefore if conflicting knowledges were instilled into us by God, our intellect would thereby be hindered from knowing the truth. And this cannot be ascribed to God.

Furthermore. Things that are natural are unchangeable so long as nature remains. Now contrary opinions alone cannot be together in the same subject. Therefore God does not instill into man any opinion or belief contrary to natural knowledge.

Hence the Apostle says (Rom. x. 8): *Thy word is nigh thee even in thy heart and in thy mouth. This is the word of faith which we preach.* Yet because it surpasses reason some look upon it as though it were contrary thereto; which is impossible.

This is confirmed also by the authority of Augustine who says *That which truth shall make known can nowise be in opposition to the holy books whether of the Old or of the New Testament.*

From this we may evidently conclude that whatever arguments are alleged against the teachings of faith, they do not rightly proceed from the first self-evident principles instilled by nature. Wherefore they lack the force of demonstration, and are either probable or sophistical arguments, and consequently it is possible to solve them.

Ssu-ma Kwang

Ancestor worship has formed a part of the religious traditions of many societies but none more so than that of China, where it has persisted from earliest times down to the twentieth century. From written records that survive from the Shang dynasty of the second millennium B.C. it would seem that the practice was at first confined to the nobility, perhaps because this class was the only one that possessed ancestors worthy of note. But the practice gradually spread so that later people at all levels of society engaged in it. It was "officially" sanctioned in the fifth century B.C. by Confucius who, in his treatise *The Doctrine of the Mean*, said:

> To gather in the same places where our fathers before us have gathered; to perform the same ceremonies which they before us have performed; to play the same music which they before us have played; to pay respect to those whom they have honored; to love those who were dear to them—in fact, to serve those now dead as if they were living, and now departed as if they were still with us; this is the highest achievement of true filial piety.

Ancestor worship is actually an aspect of a larger, and very important feature of Chinese society—the family. For the Chinese, the family has always been the center of life and family ties much stronger than in most other societies. Also, the family is a larger entity than elsewhere, for included in it, as an integral part of it, are departed ancestors. L]iving families have regularly sought the advice of ancestors before undertaking new enterprises, as well as approval for their conduct. When family finances permitted, special shrines were built where elaborate ceremonials were conducted and offerings made to the ancestors.

Early in Chinese history rules governing the ritual to be followed in ceremonies honoring ancestors were developed. With the passage of time and changes in society these ritualistic rules also changed. By the Sung dynasty (960–1279) the standard ritual was fully elaborated. It is laid out in detail in the following selection from the works of Ssu-ma Kwang (1019–1056) who was a distinguished historian and statesman, as well as the author of guides prescribing the proper procedures to be followed on a variety of social and ceremonial occasions.

1.   What does the elaborate ceremony surrounding ancestor worship tell us about Sung culture and its values?

2.   What effect do you think repeated participation in such a ritual might have had on a Chinese child?

Ancestral Rites

All ancestor worship should be conducted in the second month of a season [the first month being reserved for imperial ceremonies].

First, the master of the household, his younger brothers, sons, and grandsons, dressed in their formal attire, attend to the divination of an auspicious day for the ceremony. This is done outside of the Image Hall. The master of the household stands facing west, and all the others file behind him in one line, ordered according to their ranks in the family, from north to south. A table is set in front of the master on which are placed incense burners, incense boxes, and milfoil stalks. The master inserts his official tablet in his girdle, lights the incense, and addresses the diviner as follows:

"I would like to present a yearly offering to my ancestors on such-and-such a day. Please determine whether it is an auspicious day."

Then he steps back and hands the milfoil stalks to the diviner, who then performs the divination, facing west. If the proposed date turns out to be inauspicious, then the master of the household names another. When finally an auspicious day is found, all present enter the Image Hall. The master now stands facing north, with his sons and grandsons in file behind him as before, except that now they are ordered according to their ranks from west to east.

The master inserts the official tablet in his girdle, advances to light the incense, then returns to his former position. The deliverer of prayers now comes out from the left of the master, turns to face east, inserts his official tablet in his girdle, takes out the written prayer from his breast pocket, and kneels down to read: "Your filial grandson, officially entitled such-and-such, will on such-and-such a day offer the yearly sacrifice to his departed grandparents. This is to report to you that the date has been found auspicious and that the offering will be made." He then puts the prayer sheet away in his pocket, takes out his official tablet, and rises. After he has returned to his former position, the master of the household bows to the memorial tablets of the ancestors, and everyone exits.

Three days before the date set for the ceremony, the master of the household leads all the male members of the family (above ten years of age)

Trans. Clara Yu.
Reprinted with the permission of The Free Press, a Division of Macmillan, Inc. from *Chinese Civilization and Society: A Sourcebook* by Patricia Buckley Ebrey. Copyright © 1981 by The Free Press.

to the outer quarters of the house to observe abstinence, while the women do so in the inner quarters. Thus, although there is wine-drinking, there is no disorder. Meat-eating is allowed, but strong-smelling foods such as onion, leek, and garlic are prohibited. During this period the family members do not attend funerals, nor do they listen to music. All inauspicious and unclean matters are avoided, so that everyone can concentrate on the memory of the departed ancestors.

On the day before the ceremony, the master organizes all the male members of the family and the assistants to dust and sweep the place where the sacrifice will be held, to wash and clean the utensils and containers, and to arrange the furniture. The places for the departed ancestors are so arranged that each husband and wife are side by side, arranged according to proper ranking from west to east, and all facing south. The mistress of the house supervises the women of the household in cleaning the cooking utensils and preparing the food, which should include five kinds of vegetables and five kinds of fruits and not more than fifteen dishes of the following sorts: red stew, roast meat, fried meat, ribs, boiled white meat, dried meat, ground meat, special meats other than pork or lamb, foods made of flour. (If the family is poor, or if certain items cannot be obtained at a particular location or time, then merely include several items from each category, that is, vegetable, fruit, meat, flour-foods, and rice-foods.)

The assistants prepare a basin with a stand for washing hands and set it on the southeastern side of the eastern steps. To the north of the stand is set a rack of towels for drying hands. (These are for the relatives.) Then, on the east side of the eastern steps another basin and some towels are set; these, however, are without a stand or a rack. (These are for the assistants.)

On the day of the ceremony, all members of the family rise early and put on formal attire. The master and the mistress lead the assistants to the hall for the ceremony. In front of every seat, on the south side of the table, the assistants place vegetables and fruits, and on the north side, wine cups, spoons, chopsticks, teacups and saucers, and sauce bowls. Next they put a bottle of water and a bottle of wine on a table above the eastern steps. To its east is placed a table with a decanter, wine cups, knives, and towels on it. An incense table is placed in the center of the hall, with an incense burner and an incense box on it. An ash bowl is set on the east side, and a burner, a water bottle, an incense ash ladle, and a pair of tongs are set on the west side. Water is poured into the washing basins.

In the morning, when the cook reports that all the foods have been prepared, the master and mistress go to the Image Hall together. Two assistants carry the memorial tablets in a bamboo basket, and, with the master taking the lead and the mistress following him, all the members of the family form two rows, the men on the left-hand side and the women on the right-hand side. In this order they proceed to the hall of the ceremony. The basket is then placed at the top of the western steps, to the west of the burner.

The master and mistress now wash their hands and carry the memorial tablets to the seats: those of the male ancestors first, those of the female ones next. Afterwards, the master leads all the men in the family to form one line, from west to east according to their ranks, below the eastern steps, all facing north. The mistress, likewise, leads all the women in the same order, from east to west, below the western steps, also facing north. The assistants to the ceremony form another line, from west to east, behind the men. When all have taken their proper positions, they bow together to greet the spirits of the ancestors.

The master then ascends the eastern steps and goes to the south of the incense table. He puts his official tablet in his girdle and lights the incense. Then he bows and returns to his former position. The deliverer of prayers and the assistants to the ceremony now wash and dry their hands. One assistant ascends the steps, opens the wine bottle, wipes the mouth of the bottle, and pours the wine into the decanter. Then he takes the wine cup, fills it with wine from the decanter, and makes a libation toward the west.

The cook and servants have by now put the foods for offering on a table placed on the east side of the washing basin and towel rack. The men now wash their hands. Then, following the example of the master, they put down their official tablets and hold up bowls of meat—the master ascends from the eastern steps, all the others from the western steps—and place them in front of the memorial tablets of the ancestors, to the north of the vege-tables and fruits. Afterwards, they take up their official tablets and return to their former positions. Now the women wash and dry their hands. Led by the mistress, they first carry the foods made of flour, ascend the western steps, and set them down to the north of the meats. Then they carry the foods made of rice, ascend the western steps, and set them down to the north of the foods made of flour. Afterwards they descend and return to their for-mer positions.

The master now ascends the eastern steps, goes to the wine table, and turns to face west. An assistant takes the wine cup of the great-grandfather in his left hand and that of the great-grandmother in his right hand; another assistant, in the same manner, holds the cups of the grandparents and a third holds the cups of the parents. The three assistants now go to the master, who, after putting his official tablet away in his girdle, pours wine into the cups. With these cups in their hands, the assistants walk slowly back to the tables to set them down in their former positions. The master takes out his official tablet again, approaches the seats of his great-grandparents, facing north. One assistant now takes the wine cup of the great-grandfather and stands on the left side of the master; another holds the cup of the great-grandmother and stands on the right side of the master. The master, putting away his offi-cial tablet, kneels and receives the cup of the great-grandfather, offers a libation, and returns the cup to the assistant, who puts it back where it was.

The master then takes out his official tablet, prostrates himself on the floor, then rises and steps back a little.

The deliverer of prayers steps out from the left of the master, turns to face east, puts away his official tablet, takes out the written prayer, kneels down and reads:

> On such-and-such a day, of such-and-such a month, of such-and-such a year, your filial great-grandson, officially titled as such-and-such, presents the soft-haired sacrifice (for lamb; if a pig is offered, then he should say "hard-haired" sacrifice) and good wine in the yearly offering to his great-grandfather, officially titled such-and-such, and great-grandmother (give honorary title here). O that you enjoy the food!

He then rolls up the prayer sheet and puts it back into his pocket. Then he takes out his official tablet and rises. The master bows to the memorial tablets.

Next they proceed with the same ceremony at the seats of the grandparents and those of the parents, except that the prayer is slightly modified, so that for the grandparents it reads: "Your filial grandson presents the yearly offerings . . . ," and for the parents, "Your filial son . . . ", etc.

When this first round of offerings is completed, the deliverer of prayers and the master descend and return to their former positions. Now the second round of offering begins. (This is usually performed by the mistress herself or some close relative.) The offerer washes her hands if she has not done so already, ascends through the western steps, pours the wine and offers libations, just as the master has done. The only difference is that there is no reading of prayers.

When this second round of offerings is completed, the master ascends the eastern steps, takes off his official tablet, holds the decanter, and fills all the wine cups. Then he takes up his official tablet again and steps back to stand on the southeast side of the incense table, facing north. The mistress ascends the western steps, places spoons in the bowls of millet, and straightens the chopsticks. The handles of the spoons should point to the west. She now goes to stand on the southwest side of the incense table and faces north. The master bows twice at the memorial tablets and the mistress bows four times.

One assistant now removes the tea leaves and another ladles soup for the ancestors, both starting from the western end. When this is done they leave, and the deliverer of prayers closes the door for the ancestors to dine in private. The master now should stand on the east side of the closed door, facing west, with all male members of the family in a file behind him; the mistress stands on the west side of the closed door and faces east, with all female members of the family in a file behind her. In this manner all persons wait for the duration of a meal. Then the deliverer of prayers ascends and approaches the door, facing north. He coughs three times to warn the ancestors before opening the door.

The assistants now go to the north of the table with the water, and the master comes in to take his position, facing west. The deliverer of prayers ascends the western steps and approaches the seat of the great-grandfather. He puts his official tablet in his girdle and raises the wine cup, slowly walks to the right of the master, turns to face south, and offers the cup to the master, who, after putting his official tablet away in the girdle, kneels down to receive the cup and to sip the wine.

An assistant then hands a container over to the deliverer of prayers, who uses a spoon to take a few grains of millet from the bowl of each ancestor and puts them in the container. He then carries the container and walks up to the left of the master, turns to face north, and offers the master this blessing: "Your grandfather commands me to confer many blessings on you, the filial grandson, enabling you to receive prosperity from Heaven, your fields to produce abundantly, and you to live a long life."

The master places the wine cup in front of him, takes up his official tablet, prostrates himself on the floor, rises, and bows. Then he puts his official tablet away in his girdle and kneels to receive the millet. He tastes a little of it, then puts the rest in his left sleeve. An assistant is standing on his right side, and the master gives the container of the millet to him. The master then folds the edge of his left sleeve over his fingers, takes up the wine cup, and drinks from it. Another assistant is standing on his right side, to whom the master gives the cup. On the left side of the master another assistant is holding a plate. He now puts the plate on the floor, and the master lets the millet fall from his sleeve into the plate, which is then carried out. The master takes up his official tablet, prostrates himself, rises, and goes to stand at the top of the eastern steps, facing west. After the master receives the blessed millet, the deliverer of prayers holds up his official tablet and steps back to the top of the western steps, facing east. When the master has taken his position at the top of the eastern steps, the deliverer of prayers announces the completion of the ceremony. Then he descends and takes his former position. All present bow to the memorial tablets, except for the master, for he has received the blessing. Afterwards, the master descends and bows with everyone else to bid the ancestors farewell.

The ceremony having been completed, the master and mistress ascend to take down the memorial tablets and put them back into the bamboo basket, the tablets of the female ancestors being taken down first, then those of the male ancestors. Two assistants carry the basket to the Image Hall, followed by everyone in the family in the same manner as when the tablets were brought out.

At this point the mistress returns to supervise the removal of the offerings. The wine that remains in the cups, together with that in the decanter, is poured into a pot and sealed. This is the "blessed wine."

The assistants bring the offered foods back to the kitchen, where they are removed from the special containers into ordinary bowls and plates, and the special containers are carefully washed and put away under the supervision of the mistress. A small portion is taken from each item of the offered foods, and put into food boxes, which are sealed together with some "blessed wine," and dispatched, with a letter, to relatives and friends who are ardent observers of rites and rituals. This activity the master supervises. (The food sample is precious because it is left by the ancestors' spirits; it does not have to be rich in itself.)

The assistants now help set up the feast. The men and women are seated separately: the master and all the other male members of the family in the main hall, the mistress and the other female members of the family in the inner quarters. Tables and chairs are set; fruits, vegetables, sauces, wine cups, spoons, chopsticks, and knives are all placed in their proper places. Then wine is poured into decanters, and the hot foods that were offered to the spirits are warmed up.

First, the master of the household takes his seat, and all the other male members of the family offer their good wishes to him. They should stand according to their ranks in the family, just as during the preceding ceremony, and for both men and women the right side ranks higher than the left side. The eldest among them (either a younger brother of the master or his eldest son) stands a trifle ahead of everyone else. An assistant holds the wine decanter and stands on his right. Another assistant holds the wine cup and stands on his left. This eldest of the males then sticks his official tablet in his girdle, kneels, and takes the decanter in his right hand and the wine cup in his left. He then pours the wine and offers good wishes: "Now that the memorial ceremonies have been completed, our ancestors have been offered good food. We wish that you will receive all the five blessings, protect our lineage, and benefit our family."

The assistant who was holding the decanter then steps back, and the one who was holding the cup presents the wine to the master of the household. The eldest male prostrates himself, rises, and returns to his former position. Then he bows to the master together with all the other males. The master then orders the assistant to bring the decanter and the cup of the eldest male member. He pours wine into the cup himself, declaring, "Now that the offerings to our ancestors are successfully accomplished, we celebrate the good fortune of the five blessings bestowed on us; I hereby share them with all of you."

The assistant then hands the cup to the eldest male who, after putting away his official tablet in his girdle, kneels down to receive the wine. After he drinks the wine, he gives the cup back to the assistant, prostrates himself, then rises. The master then orders the assistant to pour wine for everyone. When this is done, all the males again prostrate themselves, and they are then ordered to be seated by the master.

Meanwhile, in the inner quarters, all the female members of the family salute the mistress and are in turn offered wine by her; the procedure is the same as that for the male members, except that it is all performed from a standing position with no kneeling or prostrating. When the round of drinking is over, the assistants bring in the meats. Afterwards, the women come to the main hall to offer their congratulations to the master, who then offers wine to the eldest female member (either a younger sister of his or the eldest daughter), who receives it without kneeling down. But all other procedures are the same as performed by the males. Then the men come to the inner quarters to offer their good wishes to the mistress, where the procedure is exactly as the one in the main hall.

Next the assistants bring in the foods made of flour, and all the assistants offer their good wishes to the master and mistress, in the same way that the female members saluted the mistress, but they are not offered wine.

Then the foods made of rice are brought in. After this, wine is liberally drunk, and wine games are played, and the offered food consumed. The number of rounds of wine-drinking is decided by the master. When the offered food and wine are used up, other food and wine is brought in. When the feast is over, the leftovers are given to the servants. The master distributes them to the servants of the outer quarters, and the mistress to the servants of the inner quarters, reaching down even to the lowliest in rank, so that the foods are entirely consumed on that day.

Whenever ancestor worship is performed, sincerity in one's love and respect for one's ancestors are what is most significant. Thus, those who are ill should only do as much as they can, but the young and strong should naturally follow the ceremonies closely.

Marco Polo

Early in the thirteenth century a powerful Mongolian chieftain, Genghis Khan, mounted an attack against northern China and its ruling Chin dynasty. This marked the beginning of a long process that led eventually to the occupation of China by the Mongolians, a process that was completed only toward the end of the century when the grandson of Genghis, Kublai Khan, finally broke the resistance of the Sung dynasty, which had dominated southern China, and proclaimed the Yuan dynasty, which then ruled China for the next hundred years.

The center of Chinese civilization in the Yuan period became the city of Cambaluc (now Beijing), where the emperor had his winter palace. To this imperial city came merchants from all parts of the civilized world, to trade goods and merchandise. Among the thousands of traders to arrive about the year 1275 were two brothers from Venice, Maffeo and Nicolo Polo. Accompanying them was Nicolo's son Marco, who was then a teenager. Marco Polo was to remain in China for nearly a quarter of a century. During this time he entered the Chinese bureaucracy, later performing a number of tasks for the emperor that led him to travel extensively throughout China and thus become well acquainted with the land and its people.

The Book of Ser Marco Polo, which is an account of his travels, paints a vivid picture of Chinese civilization in the thirteenth century, a civilization significantly more advanced than that of Europe. The origin of the book is an interesting story. When he finally returned home in 1295, Polo became involved in a war between the Venetians and the Genoese. He was captured in battle and thrown into prison. While incarcerated, he passed the time telling stories of his travels and adventures to his cellmate, who in turn transcribed them. The selection that follows gives a description of the person of Kublai Khan, his palace and court, the city of Cambaluc, and something of the imperial machinery for the rule of China.

---

1. Genghis Khan was the leader of a group of warrior-nomads and despised civilized, urban life. To what extent has his grandson, Kublai Khan, been influenced by the civilization he has conquered?

2. What do we learn about Chinese society during the time of Mongol domination from this document?

The Book of Ser Marco Polo

Book II

I. OF CUBLAY KAAN, THE GREAT KAAN NOW REIGNING, AND OF HIS GREAT PUISSANCE

Now am I come to that part of our Book in which I shall tell you of the great and wonderful magnificence of the Great Kaan now reigning, by name Cublay Kaan; Kaan being a title which signifyeth "The Great Lord of Lords," or Emperor. And of a surety he hath good right to such a title, for all men know for a certain truth that he is the most potent man, as regards forces and lands and treasure, that existeth in the world, or ever hath existed from the time of our first father Adam until this day. All this I will make clear to you for truth, in this book of ours, so that every one shall be fain to acknowledge that he is the greatest Lord that is now in the world, or ever hath been.

•••

VIII. CONCERNING THE PERSON OF THE GREAT KAAN

The personal appearance of the Great Kaan, Lord of Lords, whose name is Cublay, is such as I shall now tell you. He is of a good stature, neither tall nor short, but of a middle height. He has a becoming amount of flesh, and is very shapely in all his limbs. His complexion is white and red, the eyes black and fine, the nose well formed and well set on. He has four wives, whom he retains permanently as his legitimate consorts; and the eldest of his sons by those four wives ought by rights to be emperor;—I mean when the father dies. Those four ladies are called empresses, but each is distinguished also by her proper name. And each of them has a special court of her own, very grand and ample; no one of them having fewer than 300 fair and charming damsels. They have also many pages and eunuchs, and a number of other attendants of both sexes; so that each of these ladies has not less than 10,000 persons attached to her court.

When the Emperor desires the society of one of these four consorts, he will sometimes send for the lady to his apartment and sometimes visit her at her own. He has also a great number of concubines, and I will tell you how he obtains them.

You must know that there is a tribe of Tartars called Ungrat, who are noted for their beauty. Now every year an hundred of the most beautiful maidens of this tribe are sent to the Great Kaan, who commits them to the

Trans. Henry Yule.

charge of certain elderly ladies dwelling in his palace. And these old ladies make the girls sleep with them, in order to ascertain if they have sweet breath and do not snore, and are sound in all their limbs. Then such of them as are of approved beauty, and are good and sound in all respects, are appointed to attend on the Emperor by turns. Thus six of these damsels take their turn for three days and nights, and wait on him when he is in his chamber and when he is in his bed, to serve him in any way, and to be entirely at his orders. At the end of the three days and nights they are relieved by other six. And so throughout the year, there are reliefs of maidens by six and six, changing every three days and nights.

IX. CONCERNING THE GREAT KAAN'S SONS

The Emperor hath, by those four wives of his, twenty-two male children; the eldest of whom was called Chinkin for the love of the good Chinghis Kaan, the first Lord of the Tartars. And this Chinkin, as the eldest son of the Kaan, was to have reigned after his father's death; but, as it came to pass, he died. He left a son behind him, however, whose name is Temur, and he is to be the Great Kaan and Emperor after the death of his grandfather, as is but right; he being the child of the Great Kaan's eldest son. And this Temur is an able and brave man, as he hath already proven on many occasions.

The Great Kaan hath also twenty-five other sons by his concubines; and these are good and valiant soldiers, and each of them is a great chief. I tell you moreover that of his children by his four lawful wives there are seven who are kings of vast realms or provinces, and govern them well; being all able and gallant men, as might by expected. . . .

X. CONCERNING THE PALACE OF THE GREAT KAAN

You must know that for three months of the year, to wit December, January, and February, the Great Kaan resides in the capital city of Cathay [China], which is called Cambaluc [now Beijing], and which is at the northeastern extremity of the country. In that city stands his great palace and now I will tell you what it is like.

It is enclosed all round by a great wall forming a square, each side of which is a mile in length; that is to say, the whole compass thereof is four miles. This you may depend on; it is also very thick, and a good ten paces in height, whitewashed and loop-holed all round. At each angle of the wall there is a very fine and rich palace in which the war-harness of the Emperor is kept, such as bows and quivers, saddles and bridles, and bowstrings, and everything needful for an army. Also midway between every two of these corner palaces there is another of the like; so that taking the whole compass of the enclosure you find eight vast palaces stored with the Great Lord's harness of war. And you must understand that each palace is assigned to only one kind of article; thus one is stored with bows, a second with saddles, a third with bridles, and so on in succession right round.

The great wall has five gates on its southern face, the middle one being the great gate which is never opened on any occasion except when the Great Kaan himself goes forth or enters. Close on either side of this great gate is a smaller one by which all other people pass; and then towards each angle is another great gate, also open to people in general; so that on that side there are five gates in all.

Inside of this wall there is a second, enclosing a space that is somewhat greater in length than in breadth. This enclosure also has eight palaces corresponding to those of the outer wall, and stored like them with the Lord's harness of war. This wall also hath five gates on the southern face, corresponding to those in the outer wall, and hath one gate on each of the other faces, as the outer wall hath also. In the middle of the second enclosure is the Lord's great palace, and I will tell you what it is like.

You must know that it is the greatest palace that ever was. Towards the north it is in contact with the outer wall, while towards the south there is a vacant space which the barons and the soldiers are constantly traversing. The palace itself hath no upper story, but is all on the ground floor, only the basement is raised some ten palms above the surrounding soil and this elevation is retained by a wall of marble raised to the level of the pavement, two paces in width and projecting beyond the base of the palace so as to form a kind of terracewalk, by which people can pass round the building, and which is exposed to view, while on the outer edge of the wall there is a very fine pillared balustrade; and up to this the people are allowed to come. The roof is very lofty, and the walls of the palace are all covered with gold and silver. They are also adorned with representations of dragons sculptured and gilt, beasts and birds, knights and idols, and sundry other subjects. And on the ceiling too you see nothing but gold and silver and painting. On each of the four sides there is a great marble staircase leading to the top of the marble wall, and forming the approach to the palace.

The hall of the palace is so large that it could easily dine 6,000 people; and it is quite a marvel to see how many rooms there are besides. The building is altogether so vast, so rich, and so beautiful, that no man on earth could design anything superior to it. The outside of the roof also is all colored with vermilion and yellow and green and blue and other hues, which are fixed with a varnish so fine and exquisite that they shine like crystal, and lend a resplendent luster to the palace as seen for a great way round. This roof is made too with such strength and solidity that it is fit to last for ever.

On the interior side of the palace are large buildings with halls and chambers, where the Emperor's private property is placed, such as his treasures of gold, silver, gems, pearls, and gold plate, and in which reside the ladies and concubines. There he occupies himself at his own convenience, and no one else has access.

Between the two walls of the enclosure which I have described, there are fine parks and beautiful trees bearing a variety of fruits. There are beasts also of sundry kinds, such as white stags and fallow deer, gazelles and roe-bucks, and fine squirrels of various sorts, with numbers also of the animal that gives the musk, and all manner of other beautiful creatures, insomuch that the whole place is full of them, and no spot remains void except where there is traffic of people going and coming. The parks are covered with abundant grass; and the roads through them being all paved and raised two cubits above the surface, they never become muddy, nor does the rain lodge on them, but flows off into the meadows, quickening the soil and producing that abundance of herbage.

From that corner of the enclosure which is towards the northwest there extends a fine lake, containing foison of fish of different kinds which the Emperor hath caused to be put in there, so that whenever he desires any he can have them at his pleasure. A river enters this lake and issues from it, but there is a grating of iron or brass put up so that the fish cannot escape in that way.

Moreover on the north side of the palace, about a bow-shot off, there is a hill which has been made by art from the earth dug out of the lake; it is a good hundred paces in height and a mile in compass. This hill is entirely covered with trees that never lose their leaves, but remain ever green. And I assure you that wherever a beautiful tree may exist, and the Emperor gets news of it, he sends for it and has it transported bodily with all its roots and the earth attached to them, and planted on that hill of his. No matter how big the tree may be, he gets it carried by his elephants; and in this way he has got together the most beautiful collection of trees in all the world. And he has also caused the whole hill to be covered with the ore of azure, which is very green. And thus not only are the trees all green, but the hill itself is all green likewise; and there is nothing to be seen on it that is not green; and hence it is called the Green Mount; and in good sooth 'tis named well.

On the top of the hill again there is a fine big palace which is all green inside and out; and thus the hill, and the trees, and the palace form together a charming spectacle; and it is marvellous to see their uniformity of color. Everybody who sees them is delighted. And the Great Kaan had caused this beautiful prospect to be formed for the comfort and solace and delectation of his heart.

You must know that beside the palace (that we have been describing), *i.e.* the great palace, the Emperor has caused another to be built just like his own in every respect, and this he hath done for his son when he shall reign and be Emperor after him. Hence it is made just in the same fashion and of the same size, so that everything can be carried on in the same manner after his own death. It stands on the other side of the lake from the Great Kaan's palace, and there is a bridge crossing the water from one to the other. The Prince in question holds now a Seal of Empire, but not with such complete authority as the Great Kaan, who remains supreme as long as he lives.

Now I am going to tell you of the chief city of Cathay, in which these palaces stand, and why it was built, and how.

XI. CONCERNING THE CITY OF CAMBALUC

Now there was on that spot in old times a great and noble city called Cambaluc, which is as much as to say in our tongue "The city of the Emperor." But the Great Kaan was informed by his astrologers that this city would prove rebellious and raise great disorders against his imperial authority. So he caused the present city to be built close beside the old one, with only a river between them. And he caused the people of the old city to be removed to the new town that he had founded, and this is called Taidu. However, he allowed a portion of the people which he did not suspect to remain in the old city because the new one could not hold the whole of them, big as it is.

As regards the size of this new city you must know that it has a compass of 24 miles, for each side of it hath a length of 6 miles, and it is foursquare. And it is all walled round with walls of earth which have a thickness of full ten paces at bottom and a height of more than 10 paces; but they are not so thick at top for they diminish in thickness as they rise so that at top they are only about 3 paces thick. And they are provided throughout with loop-holed battlements which are all whitewashed.

There are 12 gates and over each gate there is a great and handsome palace, so that there are on each side of the square three gates and five palaces for (I ought to mention) there is at each angle also a great and handsome palace. In those palaces are vast halls in which are kept the arms of the city garrison.

The streets are so straight and wide that you can see right along them from end to end and from one gate to the other. And up and down the city there are beautiful palaces and many great and fine hostelries and fine houses in great numbers. All the plots of ground on which the houses of the city are built are foursquare and laid out with straight lines, all the plots being occupied by great and spacious palaces with courts and gardens of proportionate size. All these plots were assigned to different heads of families. Each square plot is encompassed by handsome streets for traffic and thus the whole city is arranged in squares just like a chess board and disposed in a manner so perfect and masterly that it is impossible to give a description that should do it justice.

Moreover, in the middle of the city there is a great clock—that is to say, a bell—which is struck at night. And after it has struck three times no one must go out in the city, unless it be for the needs of a woman in labor, or of the sick. And those who go about on such errands are bound to carry lanterns with them. Moreover, the established guard at each gate of the city is 1000 armed men, not that you are to imagine the guard is kept up for fear of any attack, but only as a guard of honor for the sovereign, who resides there, and to prevent thieves from doing mischief in the town.

•••

XIII. THE FASHION OF THE GREAT KAAN'S TABLE AT HIS HIGH FEASTS

And when the Great Kaan sits at table on any great court occasion, it is in this fashion. His table is elevated a good deal above the others, and he sits at the north end of the hall, looking towards the south, with his chief wife besides him on the left. On his right sit his sons and his nephews, and other kinsmen of the blood imperial, but lower, so that their heads are on a level with the Emperor's feet. And then the other barons sit at other tables lower still. So also with the women; for all the wives of the Lord's sons, and of his nephews and other kinsmen, sit at the lower table to his right; and below them again the ladies of the other barons and knights, each in the place assigned by the Lord's orders. The tables are so disposed that the Emperor can see the whole of them from end to end, many as they are. Further, you are not to suppose that everybody sits at table; on the contrary, the greater part of the soldiers and their officers sit at their meal in the hall on the carpets. Outside the hall will be found more than 40,000 people; for there is a great concourse of folk bringing presents to the Lord, or come from foreign countries with curiosities.

In a certain part of the hall near where the Great Kaan holds his table, there is set a large and very beautiful piece of workmanship in the form of a square coffer, or buffet, about three paces each way, exquisitely wrought with figures of animals, finely carved and gilt. The middle is hollow, and in it stands a great vessel of pure gold, holding as much as an ordinary butt; and at each corner of the great vessel is one of smaller size of the capacity of a firkin, and from the former the wine or beverage flavored with fine and costly spices is drawn off into the latter. And on the buffet aforesaid are set all the Lord's drinking vessels, among which are certain pitchers of the finest gold, which are called verniques, and are big enough to hold drink for eight or ten persons. And one of these is put between every two persons, besides a couple of golden cups with handles, so that every man helps himself from the pitcher that stands between him and his neighbor. And the ladies are supplied in the same way. The value of these pitchers and cups is something immense; in fact, the Great Kaan has such a quantity of this kind of plate, and of gold and silver in other shapes, as no one ever before saw or heard tell of, or could believe.

There are certain barons specially deputed to see that foreigners who do not know the customs of the court are provided with places suited to their rank and these barons are continually moving to and fro in the hall, looking to the wants of the guests at table and causing the servants to supply them promptly with wine, milk, meat, or whatever they lack. At every door of the hall (or, indeed, wherever the Emperor may be) there stand a couple of big men like giants, one on each side, armed with staves. Their business is to see that no one steps upon the threshold in entering, and if this does happen they strip the offender of his clothes and he must pay a forfeit to have them back again, or in lieu of taking his clothes they give him a certain number of blows. If they are foreigners ignorant of the order, then there are barons appointed to introduce them and explain it to them. They think, in fact, that it brings bad luck if any one touches the threshold. Howbeit, they are not expected to stick at this in going forth again, for at that time some are like to be the worse for liquor and incapable of looking to their steps.

And you must know that those who wait upon the Great Kaan with his dishes and his drink are some of the great barons. They have the mouth and nose muffled with fine napkins of silk and gold, so that no breath nor odor from their persons should taint the dish or the goblet presented to the Lord. And when the Emperor is going to drink, all the musical instruments, of which he has vast store of every kind, begin to play. And when he takes the cup all the barons and the rest of the company drop on their knees and make the deepest obeisance before him, and then the Emperor doth drink. But each time that he does so the whole ceremony is repeated.

I will say nought about the dishes, as you may easily conceive that there is a great plenty of every possible kind. But you should know that in every case where a baron or knight dines at those tables, their wives also dine there with the other ladies. And when all have dined and the tables have been removed, then come in a great number of players and jugglers, adepts at all sorts of wonderful feats, and perform before the Emperor and the rest of the company, creating great diversion and mirth, so that everybody is full of laughter and enjoyment. And when the performance is over, the company breaks up and every one goes to his quarters.

XIV. CONCERNING THE GREAT FEAST HELD BY THE GRAND KAAN EVERY YEAR ON HIS BIRTHDAY

You must know that the Tartars keep high festival yearly on their birthdays. And the Great Kaan was born on the 28th day of the September moon, so on that day is held the greatest feast of the year at the Kaan's court, always excepting that which he holds on New Year's Day, of which I shall tell you afterwards. Now, on his birthday the Great Kaan dresses in the best of his robes, all wrought with beaten gold; and full 12,000 barons and knights on that day come forth dressed in robes of the same color and precisely like those of the Great Kaan, except that they are not so costly, but still they are all of the same color as his and are also of silk and gold. Every man so clothed has also a girdle of gold and this as well as the dress is given him by the sovereign. And I will aver that there are some of these decked with so many pearls and precious stones that a single suit shall be worth full 10,000 golden bezants.

And of such raiment there are several sets. For you must know that the Great Kaan thirteen times in the year presents to his barons and knights such suits of raiment as I am speaking of. And on each occasion they wear the same color that he does, a different color being assigned to each festival. Hence you may see what a huge business it is and that there is no prince in the world but he alone who could keep up such customs as these.

On his birthday also all the Tartars in the world and all the countries and governments that owe allegiance to the Kaan offer him great presents according to their several ability and as prescription or orders have fixed the amount. And many other persons also come with great presents to the Kaan, in order to beg for some employment from him. And the Great Kaan has chosen twelve barons on whom is laid the charge of assigning to each of these supplicants a suitable answer.

On this day likewise all the idolaters, all the Saracens, and all the Christians and other descriptions of people make great and solemn devotions with much chanting and lighting of lamps and burning of incense, each to the God whom he doth worship, praying that he would save the Emperor and grant him long life and health and happiness.

And thus, as I have related, is celebrated the joyous feast of the Kaan's birthday.

Now I will tell you of another festival which the Kaan holds at the New Year and which is called the White Feast.

XV. OF THE GREAT FESTIVAL WHICH THE KAAN HOLDS ON NEW YEAR'S DAY

The beginning of their New Year is the month of February, and on that occasion the Great Kaan and all his subjects made such a Feast as I now shall describe.

It is the custom that on this occasion the Kaan and all his subjects should be clothed entirely in white so that day everybody is in white, men and women, great and small. And this is done in order that they may thrive all through the year for they deem that white clothing is lucky. On that day also all the people of all the provinces and governments and kingdoms and countries that owe allegiance to the Kaan bring him great presents of gold and silver, and pearls and gems, and rich textures of divers kinds. And this they do that the Emperor throughout the year may have abundance of treasure and enjoyment without care. And the people also make presents to each other of white things and embrace and kiss and make merry and wish each other happiness and good luck for the coming year. On that day, I can assure you, among the customary presents there shall be offered to the Kaan from various quarters more than 100,000 white horses, beautiful animals, and richly caparisoned. And you must know 'tis their custom in offering presents to the Great Kaan (at least when the province making the present is able to do so), to present nine times nine articles. For instance, if a province sends horses, it sends nine times nine or 81 horses; of gold, nine times nine pieces of gold, and so with stuffs or whatever else the present may consist of.

On that day also the whole of the Kaan's elephants, amounting fully to 5,000 in number, are exhibited, all covered with rich and gay housings of inlaid cloth representing beasts and birds, while each of them carries on his back two splendid coffers, all of these being filled with the Emperor's plate and other costly furniture required for the court on the occasion of the White Feast. And these are followed by a vast number of camels which are likewise covered with rich housings and laden with things needful for the Feast. All these are paraded before the Emperor and it makes the finest sight in the world.

Moreover, on the morning of the Feast, before the tables are set, all the kings and all the dukes, marquesses, counts, barons, knights, and astrologers, and philosophers, and leeches, and falconers, and other officials of sundry kinds from all the places round about present themselves in the Great Hall before the Emperor, while those who can find no room to enter stand outside in such a position that the Emperor can see them all well. And the whole company is marshalled in this wise. First are the Kaan's sons, and his nephews, and the other princes of the blood imperial; next to them all kings; then dukes, and then all others in succession according to the degree of each. And when they are all seated, each in his proper place, then a great prelate rises and says with a loud voice: "Bow and adore!" And as soon as he has said this the company bow down until their foreheads touch the earth in adoration towards the Emperor as if he were a god. And this adoration they repeat four times, and then go to a highly decorated altar on which is a vermilion tablet with the name of the Grand Kaan inscribed thereon, and a beautiful censer of gold. So they incense the tablet and the altar with great reverence and then return each man to his seat.

When all have performed this then the presents are offered, of which I have spoken as being so rich and costly. And after all have been offered and been seen by the Emperor the tables are set and all take their places at them with perfect order as I have already told you. And after dinner the jugglers come in and amuse the court as you have heard before and when that is over every man goes to his quarters.

•••

XXII. CONCERNING THE CITY OF CAMBALUC AND ITS GREAT TRAFFIC AND POPULATION

You must know that the city of Cambaluc hath such a multitude of houses, and such a vast population inside the walls and outside, that it seems quite past all possibility. There is a suburb outside each of the gates, which are twelve in number; and these suburbs are so great that they contain more people than the city itself for the suburb of one gate spreads in width till it meets the suburb of the next, while they extend in length some three or four miles. In those suburbs lodge the foreign merchants and travellers, of whom there are always great numbers who have come to bring presents to the Emperor, or to sell articles at court, or because the city affords so good a mart to attract traders. There are in each of the suburbs, to a distance of a mile from the city, numerous fine hostelries for the lodgement of merchants from different parts of the world, and a special hostelry is assigned to each description of people, as if we should say there is one for the Lombards, another for the Germans, and a third for the Frenchmen. And thus there are as many good houses outside of the city as inside, without counting those that belong to the great lords and barons, which are very numerous.

You must know that it is forbidden to bury any dead body inside the city. If the body be that of an idolater it is carried out beyond the city and suburbs to a remote place assigned for the purpose, to be burnt. And if it be of one belonging to a religion the custom of which is to bury, such as the Christian, the Saracen, or what not, it is also carried out beyond the suburbs to a distant place assigned for the purpose. And thus the city is preserved in a better and more healthy state.

Moreover, no public woman resides inside the city, but all such abide outside in the suburbs. And 'tis wonderful what a vast number of these there are for the foreigners; it is a certain fact that there are more than 20,000 of them living by prostitution. And that so many can live in this way will show you how vast is the population.

Guards patrol the city every night in parties of 30 or 40, looking out for any persons who may be abroad at unseasonable hours, i.e. after the great bell hath stricken thrice. If they find any such person he is immediately taken to prison, and examined next morning by the proper officers. If these find him guilty of any misdemeanor they order him a proportionate beating with the stick. Under this punishment people sometimes die; but they adopt it in order to eschew bloodshed; for their Bacsis say that it is an evil thing to shed man's blood.

To this city also are brought articles of greater cost and rarity, and in greater abundance of all kinds, than to any other city in the world. For people of every description, and from every region, bring things including all the costly wares of India, as well as the fine and precious goods of Cathay itself with its provinces, some for the sovereign, some for the court, some for the city which is so great, some for the crowds of barons and knights, some for the great hosts of the Emperor which are quartered round about; and thus between court and city the quantity brought in is endless.

As a sample, I tell you, no day in the year passes that there do not enter the city 1,000 cart loads of silk alone, from which are made quantities of cloth of silk and gold, and of other goods. And this is not to be wondered at; for in all the countries round about there is no flax, so that everything has to be made of silk. It is true, indeed, that in some parts of the country there is cotton and hemp, but not sufficient for their wants. This, however, is not of much consequence, because silk is so abundant and cheap, and is a more valuable substance than either flax or cotton.

Round about this great city of Cambaluc there are some 200 other cities at various distances, from which traders come to sell their goods and buy others for their lords; and all find means to make their sales and purchases, so that the traffic of the city is passing great.

•••

XXIV. HOW THE GREAT KAAN CAUSETH THE BARK OF TREES, MADE INTO SOMETHING LIKE PAPER, TO PASS FOR MONEY OVER ALL HIS COUNTRY

Now that I have told you in detail of the splendor of the city of the Emperor's, I shall proceed to tell you of the mint which he hath in the same city, in which he hath his money coined and struck, as I shall relate to you. And in doing so I shall make manifest to you how it is that the Great Lord may well be able to accomplish even much more than I have told you, or am going to tell you, in this Book. For, tell it how I might, you never would be satisfied that I was keeping within truth and reason.

The Emperor's mint then is in this same city of Cambaluc and the way it is wrought is such that you might say he hath the secret of alchemy in perfection, and you would be right. For he makes his money after this fashion.

He makes them take of the bark of a certain tree, in fact of the mulberry tree, the leaves of which are the food of the silkworms,—these trees being so numerous that whole districts are full of them. What they take is a certain fine white bast or skin which lies between the wood of the tree and the thick outer bark, and this they make into something resembling sheets of paper, but black. When these sheets have been prepared they are cut up into pieces of different sizes. The smallest of these sizes is worth a half tornesel; the next, a little larger, one tornesel; one, a little larger still, is worth half a silver groat of Venice; another a whole groat; others yet two groats, five groats, and ten groats. There is also a kind worth one bezant of gold, and others of three bezants, and so up to ten. All these pieces of paper are issued with as much solemnity and authority as if they were of pure gold or silver; and on every piece a variety of officials, whose duty it is, have to write their names, and to put their seals. And when all is prepared duly, the chief officer deputed by the Kaan smears the seal entrusted to him with vermilion, and impresses it on the paper, so that the form of the seal remains printed upon it in red; the money is then authentic. Any one forging it would be punished with death. And the Kaan causes every year to be made such a vast quantity of this money, which costs him nothing, that it must equal in amount all the treasure in the world.

With these pieces of paper, made as I have described, he causes all payments on his own account to be made; and he makes them to pass current universally over all his kingdoms and provinces and territories, and whithersoever his power and sovereignty extends. And nobody, however important he may think himself, dares to refuse them on pain of death. And indeed everybody takes them readily, for wheresoever a person may go throughout the Great Kaan's dominions he shall find these pieces of paper current, and shall be able to transact all sales and purchases of goods by means of them just as well as if they were coins of pure gold. And all the while they are so light that ten bezants' worth does not weigh one golden bezant.

• • •

XXVI. HOW THE KAAN'S POSTS AND RUNNERS ARE SPED THROUGH MANY LANDS AND PROVINCES

Now you must know that from this city of Cambaluc proceed many roads and highways leading to a variety of provinces, one to one province, another to another; and each road receives the name of the province to which it leads; and it is a very sensible plan. And the messengers of the Emperor in travelling from Cambaluc, be the road whichsoever they will, find at every twenty-five miles of the journey a station which they call *Yamb*, or, as we should say, the "Horse-Post-House." And at each of those stations used by the messengers, there is a large and handsome building for them to put up at, in which they find all the rooms furnished with fine beds and all other necessary articles in rich silk, and where they are provided with everything they can want. If even a king were to arrive at one of these, he would find himself well lodged.

At some of these stations, moreover, there shall be posted some four hundred horses standing ready for the use of the messengers; at others there shall be two hundred, according to the requirements, and to what the Emperor has established in each case. At every twenty-five miles, as I said, or anyhow at every thirty miles, you find one of these stations, on all the principal highways leading to the different provincial governments; and the same is the case throughout all the chief provinces subject to the Great Kaan. Even when the messengers have to pass through a roadless tract where neither house nor hostel exists, still there the station-houses have been established just the same, excepting that the intervals are somewhat greater and the day's journey is fixed at thirty-five to forty-five miles, instead of twenty-five to thirty. But they are provided with horses and all the other necessaries just like those we have described, so that the Emperor's messengers, come they from what region they may, find everything ready for them.

And in sooth this is a thing done on the greatest scale of magnificence that ever was seen. Never had emperor, king, or lord such wealth as this manifests. For it is a fact that on all these posts taken together there are more than 300,000 horses kept up, specially for the use of the messengers. And the great buildings that I have mentioned are more than 10,000 in number, all richly furnished, as I told you. The thing is on a scale so wonderful and costly that it is hard to bring oneself to describe it.

But now I will tell you another thing that I had forgotten, but which ought to be told while I am on this subject. You must know that by the Great Kaan's orders there has been established between those post-houses, at every interval of three miles, a little fort with some forty houses round about it, in which dwell the people who act as the Emperor's foot-runners. Every one of those runners wears a great wide belt, set all over with bells, so that as they run the three miles from post to post their bells are heard jingling a long way off. And thus on reaching the post the runner finds another man similarly equipt, and all ready to take his place, who instantly takes over whatsoever he has in charge, and with it receives a slip of paper from the clerk, who is always at hand for the purpose; and so the new man sets off and runs his three miles. At the next station he finds his relief ready in like manner; and so the post proceeds, with a change at every three miles. And in this way the Emperor, who has an immense number of these runners, receives despatches with news from places ten day's journey off in one day and night; or, if need be, news from a hundred days off in ten days and nights; and that is no small matter. In fact in the fruit season many a fine fruit shall be gathered one morning in Cambaluc and the evening of the next day it shall reach the Great Kaan in Chandu, a distance of ten days' journey. The clerk at each of the posts notes the time of each courier's arrival and departure; and there are often other officers whose business it is to make monthly visitations of all the posts, and to punish those runners who have been slack in their work. The Emperor exempts these men from all tribute, and pays them besides.

Moreover, there are also at those stations other men equipt similarly with girdles hung with bells, who are employed for expresses when there is a call for great haste in sending despatches to any governor of a province, or to give news when any baron has revolted, or in other such emergencies; and these men travel a good two hundred or two hundred and fifty miles in the day and as much in the night. I'll tell you how it stands. They take a horse from those at the station which are standing ready saddled, all fresh and in wind, and mount and go at full speed, as hard as they can ride in fact. And when those at the next post hear the bells they get ready another horse and a man equipt in the same way, and he takes over the letter or whatever it be, and is off full-speed to the third station, where again a fresh horse is found all ready, and so the despatch speeds along from post to post, always at full gallop, with regular change of horses. And the speed at which they go is marvellous.

•••

XXVIII. HOW THE GREAT KAAN CAUSES TREES TO BE PLANTED BY THE HIGHWAYS

The Emperor moreover hath taken order that all the highways travelled by his messengers and the people generally should be planted with rows of great trees a few paces apart; and thus these trees are visible a long way off, and no one can miss the way by day or night. Even the roads through uninhabited tracts are thus planted, and it is the greatest possible solace to travellers. And this is done on all the ways, where it can be of service. The Great Kaan plants these trees all the more readily, because his astrologers and diviners tell him that he who plants trees lives long.

But where the ground is so sandy and desert that trees will not grow, he causes other landmarks, pillars or stones, to be set up to show the way.

XXIX. CONCERNING THE RICE WINE DRUNK BY THE PEOPLE OF CATHAY

Most of the people of Cathay drink wine of the kind that I shall now describe. It is a liquor which they brew of rice with a quantity of excellent spice, in such fashion that it makes better drink than any other kind of wine; it is not only good, but clear and pleasing to the eye. And being very hot stuff, it makes one drunk sooner than any other wine.

XXX. CONCERNING THE BLACK STONES THAT ARE DUG IN CATHAY AND ARE BURNT FOR FUEL

It is a fact that all over the country of Cathay there is a kind of black stones existing in beds in the mountains, which they dig out and burn like firewood. If you supply the fire with them at night, and see that they are well kindled, you will find them still alight in the morning; and they make such capital fuel that no other is used throughout the country. It is true that they have plenty of wood also, but they do not burn it, because those stones burn better and cost less.

Moreover with that vast number of people, and the number of hot baths that they maintain—for every one has such a bath at least three times a week, and in winter if possible every day, while every nobleman and man of wealth has a private bath for his own use—the wood would not suffice for the purpose.

XXXI. HOW THE GREAT KAAN CAUSES STORES OF CORN TO BE MADE, TO HELP HIS PEOPLE WITHAL IN TIME OF DEARTH

You must know that when the Emperor sees that corn is cheap and abundant, he buys up large quantities, and has it stored in all his provinces in great granaries, where it is so well looked after that it will keep for three or four years.

And this applies, let me tell you, to all kinds of corn, whether wheat, barley, millet, rice, panic, or what not, and when there is any scarcity of a particular kind of corn, he causes that to be issued. And if the price of the corn is at one bezant the measure, he lets them have it at a bezant for four measures, or at whatever price will produce general cheapness; and every one can have food in this way. And by this providence of the Emperor's, his people can never suffer from dearth. He does the same over his whole Empire; causing these supplies to be stored everywhere, according to calculation of the wants and necessities of the people.

XXXII. ON THE CHARITY OF THE EMPEROR TO THE POOR

I have told you how the Great Kaan provides for the distribution of necessaries to his people in time of dearth, by making store in time of cheapness. Now I will tell you of his alms and great charity to the poor of his city of Cambaluc.

You see he causes selection to be made of a number of families in the city which are in a state of indigence, and of such families some may consist of six in the house, some of eight, some of ten, more or fewer in each as it may hap, but the whole number being very great. And each family he causes annually to be supplied with wheat and other corn sufficient for the whole year. And this he never fails to do every year. Moreover, all those who choose to go to the daily dole at the court receive a great loaf apiece, hot from the baking, and nobody is denied; for so the Lord hath ordered. And so some 30,000 people go for it every day from year's end to year's end. Now this is a great goodness in the Emperor to take pity of his poor people thus. And they benefit so much by it that they worship him as he were God.

He also provides the poor with clothes. For he lays a tithe upon all wool, silk, hemp, and the like from which clothing can be made and he has these woven and laid up in a building set apart for the purpose and as all artisans are bound to give a day's labor weekly, in this way the Kaan has these stuffs made into clothing for those poor families, suitable for summer or winter, according to the time of year. He also provides the clothing for his troops and has woolens woven for them in every city, the material for which is furnished by the tithe aforesaid. You should know that the Tartars, before they were converted to the religion of the idolaters, never practised alms-giving. Indeed, when any poor man begged of them they would tell him, "Go with God's curse, for if he loved you as he loves me he would have provided for you." But the sages of the idolaters told the Great Kaan that it was a good work to provide for the poor and that his idols would be greatly pleased if he did so. And since then he has taken to do so for the poor so much as you have heard.

XXXIII. CONCERNING THE ASTROLOGERS IN THE CITY OF CAMBALUC

There are in the city of Cambaluc, what with Christians, Saracens, and Cathayans, some five thousand astrologers and soothsayers, whom the Great Kaan provides with annual maintenance and clothing, just as he provides the poor of whom we have spoken, and they are in the constant exercise of their art in this city.

They have a kind of astrolabe on which are inscribed the planetary signs, the hours and critical points of the whole year. And every year these Christian, Saracen, and Cathayan astrologers, each sect apart, investigate by means of this astrolabe the course and character of the whole year, according to the indications of each of its Moons, in order to discover by the natural course and disposition of the planets and the other circumstances of the heavens what shall be the nature of the weather, and what peculiarities shall be produced by each Moon of the year as, for example, under which Moon there shall be thunderstorms and tempests, under which there shall be disease, murrain, wars, disorder, and treasons, and so on, according to the indications of each, but always adding that it lies with God to do less or more according to his pleasure. And they write down the results of their examination in certain little pamphlets for the year, which are called *Tacuin*, and these are sold for a groat to all who desire to know what is coming. Those of the astrologers, of course, whose predictions are found to be most exact are held to be the greatest adepts in their art and get the greater fame.

And if any one have some great matter in hand, or proposing to make a long journey for traffic or other business, desires to know what will be the upshot, he goes to one of these astrologers and says: "Turn up your books and see what is the present aspect of the heavens for I am going away on such and such a business." Then the astrologer will reply that the applicant must also tell the year, month, and hour of his birth, and when he has got that information he will see how the horoscope of his nativity combines with the indications of the time when the question is put, and then he predicts the result, good or bad, according to the aspect of the heavens.

You must know, too, that the Tartars reckon their years by twelves, the sign of the first year being the Lion, of the second the Ox, of the third the Dragon, of the fourth the Dog, and so forth up to the twelfth, so that when one is asked the year of his birth he answers that it was in the year of the Lion (let us say), on such a day or night, at such an hour, and such a moment. And the father of a child always takes care to write these particulars down in a book. When the twelve yearly symbols have been gone through then they come back to the first and go through with them again in the same succession.

XXXIV. CONCERNING THE RELIGION OF THE CATHAYANS, THEIR VIEWS AS TO THE SOUL, AND THEIR CUSTOMS

As we have said before, these people are idolaters and, as regards their gods, each has a tablet fixed high up on the wall of his chamber on which is inscribed a name which represents the most high and heavenly God, and before this they pay daily worship, offering incense from a thurible, raising their hands aloft and gnashing their teeth three times, praying him to grant them health of mind and body, but of him they ask nought else. And below on the ground there is a figure which they call *Natigai*, which is the god of things terrestrial. To him they give a wife and children and they worship him in the same manner, with incense and gnashing of teeth and lifting up of hands, and of him they ask seasonable weather and the fruits of the earth, children, and so forth.

Their view of the immortality of the soul is after this fashion. They believe that as soon as a man dies his soul enters into another body, going from a good to a better, or from a bad to a worse, according as he hath conducted himself well or ill. That is to say, a poor man, if he have passed through life good and sober, shall be born again of a gentlewoman, and shall be a gentleman, and on a second occasion shall be born of a princess and shall be a prince, and so on, always rising, til he be absorbed into the Deity. But if he have borne himself ill he who was the son of a gentleman shall be reborn as the son of a boor, and from a boor shall become a dog, always going down lower and lower.[1]

The people have an ornate style of speech; they salute each other with a cheerful countenance and with great politeness; they behave like gentlemen,

---

[1]Buddhism had penetrated China more than a thousand years before.— *Ed.*

and eat with great propriety. They show great respect to their parents and should there be any son who offends his parents or fails to minister to their necessities there is a public office which has no other charge but that of punishing unnatural children, who are proved to have acted with ingratitude towards their parents.

Criminals of sundry kinds who have been imprisoned are released at a time fixed by the Great Kaan (which occurs every three years), but on leaving prison they are branded on one cheek that they may be recognized.

The Great Kaan hath prohibited all gambling and sharping, things more prevalent there than in any other part of the world. In doing this he said: "I have conquered you by force of arms and all that you have is mine; if, therefore, you gamble away your property it is in fact my property that you are gambling away." Not that he took anything from them however.

I must not omit to tell you of the orderly way in which the Kaan's barons and others conduct themselves in coming to his presence. In the first place, within a half mile of the place where he is, out of reverence for his exalted majesty, everybody preserves a mien of the greatest meekness and quiet, so that no noise of shrill voices or loud talk shall be heard. And every one of the chiefs and nobles carries always with him a handsome little vessel to spit in while he remains in the Hall of Audience—for no one dares spit on the floor of the hall—and when he hath spitten he covers it up and puts it aside. So also they all have certain handsome buskins of white leather, which they carry with them, and, when summoned by the sovereign, on arriving at the entrance to the hall they put on these white buskins, and give their others in charge to the servants, in order that they may not foul the fine carpets of silk and gold and divers colors.

Southeast Asia

The Thai people originally dwelt in what is now southern China. Driven south by Chinese and Mongol expansion in the twelfth and thirteenth centuries, they built a powerful empire in Southeast Asia in the thirteenth and fourteenth centuries. During this time, they came into contact with the Burmese and the Khmer. Both the Burmese and Khmer had built civilizations based on the example of classical India, often with the guidance of Indian advisors. This Indian influence was then transmitted to the Thai. From the Burmese they learned Theravadan Buddhism and, from the Khmer, whom they conquered, they inherited a sophisticated political, intellectual, and artistic culture based on Indian models. Although none of these three cultures remained independent for long, they left a lasting impact on Southeast Asia. While Buddhism died out in its homeland of India and was transformed beyond recognition in Central and Eastern Asia, in modern Southeast Asian countries such as Cambodia, Burma, Thailand, and Laos, traditional Theravadan Buddhism is still widely practiced today. Beyond Buddhism, these early Southeast Asian civilizations assured that the region would look to classical India for its cultural roots.

The following selection commemorates the reign of Ram Khamaeng, a powerful and influential Thai king who died in 1307.

---

1. For what accomplishments does the king want to be remembered?

2. To what extent do you think Ram Khamaeng has been influenced by the ideal of the Buddhist ruler exemplified by Ashoka?

My father was named Sī Intharāthit, my mother was named Nāng Süang, and my elder brother was named Bān Müang. There were five of us children, born of the same womb: three boys and two girls. Our first-born brother died when he was still small. When I had grown up and attained the age of nineteen, Khun Sām Chon, chieftain of the city of Chōt, came to attack the city of Tāk. My father went into combat on Khun Sām Chon's left. Khun Sām Chon made a massive charge; my father's men fled and dispersed in a complete rout. But as for me, I did not take flight. I mounted the elephant "Anekphon" and I urged it on before my father. I engaged Khun Sām Chon in an elephant duel: I rode in quickly against Khun Sām Chon's elephant, "Māt Müang," and put him out of combat. Khun Sām Chon fled. Then my father conferred upon me the title Phra Rām Khamhāēng because I had defeated Khun Sām Chon's elephant.

During my father's life I served my father and I served my mother. If I got a bit of meat or a bit of fish, I took it to my father; if I had any sort of fruit, sour or sweet, anything delicious and good to eat, I took it to my father. If I went on an elephant hunt and caught any, I took them to my father. If I went to attack a village or a city and collected some elephants and ivory, men and women, silver and gold, I gave them to my father. Then my father died—only my elder brother remained. I continued to serve my elder brother, as I had served my father. When my elder brother died the kingdom in its entirety fell to me.

During the life of King Rām Khamhāēng this city of Sukhōthai has prospered. In the water there are fish; in the fields there is rice. The lord of the country levies no tolls on his subjects as they travel along the roads, driving cattle to go trade, riding horses to go sell. Whoever desires to trade elephants does so; whoever desires to trade horses, does so; whoever desires to trade silver or gold does so. If a commoner, a nobleman, a chieftain, or anyone at all falls ill, dies, and disappears, the house of his ancestors, his clothing, his elephants, his family, his granaries, his servants, his ancestors' areca and betel orchards are transmitted as a whole to his children. If some commoners, nobles, or chieftains are in disagreements, (the king) makes a true inquiry, and settles the matter for his subjects in an equitable fashion; he is never in collusion with practicers of thievery and deceit. If he sees someone else's wealth he does not interfere. He accords aid and assistance to whomever comes riding an elephant to find him, requesting his protection for their country. If they have neither elephants nor horses, neither male servants nor female, neither silver nor gold, he gives them some and helps them to lay out their own villages and cities. If he captures some enemy soldiers or warriors he neither kills them nor beats them. In the (palace) doorway a bell is suspended—if an inhabitant of the kingdom has any complaint or any matter which irritates his stomach and torments his mind, and he desires to expose it to the king it is not difficult: he has only to ring the bell that the king has hung there. Every time that King Rām Khamhāēng hears the sound of the bell he questions (the complainant) on his case and settles it in an equitable fashion. Consequently the inhabitants of this city of Sukhōthai admire him.

There are areca and betel orchards in all areas of the country. There are many coconut orchards in this country, many jack-fruit orchards in this country, many mango orchards in this country, and many tamarind orchards in this country. Whoever starts an orchard is permitted to do so by the king. In the middle of this city of Sukhōthai there is a marvelous well, with clean and delicious water like that of the Mekong during the dry season. Around this city of Sukhōthai there is a triple rampart measuring 3,400 wā (= 20,400 feet). The inhabitants of this city of Sukhōthai are fond of almsgiving, charity, and the maintenance of the precepts. King Rām Khamhāēng, the sovereign of this city of Sukhōthai, the princes as well as the princesses, the men as well as the women, the nobles, and the chieftains, all without exception, without distinction of rank or of sex, practice the religion of the Buddha with devotion and observe the precepts during the rainy season retreat. At the close of the rainy season, the Kathin ceremonies take place, lasting one month. At the time of the Kathin ceremonies offerings are made of stacks of cowry shells, of stacks of areca, of stacks of flowers, of cushions, and of pillows. The Kathin offerings made each year amount to two million. Chanting, (the people) go off to perform the Kathin ceremonies at the monastery of the Aranyik, and when they return to the city the procession forms at the monastery of the Aranyik and stretches as far as the border of the plain. There everyone prostrates himself, while lutes and guitars, hymns and songs resound. Whoever wants to play, plays; whoever wants to laugh, laughs; whoever wants to sing, sings. This city of Sukhōthai has four main gates—each year a great crowd presses against them in order to enter and see the king light candles and gesture with the fire. And this city of Sukhōthai is filled with people to the bursting point!

In the middle of this city of Sukhōthai there are sanctuaries. There are some gold statues of the Buddha, there is a statue of the Buddha which measures eighteen cubits, there are some statues of the Buddha which are large, and there are some which are of moderate size. There are large sanctuaries, and there are moderate-sized ones; there are monks, both theras and mahātheras.

To the west of this city of Sukhōthai is found the monastery of the Aranyik. King Rām Khamhāēng founded it and offered it to the patriarch, to the chief monk, a scholar who has studied completely the Three Scriptures and who is more learned than all the other monks of the country, having come from Nakhōn Sī Thammarāt. In the middle of this monastery of the Aranyik there is a great, lofty sanctuary, beautifuly situated, which contains a statue of the standing Buddha, with a height of eighteen cubits.

To the east of this city of Sukhōthai there are sanctuaries and monks. There is a large lake, areca and betel orchards, dry fields and paddy fields, hamlets, large and small villages, and there are mango and tamarind orchards. All of this is as beautiful as in a picture.

To the north of this city of Sukhōthai there is a market, there is a Buddha image, and there is a prāsāt. There are areca and jack-fruit orchards, dry fields and paddy fields, hamlets, and villages large and small.

To the south of this city of Sukhōthai there are hermitages and sanctuaries, and monks who live there. There is a dam; coconut, jack-fruit, mango, and areca orchards; and there is a spring from a hillside. There is Phra Khaphung—the spirit and divinity of this mountain, superior to all the spirits of the country. If a prince, whoever he might be, governing this city of Sukhōthai deals with (the spirit's) cult in a dignified way and presents ritual offerings to him, then this country is stable and prospers; but if (the sovereign) does not follow the prescribed cult and does not present ritual offerings properly then the spirit of this mountain no longer protects nor respects this country which [consequently] falls into decadence.

In 1214, the year of the dragon, King Rām Khamhāēng, sovereign of the cities of Sī Satchanālay and Sukhōthai, who had had sugar palms planted fourteen years earlier, ordered some artisans to cut a stone slab (a dais) and place it in the midst of these sugar palms. On the day of the new moon, the eighth day of the waxing moon, the day of the full moon, and the eighth day of the waning moon a group of monks, theras and mahātheras, mounts and sits down upon that dais, and recites the Law there to the laity and to the assembly of the faithful, observing the precepts. On days other than those for the recitation of the Law, King Rām Khamhāēng, sovereign of the cities of Sī Satchanālay and Sukhōthai, mounts the stone dais and sits down, and together with the assembled nobles and dignitaries governs the affairs of the country. On the days of the new moon and the full moon the king has the white elephant Rūcāsī harnessed. . . and the right (and left) tusks all decorated with gold and ivory. The king then mounts it and goes to make his devotions to the venerable chief of the Aranyik, then he returns.

There is an inscription in the city of Chaliang situated near the holy Sī Ratanathāt relic. (Also) there is an inscription in the cave called "King's Cave" situated on the bank of the Samphāy River. (In addition) there is an inscription in the Ratanathān Cave.

In the middle of the sugar palm (grove) there are two pavilions: One is called "The Pavilion of the Gold Buddha," the other "The Pavilion of the Buddha." The stone dais is called Manangkhasilābāt—it has been put in that place so that everyone can see (it).

King Rām Khamhāēng, the son of King Sī Intharāthit, is the sovereign of the cities of Sī Satchanālay and Sukhōthai, as well as the Mā, the Kāw, the Lao, and the Thai who live under the celestial vault. Both the river Thai of the U River and the river people of the Khōng have submitted and pay him homage. In 1207, the year of the pig, he had the holy relics exhumed so that everyone could contemplate them. He worshiped and venerated these relics for one month and six days, then he had them buried in the middle of the city of Sī Satchanālay; there he erected a cetiya (or "chadi") which was finished in six years; he surrounded the Great Relic with a stone fort which was built in three years.

This alphabet for writing Thai did not exist previously. In 1205, the year of the goat, King Rām Khamhāēng with great concentration and meditation devised this alphabet for writing Thai, and this Thai alphabet exists because the king developed it.

This king, Rām Khamhāēng, seeks to be the chief and the sovereign of all the Thai. He is the master who instructs all of the Thai so that they may know about merit and the true Law. Among all the men who live in this Thai country none is his equal in knowledge and in wisdom, in bravery and in hardiness, in force and in energy. He has vanquished the crowd of his enemies who possess broad cities and numerous elephants. . . .

D. T. Niane

Mali is a country in western Africa. During the Middle Ages it gained ascendency over a number of neighboring lands, thus creating the Mali Empire, which reached its height in the fourteenth century. This expansion of Mali's territory and power was accomplished in part by the great king and later emperor, Sundiata, who flourished in the early part of the thirteenth century. The epic, *Sundiata*, is an account of his life and exploits. Although for obvious reasons it gives a somewhat romanticized picture of this great leader, it also offers glimpses into life as it was really lived in the Africa of his time. Of special interest are descriptions of royal court life, religious beliefs and practices, agriculture and industry, politics, trade, and warfare.

It is possible in the selection that follows to include only an excerpt from the epic of *Sundiata*. Born the son of the king of Mali, on his father's death Sundiata was forced, with his mother, Sogolon, and his brother and sister, to flee the country at the age of ten through the machinations of another wife of the late king, who put her own son on the throne. For the next seven years Sundiata wandered around west Africa. But he had made a vow to return to Mali. In the meantime Soumaoro, the sorcerer-king of the land of Sosso, had gained great power, conquering Mali and destroying its capital city of Niani. Before he could return to Mali, therefore, Sundiata had to defeat Soumaoro. Befriended by the king of Mema, Sundiata developed into a great warrior. He gathered together an army and, after defeating a Sosso contingent under Soumaoro's son, Sosso Balla, at the stronghold of Tabon, Sundiata and his forces advanced to the plain of Krina, where Soumaoro lay in wait for him with his great army. The selection begins at this point. The following individuals need special mention: Sundiata (also referred to as Djata); his half-brother, Manding Bory; his half-sister, Nana Triban, who had learned the secret of Soumaoro's magical power while held captive in Sosso; Balla Fasséké, Sundiata's griot; and Fakoli, the nephew of Soumaoro, who had turned against his uncle after the latter stole his wife, Keleya, from him.

A special word needs to be added about griots. These were highly trained specialists who were the historians of Africa; they memorized the past and repeated it orally generation after generation. But a griot was more than simply a narrator of past events. As the current author of *Sundiata*, D. T. Niane, who translated the epic from the words of a griot, puts it: "If today the griot is reduced to turning his musical art to account or even to working with his hands in order to live, it was not always so in ancient Africa. Formerly 'griots' were the counsellors of kings, they conserved the constitutions of kingdoms by memory work alone; each princely family had its griot appointed to preserve tradition."

1. What virtues does Sundiata exemplify?

2. Compare and contrast Sundiata and Charlemagne.

Sundiata

The Battle of Krina

Sundiata wanted to have done with Soumaoro before the rainy season, so he struck camp and marched on Krina where Soumaoro was encamped. The latter realized that the decisive battle had come. Sundiata deployed his men on the little hill that dominates the plain. The great battle was for the next day.

In the evening, to raise the men's spirits, Djata gave a great feast, for he was anxious that his men should wake up happy in the morning. Several oxen were slaughtered and that evening Balla Fasséké, in front of the whole army, called to mind the history of old Mali. He praised Sundiata, seated amidst his lieutenants, in this manner:

"Now I address myself to you, Maghan Sundiata, I speak to you king of Mali, to whom dethroned monarchs flock. The time foretold to you by the jinn is now coming. Sundiata, kingdoms and empires are in the likeness of man; like him they are born, they grow and disappear. Each sovereign embodies one moment of that life. Formerly, the kings of Ghana extended their kingdom over all the lands inhabited by the black man, but the circle has closed and the Cissés of Wagadou are nothing more than petty princes in a desolate land. Today, another kingdom looms up, powerful, the kingdom of Sosso. Humbled kings have borne their tribute to Sosso, Soumaoro's arrogance knows no more bounds and his cruelty is equal to his ambition. But will Soumaoro dominate the world? Are we, the griots of Mali, condemned to pass on to future generations the humiliations which the king of Sosso cares to inflict on our country? No, you may be glad, children of the 'Bright Country,' for the kingship of Sosso is but the growth of yesterday, whereas that of Mali dates from the time of Bilali. Each kingdom has its childhood, but Soumaoro wants to force the pace, and so Sosso will collapse under him like a horse worn out beneath its rider.

Niane, D. T., *Sundiata*, trans. G. D. Pickett (Harlow: Longman, 1965). Courtesy of Presence Africaine.

"You, Maghan, you are Mali. It has had a long and difficult childhood like you. Sixteen kings have preceded you on the throne of Niani, sixteen kings have reigned with varying fortunes, but from being village chiefs the Keitas have become tribal chiefs and then kings. Sixteen generations have consolidated their power. You are the outgrowth of Mali just as the silk-cotton tree is the growth of the earth, born of deep and mighty roots. To face the tempest the tree must have long roots and gnarled branches. Maghan Sundiata, has not the tree grown?

"I would have you know, son of Sogolon, that there is not room for two kings around the same calabash of rice. When a new cock comes to the poultry run the old cock picks a quarrel with him and the docile hens wait to see if the new arrival asserts himself or yields. You have come to Mali. Very well, then, assert yourself. Strength makes a law of its own self and power allows no division.

•••

"Griots are men of the spoken word, and by the spoken word we give life to the gestures of kings. But words are nothing but words; power lies in deeds. Be a man of action; do not answer me any more with your mouth, but tomorrow, on the plain of Krina, show me what you would have me recount to coming generations. Tomorrow allow me to sing the 'Song of the Vultures' over the bodies of the thousands of Sossos whom your sword will have laid low before evening."

It was on the eve of Krina. In this way Balla Fasséké reminded Sundiata of the history of Mali so that, in the morning, he would show himself worthy of his ancestors.

At break of day, Fakoli came and woke up Sundiata to tell him that Soumaoro had begun to move his sofas out of Krina. The son of Sogolon appeared dressed like a hunter king. He wore tight-fitting, ochre-coloured trousers. He gave the order to draw up the sofas across the plain, and while his chiefs bustled about, Manding Bory and Nana Triban came into Djata's tent.

"Brother," said Manding Bory, "have you got the bow ready?"

"Yes," replied Sundiata. "Look."

He unhooked his bow from the wall, along with the deadly arrow. It was not an iron arrow at all, but was made of wood and pointed with the spur of a white cock. The cock's spur was the Tana of Soumaoro, the secret which Nana Triban had managed to draw out of the king of Sosso.

"Brother," said Nana Triban, "Soumaoro now knows that I have fled from Sosso. Try to get near him for he will avoid you the whole battle long."

These words of Nana Triban left Djata worried, but Balla Fasséké, who had just come into the tent, said to Sundiata that the soothsayer had seen the end of Soumaoro in a dream.

The sun had risen on the other side of the river and already lit the whole plain. Sundiata's troops deployed from the edge of the river across the plain, but Soumaoro's army was so big that other sofas remaining in Krina had ascended the ramparts to see the battle. Soumaoro was already distinguishable in the distance by his tall headdress, and the wings of his enormous army brushed the river on one side and the hills on the other. As at Neguéboria, Sundiata did not deploy all his forces. The bowmen of Wagadou and the Djallonkés stood at the rear ready to spill out on the left towards the hills as the battle spread. Fakoli Koroma and Kamandjan were in the front line with Sundiata and his cavalry.

With his powerful voice Sundiata cried "An gnewa." The order was repeated from tribe to tribe and the army started off. Soumaoro stood on the right with his cavalry.

Djata and his cavalry charged with great dash but they were stopped by the horsemen of Diaghan and a struggle to the death began. Tabon Wana and the archers of Wagadou stretched out their lines towards the hills and the battle spread over the entire plain, while an unrelenting sun climbed in the sky. The horses of Mema were extremely agile, and they reared forward with their fore hooves raised and swooped down on the horsemen of Diaghan, who rolled on the ground trampled under the horses' hooves. Presently the men of Diaghan gave ground and fell back towards the rear. The enemy centre was broken.

It was then that Manding Bory galloped up to announce to Sundiata that Soumaoro, having thrown in all his reserve, had swept down on Fakoli and his smiths. Obviously Soumaoro was bent on punishing his nephew. Already overwhelmed by the numbers, Fakoli's men were beginning to give ground. The battle was not yet won.

His eyes red with anger, Sundiata pulled his cavalry over to the left in the direction of the hills where Fakoli was valiantly enduring his uncle's blows. But wherever the son of the buffalo passed, death rejoiced. Sundiata's presence restored the balance momentarily, but Soumaoro's sofas were too numerous all the same. Sogolon's son looked for Soumaoro and caught sight of him in the middle of the fray. Sundiata struck out right and left and the Sossos scrambled out of his way. The king of Sosso, who did not want Sundiata to get near him, retreated far behind his men, but Sundiata followed him with his eyes. He stopped and bent his bow. The arrow flew and grazed Soumaoro on the shoulder. The cock's spur no more than scratched him, but the effect was immediate and Soumaoro felt his powers leave him. His eyes met Sundiata's. Now trembling like a man in the grip of a fever, the vanquished Soumaoro looked up towards the sun. A great black bird flew over above the fray and he understood. It was a bird of misfortune.

"The bird of Krina," he muttered.

The Pursuit of Soumaoro

The king of Sosso let out a great cry and, turning his horse's head, he took to flight. The Sossos saw the king and fled in their turn. It was a rout. Death hovered over the great plain and blood poured out of a thousand wounds. Who can tell how many Sossos perished at Krina? The rout was complete and Sundiata then dashed off in pursuit of Soumaoro. The sun was at the middle of its course. Fakoli had caught up with Sundiata and they both rode in pursuit of the fugitives. Soumaoro had a good start. Leaving the plain, the king of Sosso had dashed across the open bush followed by his son Balla and a few Sosso chiefs. When night fell Sundiata and Fakoli stopped at a hamlet. There they took a little food and rest. None of the inhabitants had seen Soumaoro. Sundiata and Fakoli started off in pursuit again as soon as they were joined by some horsemen of Mema. They galloped all night and at daybreak Djata learnt from some peasants that some horsemen had passed that way when it was still dark. The king of Sosso shunned all centres of population for he knew that the inhabitants, seeing him on the run, would no longer hesitate to lay hands on him in order to get into favour with the new master. Soumaoro was followed by none but his son Balla. After having changed his mount at daybreak, the king of Sosso was still galloping to the north.

With difficulty Sundiata found the trail of the fugitives. Fakoli was as resolute as Djata and he knew this country better. It was difficult to tell which of these two men harboured the greatest hatred towards Soumaoro. The one was avenging his humiliated country while the other was prompted by the love of a wife. At noon the horses of Sundiata and Fakoli were out of breath and the pursuers halted at Bankoumana. They took a little food and Djata learnt that Soumaoro was heading for Koulikoro. He had only given himself enough time to change horses. Sundiata and Fakoli set off again straight away. Fakoli said, "I know a short cut to Koulikoro, but it is a difficult track and our horses will be tried."

"Come on," said Djata.

They tackled a difficult path scooped out by the rain in a gully. Cutting across country they now crossed the bush until, pointing a finger in front of him, Fakoli said, "Look at the hills over there which herald Koulikoro. We have made up some time."

"Good," replied Djata simply.

However, the horses were fatigued, they went more slowly and painfully lifted their hooves from the ground. As there was no village in sight, Djata and Fakoli dismounted to let their mounts get their wind back. Fakoli, who had a small bag of millet in his saddle, fed them. The two men rested under a tree. Fakoli even said that Soumaoro, who had taken an easy but lengthy route, would not arrive at Koulikoro until nightfall. He was speaking like a man who had ridden over the whole country.

They continued on their way and soon climbed the hills. Arrived at the top, they saw two horsemen at the bottom of the valley going towards the mountain.

"There they are," cried Djata.

Evening was coming on and the sun's rays were already kissing the summit of Koulikoro mountain. When Soumaoro and his son saw the two riders behind them, they broke off and began to climb the mountain. The king of Sosso and his son Balla seemed to have fresher horses. Djata and Fakoli redoubled their efforts.

The fugitives were within spear range when Djata shouted to them, "Stop, stop."

Like Djata, Fakoli wanted to take Soumaoro alive. Keleya's husband sheered off and outflanked Soumaoro on the right, making his horse jump. He was going to lay hands on his uncle but the latter escaped him by a sudden turn. Through his impetus Fakoli bumped into Balla and they both rolled on the ground. Fakoli got up and seized his cousin while Sundiata, throwing his spear with all his might, brought Soumaoro's horse tumbling down. The old king got up and the foot race began. Soumaoro was a sturdy old man and he climbed the mountain with great agility. Djata did not want either to wound him or kill him. He wanted to take him alive.

The sun had just disappeared completely. For a second time the king of Sosso escaped from Djata. Having reached the summit of Koulikoro, Soumaoro hurried down the slope followed by Djata. To the right he saw the gaping cave of Koulikoro and without hesitation he entered the black cavern. Sundiata stopped in front of the cave. At this moment arrived Fakoli who had just tied the hands of Sosso Balla, his cousin.

"There," said Sundiata, "he has gone into the cave."

"But it is connected to the river," said Fakoli.

The noise of horses' hooves was heard and it turned out to be a detachment of Mema horsemen. Straight away the son of Sogolon sent some of them towards the river and had all the mountain guarded. The darkness was complete. Sundiata went into the village of Koulikoro and waited there for the rest of his army.

The Destruction of Sosso

The victory of Krina was dazzling. The remains of Soumaoro's army went to shut themselves up in Sosso. But the empire of Sosso was done for. From everywhere around kings sent their submission to Sundiata. The king of Guidimakhan sent a richly furnished embassy to Djata and at the same time gave his daughter in marriage to the victor. Embassies flocked to Koulikoro, but when Djata had been joined by all the army he marched on Sosso.

Soumaoro's city, Sosso, the impregnable city, the city of smiths skilled in wielding the spear.

In the absence of the king and his son, Noumounkeba, a tribal chief, directed the defence of the city. He had quickly amassed all that he could find in the way of provisions from the surrounding countryside.

Sosso was a magnificent city. In the open plain her triple rampart with awe-inspiring towers reached into the sky. The city comprised a hundred and eighty-eight fortresses and the palace of Soumaoro loomed above the whole city like a gigantic tower. Sosso had but one gate; colossal and made of iron, the work of the sons of fire. Noumounkeba hoped to tie Sundiata down outside of Sosso, for he had enough provisions to hold out for a year.

The sun was beginning to set when Sogolon-Djata appeared before Sosso the Magnificent. From the top of a hill, Djata and his general staff gazed upon the fearsome city of the sorcerer-king. The army encamped in the plain opposite the great gate of the city and fires were lit in the camp. Djata resolved to take Sosso in the course of a morning. He fed his men a double ration and the tamtams beat all night to stir up the victors of Krina.

At daybreak the towers of the ramparts were black with sofas. Others were positioned on the ramparts themselves. They were the archers. The Mandingoes were masters in the art of storming a town. In the front line Sundiata placed the sofas of Mali, while those who held the ladders were in the second line protected by the shields of the spearmen. The main body of the army was to attack the city gate. When all was ready, Djata gave the order to attack. The drums resounded, the horns blared and like a tide the Mandingo front line moved off, giving mighty shouts. With their shields raised above their heads the Mandingoes advanced up to the foot of the wall, then the Sossos began to rain large stones down on the assailants. From the rear, the bowmen of Wagadou shot arrows at the ramparts. The attack spread and the town was assaulted at all points. Sundiata had a murderous reserve; they were the bowmen whom the king of the Bobos had sent shortly before Krina. The archers of Bobo are the best in the world. On one knee the archers fired flaming arrows over the ramparts. Within the walls the thatched huts took fire and the smoke swirled up. The ladders stood against the curtain wall and the first Mandingo sofas were already at the top. Seized by panic through seeing the town on fire, the Sossos hesitated a moment. The huge tower surmounting the gate surrendered, for Fakoli's smiths had made themselves masters of it. They got into the city where the screams of women and children brought the Sossos' panic to a head. They opened the gates to the main body of the army.

Then began the massacre. Women and children in the midst of fleeing Sossos implored mercy of the victors. Djata and his cavalry were now in front of the awesome tower palace of Soumaoro. Noumounkeba, conscious that he was lost, came out to fight. With his sword held aloft he bore down on Djata, but the latter dodged him and, catching hold of the Sosso's braced arm, forced him to his knees whilst the sword dropped to the ground. He did not kill him but delivered him into the hands of Manding Bory.

Soumaoro's palace was now at Sundiata's mercy. While everywhere the Sossos were begging for quarter, Sundiata, preceded by Balla Fasséké, entered Soumaoro's tower. The griot knew every nook and cranny of the palace from his captivity and he led Sundiata to Soumaoro's magic chamber.

When Balla Fasséké opened the door to the room it was found to have changed its appearance since Soumaoro had been touched by the fatal arrow. The inmates of the chamber had lost their power. The snake in the pitcher was in the throes of death, the owls from the perch were flapping pitifully about on the ground. Everything was dying in the sorcerer's abode. It was all up with the power of Soumaoro. Sundiata had all Soumaoro's fetishes taken down and before the palace were gathered together all Soumaoro's wives, all princesses taken from their families by force. The prisoners, their hands tied behind their backs, were already herded together. Just as he had wished, Sundiata had taken Sosso in the course of a morning. When everything was outside of the town and all that there was to take had been taken out, Sundiata gave the order to complete its destruction. The last houses were set fire to and prisoners were employed in the razing of the walls. Thus, as Djata intended, Sosso was destroyed to its very foundations.

Yes, Sosso was razed to the ground. It has disappeared, the proud city of Soumaoro. A ghastly wilderness extends over the places where kings came and humbled themselves before the sorcerer king. All traces of the houses have vanished and of Soumaoro's seven-storey palace there remains nothing more. A field of desolation, Sosso is now a spot where guinea fowl and young partridges come to take their dust baths.

Many years have rolled by and many times the moon has traversed the heaven since these places lost their inhabitants. The bourein, the tree of desolation, spreads out its thorny undergrowth and insolently grows in Soumaoro's capital. Sosso the Proud is nothing but a memory in the mouths of griots. The hyenas come to wail there at night, the hare and the hind come and feed on the site of the palace of Soumaoro, the king who wore robes of human skin.

Sosso vanished from the earth and it was Sundiata, the son of the buffalo, who gave these places over to solitude. After the destruction of Soumaoro's capital the world knew no other master but Sundiata.

• • •

The Mali Empire

Ka-ba was a small town founded by Niagalin M'Bali Faly, a hunter of Sibi, and by Sounoumba Traore, a fisherman. Ka-ba belonged to the king of Sibi and nowadays you can also find Keitas at Ka-ba, but the Keitas did not come there until after Sundiata's time. Ka-ba stands on the left bank of the Niger and it is through Ka-ba that the road to old Mali passes.

To the north of the town stretches a spacious clearing and it is there that the great assembly was to foregather. King Kamandjan had the whole clearing cleaned up and a great dais was got ready. Even before Djata's arrival the delegations from all the conquered peoples had made their way to Ka-ba. Huts were hastily built to house all these people. When all the armies had reunited, camps had to be set up in the big plain lying between the river and the town. On the appointed day the troops were drawn up on the vast square that had been prepared. As at Sibi, each people was gathered round its king's pennant. Sundiata had put on robes such as are worn by a great Muslim king. Balla Fasséké, the high master of ceremonies, set the allies around Djata's great throne. Everything was in position. The sofas, forming a vast semicircle bristling with spears, stood motionless. The delegations of the various peoples had been planted at the foot of the dais. A complete silence reigned. On Sundiata's right, Balla Fasséké, holding his mighty spear, addressed the throng in this manner:

"Peace reigns today in the whole country; may it always be thus. . . ."

"Amen," replied the crowd, then the herald continued:

"I speak to you, assembled peoples. To those of Mali I convey Maghan Sundiata's greeting; greetings to those of Do, greetings to those of Ghana, to those from Mema greetings, and to those of Fakoli's tribe. Greetings to the Bobo warriors and, finally, greetings to those of Sibi and Ka-ba. To all the peoples assembled, Djata gives greetings.

"May I be humbly forgiven if I have made any omission. I am nervous before so many people gathered together.

"Peoples, here we are, after years of hard trials, gathered around our saviour, the restorer of peace and order. From the east to the west, from the north to the south, everywhere his victorious arms have established peace. I convey to you the greetings of Soumaoro's vanquisher, Maghan Sundiata, king of Mali.

"But in order to respect tradition, I must first of all address myself to the host of us all, Kamandjan, king of Sibi; Djata greets you and gives you the floor."

Kamandjan, who was sitting close by Sundiata, stood up and stepped down from the dais. He mounted his horse and brandished his sword, crying "I salute you all, warriors of Mali, of Do, of Tabon, of Mema, of Wagadou, of Bobo, of Fakoli. . . ; warriors, peace has returned to our homes, may God long preserve it."

"Amen," replied the warriors and the crowd. The king of Sibi continued.

"In the world man suffers for a season, but never eternally. Here we are at the end of our trials. We are at peace. May God be praised. But we owe this peace to one man who, by his courage and his valiance, was able to lead our troops to victory.

"Which one of us, alone, would have dared face Soumaoro? Ay, we were all cowards. How many times did we pay him tribute? The insolent rogue thought that everything was permitted him. What family was not dishonoured by Soumaoro? He took our daughters and wives from us and we were more craven than women. He carried his insolence to the point of stealing the wife of his nephew Fakoli! We were prostrated and humiliated in front of our children. But it was in the midst of so many calamities that our destiny suddenly changed. A new sun arose in the east. After the battle of Tabon we felt ourselves to be men, we realized that Soumaoro was a human being and not an incarnation of the devil, for he was no longer invincible. A man came to us. He had heard our groans and came to our aid, like a father when he sees his son in tears. Here is that man. Maghan Sundiata, the man with two names foretold by the soothsayers.

"It is to you that I now address myself, son of Sogolon, you, the nephew of the valorous warriors of Do. Henceforth it is from you that I derive my kingdom for I acknowledge you my sovereign. My tribe and I place ourselves in your hands. I salute you, supreme chief, I salute you, Fama of Famas. I salute you, Mansal."

The huzza that greeted these words was so loud that you could hear the echo repeat the tremendous clamour twelve times over. With a strong hand Kamandjan stuck his spear in the ground in front of the dais and said, "Sundiata, here is my spear, it is yours."

Then he climbed up to sit in his place. Thereafter, one by one, the twelve kings of the bright savanna country got up and proclaimed Sundiata "Mansa" in their turn. Twelve royal spears were stuck in the ground in front of the dais. Sundiata had become emperor. The old tabala of Niani announced to the world that the lands of the savanna had provided themselves with one single king. When the imperial tabala had stopped reverberating, Balla Fasséké, the grand master of ceremonies, took the floor again following the crowd's ovation.

"Sundiata, Maghan Sundiata, king of Mali, in the name of the twelve kings of the 'Bright Country,' I salute you as 'Mansa.'"

The crowd shouted "Wassa, Wassa. . . . Ayé."

It was amid such joy that Balla Fasséké composed the great hymn "Niama" which the griots still sing:

> Niama, Niama, Niama,
> You, you serve as a shelter for all,
> All come to seek refuge under you.
> And as for you, Niama,
> Nothing serves you for shelter,
> God alone protects you.

The festival began. The musicians of all the countries were there. Each people in turn came forward to the dais under Sundiata's impassive gaze. Then the war dances began. The sofas of all the countries had lined themselves up in six ranks amid a great clatter of bows and spears knocking together. The war chiefs were on horseback. The warriors faced the enormous dais and at a signal from Balla Fasséké, the musicians, massed on the right of the dais, struck up. The heavy war drums thundered, the bolons gave off muted notes while the griot's voice gave the throng the pitch for the "Hymn to the Bow." The spearmen, advancing like hyenas in the night, held their spears above their heads; the archers of Wagadou and Tabon, walking with a noise-less tread, seemed to be lying in ambush behind bushes. They rose suddenly to their feet and let fly their arrows at imaginary enemies. In front of the great dais the Kéakéa-Tigui, or war chiefs, made their horses perform dance steps under the eyes of the Mansa. The horses whinnied and reared, then, overmastered by the spurs, knelt, got up and cut little capers, or else scraped the ground with their hooves.

The rapturous people shouted the "Hymn to the Bow" and clapped their hands. The sweating bodies of the warriors glistened in the sun while the exhausting rhythm of the tamtams wrenched from them shrill cries. But presently they made way for the cavalry, beloved by Djata. The horsemen of Mema threw their swords in the air and caught them in flight, uttering mighty shouts. A smile of contentment took shape on Sundiata's lips, for he was happy to see his cavalry manoeuvre with so much skill.

$$\bullet \bullet \bullet$$

The Return to Niani

But it was time to return to his native Mali. Sundiata assembled his army in the plain and each people provided a contingent to accompany the Mansa to Niani. At Ka-ba all the peoples separated in friendship and in joy at their new-found peace.

Sundiata and his men had to cross the Niger in order to enter old Mali. One might have thought that all the dug-out canoes in the world had arranged to meet at the port of Ka-ba. It was the dry season and there was not much water in the river. The fishing tribe of Somono, to whom Djata had given the monopoly of the water, were bent on expressing their thanks to the son of Sogolon. They put all their dug-outs side by side across the Niger so that Sundiata's sofas could cross without wetting their feet.

When the whole army was on the other side of the river, Sundiata ordered great sacrifices. A hundred oxen and a hundred rams were sacrificed. It was thus that Sundiata thanked God on returning to Mali.

The villages of Mali gave Maghan Sundiata an unprecedented welcome. At normal times a traveller on foot can cover the distance from Kaba to Niani with only two halts, but Sogolon's son with his army took three days. The road to Mali from the river was flanked by a double human hedge. Flocking from every corner of Mali, all the inhabitants were resolved to see their saviour from close up. The women of Mali tried to create a sensation and they did not fail. At the entrance to each village they had carpeted the road with their multi-coloured pagnes so that Sundiata's horse would not so much as dirty its feet on entering their village. At the village exits the children, holding leafy branches in their hands, greeted Djata with cries of "Wassa, Wassa, Ayé."

Sundiata was leading the van. He had donned his costume of a hunter king—a plain smock, skin-tight trousers and his bow slung across his back. At his side Balla Fasséké was still wearing his festive garments gleaming with gold. Between Djata's general staff and the army Sosso Balla had been placed, amid his father's fetishes. But his hands were no longer tied. As at Ka-ba, abuse was everywhere heaped upon him and the prisoner did not dare look up at the hostile crowd. Some people, always ready to feel sympathy, were saying among themselves:

"How few things good fortune prizes!"

"Yes, the day you are fortunate is also the day when you are the most unfortunate, for in good fortune you cannot imagine what suffering is."

The troops were marching along singing the "Hymn to the Bow," which the crowd took up. New songs flew from mouth to mouth. Young women offered the soldiers cool water and cola nuts. And so the triumphal march across Mali ended outside Niani, Sundiata's city.

It was a ruined town which was beginning to be rebuilt by its inhabitants. A part of the ramparts had been destroyed and the charred walls still bore the marks of the fire. From the top of the hill Djata looked on Niani, which looked like a dead city. He saw the plain of Sounkarani, and he also saw the site of the young baobab tree. The survivors of the Catastrophe were standing in rows on the Mali road. The children were waving branches, a few young women were singing, but the adults were mute.

"Rejoice," said Balla Fasséké to Sundiata, "for your part you will have the bliss of rebuilding Niani, the city of your fathers, but nevermore will anyone rebuild Sosso out of its ruins. Men will lose recollection of the very site of Soumaoro's city."

With Sundiata peace and happiness entered Niani. Lovingly Sogolon's son had his native city rebuilt. He restored in the ancient style his father's old enclosure where he had grown up. People came from all the villages of Mali to settle in Niani. The walls had to be destroyed to enlarge the town, and new quarters were built for each kin group in the enormous army.

• • •

Djata's justice spared nobody. He followed the very word of God. He protected the weak against the strong and people would make journeys lasting several days to come and demand justice of him. Under his sun the upright man was rewarded and the wicked one punished.

In their new-found peace the villages knew prosperity again, for with Sundiata happiness had come into everyone's home. Vast fields of millet, rice, cotton, indigo and fonio surrounded the villages. Whoever worked always had something to live on. Each year long caravans carried the taxes in kind to Niani. You could go from village to village without fearing brigands. A thief would have his right hand chopped off and if he stole again he would be put to the sword.

New villages and new towns sprang up in Mali and elsewhere. "Dyulas," or traders, became numerous and during the reign of Sundiata the world knew happiness.

There are some kings who are powerful through their military strength. Everybody trembles before them, but when they die nothing but ill is spoken of them. Others do neither good nor ill and when they die they are forgotten. Others are feared because they have power, but they know how to use it and they are loved because they love justice. Sundiata belonged to this group. He was feared, but loved as well. He was the father of Mali and gave the world peace. After him the world has not seen a greater conqueror, for he was the seventh and last conqueror. He had made the capital of an empire out of his father's village, and Niani became the navel of the earth.

THINKING ACROSS CULTURES

1. What aspects of classical civilizations were most likely to be borrowed by their post-classical heirs? Why?

2. In purely military terms, the groups such as the Franks and Arabs defeated the classical Mediterranean civilizations and the Mongols conquered China. In what sense did the classical civilizations conquer the invaders?

3. What roles did religions such as Christianity, Islam, and Buddhism play in spreading civilization?

4. If you lived in the year 1000 and were told that one of the following civilizations would dominate the rest of the world in seven hundred years, which one would you pick: Sung China, Japan, India, Islamic Middle East, Byzantine Empire, or Western Europe? Why?

5. Today "Western Civilization" and "Islamic Civilization" are depicted as incompatible enemies. Given that "Western Civilization" derives from post-classical Western Europe and "Islamic Civilization" derives from post-classical Arabic and Persian civilizations, what do Western Civilization and Islamic Civilization have in common?